2011

Social Media Directory

The Ultimate Guide
to Facebook®, Twitter®,
and LinkedIn® Resources

Jeffery A. Riley

que®

800 East 96th Street, Indianapolis, Indiana 46240 USA

2011 Social Media Directory

ISBN-13: 978-0-7897-4711-2

ISBN-10: 0-7897-4711-1

Library of Congress Cataloging-in-Publication data is on file.

Printed in the United States of America

First Printing: July 2010

Trademarks

All terms mentioned in this book that are known to be trademarks or service marks have been appropriately capitalized. Que Publishing cannot attest to the accuracy of this information. Use of a term in this book should not be regarded as affecting the validity of any trademark or service mark.

Warning and Disclaimer

Every effort has been made to make this book as complete and as accurate as possible, but no warranty or fitness is implied. The information provided is on an "as is" basis. The author and the publisher shall have neither liability nor responsibility to any person or entity with respect to any loss or damages arising from the information contained in this book.

Bulk Sales

Que Publishing offers excellent discounts on this book when ordered in quantity for bulk purchases or special sales. For more information, please contact

U.S. Corporate and Government Sales
1-800-382-3419
corpsales@pearsontechgroup.com

For sales outside of the U.S., please contact

International Sales
international@pearson.com

Associate Publisher
Greg Wiegand

Acquisitions Editor
Michelle Newcomb

Development Editor
Mark Reddin

Managing Editor
Sandra Schroeder

Project Editor
Seth Kerney

Copy Editor
Cheri Clark

Indexer
Cheryl Lenser

Proofreader
Kathy Ruiz

Technical Editor
Mark Reddin

Publishing Coordinator
Cindy Teeters

Book Designer
Anne Jones

Compositor
Studio Galou, LLC

CONTENTS AT A GLANCE

TABLE OF CONTENTS

ACKNOWLEDGMENTS

It takes a village to raise a *2011 Social Media Directory*…

Thanks to the contributors: Susan Hobbs, Jason Hughey, Matthew Hughey, Mike LaBonne, Kelly Maish, Susan Nixon, and last—but most certainly *never* least—Deborah Riley.

Thanks to the editorial and production staff: Michelle Newcomb (acquisitions), Anne Jones (design), Kourtnaye Sturgeon (marketing), Sandra Schroeder (managing editor), Seth Kerney (project editor), Mark Reddin (technical editor), Louisa Adair (layout technician), Cheryl Lenser (indexer), Cheri Clark (copy editor), and Kathy Ruiz (proofreader).

A special thanks to Jeff Taylor, the National Account Manager at Pearson who is probably the single most talented sales rep in the industry. To nobody's
surprise, he sold the first batch of these books, maybe even putting this very copy in your hands. How do I know these things? He pinged me on Facebook, of course!

And nothing gets done around here without the love and support of my wonderful family: Deborah, Keenan, Griffen, and Cooper!

AUTHOR BIO

Jeffery A. Riley, President of Box Twelve Communications, Inc. (www.boxtwelve.com), earned a technical journalism degree from Oregon State University in 1989 and is a former staff writer of the *Los Angeles Times*. A 15-year veteran of the information technology publishing industry, Jeff has had a hand in—as copy editor, production editor, development editor, acquisitions editor, executive editor, and author—hundreds of books covering IT topics. He is the author of *Introduction to OpenOffice.org* (Prentice Hall) and *Picture Yourself Learning Microsoft Excel 2010* (Cengage Learning). As president of Box Twelve, he manages the day-to-day operations of a content solutions firm outside Hilton Head, South Carolina.

You can follow his tweets at box12comm and view his LinkedIn profile at www.linkedin.com/in/jefferyriley.

CONTRIBUTORS

Susan Hobbs is an Indianapolis writer and editor. She spent several years working for Macmillan Publishing and has been a freelancer for more than a decade. When she doesn't have her nose in a book, she's active with Indianapolis-area animal welfare organizations and currently fosters adoptable cats and dogs.

Mike LaBonne, a retired Marine and Vietnam veteran, worked in computer book publishing as a senior project editor/team leader from 1989 to 2003. He has been a freelance copy editor since 2004.

Deborah Riley is the Coordinator of Prison Ministries for the Diocese of Charleston (South Carolina). She is a founding partner of Box Twelve Communications, Inc., and serves as Vice President of Marketing.

Introduction

The Internet community has changed dramatically in the past few years. Connection speeds have become faster. Almost every laptop comes loaded with a wireless card, and free wireless is slowly becoming the norm for a lot of restaurants and other businesses. It's never been easier to get—and stay—connected.

In addition to those advances in hardware technology, software technology has improved as well. It's never been easier to get—and stay—connected with your friends and your family, as well as those who share common interests with you. As we all know, the Internet is a plethora of information—some valuable, some not so valuable, some that downright irks us. But that's the fun of the Internet, and because of some excellent tools like Facebook, LinkedIn, and Twitter, the Internet has never been a better resource for us. Experts call it social media. Whether you're posting your big-hair photos to your Facebook page for old high-school chums to view, refining your LinkedIn profile to make sure your professional networking efforts are effective, or just tweeting your latest quirky thoughts about *Dancing with the Stars*, it's a perfect mix of entertainment and value—and we can't seem to get enough of it.

But it's often difficult to pore over the abundance of information available to us. And this type of information isn't easily located with a Google search—in fact, in most cases, you can't find this information in Google at all. The 2011 Social Media Directory solves that problem by organizing the Top 15 information categories into a comprehensive resource that helps you quickly find the Facebook, Twitter, and LinkedIn connections that match your interests. Additionally, by providing you with the exact search phrase you need to locate a resource, the 2011 Social Media Directory saves you a lot of time and hassle.

Business, computers and electronics, current events, politics, news, entertainment, health, hobbies, sports, travel, religion—this book provides quick, easy access to the top Facebook, Twitter, and LinkedIn resources, ensuring that you have the latest information about the topics that interest you most. Don't waste your valuable time searching through all these sites in an effort to find this information. We've already done this work for you! Simply use this book to make sure you're connected to the top Facebook, Twitter, and LinkedIn information for the following categories:

n o t e

As you well know, information changes rapidly on the Internet. If a particular category or website is not yet hooked into LinkedIn, Facebook, or Twitter, we encourage you to search LinkedIn, Facebook, or Twitter for the website or topic you're looking for.

- **Blogs:** Personal or corporate weblogs, which are web-based but are frequently updated with new content.

- **Videos:** Media clips containing both sound and video, such as archives of TV shows or content prepared exclusively for online distribution.

- **Podcasts:** Audio presentations and archived radio shows you can play on your computer or download to a portable digital music player.

- **Wikis:** Web-based collaborative knowledge bases, like encyclopedias for the masses.

- **Social Networking:** Discussion groups on social networking sites.

- **Forums/Discussions:** Web-based bulletin board systems where you can exchange public messages with others.

EASY BROWSING BY TOPIC

Spare yourself the time-consuming burden of searching the Top 15 information categories on the Internet. We've already done this work for you! Simply use this book to make sure you're connected to the top Facebook, Twitter, and LinkedIn information for the following categories:

Chapter 1, "Business": This covers everything you need in order to start and manage a business or advance your career. It includes sections on patents and trademarks, office management, international business, and customer service.

Chapter 2, "Computers and Electronics": This chapter has topics for the gear and

gadget enthusiast, including home stereos, computers, and TV/video recording.

Chapter 3, "Current Events/Political/Science/News": Here you'll find the best news and information sources for national, international, political, and scientific events and discoveries.

Chapter 4, "Education": This chapter provides resources for students of all ages, teachers, and home-schooling parents, as well as lifelong learners who want to know more about academic subjects for their own personal benefit.

Chapter 5, "Entertainment": Here you'll find topics such as movies and music, games, celebrities, science fiction, and theaters—everything you need in order to keep yourself (and others) entertained.

Chapter 6, "Family/Parenting": This chapter focuses on family roles and parenting, with sections on adoption, pregnancy and childbirth, single parenting, teens, and child custody.

Chapter 7, "Food and Drink": In this chapter, you'll find resources for special diets, restaurants, cooking and recipes, and all kinds of beverages, both alcoholic and nonalcoholic.

Chapter 8, "Going Green/Environment": Here you'll find all the information you need about environmental protection, energy savings, alternative fuels, and other earth-friendly topics.

Chapter 9, "Health": In this chapter are resources for getting and keeping healthy and fit, researching disease symptoms, finding good deals on health insurance, and providing first aid and emergency care.

Chapter 10, "Hobbies": This chapter contains resources for pursuing your passions, whether that means reading, stamp collecting, antiques, or any of dozens of other pursuits.

Chapter 11, "Home": This chapter covers topics related to home ownership, including insurance, mortgages and real estate, landscaping, decorating, and maintenance.

Chapter 12, "Religion/Philosophy": Whether you are shopping for a religion or are firm in your current beliefs, this chapter provides resources for understanding various spiritual practices and beliefs, including Christianity, Judaism, Hinduism, Buddhism, New Thought, and atheism.

Chapter 13, "Shopping/Fashion": Love to shop or make your own clothes? This chapter provides the links for your hobby, with sections for high fashion, bargain hunting, shoes, accessories, sewing, lingerie, and more.

Chapter 14, "Sports": Whether you're looking for the latest cricket scores, tickets to a hockey game, or a good scuba diving instructor, this chapter can hook you up, with links for almost every sport you can imagine.

Chapter 15, "Travel": Planning a trip? In this chapter you'll find resources for making your reservations, deciding where to go and what to see, and locating the best discounts, guides, and bargains.

SPECIAL FEATURES

This book is all about quick, easy access to comprehensive information about your social media pursuits. That's why it includes unique features that only the world's leading technology publisher can provide:

- Each topic includes **a separate listing for Facebook, Twitter, and LinkedIn,** including each organization's company logo for quick visual reference!

- **Easy browsing by topic.** Some directories organize information alphabetically by topic, and that approach can be frustrating when you're trying to find a subject that is known by more than one name. This book organizes listings by broad topic, with only one topic per chapter, grouping the listings logically.

- Each listing includes a **brief summary** that provides readers with insight into the listing. We go the extra mile so that the reader isn't forced to click links blindly, wondering what information, exactly, is provided at the site.

SPECIAL ICONS

Throughout this directory, the following icons indicate special features or restrictions:

The Best of the Best icon marks the authors' picks for top-quality sites.

This icon marks sites where you must pay to access the content.

These sites require you to register to use their content (but not necessarily pay).

This Not for Kids icon marks sites that contain content that may not be suitable for children.

ABOUT THE TECHNOLOGIES

So, who are you and how do these technologies serve your needs?

At the writing of this book, Facebook users numbered 350 million worldwide. Early 2009 demographics showed that 40% were between the ages of 18 and 24. Sixty-six percent were 34 and younger. The 25-to-34 age group has been doubling approximately every six months. The 35-to-54 demographic was the fastest growing at 276%. Parents and professionals are the fastest-growing audience.

LinkedIn users numbered 50 million. This audience tends to be a bit older (they have an average age of 41), they are more educated (80% are college graduates), and they have more expendable income (with an average household income of $109K). Many look to add groups to their online résumé to add to their credibility. They also want to be informed of the new or popular groups. Social media experts recommend that LinkedIn users actively participate in groups to display their expertise to their markets.

Twitter users number 5 to 80 million, with an estimated 21% of those accounts inactive (users who don't post regularly). Sixty-five percent of Twitter users are less than 24 years old; 81% are less than 30. As expected, most Twitter activity is concentrated on celebrities.

LINKEDIN

LinkedIn is an interconnected network of experienced professionals from around the world, representing 170 industries and 200 countries. You can find, be introduced to, and collaborate with qualified professionals whom you need to work with to accomplish your goals. According to LinkedIn, there are more than 50 million LinkedIn members across 200 countries and territories worldwide. A new member joins LinkedIn every second, and about half of its members live outside the U.S. Executives from each Fortune 500 company are represented in LinkedIn.

There are nearly 500,000 LinkedIn Groups, which is your destination to find and join communities of professionals based on common interest, experience, affiliation, and goals. You can stay in touch with organizations, schools, and companies that you are and were a part of; network with professionals with similar interests and goals; and collaborate in a professional community online. LinkedIn Groups allows group organizations to extend their brand's reach and strengthen the brand with existing users by providing additional value through LinkedIn's features. Group categories include these:

- *Alumni groups* (82,947 groups): Examples include GreaterIBM Connection, Quant Finance, Univ. of Michigan Alumni, University of Texas Alumni, Penn State Alumni, Cornell Alumni, Beta Gamma Sigma, The Big 4 Firms, Accenture, Citi Global.

- *Corporate groups* (45,696): HP Connections, Deloitte, Cisco,

PricewaterhouseCoopers, Siemens, EDS Alumni, Ernst & Young, IBM, Microsoft, Motorola.

- *Conference groups* (9,430): Future Social Media, TED, Search Engine Strategies, BIO International Convention, Speakers and Panelists, Google Android, Black Hat, International Outsourcing Forum, Free Resume Drop Box, Harvard Business Review.

- *Networking groups* (132,110): Human Resources, eMarketing Association, OnStartups, Consultants Network, Bio Tech & Pharma, The Recruitment Network, TopLinked.com, Jobs, Green, Media Professionals Worldwide.

- *Nonprofit groups* (38,389): Christian Professionals, Business Process Improvement, Non-Profit Network, JobAngels, Ubuntu Users, World Wildlife Fund, IEEE, Agile Alliance, Toastmasters, Slow Food.

- *Professional groups* (124,657): Executive Suite, Telecom Professionals, RecruitingBlogs, Project Manager Networking Group, Marketing & PR Innovators, ThoseInMedia, Information Security Community, Online Advertising Professionals, Social Media Marketing, SAP Community.

- *Other groups* (28,299): India Leadership Network, Global Jobs Network, Obama for America, India Jobs Network, Innovative Recruitment Forum, Canon EOS Digital Photography, White House, A Job Needed—A Job Posted, Women's Wear Daily.

Additionally, you can create your own group!

FACEBOOK

Facebook is a global social networking website that boasts 350 million registered users. Facebook users add friends to their Facebook network to whom they send messages, profile updates, pictures, and the like. Additionally, users can join networks organized by city, workplace, school, and region. With 340 million unique visitors each month, Facebook ranks as the fourth-most-popular website in the world, behind only Google (844 million unique visitors), Microsoft (691 million), and Yahoo! (581 million). Facebook eclipsed MySpace in April 2008; MySpace has stagnated at 100,000 unique visitors and has endured 30% layoffs and management upheaval throughout much of 2009.

According to Facebook, 150 million users log in to Facebook each day. The fastest-growing demographic is composed of users 35 years and older. More than 10 million users become fans of Pages each day. There are more than 45 million active user groups. Page categories include Places, Products, Services, Stores, Restaurants, Bars & Clubs, Organizations, Politicians, Government Officials, Non-Profits, TV Shows, Films, Games, Sports Teams, Celebrities/Public Figures, Music, and Websites. The top 10 pages change almost daily, but an example of the top 10 pages in April 2010 is shown here:

1. Michael Jackson (10.40 million fans)

2. Vin Diesel (7.05 million)

3. Barack Obama (6.94 million)

4. Mafia Wars (5.91 million)

5. Facebook (5.82 million)

6. Megan Fox (5.12 million)

7. Starbucks (5.15 million)

8. RIP Michael Jackson (4.67 million)

9. I (heart) Sleep (4.59 million)

10. Pizza (4.59 million)

TWITTER

Twitter is notoriously protective of its user information and usage numbers, so an exact number is difficult to come by. Membership estimates range from as few as 5 million users to more than 80 million. It should be noted, however, that more than one-fifth (21%) of the user accounts are inactive (users who simply aren't posting anything). As expected, most Twitter activity is concentrated on celebrities—evident in the top 10

"Twitterholics" (based on followers) listed at http://twitterholic.com:

1. Ashton Kutcher (4.04 million followers)

2. Britney Spears (3.87 million)

3. Ellen DeGeneres (3.81 million)

4. CNN Breaking News (2.81 million)

5. Barack Obama (2.76 million)

6. Oprah (2.71 million)

7. Twitter (2.70 million)

8. John Mayer (2.67 million)

9. Ryan Seacrest (2.65 million)

10. Kim Kardashian (2.64 million)

BUSINESS

Many of the sites featured in this chapter allow you to do more than simply retrieve information. They stimulate the notion that together we can do more, learn more, and mean more to others. And although it's true that you'll find excellent sites throughout this directory, some of the ones featured in this chapter display perhaps the best use of technology, creativity, and collaboration you're likely to find anywhere. Whether you own a business, work for one, or plan to start a company of your own, the organizations and web-based resources found in this chapter are bound to give you a leg up on your competition.

ACCOUNTING

AccountantsWorld

One of the oldest and most popular online destinations for accounting professionals, offering a vast array of free resources, tools, and services.

Web: www.accountantsworld.com
Facebook: Accountants World (Group)
Twitter: (None)
LinkedIn: AccountantsWorld (Company)

AccountingCoach

Free online educational material to help you learn the accounting concepts practiced in the United States. The site provides hundreds of pages of explanations, drills, exams, crossword puzzles, insight from accounting guru Harold Averkamp, and even a glossary of more than 1,000 terms.

Web: www.accountingcoach.com
Facebook: Accounting Coach (Page)
Twitter: (None)
LinkedIn: Harold Averkamp (People)

Accounting Terminology Guide

If you need to know what a specific accounting term means, no matter how obscure, this is the site for you. Hosted and maintained by the New York State Society of CPAs, this site defines nearly 500 accounting terms, all sorted in an easy-to-use alphabetical list.

Web: www.nysscpa.org/glossary
Facebook: NYSSCPA / FAE (Page), Nysscpa Fae (People)
Twitter: nysscpa
LinkedIn: NYSSCPA (Company), New York State Society of CPAs (Group)

AccountingWEB

Updated daily, this website offers accounting industry news, information, tips, tools, resources, and insight—everything you need to prosper and interact with other accounting professionals.

Web: www.accountingweb.com
Facebook: AccountingWEB (Page)
Twitter: AccountingWEB
LinkedIn: AccountingWEB, Inc. (Company), AccountingWEB (Group)

1

The CPA Journal Online

Read what the accounting industry reads, for free. Published by the New York State Society of CPAs, the CPA Journal Online is a great resource for anyone interested in going in-depth, especially public practitioners, management, educators, and other accounting professionals.

Web: www.cpajournal.com
Facebook: (None)
Twitter: cpajournal
LinkedIn: The CPA Journal (Group)

CPA Success

CPA-related success stories from the Maryland Association of CPAs.

Web: www.cpasuccess.com
Facebook: Maryland Association of CPAs. Includes a Page and a Group.
Twitter: MACPA
LinkedIn: Maryland Association of CPAs. Includes a Company and a Group.

FreshBooks ⑤

FreshBooks is an online invoicing and time-tracking service that helps businesses of all sizes save time, get paid faster, and look professional.

Web: www.freshbooks.com
Facebook: FreshBooks (Page)
Twitter: freshbooks
LinkedIn: FreshBooks (Company)

BRANDING

Brand Autopsy

Blogger John Moore spent years implementing marketing and branding for Whole Foods Market and Starbucks. Today, he shares his marketing advice to those companies looking to be the next big thing.

Web: http://brandautopsy.typepad.com
Facebook: (None)
Twitter: BrandAutopsy
LinkedIn: john moore (Marketing Strategist)

BrandChannel.com

Run by internationally acclaimed brand consultancy Interbrand, BrandChannel.com provides a global perspective on brands and the art of branding. Site features include in-depth feature articles, conference announcements, career resources, and access to white papers.

Web: www.brandchannel.com/home/
Facebook: brandchannel (Page)
Twitter: brandchannelhub
LinkedIn: Hub brandchannel (Group)

Brand Noise

Tim Stock's blog about the business of branding. Stock, a partner in the creative strategy shop scenarioDNA, uses this blog to provide critical insight and ideas for brand managers and planners.

Web: http://brandnoise.typepad.com
Facebook: Tim Stock (People)
Twitter: timstock
LinkedIn: Tim Stock (People)

Brandweek

A leading source of news and information for the branding industry and the only online trade magazine to offer saturation coverage at all levels of the brand-activation process.

Web: www.brandweek.com
Facebook: Brandweek (Page)
Twitter: BrandweekDotCom
LinkedIn: Brandweek (Company), Brandweek's Marketer of the Year (Group)

Wireality 📖

Wireality is the leading online forum about branding and identity. Wireality's members come from several dozen countries across the world for what can only be described as highly focused and relevant discussions about all things branding.

Web: http://wireality.com/index.wire
Facebook: (None)
Twitter: Wireality
LinkedIn: (None)

CAREERS

Jibber Jobber

Jibber Jobber has many helpful career tools for the job hunter, including a listing of career coaches, recruiters, and many interesting articles chock-full of constructive career information.

Web: www.jibberjobber.com/blog
Facebook: Jibber Jobber (Page)
Twitter: JibberJobber
LinkedIn: JibberJobber – Career Management (Group)

Jobfox 📖

Started by the former CEO of CareerBuilder.com, Jobfox walks you through creating a skills inventory and then tells you which employers are looking for people with those skills. The Jobfox site also provides a free trackable résumé and career web page to showcase your skills, experience, and work samples.

Web: www.jobfox.com
Facebook: JobFox (Group)
Twitter: Jobfox
LinkedIn: Jobfox (Company)

LinkedIn Jobs 📖

Whether you're looking for a new job or trying to help someone else find his or her perfect job, LinkedIn can help you find and get in touch with the people you need to contact. Create a profile and click the Jobs tab to get started.

Web: www.linkedin.com/jobs
Facebook: LinkedIn. Includes a Page and a Group.
Twitter: LinkedIn_jobs
LinkedIn: Linked:HR (Group)

Manpower

Manpower Island is a place where job seekers, employers, and entrepreneurs can come together to learn about and explore the World of Virtual Work, share ideas, and identify new opportunities. Built as a learning community, Manpower Island features a variety of virtual work resources and a series of work-related stations offering advice on creating a virtual résumé, preparing for both Real Life and Second Life job interviews, obtaining appropriate attire, and finding a job in the virtual world.

Web: http://world.secondlife.com/place/b1fc979c-eb94-e4de-bde3-23c5bf3866cb
Facebook: Manpower US (Page), Manpower (Group)
Twitter: manpower
LinkedIn: Manpower SA (Company)

NotchUP 📖

Instead of sorting through hundreds of job postings, you can take advantage of NotchUP, which enables top companies to find you and pays you to interview for available jobs.

Web: www.notchup.com/c/home
Facebook: NotchUp (Page)
Twitter: NotchUp
LinkedIn: NotchUp, Inc. (Company), NotchUp users (Group)

Penelope Trunk's Brazen Careerist

Penelope focuses on helping you find success at the intersection of life and work. Topics she covers range from career fulfillment and networking to promoting yourself and working from home.

Web: http://blog.penelopetrunk.com
Facebook: Penelope Trunk (Page)
Twitter: penelopetrunk
LinkedIn: Brazen careerist (People)

Simply Hired 📰

With an average of seven million listings, Simply Hired is one of the world's largest employment search engines and a unique recruitment/advertising network for employers and recruiters.

Web: www.simplyhired.com
Facebook: Simply Hired (Page)
Twitter: SimplyHired
LinkedIn: Simply Hired (Company), Job Search Made Simple by Simply Hired (Group)

Standout Jobs 📰

Standout Jobs helps employers produce a video job ad to show prospective job candidates more about their company. In a two-to-four-minute video, Standout Jobs helps your company show people why they should work for you, demonstrating your culture, your team, and what your company is all about.

Web: http://standoutjobs.com
Facebook: Standout Jobs (Page)
Twitter: Standout_Jobs
LinkedIn: Standout Jobs (Company)

TheLadders.com 📰

TheLadders.com is the world's largest website catering exclusively to the $100K-plus job market. Each week, site administrators screen 50,000-plus job listings and hand select approximately 5,000 that meet the company's strict criteria.

Web: www.theladders.com
Facebook: TheLadders.com (Group)
Twitter: TheLadders
LinkedIn: TheLadders.com (Company)

Twitter: CareerPro

Daily—sometimes hourly—thoughts of John M. O'Connor, President and CEO of Career Pro, Inc., a North Carolina–based executive recruitment and placement firm, delivered via Twitter.com. Great for anyone looking for quick job search–related tips, strategies, and warnings.

Web: http://twitter.com/CareerPro
Facebook: (None)
Twitter: CareerPro
LinkedIn: (None)

Twitter: careertips

Daily career tips from Douglas E. Walsh, writer and computer consultant, whose work has been published in *Wired*, *MacWorld*, and the *Los Angeles Times*, delivered via Twitter.com.

Web: http://twitter.com/careertips
Facebook: (None)
Twitter: careertips
LinkedIn: (None)

VisualCV 🏅 📰

VisualCV reinvents your résumé using technologies that transform the way in which résumé data is presented, accessed, and shared. VisualCV allows you to easily build and manage online career portfolios that come alive with informational keyword pop-ups, video, pictures, and professional networking.

Web: www.visualcv.com/www/indexc.html
Facebook: VisualCV (Page)
Twitter: visualcv, visualcvjobs
LinkedIn: VisualCV (Company), VisualCV (Group), VisualCV Job Assistant (Group)

CUSTOMER SERVICE

BusinessWeek Podcast

BusinessWeek magazine's podcast on improving the customer experience.

Web: www.businessweek.com/search/podcasting.htm
Facebook: (None)
Twitter: bweek
LinkedIn: BusinessWeek (Company), BusinessWeek Group (Group)

Call Center Network Group

The Call Center Network Group (CCNG) provides customer-care professionals with the opportunity to give and get both knowledge and support from peers and trusted advisors. From salary benchmarking and industry white papers and reports, to information on local networking meetings and an online career center, CCNG's website has it all.

Web: www.ccng.com/i4a/pages/index.cfm?pageid=1
Facebook: (None)
Twitter: dhadobas
LinkedIn: CCNG (Company), CCNG - Contact Center Network Group (Group)

Yelp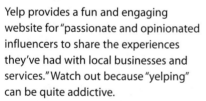

Yelp provides a fun and engaging website for "passionate and opinionated influencers to share the experiences they've had with local businesses and services." Watch out because "yelping" can be quite addictive.

Web: www.yelp.com
Facebook: Yelp (Page)
Twitter: Yelp
LinkedIn: Yelp.com (Company), Yelp Elite (Group)

ENTREPRENEURSHIP AND SMALL BUSINESS

Better Business Bureau

Browse or search for a business or charity's reputation. Included are instructions for how to file a consumer or business-to-business complaint. Be sure to search Twitter and LinkedIn for links to specific cities or organizations.

Web: www.bbb.org/us/
Facebook: Better Business Bureau (Page)
Twitter: (None)
LinkedIn: (None)

Biznik

Biznik connects people who have built or are building their own businesses. Connect with other entrepreneurs and take part in events and discussions.

Web: www.biznik.com
Facebook: Biznik (Group)
Twitter: (None)
LinkedIn: Biznik: business networking that doesn't suck (Group)

Business.com

A comprehensive, browsable, and searchable business directory that helps you or your company find the products and services you need.

Web: www.business.com
Facebook: Business.com (Page)
Twitter: businessdotcom
LinkedIn: Business.com (Company)

1

Business Owners Idea Cafe

Managed by successful entrepreneurs and the authors of several guides on forming and running a business, this site includes numerous award-winning resources, along with practical advice, business news, and humor.

Web: www.businessownersideacafe.com
Facebook: Business Owners Idea Cafe (Page)
Twitter: boic
LinkedIn: Business Owners Idea Cafe (Group)

Business Owner's Tool Kit

With an emphasis on problem solving, this site features more than 5,000 pages of free cost-cutting tips, step-by-step checklists, real-life case studies, startup advice, and business templates to small-business owners and entrepreneurs.

Web: www.toolkit.com
Facebook: The Business Owner's Toolkit (Group)
Twitter: (None)
LinkedIn: Business Owner's Toolkit (Group)

BusinessWeek Small Biz

This site, which is maintained by the staff of *Business Week* magazine, provides articles, video, answers to commonly asked questions, and numerous special reports on starting and managing a small business.

Web: www.businessweek.com/small-business/
Facebook: (None)
Twitter: bweek
LinkedIn: BusinessWeek (Company), BusinessWeek Group (Group)

Dane Carlson's Business Opportunities Weblog

The mission of this website is "to help entrepreneurs like yourself find the business that's right for YOU!" Included is a listing of legitimate business opportunities, business tips, and success stories.

Web: www.business-opportunities.biz
Facebook: Dane Carlson's Business Opportunities Weblog (Page)
Twitter: danec
LinkedIn: (None)

Doba

The world's leading online product sourcing marketplace for retailers. Doba's web-based inventory-on-demand platform automates the e-commerce supply chain through virtual inventory management and direct merchandise fulfillment.

Web: www.doba.com
Facebook: Doba (Page)
Twitter: doba
LinkedIn: Doba (Company)

Entrepreneur Wiki

Not nearly as populated with content as Wikipedia's Entrepreneurship page, this page enables you to really make a dent by sharing what you know about starting and managing your business.

Web: http://evp.wikia.com/wiki/Main_Page
Facebook: Wikia. (Page, Group)
Twitter: wikia
LinkedIn: Wikia (Company)

Go BIG Network

The Go BIG Network is an online marketplace that connects entrepreneurs with investors, advisors, service providers, and job seekers. Find help writing a business plan, or network with potential investors by registering to use this free fast-growing website for business leaders and entrepreneurs.

Web: www.gobignetwork.com
Facebook: GoBig Network (Page)
Twitter: (None)
LinkedIn: GoBigNetwork Startup Community (Group)

Hoover's

Hoover's gives you access to up-to-date information about industries, companies, and key decision makers. Great for professionals working in sales, marketing, business development, and others who need intelligence on U.S. and global companies, industries, and the people who lead them.

Web: www.hoovers.com
Facebook: Hoover's (Page)
Twitter: hoovers
LinkedIn: Hoover's Users (Group)

How to Change the World

Über-popular entrepreneur, venture capitalist, and blogger Guy Kawasaki understands business. Guy is a managing director of Garage Technology Ventures, a columnist for *Entrepreneur* magazine, and the author of eight books on innovative business practices.

Web: http://blog.guykawasaki.com
Facebook: Guy Kawasaki (Page)
Twitter: GuyKawasaki
LinkedIn: (None)

iinnovate

The iinnovate site is a podcast written and produced by students at Stanford University's Business and Design schools, and features interviews with leading business thinkers, authors, and venture capitalists.

Web: http://iinnovate.blogspot.com
Facebook: iinnovate (Group)
Twitter: (None)
LinkedIn: (None)

JaredReitzin.com

For anyone thinking about starting a business, this blog provides the tips and information needed to be a successful entrepreneur. Jared's mission is to "give you real-life tools, examples, and suggestions on how to run an efficient business without much capital."

Web: www.jaredreitzin.com
Facebook: Jared Reitzin (People)
Twitter: JaredReitzin
LinkedIn: Jared Reitzin (People)

Jott

Jott is a voice-to-text service that allows you to create and send emails and text messages and post information to web services all with a simple toll-free call from your phone. Regardless of where you are, Jott helps you stay connected by converting your voice into timely messages and more.

Web: http://jott.com/default.aspx
Facebook: Jott (Application)
Twitter: JottNetworks
LinkedIn: Jott Networks (Company)

Kauffman Foundation

An up-to-date and relevant website dedicated to furthering our understanding of the phenomenon of entrepreneurship and to advancing entrepreneurship education and training. Check out the Resource Center for getting-started information on business operations, sales and marketing, human resources, finance and accounting, and the like.

Web: www.kauffman.org
Facebook: Ewing Marion Kauffman Foundation (Page)
Twitter: KauffmanFDN
LinkedIn: Kauffman Foundation (Company), The Kauffman Foundation for Entrepreneurship (Group)

LinkedIn

LinkedIn is a leading online network of more than 25 million professionals from around the world, representing more than 150 industries. When you join, you create a profile summarizing your professional accomplishments, which is then linked to current and former colleagues, clients, and partners.

Web: www.linkedin.com
Facebook: LinkedIn (Page, Group)
Twitter: LinkedIn, LinkedInNews
LinkedIn: Linkedin (Company)

1

The Long Tail

Wired magazine editor in chief Chris Anderson's blog about business and the impact of the "Long Tail"—Andersen's theory that the economy is shifting from mass markets to million of niches.

Web: www.longtail.com
Facebook: The Long Tail (Group)
Twitter: (None)
LinkedIn: (None)

MAKING IT! Minority Success Stories

A weekly half-hour magazine-format webcast highlighting the challenges and contributions of minority-owned and -managed businesses. Each episode includes two entrepreneurs' stories, profiling the efforts of minority men and women who strive to improve their communities through business ownership.

Web: www.makingittv.com/homepage.html
Facebook: Nelson Davis (People)
Twitter: (None)
LinkedIn: Nelson Davis (People)

Microsoft Small Business Center

A vehicle for selling various Microsoft small-business products, this site also provides plenty of excellent information and advice entirely free. If you're starting or running your own small business, Microsoft's Small Business Center is an excellent place to learn from the experts.

Web: www.microsoft.com/smallbusiness/hub.mspx
Facebook: Microsoft (Page)
Twitter: Microsoft
LinkedIn: Microsoft (Company)

My Business Credit Journey

If your business is having difficulties establishing a line of credit, or if you'd like to know more about how credit can impact your new or existing business, this blog is for you. You will find tips, tricks, strategies, and warnings about establishing and maintaining business-related credit, which along with customers is the lifeblood of any business.

Web: www.mybusinesscreditblog.com
Facebook: (None)
Twitter: MyBCBlog
LinkedIn: (None)

Plaxo

Think of Plaxo as a dashboard for viewing what the people you do business with are creating and sharing via the Web. Features include an address book, a friend list, and video and photo sharing.

Web: www.plaxo.com
Facebook: Plaxo (Page), PLAXO (Group)
Twitter: plaxo, Plaxo_Jobs
LinkedIn: Plaxo (Company)

Review Fuse

Review Fuse provides a unique service for businesses and individuals who find value in having their work reviewed by noncompetitive third parties prior to turning it in. Great for management consultants, writers, and others who work alone and value the opinions of trusted peers.

Web: www.reviewfuse.com
Facebook: Review Fuse (People)
Twitter: ReviewFuse
LinkedIn: (None)

Small Business Administration

Here you can learn how to start your own business and finance it. The site also provides information on business opportunities, local SBA offices, laws and regulations, and much more.

Web: www.sba.gov
Facebook: (None)
Twitter: (None)
LinkedIn: US Small Business Administration (Company)

Small Business School

The award-winning weekly half-hour PBS television show that began in 1995 and has been airing ever since is now available online. At this website, the key ideas of every episode of the show come alive within an executive summary, transcript, case-study guide, and streaming video.

Web: www.smallbusinessschool.org
Facebook: Small Business School (Group)
Twitter: (None)
LinkedIn: (None)

Small Business Trends

Get updated on the latest small-business trends, find marketing tips, and read information from the small-business experts. You will also find podcasts available for downloading.

Web: www.smallbiztrends.com
Facebook: Anita Campbell (People), Small Biz Trends (Group)
Twitter: smallbiztrends
LinkedIn: Anita Campbell (People), Small Business Trends (Group)

VentureDeal

Easy-to-use database with the latest information on U.S.-based venture-backed technology companies, senior management, company financings, and M&A transactions. Updated daily, this site offers a convenient way of accessing critical information related to business development, funding searches, and venture capital investment goals.

Web: www.venturedeal.com
Facebook: VentureDeal Venture Capital Database (Page)
Twitter: VentureDeal
LinkedIn: (None)

Venture Voice

The Venture Voice podcast explores how entrepreneurs build their businesses, manage their companies, and live their lives. Nearly 50 interviews from some of the most fascinating entrepreneurs are available for download.

Web: www.venturevoice.com
Facebook: Venture Voice (Page)
Twitter: venturevoice
LinkedIn: (None)

Work.com

The small-business entrepreneur's owner's manual on where to go, what to know, and how to get the most value from the ever-growing array of web resources for business. The site features more than 2,000 how-to guides authored by business experts and organized by common business tasks and challenges.

Web: www.work.com
Facebook: (None)
Twitter: whatworks
LinkedIn: (None)

Young Entrepreneur

This blog provides information and advice to worldwide entrepreneurs. There are many great articles, including "How to Create a Budget," "Don't Try to Be Perfect—by Anthony Robbins," and "10 Things You Should Know When Marketing Your Business."

Web: www.youngentrepreneur.com/blog
Facebook: Young Entrepreneur (Page)
Twitter: thebizguy
LinkedIn: (None)

FRANCHISING

Federal Trade Commission: Franchise and Business Opportunities

This site has lots of information, including a FAQs section, Guide to the FTC Franchise Rule, consumer alerts, Before You Buy pamphlets, and state disclosure requirements.

Web: www.ftc.gov/bcp/franchise/netfran.htm
Facebook: (None)
Twitter: ftcnews
LinkedIn: Federal Trade Commission (Company)

1

Franchise.com

Learn more about available franchise opportunities or advertise your franchise to potential buyers at this site, which aims to connect franchise buyers and sellers, as well as anyone thinking of starting a franchise.

Web: www.franchise.com
Facebook: (None)
Twitter: franchisedotcom
LinkedIn: (None)

The Franchise King

Rated as a Top 50 Blog for Franchise Startups, this blog covers a variety of topics, including tips, tricks, and trends for the franchise owner.

Web: http://thefranchiseking.typepad.com
Facebook: The Franchise King (Page)
Twitter: FranchiseKing
LinkedIn: Joel Libava (People)

Franchise Solutions

Find franchise and business opportunities at this site. It's a good collection of articles, tips, and advice from franchise experts, along with FAQs, a glossary, and a suggested reading list.

Web: www.franchisesolutions.com
Facebook: Franchise Solutions (Page)
Twitter: francisesale
LinkedIn: Franchise Solutions (Company)

Franchise Talk Radio Show and Podcast

Podcast featuring information on franchise opportunities from top business leaders and entrepreneurs.

Web: www.franradio.com
Facebook: FranRadio - Franchise Talk Radio Show (Page)
Twitter: (None)
LinkedIn: (None)

Franchise Update

Check out detailed articles about franchising, find experienced franchise attorneys, and learn more about available franchises at the site.

Web: www.franchise-update.com
Facebook: Franchise UPDATE Magazine (Page)
Twitter: (None)
LinkedIn: Franchise Update Media Group (Company)

Franchise Zone by Entrepreneur.com

Dedicated to linking enthusiastic entrepreneurs with the top franchises, this site provides all the information you need to find the best franchises and become a successful franchisee. How-to articles, advice from experts, and lists of the top franchises in various categories make this the first site to turn to for those considering the purchase of a franchise.

Web: www.entrepreneur.com/franchises
Facebook: Entrepreneur Magazine (Page, Group)
Twitter: EntMagazine
LinkedIn: Entrepreneur (Company)

Franchising.com

Franchising.com features a collection of top franchising opportunities, along with the information and tools you need to successfully operate your own franchise. The extensive Franchise Opportunities Directory can help you find the right business opportunity.

Web: www.franchising.com
Facebook: Frachising.com (Page)
Twitter: Franchising_com
LinkedIn: Franchise Business Opportunities by Franchising.com (Group)

FranNet

This site is all about franchising and whether you're suited for it. Some excellent resources include information on the history of franchising and what it's all about, as well as a guide to selecting the right franchise for you. A great place to look when you're just starting to consider becoming a franchise owner.

Web: www.frannet.com
Facebook: FranNet (Page, Group)
Twitter: FranNet_Team
LinkedIn: FranNet (Company), FranNet Group (Group)

HOME-BASED BUSINESS

Bizymoms

Business ideas, recommended books and resources, and work-at-home scams and how to avoid them. Check out the message board for ideas on a variety of topics!

Web: www.bizymoms.com/index.html
Facebook: Bizy Moms (Group), Bizymoms Experts Corner (Group)
Twitter: Bizymoms
LinkedIn: Bizymoms Work At Home Moms (Group), Bizymoms Forums (Group), Bizymoms Cities (Group)

HomeBasedBusiness.com

This is a very impressive blog about owning and operating a home-based business. Create a free profile for your business, participate in a forum discussion, and even create a blog of your own.

Web: www.homebasedbusiness.com
Facebook: (None)
Twitter: Home_Business
LinkedIn: (None)

Legitimate Home-Based Business

Home-based business owner and coach Kirk Bannerman's website dedicated to helping new home business owners make the most of every opportunity.

Web: www.business-at-home.us
Facebook: Legitimate Home-Based Business Network (Group)
Twitter: (None)
LinkedIn: (None)

PowerHomeBiz.com 🏅

A great website for those who are just considering the opportunity of starting their own home-based business and for those who already have a business in place. This site features step-by-step instructions on getting started, links to home-based business blogs, and tips and hints for gaining an edge in the competitive marketplace.

Web: www.powerhomebiz.com
Facebook: PowerHomeBiz.com: Home Business and Small Business Entrepreneurs (Page)
Twitter: powerhomebiz
LinkedIn: (None)

INTELLECTUAL PROPERTY

American Intellectual Property Law Association

The American Intellectual Property Law Association leads and serves a diverse intellectual property (IP) community by enhancing knowledge and shaping the future of IP law.

Web: www.aipla.org
Facebook: American Intellectual Property Law Association (AIPLA) (Page)
Twitter: aipla
LinkedIn: American Intellectual Property Law Association (Page, Group)

Daily Dose of IP

Patent attorney Mark Reichel's daily dose of intellectual property law news, opinion, and more.

Web: http://dailydoseofip.blogspot.com
Facebook: (None)
Twitter: markreichel
LinkedIn: Mark Reichel (People)

Electronic Frontier Foundation (EFF): Intellectual Property 🏅

EFF works to preserve balance and ensure that the Internet and digital technologies empower consumers, creators, innovators, scholars, and average citizens. This section of the EFF website

1

spotlights current challenges and solutions facing intellectual property rights.

Web: www.eff.org/issues/intellectual-property
Facebook: EFF (The Electronic Frontier Foundation) (Page), Electronic Frontier Foundation (Page, Group)
Twitter: EFF
LinkedIn: Electronic Frontier Foundation (Company), Electronic Frontier Foundation (EFF) (Group)

Nolo's Patent, Copyright, and Trademark Blog 🏅

Nolo book editor Rich Stim's blog about patents, copyright, trademarks, and more.

Web: www.patentcopyrighttrademarkblog.com
Facebook: Nolo (Page)
Twitter: NoloLaw
LinkedIn: Nolo & Friends (Group), Nolo Lawyers (Group)

World Intellectual Property Organization

Agency of the United Nations dedicated to developing a balanced and accessible international intellectual property system, which rewards creativity, stimulates innovation, and contributes to economic development while safeguarding the public interest.

Web: www.wipo.int/portal/index.html.en
Facebook: WIPO (Group)
Twitter: wiponews
LinkedIn: WIPO (Company)

INTERNATIONAL BUSINESS

Export-Import Bank of the United States

This independent U.S. government agency helps finance the overseas sales of U.S. goods and services. In more than 65 years, Export-Import Bank has supported more than $400 billion in U.S. exports, primarily to emerging markets worldwide.

Web: www.exim.gov
Facebook: (None)
Twitter: (None)
LinkedIn: Export-Import Bank of the United States (Company)

Finfacts Ireland

Extensive information on Irish finance and business.

Web: www.finfacts.ie
Facebook: (None)
Twitter: Finfacts
LinkedIn: (None)

globalEDGE

This site serves as an index of business, economics, trade, marketing, and government sites with an international focus. Great if you're thinking of expanding or moving your business to another country.

Web: http://globaledge.msu.edu/resourcedesk/
Facebook: globalEDGE (Page)
Twitter: globalEDGEmsu
LinkedIn: GlobalEDGE Marketing Consultants (Company)

Latin Trade

Excellent, up-to-date articles, a business-to-business directory, and other resources make this site a must-visit for anyone doing business or planning to do business in Latin America.

Web: http://latintrade.com
Facebook: Latin Trade (Page)
Twitter: latintrade
LinkedIn: Latin Trade (Company)

United States Council for International Business

A website for encouraging and assisting companies to succeed abroad by working together to influence laws, rules, and policies that may undermine U.S. competitiveness. In other words, this organization helps U.S. companies break down trade barriers in other countries.

Web: www.uscib.org
Facebook: USCIB (Page)
Twitter: USCIB
LinkedIn: USCIB-United States Council for International Business (Company), USCIB - United States Council for International Business (Group)

World Bank Group

The World Bank website offers information on loans and an array of customized resources.

Web: www.worldbank.org
Facebook: The World Bank (Page)
Twitter: WorldBankNews
LinkedIn: The World Bank (Company)

MANAGEMENT CONSULTING

American Society of Training and Development

ASTD is the world's largest professional association dedicated to workplace learning and performance professionals. Use this site to find industry conferences, news, publications, research reports, and more.

Web: www.astd.org
Facebook: ASTD (Page, Group)
Twitter: ASTD
LinkedIn: ASTD (Company), ASTD National (Group)

Association of Management Consulting Firms

The top international association of firms engaged in management consulting. This website is at the forefront of promoting excellence and integrity in the profession.

Web: www.amcf.org/amcf
Facebook: AMCF - Association of Management Consulting Firms (Group)
Twitter: (None)
LinkedIn: Association of Management Consulting Firms (AMCF) (Group)

Guerrilla Consulting

This blog is an extension of Jay Conrad Levinson's best-selling book, *Guerrilla Marketing for Consultants*. Gain tons of knowledge and get hands-on advice for all you need to know about consulting.

Web: http://guerrillaconsulting.typepad.com
Facebook: Jay Conrad Levinson (Page)
Twitter: GMarketingAssoc
LinkedIn: Guerrilla Marketing Tips for Small Businesses (Group), Guerrilla_Marketing (Group)

Manager Tools Podcast

Manager Tools is a weekly podcast focused on helping business professionals become more effective managers and leaders.

Web: www.manager-tools.com
Facebook: Manager Tools (Page)
Twitter: askmanagertools
LinkedIn: Manager Tools (Group)

The Project Management Podcast

Weekly podcast on how project management shapes the business world of today and tomorrow and helps you achieve the level of skill you will need in order to succeed.

Web: www.project-management-podcast.com
Facebook: The Project Management Podcast (Page)
Twitter: corneliusficht
LinkedIn: The Project Management Podcast (Group)

Tom Peters

Tom Peters doles out tons of innovative ideas and information on leadership, PR, and management training via this blog. Categories include branding, leadership, marketing, strategies, and success tips.

Web: www.tompeters.com
Facebook: Tom Peters (Page), Tom Peters Fan Club (Group)
Twitter: tom_peters
LinkedIn: Tom Peters Company (Company), TOM PETERS MENTORING GROUP (Group), Tom Peters Company Future Shape of the Winner (Group)

NONPROFIT BUSINESS RESOURCES

Big Duck

Insight into issues facing nonprofits; includes helpful resources and simple actions you can take to improve your nonprofit organization's communication efforts.

Web: www.bigducknyc.com
Facebook: Big Duck (Page)
Twitter: bigduck
LinkedIn: Big Duck (Company)

BoardSource

If you need to assemble or energize a board of directors for your nonprofit organization, this is the place to go. Features books, training, board Q&As, and membership information.

Web: www.boardsource.org
Facebook: BoardSource (Page)
Twitter: BoardSource
LinkedIn: BoardSource (Company, Group)

Care2

Whatever your nonprofit organization is passionate about—green living, health, human rights, or protecting the environment—Care2 puts the tools for change in your hands.

Web: www.care2.org
Facebook: Care2 (Page, Application)
Twitter: Care2
LinkedIn: Care2 (Company)

The Chronicle of Philanthropy

Summaries of articles published in the Chronicle's print version. Browse the site to find information on gifts and grants, fundraising, management, and technology of interest to nonprofit organizations.

Web: www.philanthropy.com
Facebook: Philanthropy.com (Page), The Chronicle of Philanthropy (Group)
Twitter: Philanthropy
LinkedIn: The Chronicle of Philanthropy (Group)

Citizendium

This wiki—which features lots of information for nonprofit organizations—has the ambitious goal of finding a better way for all of us to come together to make an encyclopedia. An alternative to Wikipedia, Citizendium, short for The Citizens' Compendium, is worth a look, especially if you work for or serve on the Board of Directors of a nonprofit organization.

Web: http://en.citizendium.org/wiki/Welcome_to_Citizendium
Facebook: Citizendium (Page)
Twitter: citizendium
LinkedIn: Citizendium Wiki (Group), Citizendium (Group)

Council on Foundations

A membership association of more than 2,000 grant-making foundations and giving programs from around the world (independent, corporate, and public). COF provides leadership expertise, legal services, and networking opportunities to its members.

Web: www.cof.org
Facebook: Council on Foundations (Page)
Twitter: COF_
LinkedIn: Council on Foundations (Company, Group)

Foundation Center

For grant seekers and grant makers, this site contains information on training and seminars, fundraising trends and analyses, the fundraising process, and publications. Also included are a searchable database and an online reference desk.

Web: http://foundationcenter.org
Facebook: Foundation Center (Page, Group)
Twitter: fdncenter
LinkedIn: The Foundation Center (Company)

IRS: Charities

If you run a nonprofit organization, you must file the proper forms with the IRS to establish and maintain your tax-exempt status. This site provides information and guidance from the IRS on how to handle all the important paperwork and more.

Web: www.irs.gov/charities
Facebook: IRS (Group)
Twitter: IRStaxpros
LinkedIn: Internal Revenue Service (Company)

Nonprofit Communications

Kivi Leroux Miller believes that "even the smallest nonprofit staffs with the most modest budgets can achieve tremendous results through savvy marketing and communications." Here you will find many useful resources to help you market your nonprofit.

Web: www.nonprofitmarketingguide.com/blog
Facebook: Nonprofit Marketing Guide (Page)
Twitter: kivilm
LinkedIn: Kivi Leroux Miller (People)

The NonProfit Times

The *NonProfit Times* is a leading business publication for nonprofit professionals. The website offers topics that focus on fundraising, financial management, marketing, web tools, nonprofit news, and careers.

Web: http://nptimes.blogspot.com
Facebook: The NonProfit Times (Page)
Twitter: NonProfitTimes
LinkedIn: (None)

A Small Change

This blog is dedicated to answering your nonprofit fundraising questions. Numerous topics are addressed, including major donors, business and foundation relations, technology, and online fundraising.

Web: www.asmallchange.net
Facebook: A Small Change- Fundraising Blog (Page)
Twitter: (None)
LinkedIn: A Small Change- Fundraising Blog (Group)

Social Innovation Conversations

Coproduced with the Center for Social Innovation at the Stanford Graduate School of Business, this podcast cover lots of ground, including social entrepreneurship, corporate responsibility, and responsible investing.

Web: http://sic.conversationsnetwork.org
Facebook: Social Innovation Conversations (Page, Group)
Twitter: SIConversations
LinkedIn: (None)

Tech Soup

This site offers nonprofits a one-stop resource for technology needs by providing free information, resources, and support.

Web: http://home.techsoup.org/pages/default.aspx
Facebook: TechSoup (Page)
Twitter: TechSoup
LinkedIn: TechSoup Global (Company), TechSoup (now TechSoup Global) (Group)

USA.gov For Nonprofits

Learn about government support for nonprofit groups by clicking federal government agency names at this simple site that's packed with valuable information.

Web: www.usa.gov/Business/Nonprofit.shtml
Facebook: USA.gov (Page)
Twitter: USAgov
LinkedIn: (None)

1

1

OFFICE MANAGEMENT

AtTask

AtTask offers Internet-based project management software that helps companies schedule and manage multiple projects and resources and improve workflow and productivity.

Web: www.attask.com
Facebook: @task (Page)
Twitter: AtTask
LinkedIn: AtTask, Inc. (Company), AtTask User's Group (Group), AtTask Community (Group)

G.ho.st

G.ho.st, pronounced "ghost," stands for Global Hosted Operating System. It provides a free web-based virtual computer to everyone who needs one. The G.ho.st service includes a personal desktop, files, and applications, and is available from any browser.

Web: http://ghost.cc/
Facebook: G.ho.st - A Free Virtual PC For All Mankind! (Group)
Twitter: ghostvc
LinkedIn: G.ho.st Global Hosted Operating SysTem (Company)

Google Docs

Free web-based word processor and spreadsheet, which allow you to share and collaborate online. Google Docs accepts most popular file formats, including DOC, XLS, ODT, ODS, RTF, CSV, PPT, and more.

Web: www.docs.google.com
Facebook: Google Docs (Page, Application)
Twitter: (None)
LinkedIn: Google Docs (Group)

Mozy

Mozy offers automatic and secure data backup via the Internet for individuals and businesses. If you or your business is looking for a simple and safe data backup solution, this service is for you.

Web: www.mozy.com
Facebook: Mozy (Page, Group)
Twitter: mozy, mozysupport, mozybackup, MozyCode
LinkedIn: Mozy (Company)

Salesforce.com ⬢

Easy-to-use web-based customer relation management tools for your entire company, including online solutions for sales, service, marketing, and call-center operations.

Web: www.salesforce.com
Facebook: Salesforce Global (Group), Salesforce (Page)
Twitter: salesforce
LinkedIn: SalesForce (Company), Salesforce Power Users Group (Group)

Wufoo

Wufoo is a web-based application that removes inefficiency and tediousness from the form-building process. Wufoo reduces what used to take days (if not weeks) by trained professionals to something that can be done by anyone in minutes.

Web: www.wufoo.com
Facebook: Wufoo (Page)
Twitter: Wufoo
LinkedIn: (None)

Zoho

Zoho offers a suite of office productivity tools online, including a word processor, a spreadsheet program, an invoicing tool, a presentation creator, web-conferencing functions, and calendar organizers.

Web: www.zoho.com
Facebook: Zoho (Page, Group)
Twitter: zoho
LinkedIn: Zoho Corporation (Company), Zoho World (Group)

PATENTS AND TRADEMARKS

All About Trademarks

A detailed online directory offering an overview of trademarks and their use, along with hundreds of links to federal and international laws, journals, and organizations.

Web: www.ggmark.com
Facebook: (None)
Twitter: ggmark
LinkedIn: (None)

Idea Locker 🏅 📑

One of the best invention/patent sites on the Web for novice innovators of all ages, this site is specifically designed for kids. Provides information on how to invent, famous inventors, and discoveries.

Web: www.bkfk.com
Facebook: BKFK (Page)
Twitter: bykidsforkids
LinkedIn: (None)

Patently-O

Must-read read blog for more than 10,000 patent law professionals. With categories covering all aspects of patents and patent law, this blog is sure to please.

Web: www.patentlyo.com
Facebook: Patently-O etc. (Group)
Twitter: patentlyo
LinkedIn: (None)

Peter Zura's 271 Patent Blog

A great source for up-to-date news and analysis on patent law. Managed by Chicago attorney Peter Zura.

Web: http://271patent.blogspot.com
Facebook: (None)
Twitter: pzura
LinkedIn: Peter Zura (People)

U.K. Intellectual Property Office

The U.K. Intellectual Property Office has a well-designed site that makes it easy to navigate to the main sections: Trade Marks, Copyright, Designs, and Patents. The Patents page covers everything from the definition of a patent, instructions on how to apply, and detailed patent information that might appeal to lawyers more than the average citizen.

Web: www.ipo.gov.uk
Facebook: Intellectual Property Office (IPO) (Page)
Twitter: (None)
LinkedIn: (None)

Your Legal Companion—Law and Business

Nolo writer and attorney Richard Stim presents dynamic discussions of the law, interviews with authors and other experts, and answers to everyday questions in plain English.

Web: www.nolocast.com
Facebook: Nolo (Page)
Twitter: NoloLaw
LinkedIn: Nolo & Friends (Group), Nolo Lawyers (Group)

SALES AND MARKETING

Adweek Online

Online edition of *Adweek*, a popular print magazine focusing on all things advertising and marketing. This site features the inside scoop on what's going on in the marketing departments of high-profile companies and corporations.

Web: www.adweek.com/aw/index.jsp
Facebook: Adweek (Page)
Twitter: AdweekDotCom
LinkedIn: Adweek (Company), Buzz Awards (Group)

Chief Marketer

A very rich website that provides marketing executives with insights into key marketing issues, innovations, and practical solutions.

Web: www.chiefmarketer.com
Facebook: Chief Marketer (Page)
Twitter: chief_marketer
LinkedIn: (None)

ClickZ Network

ClickZ is the "largest resource of interactive marketing news, information, commentary, advice, opinion, research, and reference in the world, online or off."

Web: www.clickz.com
Facebook: Clickz (Application)
Twitter: ClickZ
LinkedIn: ClickZ Network (Company)

Culture Scout Blog

Marketing author, speaker, and consultant Patricia Martin's blog about consumer behavior and culture—two critical components of all marketing efforts.

Web: http://blog.patricia-martin.com
Facebook: (None)
Twitter: PatriciaMartin
LinkedIn: (None)

Direct Marketing Association

The Direct Marketing Association (DMA) is the largest trade association for businesses that are interested and involved in direct, database, and interactive global marketing. Here you can learn more about the DMA, become a member, and access its services.

Web: www.the-dma.org/index.php
Facebook: Direct Marketing Association - DMA (Page)
Twitter: DMASocialMedia
LinkedIn: Direct Marketing Association "Official" (Group)

Duct Tape Marketing

Chock-full of information to help with small-business marketing, this blog has categories covering many useful topics, including marketing materials, marketing plans, strategy, and web marketing.

Web: www.ducttapemarketing.com/blog
Facebook: Duct Tape Marketing (Page)
Twitter: ducttape
LinkedIn: Duct Tape Marketing (Group)

GreenBook

Looking for a marketing research firm? GreenBook should be your first stop. It is the annual directory of marketing research firms; it can be ordered in print form here or searched free online.

Web: www.greenbook.org
Facebook: (None)
Twitter: ResearchShare
LinkedIn: (None)

Guerrilla Marketing

Read daily or bimonthly material from Jay Conrad Levinson, Mr. Guerrilla Marketing, and search the site's archives for useful guerrilla marketing strategies detailed by other marketing pros.

Web: www.gmarketing.com
Facebook: Guerrilla Marketing (Group)
Twitter: GMarketingAssoc
LinkedIn: Guerrilla_Marketing (Group)

Internet Business Mastery

Learn how to create an Internet-based business, unleash a flood of traffic, and trigger explosive profits in the new social media age.

Web: http://internetbusinessmastery.com/category/podcast
Facebook: Internet Business Mastery (Page)
Twitter: (None)
LinkedIn: (None)

KnowThis.com

Take the free Principles of Marketing Tutorial or delve deep to find out what an effective website looks like. Whether you're a marketing student or a professional, you can find plenty of excellent, up-to-date information at this site.

Web: www.knowthis.com
Facebook: KnowThis.com (Page)
Twitter: (None)
LinkedIn: (None)

MarketingProfs Know-How Exchange

The Internet's most vibrant marketing forum, featuring nearly 25,000 searchable questions and five times as many answers.

Web: www.marketingprofs.com/ea/
Facebook: MarketingProfs (Page)
Twitter: marketingprofs
LinkedIn: MarketingProfs (Company, Group)

Marketing Research Association

Dedicated to advancing the practical application, use, and understanding of the opinion and marketing research profession, MRA's website features research tools, publications about marketing and opinion polls, software tools, and so on.

Web: www.mra-net.org
Facebook: Marketing Research Association (Page)
Twitter: MRA_National
LinkedIn: Marketing Research Association (Group)

Marketing Resource Center

From the same people who publish *Inc. Magazine*, this site features a bevy of resources for the marketer, including recent articles, streaming video, blog entries, and links to additional resources.

Web: www.inc.com/marketing
Facebook: Inc. Magazine (Page)
Twitter: incmagazine
LinkedIn: (None)

Sales and Marketing Management Magazine

This website is devoted to providing its readers with "easy access to the most relevant trends, strategies, exclusive research, expert voices, and cutting-edge case studies designed to help them sell more, manage better, and market smarter." Here, you can read sample articles and sign up for a subscription.

Web: www.salesandmarketing.com/msg/publications/smm.jsp
Facebook: (None)
Twitter: SMM_Pub
LinkedIn: Sales & Marketing Management (Group)

Sales Guy: Quick and Dirty Tips For Getting the Deal Done

Actionable tips designed to help you close more business, advance your sales career, and put more money in your wallet.

Web: http://sales.quickanddirtytips.com
Facebook: Sales Guy (Page)
Twitter: (None)
LinkedIn: (None)

Sales Resource Center

Inc.com's resource center for all things related to sales. You can find articles, streaming video, blog entries, links to additional resources, and so on.

Web: www.inc.com/sales
Facebook: Inc. Magazine (Page)
Twitter: incmagazine
LinkedIn: (None)

Wonder Branding: Marketing to Women

Find blog posting with such titles as "Four Fallacies About Female Consumers" and "Beyond The Pink Ribbon: Cause Marketing." The blog also features many useful and interesting links.

Web: www.wonderbranding.com
Facebook: Michele Miller (People)
Twitter: MicheleMiller
LinkedIn: Michele Miller (People)

Word of Mouth Marketing Association ⬥BEST⬥

Official website of WOMMA, where you can find the latest thinking on a variety of Internet marketing strategies, including word-of-mouth marketing.

Web: http://womma.org/main/
Facebook: WOMMA Education Council (Group)
Twitter: WOMMA
LinkedIn: WOMMA (Company), Word of Mouth Marketing Association (Group), Fan of Word of Mouth Marketing (Group)

TRADE PUBLICATIONS

Entrepreneur.com's Trade Publication Directory

One of the Internet's largest searchable databases of trade publications. From agriculture and biotech to purchasing and procurement, Entrepreneur.com has your industry's trade publication listed here.

Web: www.entrepreneur.com/tradepublication/category/index.html
Facebook: Entrepreneur Magazine (Page, Group)
Twitter: EntMagazine
LinkedIn: Entrepreneur (Company), Entrepreneur Magazine (Group)

TradePub.com ⬥BEST⬥

If you're looking for a trade publication, you're likely to find it here. This site features an extensive list of free business, computer, and engineering trade newsletters and magazines, all of which you can subscribe to for free.

Web: www.tradepub.com
Facebook: (None)
Twitter: TradePub
LinkedIn: (None)

VIDEOCONFERENCING

Cisco

If you work for a large company that can afford a top-of-the-line telepresence room, take a serious look at Cisco's telepresence solutions.

Web: www.cisco.com/en/US/products/ps7060/index.html
Facebook: Cisco Press Products (Page), Cisco (Page)
Twitter: CiscoSystems, CiscoPress
LinkedIn: Cisco Systems (Company)

Face to Face Live ⬥BEST⬥

A leading provider of low-cost, high-definition, managed, point-to-point videoconferencing and telepresence solutions. The only managed services provider for LifeSize Communication's award-winning videoconferencing systems.

Web: www.f2fl.com
Facebook: Face to Face Live (Page)
Twitter: F2FL
LinkedIn: Face to Face Live (Company)

Face to Face Live Blog

On videoconferencing company Face to Face Live's blog, you can find information about the role videoconferencing plays in small, medium, and large businesses and nonprofit organizations.

Web: www.facetofaceliveblog.com
Facebook: Face to Face Live (Page)
Twitter: F2FL
LinkedIn: Face to Face Live (Company)

HP Halo

Hewlett-Packard sells more than just computers. Large corporations that can spend the big bucks favor HP's Halo line of videoconferencing and telepresence systems.

Web: http://h71028.www7.hp.com/enterprise/us/en/halo/index.html
Facebook: (None)
Twitter: HP_Halo
LinkedIn: HP HALO Telepresence Professional Group (Group)

LifeSize Communications

Manufacturer of award-winning high-definition videoconferencing systems for businesses of all sizes. Now a division of Logitech, LifeSize empowers you to be more productive by helping you travel less and do more.

Web: www.lifesize.com
Facebook: LifeSize Communications (Page)
Twitter: lifesizehd
LinkedIn: LifeSize Communications (Company)

Polycom

Best known for their telephones, Polycom also offers a line of videoconferencing systems for corporations around the globe.

Web: www.polycom.com
Facebook: Polycom (Page, Group)
Twitter: (None)
LinkedIn: Polycom (Company), Polycom Community (Group)

Tandberg

Tandberg is a leading global provider of telepresence, videoconferencing, and mobile video products and services.

Web: www.tandberg.com
Facebook: TANDBERG (Group)
Twitter: TANDBERG_Video, TANDBERG_News, TANDBERG_Events
LinkedIn: TANDBERG (Company)

Telepresence Options

Productivity-focused technologist Howard S. Lichtman's website about all things telepresence. This site covers the leading companies, solutions, and technologies behind the communications revolution that is videoconferencing.

Web: www.telepresenceoptions.com
Facebook: Telepresence Options (Page)
Twitter: TelepresenceVTC
LinkedIn: Telepresence Options (Company)

Videoconferencing Tips and Techniques

Australian blogger Carol Daunt Skyring's blog about taking your videoconferencing skills to the next level.

Web: http://videoconference.edublogs.org
Facebook: Carol Skyring (People)
Twitter: caroldaunt
LinkedIn: Carol Skyring (People)

WOMEN IN BUSINESS

The Boss of You

From the authors of the book *The Boss of You*, this blog features expanded information on running a woman-owned business. Categories include profiles, business advice, and resources for women in business and more.

Web: http://laurenandemira.com
Facebook: The Boss of You (Page)
Twitter: laurenbacon, emiramears
LinkedIn: (None)

Catalyst

Catalyst is a leading corporate research and advisory organization that works with businesses to build inclusive environments and expand professional opportunities for women.

Web: www.catalyst.org
Facebook: Catalyst (Page)
Twitter: CatalystInc
LinkedIn: Catalyst Inc (Company, Group)

1

Diva Marketing Blog

Toby Bloomberg, an expert marketer, uses this blog to share her opinions and views on marketing to women.

Web: http://bloombergmarketing.blogs.com/bloomberg_marketing
Facebook: Toby Bloomberg (People)
Twitter: TobyDiva
LinkedIn: Toby Bloomberg (People)

The Lip-Sticking Blog

Interested in marketing to women online? This blog features articles written by successful women entrepreneurs, bloggers, authors, and media specialists, all geared toward helping you market your products and services to women.

Web: http://windsormedia.blogs.com
Facebook: (None)
Twitter: y2vonne
LinkedIn: (None)

National Association for Female Executives

NAFE provides education, networking, and public advocacy to empower its members to achieve career success and financial security.

Web: www.nafe.com/?service=vpage/1474
Facebook: (None)
Twitter: _NAFE_
LinkedIn: National Association for Female Executives (NAFE) (Group), National Association for Female Executives (Group)

Office of Women's Business Ownership

Part of the U.S. Small Business Administration, this office/website assists women in achieving their goals by helping them start and run successful businesses.

Web: www.sba.gov/aboutsba/sbaprograms/onlinewbc
Facebook: (None)
Twitter: (None)
LinkedIn: US Small Business Administration (Company)

Women's Work

Women's Work is dedicated to helping women move from standard 9-to-5 jobs to flex careers—telecommuting, small business, and other options. This site is packed with articles, advice, how-to guides, flexible career choices, and success stories to inspire and motivate.

Web: www.wwork.com
Facebook: Women's Work (Page, Group)
Twitter: WomensWork
LinkedIn: (None)

COMPUTERS AND ELECTRONICS

While this book helps you travel the worldwide network known as the Internet, this chapter details specific places that will make your Internet experience more interesting. In particular, each entry is designed to give you access to top computer and electronic resources that use the big three social media sites: Facebook, Twitter, and LinkedIn.

COMPUTER MANUFACTURERS

Acer

The Acer Group is a family of four brands—Acer, Gateway, Packard Bell, and eMachines.

Web: http://www.acer-group.com/public/
Facebook: Acer (Page), Acer (Group)
Twitter: AcerGroup, aspireonenews
LinkedIn: Acer America Corp. (Company), Acer fans (Group)

Apple

Among other products, Apple gives you the Mac, iPod, iPhone, iPad, iTunes, and Support.

Web: www.apple.com
Facebook: Fans of Apple (Page), :Apple Ipod: (Page), Macintosh Computers (Page), #Macintosh (Group)
Twitter: macTweeter, apple_app_store, AppleSupportRSS, iPadSupport
LinkedIn: Apple Professionals (Group), Mac Users (Group), MacUser (Group), Apple fans (Group), Apple Inc. (Company)

ELECTRONICS

Best Buy

A place where you can go to get the electronics that you want, either online or in the "real world." Enroll in their free Reward Zone program to get discount coupons and more to make your dollars go just a bit further.

Web: www.bestbuy.com
Facebook: Best Buy (Page)
Twitter: BestBuy_Deals
LinkedIn: Best Buy (Company)

CNET ⬛

A tech product review, news, and blog site. You'll find not only words and pictures but also video coverage of the latest and greatest on the market.

Web: www.cnet.com
Facebook: CNET (Page)
Twitter: CNETNews
LinkedIn: CNET Technology (Page)

Engadget

The latest and greatest in the world of electronics appear here well before hitting the stores. Also has a sister site, Engadget HD, that covers hi-def television topics exclusively.

Web: www.engadget.com
Facebook: Engadget (Page)
Twitter: engadget
LinkedIn: Engadget Users Group (Group)

2

EMAIL

Gmail

Gmail is Google's entry into the web mail arena. Google was one of the first to offer mailboxes that can hold more than one gigabyte. Currently, mailbox sizes start at more than five gigabytes for free, with additional storage available for a fee.

Web: www.gmail.com
Facebook: Gmail (Page), Gmail (Group)
Twitter: Gmail_team
LinkedIn: Gmail Users (Group)

Mail2Web

This site provides a nice web interface for your Internet standard email in the event your provider doesn't have one. You'll need to know some technical details, such as your mail server's name, login, and password.

Web: www.mail2web.com
Facebook: mail2web.com (Page)
Twitter: (None)
LinkedIn: (None)

Windows Live Hotmail

Hotmail was one of the pioneers in the web-based email market. Now owned by Microsoft, it is part of the larger Windows Live product line. Offers five gigabytes of storage.

Web: http://mail.live.com
Facebook: Windows Live Hotmail (Page)
Twitter: (None)
LinkedIn: (None)

EngadgetHD

This site covers hi-def television topics exclusively.

Web: www.engadgethd.com
Facebook: (None)
Twitter: engadgethd
LinkedIn: (None)

Gizmodo

News, reviews, and rumors for the lover of all types of electronic gadgets.

Web: http://gizmodo.com/
Facebook: Gizmodo (Page)
Twitter: GizmodoFeed
LinkedIn: (None)

Gizmo Lovers

A site with a focus on television-related devices, particularly TiVo digital video recorders.

Web: www.gizmolovers.com
Facebook: (None)
Twitter: GizmoLovers
LinkedIn: (None)

Radio Shack

Home site for one of the older retailers in the electronics space. You can probably find the parts you need here.

Web: www.radioshack.com
Facebook: RadioShack (Page)
Twitter: The_Shack
LinkedIn: RadioShack (Company)

Tom's Guide

A site that hosts reviews of home computing and networking gear. You'll also find a good section on bargain hunting to get the most for your money.

Web: www.tomsguide.com
Facebook: Tom's Guide (Page)
Twitter: Tomsguide
LinkedIn: None

GAMES

Addicting Games

Site features a broad and extensive list of games that you can play within your browser, as long as it supports Adobe Flash.

Web: www.addictinggames.com
Facebook: Addicting Games (Page), Addicting Games (Group)
Twitter: Addicting_Games
LinkedIn: (None)

IGN

The Internet Gaming Network covers all home video game systems, along with game previews, reviews, guides, and cheats.

Web: www.ign.com
Facebook: IGN (Page)
Twitter: IGNcom
LinkedIn: IGN Entertainment (Page)

Joystiq

An independent news and review site that serves as the hub for a cluster of sites covering each of the major gaming systems.

Web: www.joystiq.com
Facebook: Joystiq (Group)
Twitter: joystiq
LinkedIn: (None)

Kotaku

This site is a video gaming news and lifestyle site with a focus on the Japanese side of things.

Web: http://kotaku.com/
Facebook: Kotaku (Page, Group)
Twitter: kotakudotcom
LinkedIn: (None)

Massively

If you're looking for information on an MMORPG (massively multiplayer online role-playing game) that isn't WoW, this is the place to look.

Web: www.massively.com
Facebook: Massively.com (Page)
Twitter: massively
LinkedIn: Massive Online Gamer Group (Group), MMO Players (Group)

Penny Arcade

Penny Arcade started simply as a web comic with spot-on insight into the video game industry and community. It has now grown to include a forum and a store, and it's the center of activity for one of the largest video game conventions, PAX (Penny Arcade eXpo).

Web: www.penny-arcade.com
Facebook: Penny Arcade (Page, Group)
Twitter: PA_Megacorp
LinkedIn: Penny Arcade, Inc. (Company)

VGCats

A web comic that lovingly pokes fun at video games and their players.

Web: www.vgcats.com
Facebook: VGCats (Group)
Twitter: vgcats
LinkedIn: (None)

Wikia Gaming

A collection of wikis relating to video games of all types. Just about every game ever made (or about to be made) is covered in one of the sites found here.

Web: http://gaming.wikia.com/wiki/Wikia_Gaming
Facebook: Wikia Gaming (Group)
Twitter: (None)
LinkedIn: (None)

WoW Insider

This site provides news and advice regarding the world's number-one MMORPG.

Web: www.wowinsider.com
Facebook: WoW Insider (Page, Group)
Twitter: WoWInsider
LinkedIn: (None)

GENERAL BLOGGING

Blogger

Google's entry into the free-blog-site field.

Web: www.blogger.com
Facebook: Blogger (Group)
Twitter: Blogger
LinkedIn: Blogger Users (Group)

LiveJournal

One of the most popular blogging homes. It offers both free and fee blogs. LiveJournal is home to many personal and community blogs that cover a variety of topics.

Web: www.livejournal.com
Facebook: LiveJournal (Page), LiveJournal (Application)
Twitter: LiveJournal
LinkedIn: LiveJournal (Company)

Windows Live Writer

Home of Windows Live Writer, a free blog editor. Allows you to write your posts offline for later posting.

Web: http://writer.live.com
Facebook: Live Writer
Twitter: WLWriter
LinkedIn: None

WordPress

WordPress is the producer of blog-site software and is also a free blog host site.

Web: http://wordpress.com
Facebook: WordPress
Twitter: wordpressdotcom
LinkedIn: WordPress (Group)

Compaq (now a division of Hewlett-Packard)

Among other products, Compaq offers laptops, mini notebooks, desktops, all-in-ones, monitors, and accessories.

Web: www.compaq.com
Facebook: Compaq (Page), compaq (Group), COMPAQ (Group)
Twitter: (None)
LinkedIn: Compaq (Company), COMPAQ Users (Group)

Dell

Among other products, Dell offers computers for home, office, and small and medium businesses.

Web: www.dell.com
Facebook: Dell (Page), DELL (Group)
Twitter: Dell
LinkedIn: Dell (Company), The Dell Workforce (Group)

Gateway

Among other products, Gateway offers nine series of netbook and notebook computers.

Web: www.gateway.com
Facebook: Gateway (Page)
Twitter: (None)
LinkedIn: Gateway (Company)

Hewlett Packard

Among other products, Hewlett Packard offers computers designed for home, office, small and medium businesses, and large-enterprise businesses.

Web: www.hp.com
Facebook: Hewlett Packard (Company), Hewlett Packard (Group)
Twitter: HPCorp
LinkedIn: HP

Lenovo (includes IBM ThinkPads)

Among other products, Lenovo carries laptops, netbooks, desktops, all-in-ones, smartbooks, workstations, and servers.

Web: www.lenovo.com
Facebook: Official Lenovo Fan Site (Page), Lenovo (Page)
Twitter: (None)
LinkedIn: Lenovo (Company)

Sony

Among other products, Sony carries an extensive line of computers and electronics

Web: www.sony.com/vaio
Facebook: Sony (Page)
Twitter: SonyElectronics
LinkedIn: Sony (Company)

INSTANT MESSAGING

AIM

AOL Instant Messenger is AOL's popular entry. It was one of the first graphical clients for instant messaging, and for a long time it was what people were referring to when people would say, "IM me." AIM offers text, audio, and video chatting capabilities.

Web: www.aim.com
Facebook: AIM (Page)
Twitter: AIMRunningMan, aolaim
LinkedIn: (None)

Google Talk

An instant messaging client that integrates well with Google's other products, especially Gmail. It offers both text and voice chat.

Web: www.google.com/talk
Facebook: Google Talk (Page), google talk (Application)
Twitter: (None)
LinkedIn: (None)

Pidgin

So, now you've got instant messaging accounts on multiple services with friends on each of them. How do you get them together? You can use a client that connects to more than one service, like Pidgin.

Web: www.pidgin.im
Facebook: Pidgin (Page), Pidgin (Group)
Twitter: PidginIM
LinkedIn: (None)

Windows Live Messenger

Microsoft's client for text, voice, and video chatting. In addition to your Messenger contacts, you can add contacts on Yahoo! Messenger's network.

Web: http://get.live.com/messenger
Facebook: Windows Live Messenger (Page), Windows Live Messenger (Application)
Twitter: (None)
LinkedIn: (None)

Yahoo! Messenger

Another messenger client from the portal owners.

Web: http://messenger.yahoo.com
Facebook: Yahoo Messenger (Page)
Twitter: YAHOO_MESSENGER
LinkedIn: Yahoo Messenger User Group (Group)

INTERNET SECURITY

AVG Anti-Virus

Sometimes good things come with low prices, even no price. AVG offers a free version of its antivirus product.

Web: http://free.avg.com
Facebook: AVG Anti-Virus (Page)
Twitter: avg_updates
LinkedIn: AVG (Page)

ESET

Anti-virus solutions developed to deliver instant, comprehensive protection against evolving computer security threats. The self-proclaimed leader in proactive threat detection.

Web: http://www.eset.com
Facebook: ESET (Page), ESET Nod32 Smart Security (Group)
Twitter: ESET
LinkedIn: ESET Antivirus Software (Group), ESET (Company)

2

McAfee

McAfee releases a full spectrum of security software. They produce anti-virus programs for both the PC and Macintosh platforms.

Web: www.mcafee.com
Facebook: McAfee (Page)
Twitter: McAfeeNews
LinkedIn: McAfee (Page), McAfee Professionals (Group)

Security Now!

Listen to two respected voices from the Internet community, Steve Gibson and Leo Laporte, discuss matters in the world of personal computer security.

Web: www.grc.com/SecurityNow.htm
Facebook: Security Now! (Group)
Twitter: (None)
LinkedIn: (None)

Symantec

Symantec provides a variety of security-oriented software, including Norton Antivirus, Antispyware, and an Internet firewall. They've also got an extensive library of virus information to help in identifying and removing threats.

Web: www.symantec.com
Facebook: Symantec (Page, Group)
Twitter: symantec
LinkedIn: Symantec Corporation (Group)

MACINTOSH

Apple Support

Sometimes you need to go to the source to find an answer. This site would be that source for Mac-related questions. Check out the links for Support Resources on the left side of the page or use the Search Support box to find the help you need.

Web: www.apple.com/support/
Facebook: (None)
Twitter: AppleSupportRSS
LinkedIn: (None)

MacBreak Weekly

This podcast features a weekly audio gathering of Mac fans from the tech journalism community. It's known to be insightful and informative.

Web: www.thisweekintech.com/mbw
Facebook: MacBreak Weekly (Group)
Twitter: (None)
LinkedIn: (None)

Mac Rumors

A source for news, reviews, and, of course, rumors from the Apple Macintosh market. You'll also find notices of deals on Macintosh hardware and software.

Web: www.macrumors.com
Facebook: MacRumors (Page)
Twitter: MacRumorsDotCom
LinkedIn: (None)

Macworld

Macworld is one of the leading periodicals that cover the Macintosh, iPod, and iPhone. You'll find up-to-date information on the site that hasn't made it to print yet.

Web: www.macworld.com
Facebook: Macworld (Page)
Twitter: macworld
LinkedIn: Mackworld (Page)

The Unofficial Apple Weblog

This is a Mac-centric blog that brings you news that's not always blessed by Apple itself.

Web: www.tuaw.com
Facebook: The Unofficial Apple Weblog (TUAW) (Page), The Unofficial Apple Weblog (Group)
Twitter: TUAW
LinkedIn: (None)

MULTIMEDIA

BBC

If you're in Britain, you can catch up on BBC programming by using the iPlayer. Programs from the past seven days are available and, after downloading them, you've got 30 days to view them.

Web: www.bbc.co.uk/iplayer
Facebook: (None)
Twitter: BBCClick
LinkedIn: (None)

Expert Village

Billing itself as "The World's Largest How-To Video Site," this site is full of videos on a variety of topics—personal and professional. You can even submit videos for others to view. Also, you can register as an "expert" and, possibly, have a film-maker contact you about producing a series of videos on your subject. You will also find this information at ehow.com.

Web: www.expertvillage.com
Facebook: Expert Village (Group)
Twitter: (None)
LinkedIn: (None)

Hulu

A great site that hosts various U.S. television shows and movies from the past and present. Other than limited commercials, usually at the beginning of a program, the site is free.

Web: www.hulu.com
Facebook: hulu (Page), hulu (Group)
Twitter: hulu_com
LinkedIn: hulu (Company), HULU Users Group (Group)

Miro

Home of Miro (formerly known as the Democracy Player) and a vast directory of video blogs and other clips. According to the site, they offer the most high-definition programming on the Internet.

Web: www.getmiro.com
Facebook: (None)
Twitter: TheMiroFolks
LinkedIn: (None)

YouTube

YouTube came out of nowhere to become the site synonymous with video clips on the Web. Upload your own videos to share with the world or just watch what everyone else has posted. It's now part of the Google family of sites.

Web: www.youtube.com
Facebook: YouTube (Page), YouTube (Group)
Twitter: youtube
LinkedIn: YouTube (Company), YouTube innovators Innovation & Creativity You Tube Network (Group)

MUSIC RESOURCES

eMusic $

A subscription music site that specializes in tracks from independent music labels. Music is offered as MP3 files unencumbered by DRM.

Web: www.emusic.com
Facebook: eMusic (Page)
Twitter: eMusic
LinkedIn: (None)

iTunes

iTunes is the industry leader in digital music and continues to attract fans with its creative social media marketing efforts. For example, when you become a fan of iTunes' Facebook page, you receive an exclusive offer for 15 free songs.

Web: www.itunes.com
Facebook: iTunes (Page)
Twitter: iTunes Music, iTunes Podcasts, iTunesMovies, iTunesTV
LinkedIn: (None)

2

Napster 📖

Napster is an on-demand music service that has content agreements with the five major record labels and hundreds of independents. Napster delivers access to the largest catalog of online music, with more than seven million tracks.

Facebook: Napster (Page)
Twitter: napster
LinkedIn: Napster (Company)

Rhapsody ⑤

Rhapsody empowers you to listen to all the music you want for only $10/month. You don't pay for songs, you don't burn CDs, and you don't manage music files.

Web: www.rhapsody.com
Facebook: Rhapsody (Page)
Twitter: Rhapsody
LinkedIn: Rhapsody International (Company)

Zune 📖

Zune is another digital music provider, only Zune features The Social, an online music community that is driven by what users are listening to.

Web: www.zune.com
Facebook: Zune (Page)
Twitter: ZUNE
LinkedIn: (None)

PERSONAL COMPUTING

Motherboards.org

News, reviews, and user ranking site for PC motherboards, upgrades, and other hardware.

Web: www.motherboards.org
Facebook: (None)
Twitter: motherboardsorg
LinkedIn: (None)

MSN Tech

The MSN Tech site includes information and resources for all levels of PC/Windows users. Look here for product details, downloads, message boards, blogs, how-to instructions, tech news, and more.

Web: http://tech.msn.com
Facebook: (None)
Twitter: MSNTechGadgets
LinkedIn: (None)

PC Pitstop

A site that offers online free utilities for keeping your PC healthy. It includes programs for spyware and performance scanning.

Web: www.pcpitstop.com
Facebook: PC Pitstop (Group)
Twitter: pcoptimize
LinkedIn: (None)

PC World

Home of the popular *PC World* magazine, the site presents most of the content of the print publication free. The site also acts as a hub for blogs, buyers' guides, and podcasts.

Web: www.pcworld.com
Facebook: PC WORLD (Page)
Twitter: pcworld
LinkedIn: PC World (Company)

SEARCH ENGINES

Bing

Never content to be absent from a market, Microsoft has an entry in the search arena. Formerly known as Live Search, the semantic technology based Bing went live in 2009.

Web: www.bing.com
Facebook: Bing (Page)
Twitter: bing
LinkedIn: (None)

Google

The most popular site currently in the search-engine space. The company ensures that the engine is constantly evolving to meet the needs of the browsing population.

Web: www.google.com
Facebook: (None)
Twitter: google
LinkedIn: Google (Page), Google Group (Group)

Yahoo!

One of the pioneers in the Internet directory market, Yahoo! now maintains the directory and standard search site.

Web: www.yahoo.com
Facebook: Yahoo! (Page, Group)
Twitter: (None)
LinkedIn: Yahoo! (Company)

SOFTWARE

Adobe

Adobe is the publisher of a plethora of tools, most of them in the graphics arena. Find support and product-demo downloads at this site.

Web: www.adobe.com
Facebook: Adobe Photoshop (Page), Adobe Illustrator (Page)
Twitter: Adobe
LinkedIn: Adobe Systems (Company), Adobe Photoshop Group (Group), Adobe Software Users (Group)

Apple

If you have (or are thinking of getting) a Mac, an iPod, or an iPhone, this is the home of those popular products. Apple provides product updates and support from here.

Web: www.apple.com
Facebook: (None)
Twitter: (None)
LinkedIn: Apple Professionals (Group), Mac Users (Group), MacUser (Group)

Download Squad

This blog features updates on new and interesting software for Linux, Mac, and Windows users. Typically focuses on free software and shareware.

Web: www.downloadsquad.com
Facebook: Download Squad (Page)
Twitter: DownloadSquad
LinkedIn: (None)

FileHippo

FileHippo is another download library site, but it is notable for its Update Checker, which will check your PC and present you with a list of updates your machine may need for various major utilities.

Web: www.filehippo.com
Facebook: filehippo (Page)
Twitter: filehippo
LinkedIn: (None)

Giveaway of the Day

Every day this site offers users a free fully licensed copy of different software packages. The offer is good for one day, but the software will continue to work after the day is over.

Web: www.giveawayoftheday.com
Facebook: Giveaway of the Day (Page)
Twitter: GiveawayotDay
LinkedIn: (None)

Intuit

If you're keeping track of your finances or trying to prepare your tax return, you might already know about Intuit. They're the producers of the popular Quicken and TurboTax software packages.

Web: www.intuit.com
Facebook: Intuit (Page)
Twitter: Intuit
LinkedIn: Intuit (Company), Successful QuickBooks Consultants / Consulting - Accounting & Bookkeeping— Long for Success (Group)

2

LifeHacker

LifeHacker presents you with software and tech tips that help you improve and simplify your life.

Web: http://lifehacker.com
Facebook: Lifehacker (Page)
Twitter: Lifehacker
LinkedIn: (None)

Linux

So you have a computer but you want an alternative operating system. Linux might be the answer to that quandary. You'll find pointers to various flavors of Linux here, most of them free.

Web: www.linux.com
Facebook: Linux (Page)
Twitter: (None)
LinkedIn: Linux (Company), Open Source (Group), Linux Experts (Group) Linux Users (Group)

Microsoft

The 800-pound gorilla of the computer industry, Microsoft produces the ubiquitous Windows operating system and the Microsoft Office suite of productivity tools. Great volumes of information can be found at this site for those products and the many others that Microsoft produces.

Web: www.microsoft.com
Facebook: Microsoft (Page, Group)
Twitter: Microsoft
LinkedIn: Microsoft (Company)

VIRTUAL WORLDS

Dell Island

Ever want to walk through a personal computer? Now you can, at least virtually, by visiting Dell Island in Second Life. You can buy a computer for your avatar with Linden Dollars or buy one for the "real" you with real money. You can also visit the virtual Dell factory to watch PCs get built.

Web: www.dell.com/html/global/topics/sl/index.html
Facebook: (None)
Twitter: TeamDell
LinkedIn: Dell (Company)

IBM Real Business in 3-D

Visit IBM's outpost in Second Life to interact with IBM salespeople and partners. You can also find a technical-support library and the Virtual Green Data Center, where you can review some of IBM's energy-efficient projects.

Web: www.ibm.com/3dworlds/businesscenter/us/en
Facebook: (None)
Twitter: ibmdesign
LinkedIn: IBM (Page), IBMers (Group)

WEB BROWSERS

Firefox

The extremely popular web browser for multiple operating systems. Version 3.6 was released recently and set the newly created world record for most downloads in a day.

Web: www.mozilla.com/en-US/firefox
Facebook: Mozilla Firefox (Page)
Twitter: firefox
LinkedIn: Firefox Addicts (Group)

Opera

Officially supported group for users of the Opera web browser. This site invites users to surf the web with lightning speed, using the fastest browser ever.

Web: http://www.opera.com/
Facebook: Opera Web Browser (Page, Group)
Twitter: (None)
LinkedIn: Opera Users (Group)

CURRENT EVENTS/POLITICAL SCIENCE/NEWS 3

It's hard not to have information fatigue in the Information Age. People receive news on current events in real time and it's hard to keep up. This section provides some editorial filters designed to help you to stay connected with the social media world. Organized by topic, you'll find social media links covering news, financial information, politics, international affairs, and fringe culture.

CURRENT EVENTS

AlterNet.org

This portal compiles news from independent media sources, such as underground papers, alternative weeklies, and independent investigative journalists, to provide readers with news ignored by the mainstream media.

Web: www.alternet.org
Facebook: AlterNet (Page)
Twitter: AlterNet
LinkedIn: AlterNet (Company, Group)

Arts & Letters Daily

Arts & Letters Daily is an influential website that posts links to articles, essays, and reviews about art and literature. Although the site is affiliated with *The Chronicle of Higher Education* journal, it is not stuffy and academic. Rather, it's a key resource for bloggers, and articles posted on the site often influence many blog discussions.

Web: www.aldaily.com
Facebook: Arts & Letters Daily (Page), Arts and Letters Daily (Group)
Twitter: aldaily
LinkedIn: (None)

BoingBoing.net 🏅

BoingBoing.net rightly bills itself as "a directory of wonderful things." The site is one of the most visited blogs on a consistent basis, mainly because of the crackerjack efforts of its core stable of contributors, many of whom are published authors. Visitors won't be bored perusing the site, looking out for some new bit of weird and wonderful information, usually with a technology element, posted by one of the contributors.

Web: www.boingboing.net
Facebook: boingboing (Application, Page)
Twitter: BoingBoing
LinkedIn: (None)

Citizendium

Citizendium is a wiki encyclopedia project hoping to codify all aspects of knowledge. Users are encouraged to participate in the Citizendium online community as well as author or edit articles.

Web: http://en.citizendium.org/wiki/Main_Page
Facebook: Citizendium (Page)
Twitter: citizendium
LinkedIn: Citizendium Wiki (Group), Citizendium (Group)

DemocracyNow.org

Public radio vets Amy Goodman and Juan Gonzalez host this daily news program broadcast in video and audio formats.

Web: www.democracynow.org
Facebook: DemocracyNow.org (Group)
Twitter: (None)
LinkedIn: Democracy Now! Productions (Company)

Digg

Digg is a popular social bookmarking tool that allows readers to rate the news value of articles and share them with other readers. The more people who rate the same story, the higher it rises in popularity on the site. The site is an excellent way to take the pulse of what current events have attracted the most attention on any given day, or even hour.

Web: www.digg.com
Facebook: Digg (Page, Group)
Twitter: digg
LinkedIn: Digg (Company, Group)

Facebook

Facebook is more than a social networking site. It has encouraged many news publishers to develop applications that mesh with the site, letting millions of readers access news instantly. News applications such as the "New York Times Quiz," CNN, "The Daily Show," and Grouptivity's Social News are very popular on the site.

Web: www.facebook.com
Facebook: Facebook (Page)
Twitter: facebook, FacebookGeek, facebook_news, LatestFacebook
LinkedIn: Facebook.com (Group)

Free Republic

Free Republic is a conservative discussion forum and website, offering members instant messaging software, blog publishing platforms, and organizing tools. You must register in order to participate in the forums.

Web: www.freerepublic.com/tag/*/index
Facebook: Free Republic (Group)
Twitter: (None)
LinkedIn: (None)

Huffington Post

The Huffington Post is a popular group blog created by columnist Arianna Huffington. Her celebrity status has helped her wrangle high-profile contributors such as Barbra Streisand to post their opinions on politics, news, and culture.

Web: www.huffingtonpost.com
Facebook: The Huffington Post (Page)
Twitter: huffingtonpost
LinkedIn: HuffingtonPost.com (Company)

Learn Out Loud $

This site provides educational podcasts, audiobooks, MP3 downloads, and videos covering a wide range of current-affairs topics. Top sellers include audiobooks on meditation, the laws of attraction, and money management.

Web: www.learnoutloud.com
Facebook: Learn Out Loud (People)
Twitter: (None)
LinkedIn: (None)

The Mark Levin Show

Fans of conservative radio personality Mark Levin can download podcasts of his shows here.

Web: www.marklevinshow.com
Facebook: The Mark Levin Fan group (Group), Listen to the Mark Levin Show (Group)
Twitter: marklevinshow, Mark_Levin
LinkedIn: Mark Levin Show (Group)

MetaFilter

MetaFilter is one of the first group weblogs that allowed readers (after fulfilling membership requirements) to post comments on interesting things found on the Web. This site is an excellent filter for finding both the usual news items and other, stranger stories that may have gone unnoticed on mainstream media.

Web: www.metafilter.com
Facebook: MetaFilter (Page), Metafilter (Group)
Twitter: mefi_tweed
LinkedIn: (None)

The Michael Baisden Show

Michael Baisden hosts a popular national talk show that addresses issues affecting the African-American community. His website offers on-demand archives of all shows to registered users.

Web: http://zmba.fimc.net/Article.asp?id=437448
Facebook: michael baisden live (Page), The Michael Baisden Show (Group)
Twitter: BaisdenLive
LinkedIn: (None)

Mixx

Organized based on the same principles as Digg.com, Mixx lets readers vote on stories from around the Web. The site organizes new items based on popularity or subject matter. Visitors can also access video news on the site.

Web: www.mixx.com
Facebook: (None)
Twitter: mixx
LinkedIn: (None)

Reddit

This site has a casual interface and is computer-oriented, giving readers links to stories from around the world that cover science and tech news. Readers can track an article's popularity with handy arrow-indicator graphics.

Web: www.reddit.com
Facebook: Reddit (Page), reddit feed (Application)
Twitter: reddit, redditfeed
LinkedIn: Reddit Fans (Group), Reddit (Group)

Times Online Virtual Worlds News Portal

The London Times Online site provides a comprehensive mini-site devoted to news emanating from virtual worlds and impacting their residents. This site usually has the most recent reports on any new trends or developments occurring in Second Life or other virtual worlds.

Web:
http://technology.timesonline.co.uk/tol/news/tech_and_web/gadgets_and_gaming/virtual_worlds/
Facebook: Times Online (Group)
Twitter: TimesTech
LinkedIn: (None)

To The Point

Warren Olney's podcast of his popular radio program on KCRW in Los Angeles. Olney interviews Southern Californian newsmakers and politicians who have an impact on a national scale.

Web: www.kcrw.com
Facebook: Warren Olney Fan Club (Group)
Twitter: ToThePoint_KCRW
LinkedIn: KCRW (Company)

EMERGENCY PREPAREDNESS

American Red Cross

The well known humanitarian organization established in 1881 and headquartered in Washington, D.C.

Web: http://www.redcross.org
Facebook: American Red Cross (Page), Red Cross! (Group)
Twitter: RedCross
LinkedIn: American Red Cross (Company, Group)

WikiHow.com

This is a wiki containing articles instructing readers on how to do almost anything.

Web: www.wikihow.com
Facebook: wikiHow (Page), Wiki How (Group)
Twitter: wikiHow
LinkedIn: wikiHow (Company)

FINANCIAL NEWS

BoardCentral.com

BoardCentral.com aggregates and displays posts from top messages from one site, eliminating the necessity of monitoring individual message boards for the latest stock tips. This service syndicates data from message boards at Yahoo! Finance, RagingBull, The Motley Fool, SiliconInvestor, and ClearStation.

Web: www.boardcentral.com
Facebook: BoardCentral (Page)
Twitter: (None)
LinkedIn: (None)

Entropia Universe

Mindark, a Swedish company, has created one of the first virtual game worlds to introduce an open economy, allowing residents to trade actual currencies to purchase virtual real estate in the game, as well as using banks to increase the currency's value.

Web: www.entropiauniverse.com
Facebook: Entropia Universe (Group)
Twitter: EntropiaOnline
LinkedIn: Entropia Universe (Group)

The Fat Wallet.com Forums

Members of FatWallet.com gather to share investment advice and offer perspectives on saving money.

Web: www.fatwallet.com/forums/finance/
Facebook: Fatwallet.com (Page), FatWallet (Group)
Twitter: FatWallet, fatwalletdeals
LinkedIn: FatWallet, Inc. (Company)

Forbes.com Video

Forbes Magazine provides video on the latest financial stories on a daily basis.

Web: http://video.forbes.com/recentVideo
Facebook: Forbes (Group)
Twitter: ForbesTech
LinkedIn: Forbes.com (Company)

GStock Supercomputer

GStock is a subscription-based stock-picking service that analyzes trading and tells you the optimal time to buy or sell your stock based on recommendations from the company's computer algorithm.

Web: www.gstock.com
Facebook: GStock (Page)
Twitter: gstock
LinkedIn: (None)

Investors Hub

This forum gives investors access to all the market data while contributing to discussion groups focused on specific companies or strategies.

Web: http://investorshub.advfn.com
Facebook: (None)
Twitter: Investors_Hub
LinkedIn: (None)

Random Roger's Big Picture

Random Roger (aka Roger Nusbaum) is a portfolio manager who also writes for TheStreet.com. His blog focuses on long-term investment strategies, giving his opinion about market fluctuations.

Web: www.randomroger.blogspot.com
Facebook: (None)
Twitter: randomroger
LinkedIn: (None)

SaneBull Market Monitor

SaneBull creates widgets that let you monitor all your investment information in one place. The site provides various scripting tools for placing the widget on any Internet platform, including your desktop, Facebook, MySpace, and so on.

Web: www.sanebull.com
Facebook: SaneBull Monitor (Application)
Twitter: sanebull
LinkedIn: (None)

Seeking Alpha

Seeking Alpha is a network of blogs covering domestic and financial markets. The site is well organized and includes feeds from other stock blogs.

Web: www.seekingalpha.com
Facebook: Seeking Alpha (Group)
Twitter: (None)
LinkedIn: Seeking Alpha (Company)

SocialPicks

SocialPicks is a stock-picking community where users can share information with one another and track investments. The site offers groups and a tool for voting on financial news stories.

Web: www.socialpicks.com
Facebook: Stock Ideas on SocialPicks (Group)
Twitter: SocialPicks
LinkedIn: Socialpicks (Company)

Stockpickr

Owned by the financial news site TheStreet.com, this community of investors can provide advice and recommendations for ways to increase your investments.

Web: www.stockpickr.com
Facebook: Stockpickr (Page)
Twitter: Stockpickr
LinkedIn: (None)

Wall Street Confidential

Financial news personality Jim Cramer podcasts his opinions on the day's markets on TheStreet.com. Cramer may not always be right, but he's definitely entertaining.

Web: www.thestreet.com/podcasts/wall-street-confidential.html
Facebook: Jim Cramer (Page)
Twitter: ForbesTech
LinkedIn: (None)

Wikinvest

Wikinvest is an online community that lets users add opinion and information on the stock market by editing wiki pages on specific topics or companies.

Web: www.wikinvest.com
Facebook: Wikinvest (Group)
Twitter: wikinvest
LinkedIn: Wikinvest (Company)

GOVERNMENT

3

Congresspedia

Jointly created by the Center for Media and Democracy and the Sunlight Foundation, Congresspedia is a wiki devoted to providing accurate information on all U.S. congressional representatives. This wiki is part of a larger project to encourage civic engagement and highlight transparency in our government.

Web: http://www.opencongress.org/wiki/Wiki_Home
Facebook: Congresspedia (Page)
Twitter: (None)
LinkedIn: (None)

GovernmentExecutive.com

This site is an online magazine for management-level government employees. The site includes blogs and directories.

Web: www.govexec.com
Facebook: Government Executive Media Group (Page)
Twitter: (None)
LinkedIn: Government Executive Media Group (Company), The Government Executive Media Group Community (Group)

If I'm President

This social networking site lets you share your political views by pretending to be a candidate. The site lets you establish your platform and share your views across a network of friends on the site.

Web: www.ifimpresident.com
Facebook: (None)
Twitter: ifimpresident
LinkedIn: (None)

Judicial Watch

This site is a conservative website that keeps track of stories about the Supreme Court and the U.S. judiciary. Judicial Watch takes an activist role as well. It files lawsuits in support of causes that it supports, and publishes special projects like a financial disclosure report from all Supreme Court justices, appellate courts, and district court judges.

Web: www.judicialwatch.org
Facebook: Judicial Watch, Inc. (Page), Judicial Watch (Group)
Twitter: (None)
LinkedIn: Judicial Watch (Company)

Project On Government Oversight

The Project On Government Oversight (POGO) investigates government corruption and misconduct at the federal level. The POGO blog posts the latest news on the organization's activities and investigations.

Web: http://pogoblog.typepad.com/
Facebook: Project On Government Oversight (Page), POGO PEOPLE (Project On Government Oversight) (Group)
Twitter: POGOBlog
LinkedIn: Project On Government Oversight (Company)

SCOTUSblog

The Supreme Court of the United States blog is staffed by members of a law firm called Goldstein & Howe, one of the few Supreme Court litigation firms in the United States. SCOTUS is one of the most popular law blogs because it regularly monitors all the cases under review by the Supreme Court.

Web: www.scotusblog.com
Facebook: SCOTUSblog (Pages)
Twitter: SCOTUSblog
LinkedIn: (None)

The White House

Barack Obama's White House staffers keep the public up-to-date on the issues of our times. Article authors are unnamed.

Web: www.whitehouse.gov
Facebook: The White House (Page), THE WHITE HOUSE (Group)
Twitter: whitehouse
LinkedIn: White House (Group)

White House Watch

The *Washington Post* hosts this blog by Daniel Froomkin that collects news items about the President and his staff from blogs, news outlets, and international media.

Web: www.washingtonpost.com/wp-dyn/content/blog/2008/06/18/BL2008061801546.html
Facebook: Dan Froomkin's White House Watch (Page)
Twitter: froomkin
LinkedIn: (None)

MILITARY

America's Army

America's Army is a computer game based on the experiences of Army soldiers in combat. Players can join leagues and play against one another on the Internet.

Web: www.americasarmy.com
Facebook: America's Army: The Official U.S. Army Game (Page)
Twitter: americasarmy3
LinkedIn: (None)

Global Guerrillas

Global Guerrillas is a blog by journalist John Robb about guerrilla warfare tactics in the twenty-first century.

Web: http://globalguerrillas.typepad.com/globalguerrillas/
Facebook: (None)
Twitter: johnrobb
LinkedIn: (None)

Milblogging.com

This site is a comprehensive index of current blogs written by military personnel. The site provides a feed of top stories posted from milblogs all around the world.

Web: www.milblogging.com
Facebook: Fan of MilBlogs (Page)
Twitter: milblogging
LinkedIn: (None)

Military Podcast

MilitarySpot.com publishes this directory of the latest audio prepared by military journalists or soldier podcasters.

Web:
www.militaryspot.com/resources/item/military_podcast
Facebook: (None)
Twitter: milspot
LinkedIn: (None)

MyArmyLifeToo.com

Designed for the families of Army personnel, this Department of the Army site offers jargon-free content, resources, and tools for the families of Army members.

Web: www.myarmyonesource.com/default.aspx
Facebook: Army OneSource (Page)
Twitter: AOS_Lousiana
LinkedIn: (None)

Sean Dustman's Photoblog

This is a photoblog by a sailor stationed in Iraq on his fourth tour of duty.

Web: http://dustmans.fotopages.com/
Facebook: Sean Dustman (People)
Twitter: dustmans
LinkedIn: (None)

VAJoe.com Military Forum

VAJoe.com is a comprehensive website for current and retired military personnel. The message boards provide a sense of community for all branches of the military and their families.

Web: www.allmilitary.com/board/index.php
Facebook: AllMilitary.com (Group)
Twitter: AllMilitary
LinkedIn: (None)

Wounded Warrior Project

This website focuses on the plight of wounded soldiers and their efforts to rehabilitate their lives. The site is an excellent clearinghouse for information and resources available to wounded veterans.

Web: www.woundedwarriorproject.org
Facebook: Wounded Warrior Project (Page, Group)
Twitter: wwpinc
LinkedIn: Wounded Warrior Project (Company, Group)

MONEY MANAGEMENT

American Consumer News

This site offers content on ways to manage personal finance and reduce unsecured debt. The site includes columnists addressing travel tips, debt elimination, and money-management strategies.

Web: www.americanconsumernews.com
Facebook: (None)
Twitter: ConsumerFeed
LinkedIn: American Consumer News, LLC (Company)

Bankwide.com

This is an online magazine dedicated to offering tips on gaining financial stability and independence. The site offers community forums, research papers, and articles. Banking professionals can find news feeds from all the financial trade papers on Bankwide.com's front page.

Web: http://bankwide.com
Facebook: Aiden Michaels (People)
Twitter: bankwide
LinkedIn: (None)

Chief Family Officer

A working mom named Cathy offers her tips on finances, food, and family. She frequently shares links to freebies or other discounts.

Web: www.chieffamilyofficer.com
Facebook: (None)
Twitter: CFOblog
LinkedIn: (None)

Dave Ramsey Show

Debt-relief author Dave Ramsey shares his wisdom via his radio-show broadcast daily on the Internet. Listeners can call in and get specific advice as well.

Web: www.daveramsey.com/radio/home
Facebook: Dave Ramsey (Page)
Twitter: ramseyshow
LinkedIn: Dave Ramsey (Company), Fans of Dave Ramsey (Group)

Money Hackers Network

This website publishes posts from consumer finance blogs from around the Internet. This site is an efficient way for users to keep abreast of all the finance blogs at the same time.

Web: www.moneyhackers.net
Facebook: (None)
Twitter: mhnet
LinkedIn: (None)

No Credit Needed Podcast

This is an archive of podcasts produced by the No Credit Needed blog about debt reduction and personal finance.

Web: www.ncnpodcast.com
Facebook: (None)
Twitter: NCN
LinkedIn: (None)

Wesabe.com

Here is a community-based money-management site. Users upload their financial data, visible only to the account user, and Wesabe offers financial tips based on the experience of users with a similar balance sheet.

Web: www.wesabe.com
Facebook: (None)
Twitter: wesabe
LinkedIn: Wesabe (Company)

POLITICS

Conservapedia

This wiki site aims to publish encyclopedic articles with a conservative perspective.

Web: www.conservapedia.com/Main_Page
Facebook: Conservapedia (Page, Group)
Twitter: jay_pe
LinkedIn: (None)

Crooks and Liars

Crooks and Liars concentrates on the television news media. The site uses clever headlines and captions to mock live news reports and policy debates from Fox News, CNN, and international broadcasters.

Web: www.crooksandliars.com
Facebook: (None)
Twitter: crooksandliars
LinkedIn: (None)

Daily Kos

This group effort, hosted by blogger Markos Moulitsas Zuniga, is one of the most popular political blogs on the Internet. The liberal site offers quotations, useful links, and insightful articles about the Iraq war, terrorism, and hypocritical world leaders.

Web: www.dailykos.com
Facebook: Daily Kos (Page), The Official Daily Kos Facebook Group (Group)
Twitter: dailykos
LinkedIn: The Daily KosNetworking Group (Group)

Debate Politics Forums

This discussion board offers visitors a chance to share their views on political issues in a nonpartisan, civil forum.

Web: www.debatepolitics.com
Facebook: (None)

Twitter: debatepolitics
LinkedIn: (None)

Instapundit.com

Glenn Reynolds maintains Instapundit.com. His blog covers a bit of everything, but he's primarily interested in issues involving individual liberty and advanced technology. People love to read Mr. Reynolds's writing because, even if they don't agree with him, they admire his quick, smart, and funny posts.

Web: http://pajamasmedia.com/instapundit/
Facebook: Instapundit Fan Club (Group)
Twitter: instapundit
LinkedIn: (None)

The Living Room Candidate

The Museum of the Moving Image created this special site to share presidential campaign commercials from the past.

Web: http://livingroomcandidate.org
Facebook: Museum of the Moving Image (Page)
Twitter: (None)
LinkedIn: Museum of the Moving Image (Company)

SCIENCE/TECH NEWS

Bitesize Bio

This well-written blog covers genetic engineering and microbiology issues from the perspective of the researcher. It's a great introduction into the mechanics of working in a lab.

Web: http://bitesizebio.com/
Facebook: (None)
Twitter: BitesizeBio
LinkedIn: (None)

DNA Ancestry.com

Ancestry.com has launched this service that allows users to submit a DNA sample to the site for DNA analysis and comparison to results in its genetic database. Using this data, DNA Ancestry allows people to join others with similar genetic traits or surnames in groups to determine how they may be related.

Web: http://dna.ancestry.com/
Facebook: Ancestry.com (Page, Group)
Twitter: Ancestrydotcom
LinkedIn: Ancestry.com (Company)

Nature Network

Nature Magazine has created a social networking site for scientists. Members can connect with one another, discuss research, and participate in forums.

Web: http://network.nature.com/
Facebook: Nature Network (Group)
Twitter: NatNetNews
LinkedIn: (None)

Science@NASA

Aspiring astronauts and astronomers can listen to stories about space exploration and rocket innovation. The agency posts a new audio file each week.

Web: http://science.nasa.gov/
Facebook: Science@NASA (Page), Science in Nasa (Group)
Twitter: NASA
LinkedIn: NASA (Company), Friends of NASA (Group)

Science Daily

This site offers the latest research news. Users can access articles, blogs, and video on topics including medicine, biology, earth science, space and time, matter and energy, and computers.

Web: www.sciencedaily.com
Facebook: Science Daily (Page)
Twitter: sciencedaily
LinkedIn: (None)

Science Magazine Podcasts

Science magazine produces weekly podcasts about interesting stories in the journal and on the website.

Web: http://sciencemag.org/about/podcast.dtl
Facebook: Science Magazine Podcast (Page)
Twitter: sciencemagazine
LinkedIn: Science Magazine (Company)

3

Science News

This is the online edition of the weekly magazine published by the Society for the Science & the Public. The publication covers all aspects of scientific discovery.

Web: www.sciencenews.org
Facebook: Science News Magazine (Page)
Twitter: (None)
LinkedIn: Science News (Company)

SciLands Virtual Continent

SciLands is a minicontinent created in Second Life by residents interested in science and technology. There are more than 20 science- and technology-related organizations in the SciLands, including government agencies, universities, and museums. Members collaborate on projects, host meetings, and share ideas.

Web: www.scilands.org
Facebook: SciLands (Group)
Twitter: scilands
LinkedIn: (None)

Slashdot

Slashdot describes itself as "News for Nerds." Although the blog's focus is on news related to technology, it is an excellent resource for news on the latest cultural developments.

Web: http://slashdot.org/
Facebook: Slashdot (Application, Group)
Twitter: slashdot
LinkedIn: Slashdot (Company, Group)

TechCrunch

TechCrunch is a group blog covering technology and Internet start-ups. The site maintains a thorough archive of new company reviews. It's fun to look back and see how established Internet companies fared when they were just starting out.

Web: www.techcrunch.com
Facebook: TechCrunch (Page, Group)
Twitter: TechCrunch
LinkedIn: TechCrunch (Company, Group)

Wired.com

Wired magazine's website covers all the latest technology trends. In addition to posting articles from the paper version of the magazine, the site publishes several well-written blogs, tech and game reviews, and lots of multimedia.

Web: www.wired.com
Facebook: Wired (Page)
Twitter: wired
LinkedIn: Wired Magazine (Company), WIRED (Group)

STATE GOVERNMENTS

Capitol Inside

This blog covers Texas politics and government in a very intense way. Political junkies will enjoy the site's comprehensive news feeds from every major Texan news publication. Edited by Mike Hailey, the site publishes original articles and opinion pieces about Texas legislators and state power brokers.

Web: http://capitolinside.com/
Facebook: (None)
Twitter: capitolinside
LinkedIn: (None)

FollowTheMoney.org

This site focuses on campaign funding in state politics by tracking donations at the state congressional level.

Web: www.followthemoney.org
Facebook: FollowTheMoney.org (Page)
Twitter: MoneyInPolitics
LinkedIn: FollowTheMoney.org: The National Institute on Money in State Politics (Group)

Stateline.org

Published by the Pew Research Center, this website monitors a variety of news sources to inform readers about issues affecting various U.S. states.

Web: www.stateline.org/live/
Facebook: Stateline.org
Twitter: (None)
LinkedIn: Stateline.org (Company)

UNDERGROUND NEWS

Adbusters.org

Adbusters.org site is the electronic arm of a print magazine aimed at challenging corporate consumerism and materialistic media messages.

Web: www.adbusters.org
Facebook: Adbusters (Group)
Twitter: adbusters
LinkedIn: Adbusters Reader's Corner (Group)

Coast to Coast AM

Hosted by George Noory, Coast to Coast AM podcasts weekly shows about conspiracy theories, UFO sightings, and the paranormal.

Web: www.coasttocoastam.com
Facebook: Coast.To.Coast.AM (Group), Fan of CoasttoCoastAM (Group)
Twitter: coasttocoastam
LinkedIn: (None)

Disinformation

The logo for this blog is "Everything you know is wrong." A humorous group effort, with plenty of actual information hidden among the nuggets of wit.

Web: www.disinfo.com
Facebook: Disinformation (Page), disinformation (Group)
Twitter: disinfo
LinkedIn: The Disinformation Company Ltd. (Company)

Firedoglake

This blog is rich in multimedia demonstrating the erosion of American civil liberties from a progressive point of view.

Web: www.firedoglake.com
Facebook: Firedoglake (Page)
Twitter: firedoglake
LinkedIn: (None)

GRITtv

This Internet news show features commentary on international affairs and human rights and includes interviews conducted by Laura Flanders and Amani Noma.

Web: http://lauraflanders.firedoglake.com/
Facebook: GRITtv with Laura Flanders (Group)
Twitter: grittv
LinkedIn: (None)

History Podcast

Jason Watts podcasts weekly about odd historical figures, places, and events.

Web: http://historyonair.com/
Facebook: (None)
Twitter: historypodcast
LinkedIn: (None)

Mobile Broadcast News 🐦

This site features news stories created by a team of independent video journalists roving across the country on a bus. The site documents peace and justice issues in America.

Web: http://mobilebroadcastnews.com/
Facebook: Mobile Broadcast News (Page)
Twitter: (None)
LinkedIn: (None)

Professor Hex

Professor Hex posts news items about the weird, paranormal, or unexplainable, such as UFOs and Loch Ness monster sightings.

Web: http://professorhex.blogspot.com/
Facebook: (None)
Twitter: Professorhex
LinkedIn: (None)

3

The Raw Story

Raw Story is a news website that posts stories that do not get much attention in the mainstream media.

Web: www.rawstory.com
Facebook: The Raw Story (Group), The Raw Story on Facebook. (Page)
Twitter: RawStory
LinkedIn: (None)

WORLD AFFAIRS/DIPLOMACY

America Abroad Radio

Listeners obtain international news created by independent journalists affiliated with the America Abroad Media organization.

Web: www.americaabroadmedia.org/radio
Facebook: America Abroad Media (Page, Group)
Twitter: AAMRadioTV
LinkedIn: American Abroad Media (Company)

Council on Foreign Relations

The Council on Foreign Relations provides audio downloads, available several times a week, on the latest foreign-policy news and analysis.

Web: www.cfr.org
Facebook: CFR.org, Council on Foreign Relations (Page)
Twitter: CFR_org
LinkedIn: (None)

Diplomacy Island

Second Life residents can practice their diplomatic skills at conferences and other events on this island in the online game. Visitors can explore the island's virtual embassy (for the Maldives), library, and Museum of Diplomacy.

Web: www.diplomacy.edu/DiplomacyIsland
Facebook: (None)
Twitter: DiplomacyEdu
LinkedIn: (None)

Earth TV

This site provides video feeds from closed-circuit cameras in more than 70 countries around the world. Viewers get an eyeful.

Web: www.earthtv.com/en
Facebook: earthTV (Page), earthTV TravelBOX (Application)
Twitter: earthTV
LinkedIn: (None)

Foreign Policy Watch

This group blog provides thoughtful political analysis on issues affecting diplomatic strategy and international relations.

Web: http://fpwatch.blogspot.com/
Facebook: Foreign Policy Watch (Group)
Twitter: (None)
LinkedIn: (None)

Security Dilemmas

Professor Seth Weinberger maintains this blog dedicated to examining national security and international-relations issues.

Web: http://securitydilemmas.blogspot.com/
Facebook: Seth Weinberger (People)
Twitter: (None)
LinkedIn: Seth Weinberger (People)

TakePart.com

This social networking site aims to engage and motivate social activists from around the world. The site provides users with forums and tools for meeting in real life to foster change in the world.

Web: www.takepart.com
Facebook: TakePart.com (Page)
Twitter: TakePart
LinkedIn: (None)

WorldPress.org

To foster a broader exchange of ideas and perspectives, this website reprints articles written by journalists outside of the United States.

Web: www.worldpress.org
Facebook: (None)
Twitter: (None)
LinkedIn: Worldpress.org (Company)

3

EDUCATION

4

Whether you are a student, a parent, or an educator, a wealth of resources is just a mouse click away. Students can get help with their homework, prepare for tests, and find a college or graduate school. Parents can learn about financial aid, choosing a private school or college, and schooling their children at home. Teachers can find lesson plans, online libraries, and places to talk with other teachers. You can learn a new language, take an interesting course, or even earn a degree online. The Internet has opened up a whole new world of education, and this chapter guides you through the best of it. To make things easier for you, many of these outlets are available on one or more of the big three social media sites: Facebook, Twitter, and LinkedIn.

COLLEGES AND UNIVERSITIES

Association of American Colleges and Universities

AAC&U is a national association that works to ensure the quality and availability of liberal arts undergraduate education. Offers resources on liberal education, general education, curriculum, faculty, and more. The site's podcasts let you listen in on sessions of its annual meeting.

Web: www.aacu.org
Facebook: Association of American Colleges and Universities (Page)
Twitter: (None)
LinkedIn: (None)

College Parents of America

If you have one or more kids in college, take a look at this site. CPA is a national association that educates and advocates for parents of college students. The site's free area has a helpful parent resource center. Registered members who pay to join also have access to Deals and Discounts, Ask the Experts, Tools (such as student loan comparison and tax planning), and a Newsletter Library.

Web: www.collegeparents.org/cpa/index.htm
Facebook: College Parents of America (Page), College Parents of America (Group)
Twitter: CPofAmerica
LinkedIn: College Parent of America (Group)

Kaplan

Kaplan provides information on test preparation and college admissions, as well as undergraduate, graduate, diploma and certificate, continuing education, and international programs.

Web: www.kaplan.com
Facebook: Kaplan (Group)
Twitter: (None)
LinkedIn: Kaplan (Group)

4

Peterson's 🏅

Peterson's steps college applicants through the process of finding, choosing, and applying to colleges and universities. Register to create a My Peterson's account, where you can build a list of schools, keep track of deadlines, and take practice tests. Search for schools based on various criteria, from location and size to selectivity to degrees offered.

Web: www.petersons.com
Facebook: (None)
Twitter: (None)
LinkedIn: Peterson's (Company)

The Princeton Review

The Princeton Review is known for its test-prep programs, and that's a focus of this site. But you can also use the Counselor-O-Matic to help find the best college matches, browse school rankings, and get information about scholarships and financial aid.

Web: www.princetonreview.com
Facebook: The Princeton Review (Page), The Princeton Review (Group)
Twitter: ThePrincetonRev
LinkedIn: The Princeton Review (Company)

Second Life

A number of colleges and universities have a presence in this virtual world. Students can attend online classes, join virtual versions of student clubs and organizations, and participate in academic research about virtual worlds.

Web: http://secondlife.com/
Facebook: Second Life (Page), Second Life (Group)
Twitter: SecondLife, 2ndLife
LinkedIn: Professional Second Lifers (Group), SLED-Second Life Educators (Group), Second Life Resident (Group)

CONTINUING EDUCATION

MindEdge

Founded by Harvard and MIT educators, MindEdge focuses on online learning for business and management professionals. Choose from courses in business and leadership, communications, project management, and others offered through the Winchester Center for Management development. MindEdge also offers test prep for various professional certification exams.

Web: www.mindedge.com
Facebook: (None)
Twitter: (None)
LinkedIn: MindEdge (Company)

DISTANCE LEARNING

H. Wayne Huizenga School of Business and Entrepreneurship

Offers an internationally accredited MBA and other master's programs in business online. The Huizenga school is part of Nova Southeastern University (www.nova.edu), which offers 78 degree and certificate programs via distance learning.

Web: www.huizenga.nova.edu
Facebook: H. Wayne Huizenga School of Business and Entrepreneurship at NSU (Page)
Twitter: (None)
LinkedIn: H. Wayne Huizenga School of Business and Entrepreneurship (Company)

United States Distance Learning Association

The USDLA aims to provide leadership, advocacy, and information for distance learners and education providers. Its Distance Learning Link Program features distance-learning institutions that offer degrees, certificates, and courses in distance education. You can sign up for USDLA membership, shop the USDLA Virtual Bookstore, find a USDLA chapter in your state, and browse distance-learning programs.

Web: www.usdla.org
Facebook: United States Distance Learning Association (Group)
Twitter: USDLA (None)
LinkedIn: United States Distance Learning Association (Group)

University of Maryland University College

UMUC is one of the largest online education providers in the U.S., with more than 177,000 course enrollments in 2007. Choose from 100 degree- or certificate-granting programs for both undergraduate and graduate students. More than 700 courses are available.

Web: www.umuc.edu/online_ed.shtml
Facebook: University of Maryland University College (Page), University of Maryland University College (Group)
Twitter: (None)
LinkedIn: University of Maryland University College (Company)

University of Phoenix

The University of Phoenix is the world's largest private university, with more than 280,000 enrolled students from all over the globe. Many of those students take UOP's online courses. Programs focus on business, technology, healthcare, education, and social/behavioral science, with undergraduate and graduate degrees available.

Web: www.phoenix.edu
Facebook: University of Phoenix (Page), University of Phoenix (Group)
Twitter: UOPX
LinkedIn: University of Phoenix (Company), University of Phoenix Alumni (Group), University of Phoenix Association (Group)

Western Kentucky University Distance Learning

Listen or subscribe to lectures from online courses in a variety of subjects, including English, Business, Accounting, History, Math, Social Work, and Engineering.

Web: http://161.6.105.21:8084/nutch-0.9/login.html
Facebook: (None)
Twitter: WKUAdmissions
LinkedIn: WKU Alumni Association (Group)

FINANCIAL AID AND SCHOLARSHIPS

AmeriCorps

This government-sponsored network of community service programs lets you earn up to $4,275 toward college or paying back student loans in exchange for working with a local or national non-profit group. AmeriCorps members work with disadvantaged youth, build affordable housing, clean up parks and natural areas, work with healthcare, and more. If you're 17 or older and a U.S. citizen (or legal, permanent resident alien), you can join "America's Peace Corps."

Web: www.americorps.org
Facebook: AmeriCorps (Page), AmeriCorps (Group)
Twitter: americorps
LinkedIn: Americorps (Company)

4

FastWeb

FastWeb's database contains more than a million scholarships, worth billions of dollars to college-bound students. Create a profile, and FastWeb uses it to find scholarships for which you may qualify, taking a lot of the work out of wading through the thousands of available scholarships. The site also has tools for selecting a college and finding a job or an internship.

Web: www.fastweb.com
Facebook: FastWeb (Page), FastWeb (Group)
Twitter: FastWebdotcom
LinkedIn: (None)

Financial Aid Podcast

This site features an archive of host Christopher S. Penn, Chief Technology Officer of the Student Loan Network, discussing the latest financial-aid news and tips. The podcast is of interest to students, parents, and financial aid professionals.

Web: www.financialaidnews.com/category/podcast/
Facebook: Financial Aid Podcast (Page), Financial Aid Podcast Loyalists (Group)
Twitter: (None)
LinkedIn: (None)

Scholarships.com 🏅

The Scholarships.com database holds nearly three million scholarships and grants, worth a grand total of $19 billion in aid. This site helps you find scholarship opportunities that match your background and interests and also offers some scholarships itself. The Scholarship.com blog, updated weekdays, discusses financial-aid news and opportunities.

Web: www.scholarships.com
Facebook: (None)
Twitter: Scholarshipscom
LinkedIn: (None)

GRADUATE SCHOOLS

Graduate Guide

Search for on-campus and online graduate programs. Read about grad schools in the news, how to pay for graduate education, and admissions tests.

Web: www.graduateguide.com
Facebook: GraduateGuide (Page)
Twitter: graduateguide
LinkedIn: (None)

MBA Podcaster

If you're planning to apply to MBA programs, get the inside scoop on the admissions process from this podcast. The site delivers relevant information and advice through biweekly audio and video segments for those planning to apply for a Master in Business Administration. Topics include everything from a behind-the-scenes view of the admission process to post-MBA job opportunities and current market trends.

Web: www.mbapodcaster.com
Facebook: MBA Podcaster (Page)
Twitter: MBA Podcaster
LinkedIn: MBA Podcaster (Company)

HOME SCHOOLING

A to Z Home's Cool

Ann Zeise, who home-schooled her son and remains a keen proponent of home schooling, created a site of more than 1,000 information-packed pages. Whether you're just getting started with home schooling, want to connect with other home-schoolers, or are looking for materials, you'll find it here. Explorations 4 Kids has a great selection of kid-friendly activities and websites for all subjects. A to Z also sponsors several Yahoo-based discussion groups.

Web: http://homeschooling.gomilpitas.com
Facebook: A to Z Home's Cool (Page)
Twitter: AnnZeise
LinkedIn: (None)

California Homeschool Network

CHN's motto is "Strengthening the voice of California homeschoolers," and the group aims to do just that. Founded in 1994 by a group of home-schooling families from across the state, CHN has evolved into an advocacy group that supports a wide range of home-schooling styles and philosophies. Its site describes the group's work and also offers educational resources and advice on how to home-school. Has a blog and an online magazine.

Web: http://californiahomeschool.net
Facebook: California Homeschool Network (Page)
Twitter: (None)
LinkedIn: (None)

Enchanted Learning

For a low annual subscription fee (currently $20), you receive access to more than 20,000 pages of educational content, from printable picture books to high-school subjects. Enchanted Learning has free sample pages you can browse before you subscribe.

Web: http://www.enchantedlearning.com/Home.html
Facebook: Enchanted Learning (Page)
Twitter: (None)
LinkedIn: (None)

TheHomeSchoolMom

Mary Ann Kelley began home-schooling her kids in 2000 and decided to create a website to gather the resources she'd found and share them with other home-schooling parents. Besides free newsletters, resources, and support information, the site offers a weekly menu planner, complete with recipes and shopping lists, so busy home-schooling moms can plan ahead.

Web: www.thehomeschoolmom.com
Facebook: TheHomeSchoolMom (Page)
Twitter: MaryAnnKelley
LinkedIn: (None)

K–12 EDUCATOR RESOURCES

ABC Teach

This subscription site ($35 per year or $60 for two years) has more than 15,000 worksheets that teachers can download and print for use in K–8 classrooms. Also has a clip-art library and tools for creating your own worksheets.

Web: www.abcteach.com
Facebook: abcteach.com (Page)
Twitter: Abcteach
LinkedIn: abcteach, LLC (Company)

Classroom 2.0

With 8,000 members, Classroom 2.0 is the social networking site for teachers interested in using Web 2.0 technology in the classroom. As the site defines it, Web 2.0 fosters "contribution, collaboration, and conversation" to make education participatory and interactive. The site lets you create a profile and then link to other educators, participate in forums, help build a resources wiki, and join special-interest groups.

Web: www.classroom20.com
Facebook: Classroom 2.0 (Group)
Twitter: classroom20
LinkedIn: (None)

The Cool Cat Teacher

Georgia teacher Vicki A. Davis writes this blog, nominated for Best Teacher Blog in the 2007 edublog awards, about teaching and technology.

Web: http://coolcatteacher.blogspot.com
Facebook: (None)
Twitter: coolcatteacher
LinkedIn: Vicki Davis (People)

4

Council for Exceptional Children

The Council for Exceptional Children (CEC) advocates for children who have special needs in their education, including gifted students and those with disabilities. This site explains about the CEC's work, offers professional development resources for educators (including web seminars and online courses), and lists news and publications. Here you can join CEC or shop in its online store.

Web: www.cec.sped.org
Facebook: Council for Exceptional Children (Group)
Twitter: (None)
LinkedIn: Council for Exceptional Children (CEC) (Group)

Discovery Education

From Discovery Communications, parent company of the Discovery Channel, comes this educational site. The School Resources section holds a lesson-plan library for all subjects, as well as a puzzle maker, brain boosters, and a schedule of Discovery's educational programming. The Discovery Educator Network has blogs, forums, and educator resources.

Web: www.discoveryeducation.com
Facebook: Discovery Global Education Partnership (Page)
Twitter: DEN
LinkedIn: (None)

Education Week 📖

This site is the online home of *Education Week* newspaper and *Teacher* magazine. Get the latest education-related news or browse stories by topic. The Community section has blogs, forums, polls, and a chat room. The site also has links to a related job site for teachers and administrators. You need to register (it's free) to get full access and sign up for optional free e-newsletters.

Web: www.edweek.org/ew/index.html
Facebook: Education Week (Page)
Twitter: educationweek
LinkedIn: (None)

Education World

Founded in 1996, this site calls itself "The Educator's Best Friend"—and really lives up to the claim. Use its search engine to search educational websites only, rather than wading through pages of irrelevant search results. You can find lesson plans and practical advice on all kinds of teaching-related issues (as well as reviews of websites), sign up for a free newsletter, read teacher and school profiles, and look for a job.

Web: www.educationworld.com
Facebook: Education World (Page), Education World (Group)
Twitter: education_world
LinkedIn: Education World, Inc. (Company)

EduHound

This site boasts that it has "everything for education K12"—and if it doesn't have *everything*, it comes awfully close. You can browse the site's dozens of categories, "site sets" (educational websites grouped by topic), or subject area (for lesson plans). Also offers clip art and templates for teachers. A useful site for teachers and students alike.

Web: www.eduhound.com
Facebook: (None)
Twitter: EduHound
LinkedIn: (None)

FREE: Federal Resources for Educational Excellence

This site, maintained by the U.S. Department of Education, helps teachers find educational resources—more than 1,500 of them—offered by the federal government. Resources are organized by subject (but not grade level): Arts and Music, Health and Physical Education, History and Social Studies, Language Arts, Math, and Science. Sign up for the FREE RSS to stay abreast of new resources as they're added to the site.

Web: www.free.ed.gov
Facebook: (None)
Twitter: FreeResources
LinkedIn: (None)

Internet4Classrooms

I4C aims to help teachers use the Internet effectively. The site has a large number of links for classroom teachers: instruction- and resource-related links, assessment assistance, and online practice modules.

Web: www.internet4classrooms.com
Facebook: (None)
Twitter: internet4classr
LinkedIn: (None)

National Writing Project

The National Writing Project (NWP) supports the teaching of writing, in all subjects and at all grade levels. Find local groups, get info about national programs, and check out the site's extensive library of teaching resources. You can also sign up for E-Voice, NWP's free bimonthly e-newsletter, or shop in its online store.

Web: www.nwp.org
Facebook: National Writing Project (Page), National Writing Project (Group)
Twitter: writingproject
LinkedIn: (None)

TeachersFirst.com

All the content on this site is written and reviewed by professional educators. Resources include lesson plans (searchable by subject, grade level, or keyword), puzzles and brain twisters, tips from working teachers, and tech help. Register for free to gain access to further benefits: tag or comment on resources, build your own home page. A well-organized site rich in resources.

Web: http://www.teachersfirst.com/
Facebook: I Love TeachersFirst.com (Group)
Twitter: TeachersFirst
LinkedIn: (None)

The Teachers' Podcast

Hosts Mark Gura and Dr. Kathy King cover news, information, and resources about education technology that teachers can put right to work.

Web: www.teacherspodcast.org
Facebook: The Teachers' Podcast: A New Generation of Ed Tech of Prof Dev of Educators (Group)
Twitter: drkpking
LinkedIn: Kathleen King (People)

USA Today Education

USA TODAY aims to educate students about current events and issues. On this site, teachers will find a weekly cross-curricular activity and a place to sign up for Inside USA TODAY, a daily teaching guide delivered by email.

Web: www.usatoday.com/educate/
Facebook: USA Today K-12 Education Team (Page)
Twitter: (None)
LinkedIn: USA Today (Company)

Wikiversity

From Wikimedia (the folks who brought you Wikipedia) comes this wiki devoted to education. Covering all levels from preschool through college, the site aims to develop collaborative learning resources and communities.

Web: http://en.wikiversity.org
Facebook: (None)
Twitter: Wikiversity
LinkedIn: (None)

K–12 HOMEWORK HELP

Cliffs Notes

These yellow-and-black study guides have been around for decades, summarizing and analyzing literary and other works. The online versions are free and cover just about all academic subjects. The Ask Cliff feature lets you email a question if you can't find the answer on the site. And there's a store where you can buy Cliffs Notes products.

Web: www.cliffsnotes.com
Facebook: CliffsNotes (Page), Cliffs Notes fans (Group)
Twitter: (None)
LinkedIn: (None)

Jiskha Homework Help

Post a question and get help from one of 200 experts. Jiskha also offers links and articles related to different school subjects. If you're in a hurry for help (and you're willing to pay for it), click the Live Experts link for a real-time conversation.

Web: www.jiskha.com
Facebook: Jiskha Homework Help (Page)
Twitter: Jiskha
LinkedIn: (None)

SparkNotes 🏅

SparkNotes, started by Harvard students in 1999, quickly became the home of the most popular study guides on the Web. The site includes study guides on a plethora of subjects, No Fear Shakespeare to help you navigate the Bard's works, SparkCharts (quick facts in chart form), and test prep and college search materials. The SparkLife section is full of fun stuff: TV, movies, personality tests, message boards, and the like, for when students need a break from all that studying.

Web: http://sparknotes.com
Facebook: SparkNotes (Page), SparkNotes (Group)
Twitter: SparkNotes
LinkedIn: (None)

K–12 LANGUAGE ARTS

Between the Lions

A companion site to the popular PBS series about reading, Between the Lions aims to foster literacy skills and promote the joy of reading in young children. With stories, games, and downloadable video clips, this is a fun and engaging site for beginning readers.

Web: http://pbskids.org/lions/stories/
Facebook: Between the Lions (Page), Between the Lions (Group)
Twitter: (None)
LinkedIn: (None)

Grammar Grater

This weekly podcast from Luke Taylor focuses on grammar in the digital age. These days, email, text messaging, social networking sites, and online reviews make everyone a writer.

Web: http://minnesota.publicradio.org/radio/podcasts/grammar_grater/
Facebook: Minnesota Public Radio's Grammar Grater (Group)
Twitter: (None)
LinkedIn: (None)

Poets.org

The Academy of American Poets developed and maintains this site, which contains thousands of poems. Search for a particular poem or a poet's biography, find poetry-related events, click the National Poetry Map to see what's happening, poetrywise, in your state, e.g., local poets and events, favorite poems, history of poems. Most of the site is free, but you can also join the Academy of American Poets (for an annual subscription fee) or shop in its Poetry Store.

Web: www.poets.org
Facebook: The Academy of American Poets (Page)
Twitter: Poetsorg
LinkedIn: (None)

K–12 MATH AND SCIENCE

Cool Math

Cool Math makes math fun! Calling itself "an amusement park of math," the site combines games with clearly presented lessons to help students develop their math skills.

Web: www.coolmath.com
Facebook: Cool math is cool! (Group)
Twitter: (None)
LinkedIn: (None)

Extreme Biology

This blog is created by and for biology students at a private school in the southeastern United States.

Web: www.missbakersbiologyclass.com/blog/
Facebook: Extreme Biology (Application)
Twitter: extremebiology
LinkedIn: (None)

Extreme Science

What's the biggest spider? Where's the hottest place in the world? Which animal is the strongest? Extreme Science answers these questions and others. Site content is organized into these categories: Earth, ocean, animal kingdom, space, weather, and resources.

Web: www.extremescience.net
Facebook: Extreme Science (Page)
Twitter: (None)
LinkedIn: Extreme Science (Company)

Science Blog

If you want to keep up with science news, take a look at this blog, which gathers news stories from various sources, keeping you informed about the world of science.

Web: www.scienceblog.com
Facebook: (None)
Twitter: ScienceBlogTwit
LinkedIn: (None)

K–12 PRIVATE EDUCATION

Council for American Private Education

The Council for American Private Education (CAPE) is "a coalition of national organizations and state affiliates serving private elementary and secondary schools." CAPE's member organizations represent about 80% of private-school enrollment across the country. This site explains the benefits of a private-school education and helps parents find a suitable school. It also has information for teachers interested in a private-school career.

Web: http://capenet.org
Facebook: Council for American Private Education (CAPE) (Page)
Twitter: (None)
LinkedIn: (None)

TABS: The Association of Boarding Schools

The website of the Association of Boarding Schools (TABS) discusses the kinds of boarding schools, describes what it's like to live at school, and gives tips on applying. There's even an online application form that many of TABS's member schools accept. Browse the School Finder to get more information about particular schools.

Web: www.boardingschools.com
Facebook: Boarding Schools – The Official Home (Page)
Twitter: TABSorg
LinkedIn: The Association of Boarding Schools (Company)

K–12 PUBLIC EDUCATION

Center for Public Education

The Center for Public Education provides information about public education, including research and analysis of current education issues, to a variety of audiences: state and local policymakers, educators, community leaders, parents, and anyone with an interest in public education. Its site is divided into four main sections: The Role of Public Schools, Research and Practice, News and Reports, and Useful Resources.

Web: www.centerforpubliceducation.org
Facebook: Center for Public Education (Page)
Twitter: (None)
LinkedIn: (None)

K–12 SOCIAL STUDIES

Social Studies for Kids

Topics on this well-organized site include current events, cultures, religions, government, economics, history, archaeology, and sports. Kids who visit the site can play games related to most of these subjects.

Web: www.socialstudiesforkids.com
Facebook: (None)
Twitter: SocStudies4Kids
LinkedIn: (None)

LANGUAGE AND LINGUISTICS

italki.com

The goal of this social network is to create a community where people can learn languages by finding language partners and language resources and develop their language skills by participating in chats, groups, and forums. Dozens of languages are represented on this lively site.

Web: www.italki.com
Facebook: italki.com (Group)
Twitter: italki
LinkedIn: italki.com (Company)

The Linguist List

The Linguist List at Eastern Michigan University is primarily an email discussion list for academic linguists. Its extensive website lets you search the archives, find language resources and other language-related email lists, search its directory of linguists, find jobs and calls for papers, and so on. It's the first place for linguists to go on the Web.

Web: www.linguistlist.org
Facebook: The Linguist List (Page)
Twitter: (None)
LinkedIn: Linguist List (Company)

Sprachcaffe International

With more than 20 years of experience, Sprachcaffe runs 25 language schools all over the world. Languages offered include English, Spanish, French, Italian, German, Chinese, Arabic, and Portuguese. Gauge your skill level with a free online language test; then browse last-minute bargains and/or book your course online.

Web: www.sprachcaffe.com
Facebook: Sprachcaffe International (Page)
Twitter: (None)
LinkedIn: (None)

YourDictionary.com Foreign Language Dictionaries

A comprehensive directory of links to dictionaries for more than 300 languages. An excellent resource for linguists and language learners.
Web: www.yourdictionary.com/languages.html
Facebook: (None)
Twitter: YourDictionary
LinkedIn: (None)

LIBRARIES

American Library Association

The American Library Association (ALA) has more than 65,000 members, making it the world's largest library association. The ALA promotes high standards in libraries and wide access to the public. Here you can find information about becoming a librarian; learn about careers, events, and conferences; find professional tools; and shop in the ALA Online Store.
Web: www.ala.org
Facebook: (None)
Twitter: (None)
LinkedIn: American Library Association (Company)

Hey Jude

Judy O'Connell, head of Library and Information Services at St. Joseph's College in Sydney, Australia, writes about technology's effect on libraries and education.
Facebook: Judy O'Connell (Page)
Twitter: heyjudeonline
LinkedIn: (None)

New York Public Library, Digital Collections

NYPL's Digital Gallery contains more than half a million images from the library's collection on an astonishing variety of topics: art, dance, fashion and costume, early photographs, illuminated manuscripts, nature, and much, much more. The text collection includes articles and databases (with a tool that lets you search multiple databases at once), eNYPL (a collection of music, audiobooks, videos, and eBooks that you can download), NYPL books in Google Book Search, and more.
Web: http://www.nypl.org/collections
Facebook: The New York Public Library (Page)
Twitter: nypl
LinkedIn: (None)

Project Gutenberg

Project Gutenberg (named for Johann Gutenberg, inventor of the printing press) offers more than 25,000 free, public-domain eBooks, created by volunteers. Download a book or create one to add to the project.
Web: www.gutenberg.org/wiki/Main_Page
Facebook: Project Gutenberg (Page)
Twitter: (None)
LinkedIn: (None)

Questia $

An online library that provides round-the-clock access to a million and a half titles in the humanities and social sciences, Questia works on a subscription basis. You can subscribe to the entire collection or choose a particular specialized collection, such as history, literature, or psychology. Note, however, that Questia's collection does not include business or science titles.
Web: www.questia.com
Facebook: Questia (Page), Questia Users (Group)
Twitter: Questia
LinkedIn: Questia Media (Company)

4

WorldCat

WorldCat uses its huge network of libraries to make finding a particular book or other item easier. When you search for a book, CD, or video, WorldCat searches many libraries at once and shows you where the item is available near you. You can also find articles, audiobooks, and other digital resources available for immediate download. Register for a free account, and you can create a list of items that interest you or build a bibliography as you search. WorldCat also has a blog.

Web: www.worldcat.org
Facebook: WorldCat Fan Club (Group)
Twitter: worldcatorg
LinkedIn: (None)

PRESCHOOL

KinderCare

Nearly 2,000 KinderCare Learning Centers exist across the United States. Learn about KinderCare programs for different age groups, watch a parenting video, or shop in the KinderCare store. Enter your ZIP code to find a KinderCare center near you.

Web: www.kindercare.com
Facebook: KinderCare Learning Centers (Page)
Twitter: (None)
LinkedIn: KinderCare (Company)

REFERENCE RESOURCES

Dictionary.com

Type a word into the search box, and Dictionary.com looks it up in more than two dozen dictionaries to tell you what it means. If you misspell the word, the site makes suggestions about the correct

spelling. Besides dictionary lookups, the site has a word of the day (English and Spanish), word games, a blog, and Word Explorer podcasts, as well as links to related reference sites.

Web: http://dictionary.reference.com
Facebook: Dictionary.com (Group)
Twitter: dictionarycom
LinkedIn: (None)

The Free Dictionary 🏅

This site boasts nearly a billion visitors so far, and it's easy to see why: It brings together multiple dictionaries (including medical, legal, financial, and computer dictionaries), a thesaurus, an encyclopedia, a literature reference library, an acronym list, and a search engine. The customizable home page has a ton of content, from games, local weather, and your daily horoscope to This Day in History, Today's Birthday, and Word of the Day.

Web: www.thefreedictionary.com
Facebook: The Free Dictionary (Group)
Twitter: (None)
LinkedIn: (None)

Quoteland

Whether you're searching for a particular quotation or want to find quotes related to a topic, Quoteland can help you find it. When you find the quote you want, you can put it on a T-shirt, a coffee mug, or another product available in the online store. Quoteland has active discussion forums, a reference library, and links to related sites.

Web: www.quoteland.com
Facebook: Quoteland (Page)
Twitter: quoteland
LinkedIn: (None)

Thinkmap Visual Thesaurus

Search for a word, and the visual thesaurus creates a cool-looking, interactive map of related words. Synonyms cluster together; click any synonym to create a new map with that word at the center. Click the speaker icon to hear a word's pronunciation, or click the dot that connects a cluster of words to get that cluster's main definition. Great for visual thinkers and creative association. The site offers a free trial, or you can buy a desktop or online edition. Fun to play with—and you might just learn something at the same time.

Web: www.visualthesaurus.com
Facebook: Thinkmap Visual Thesaurus (Page)
Twitter: VisualTheasurus
LinkedIn: (None)

Wikipedia

Probably the most famous wiki on the planet, Wikipedia lets anyone write, edit, read, and discuss articles—more than two million of them—on every topic under the sun. The idea is that multiple authors will keep the information both accurate and up-to-date. You can research topics, create new articles, or edit existing ones.

Web: www.wikipedia.org
Facebook: Wikipedia (Page), If Wikipedia Says It, It Must Be True (Group)
Twitter: Wikipedia
LinkedIn: Wikimedia Foundation (Group)

YourDictionary.com

YourDictionary.com has a free dictionary and thesaurus, but it provides links to a whole lot more: more than 2,500 dictionaries and grammar guides in more than 300 languages. You'll also find language-related games and an active forum for people who love to talk about words and language.

Web: www.yourdictionary.com
Facebook: (None)
Twitter: YourDictionary
LinkedIn: YourDictionary (Company)

RESEARCH HELP

Research Help Now

The Library of Michigan has joined forces with 15 Michigan colleges to provide this online reference service. Students and patrons of participating libraries can receive free research assistance by chatting online with a librarian. During times when the chat room is closed, you can email your question. A wonderful resource for Michigan residents. Similar sites exist for residents of Ohio and Wisconsin. If you don't live in these states, use your search engine to see if a site exists for your state as well.

Web: www.researchhelpnow.org
Facebook: Research Help Now (Page)
Twitter: (None)
LinkedIn: (None)

TUTORING

GlobalScholar

Online tutoring with qualified educators with verified credentials. This site offers three ways of learning: connect with a tutor in person in a virtual classroom (you can work instantly with an online tutor or schedule a future session), get help with homework by submitting a question, or take a self-guided course. You can try out the site for $1; after that, fees vary by instructor.

Web: www.globalscholar.com
Facebook: (None)
Twitter: GlobalScholar
LinkedIn: (None)

Kaplan Tutoring

Kaplan is well known for helping students prepare for college and graduate-school admission exams. The company also offers tutoring in all subjects to students in kindergarten through grade 10. Learn about Kaplan's Advantage Program, a computer-based course, and Personal Academic Tutoring.

Web: www.kaplan.com
Facebook: Kaplan Tutoring (Page)
Twitter: Kaplan Tutoring
LinkedIn: (None)

Sylvan Learning

Sylvan Learning gives each student a skills assessment to create a customized learning plan. Choose from three tutoring methods: online, at a Sylvan Learning Center, or in your home. Prices start at $88/month, and you can choose from various payment options. The Resources for Parents section has a K–12 Tutoring Library with articles and tips for helping children learn.

Web: http://tutoring.sylvanlearning.com
Facebook: Sylvan Learning (Page)
Twitter: SylvanLearning
LinkedIn: Sylvan Learning (Company)

Tutor.com

Tutor.com provides on-demand tutoring from a network of more than 2,000 certified tutors. On-demand means that tutors are available around the clock, every day of the week, so there's no need for an appointment. Sessions take place in a virtual classroom equipped with an interactive whiteboard and text chat. Students buy a certain number of minutes. When they use minutes in a tutoring session, the minutes are deducted from the student's account. You can try out Tutor.com for 25 minutes for free.

Web: www.tutor.com
Facebook: Tutor.com Online Tutoring for Military Families (Page), Tutor.com Librarians (Group)
Twitter: Tutor.com
LinkedIn: Tutor.com (Company)

ENTERTAINMENT

There's no shortage of fun on the Internet, and this chapter highlights the best of the social media resources for the entertainment industry. Whether you're looking for movie reviews, celebrity gossip, music videos, games, television episodes—whatever— you'll find it here. You'll also find social media outlets where you can get together with other fans and make connections, discuss hot new trends, and share your views.

ACTORS AND ACTRESSES

Actors' Equity Association

Equity is a labor union for theater professionals, representing more than 45,000 actors and stage managers across the United States. Besides negotiating wages and working conditions for its members, the organization works to promote live theater in U.S. culture. Visit Equity's website to learn about membership and how to join, find auditions and jobs in its Casting Call section, and read rulebooks and other documents in the Document Library.

Web: www.actorsequity.org
Facebook: Actors' Equity Association (Page), The Official Actors' Equity Association Facebook Group (Group)
Twitter: ActorsEquity
LinkedIn: (None)

Back Stage

A resource for actors, Back Stage is a great place to connect with other actors and industry professionals. The site features lots of articles to help actors perfect their craft and build a career, as well as show-business news, theater and film reviews, a searchable database of casting notices, and numerous other resources.

Web: www.backstage.com
Facebook: Back Stage (Page), Backstagecasting (Page)
Twitter: BackStageCast
LinkedIn: (None)

Filmbug: Guide to the Movie Stars

Filmbug is a guide to more than 10,000 actors and other movie-industry professionals. When you search for an actor or actress, the resulting page has a bio, filmography, and a link to a forum where you can meet other fans and discuss the actor's work.

Web: www.filmbug.com
Facebook: Filmbug Movie Stars (Page)
Twitter: Filmbug Tweets
LinkedIn: (None)

Screen Actors Guild (SAG)

With 20 branches nationwide, SAG represents nearly 120,000 actors who work in film, television and commercials, video games, the Internet, and all new media formats. Here you'll find information about SAG's work, membership, contracts, and branches. Members can use iActor, the site's online casting directory, pay dues online, and view contracts, career seminars, and workshops.

Web: www.sag.org
Facebook: Screen Actors Guild (Page), Screen Actors' Guild Foundation (Pages), Screen Actors Guild (Group)
Twitter: ScreenActors
LinkedIn: Screen Actors Guild (SAG) (Group)

CELEBRITIES

Coolspotters

Want to look like a celebrity? Check out Coolspotters, where users link up celebrities with the fashions and products they're spotted with. Here you'll find profiles of celebrities, products, and movies, as well as "Spots," or links between two profiles. Register to add Spots, create and edit profiles, leave comments, and interact with other users.

Web: http://coolspotters.com
Facebook: Coolspotters (Page)
Twitter: coolspotters
LinkedIn: (None)

E! Online

The official website of E! dishes up celebrity news and inside information about life on the red carpet. You'll also find music and movie reviews, live-event coverage, and discussion boards, as well as blogs and podcasts. If you like to be in on the latest celebrity gossip, join the 2.5 million people who visit E! Online each month.

Web: www.eonline.com
Facebook: E! online (Page)
Twitter: eonline
LinkedIn: (None)

People Magazine 🏅

Readers of *People* magazine will want to check out its website for up-to-the-minute celebrity news and photos. Peruse sections on style, TV news, celebrity gossip, and video reports. Get celebrity quotes and fun facts and make sure you don't miss the most-read stories. You can also subscribe to *People* or sign up for free updates and newsletters.

Web: www.people.com/people
Facebook: Peoplemag (Page)
Twitter: peoplemag, People News
LinkedIn: People Magazine (Company)

TMZ 🚫

TMZ.com is a frequently updated news and gossip site that takes an irreverent peek into the lives of celebrities. Read the latest news, check the schedule for TMZ TV, and find out how to access TMZ on your cellphone. There's lots of juicy stuff here.

Web: www.tmz.com
Facebook: TMZ (Page)
Twitter: TMZ, TMZcelebs, TMZAol
LinkedIn: TMZ (Company)

COMEDIANS AND HUMOR

Clean Comedians

Looking to hire a comedian to liven up an event? Go to this website to book a comedian or another entertainer who'll amuse without offending. The site even offers a guarantee: If the act isn't funny, you'll get your money back.

Web: www.cleancomedians.com
Facebook: (None)
Twitter: cleancomedians
LinkedIn: (None)

Jokes by Kids

Kids crack each other up, and this site lets them share their favorite jokes with other kids from all over the world. All jokes are clean and appeal to kids' unique sense of humor. Jokes are sorted into categories, such as animal jokes, school jokes, cross-the-road jokes, knock-knock jokes, and a whole bunch more. There's even a section of video jokes. Kids can also sign up to receive jokes by email.

Web: www.jokesbykids.com
Facebook: (None)
Twitter: JokesByKids
LinkedIn: (None)

Last Comic Standing

In this NBC reality show, viewers vote for the comic whose act they find funniest. A comic is eliminated each week until a new king or queen of comedy is crowned. This website is where you can get the lowdown on the show, including exclusive footage and behind-the-scenes news. Keep an eye on this website—it will update to new seasons and archive old ones.

Web: www.nbc.com/casting
Facebook: lastcomic7 (Page)
Twitter: lastcomic7
LinkedIn: (None)

Stand Up Comedian for Hire

Stand-up comedian Brian Carter talks about being a comedian: how to get started, how to write funny, and more. He emphasizes clean comedy, so you don't have to wonder what's making the kids snicker.

Web: http://standupcomedianforhire.blogspot.com/
Facebook: (None)
Twitter: briancarter
LinkedIn: (None)

DVDS

Blockbuster $

Find a local store, or sign up to rent DVDs by mail. Blockbuster ships movies to you; when you're done, you can return them by mail or to a nearby Blockbuster store. Blockbuster offers recommendations, as well as trailers and clips for you to watch. You can also buy new or previously viewed DVDs.

Web: www.blockbuster.com
Facebook: BLOCKBUSTER (Page)
Twitter: blockbuster
LinkedIn: Blockbuster (Company)

Netflix $

Netflix revolutionized DVD rentals by creating a subscription-based site where you can create a list of the DVDs you'd like to see, receive them in the mail, and return them when you're ready—no late fees. Now, you can use this DVD-rental model or pick a movie and view it instantly on your PC. Browse more than 100,000 titles (10,000 for PC viewing), get recommendations, or sign up for a free trial before you commit.

Web: www.netflix.com
Facebook: Netflix (Page), Netflix Updates (Application)
Twitter: netflix, instant_netflix, netflixapi, netflix_movies
LinkedIn: Netflix (Company)

5

SwapaDVD

Lots of people have DVDs lying around that they don't really watch anymore. If your DVDs are in good condition, you can trade them for movies you *do* want to see. Create a list of DVDs you're willing to give away. When someone requests one and you mail it off (you pay postage), you get a credit on the site. Use credits to request the DVDs you want. When you get a DVD, it's yours to keep—or to swap another day.

Web: www.swapadvd.com
Facebook: SwapaDVD (Page, Application)
Twitter: swapadvd (Company)
LinkedIn: (None)

FILM FESTIVALS

Cannes Film Festival

The world's most glamorous film festival has an informative website where you can learn all about the festival's 60-plus-year history. Click the current year to find out what's happening with this year's festival: View its poster and look through photos, read about daily news and events, see who's on the juries, and (after the festival is over) see which films won. The festival archives give you the same information for previous festivals.

Web: www.festival-cannes.fr
Facebook: Cannes Film Festival (Page)
Twitter: (None)
LinkedIn: (None)

FilmFestivals.com

Every year, thousands of film festivals take place all over the world. If you're an aspiring filmmaker (or a serious movie buff), this site tells you everything you could possibly want to know about film festivals. The site collects and displays the latest festival news. It also has a bulletin board where festivals post information about entering, and sections about films, people, awards, and digital movies.

Web: www.filmfestivals.com
Facebook: Festivals Only (Page)
Twitter: (None)
LinkedIn: (None)

Film Festival Secrets

Entertainment writer Chris Holland reviews and blogs about film festivals from all over.

Web: http://www.filmfestivalsecrets.com
Facebook: Film Festival Secrets (Page)
Twitter: ffsecrets
LinkedIn: (None)

Film Festival Today Online

This comprehensive site focuses on film festivals around the world. Sections include Film Festivals, News, Interviews, Reviews, Technology, Movies That Matter, Filmmaker Resources, and Feature Articles. Whether you're looking for a film festival to attend or you're a filmmaker who wants to participate, you'll find this informative site useful.

Web: www.filmfestivaltoday.com
Facebook: (None)
Twitter: filmfestoday
LinkedIn: (None)

Sundance Film Festival

Whether you want to travel to Utah for Robert Redford's Sundance Film Festival, volunteer, catch a couple of films, or just see the winners, this informative site will help you out. Find out about the latest news and get festival info (including tickets, films, events, and venues). Check out videos and podcasts.

Web: www.sundance.org/festival/
Facebook: Sundance Film Festival (Page), Sundance Film Festival (Group)
Twitter: sundancefest
LinkedIn: Sundance Film Festival (Company), Sundance Film Festival Connection (Group)

Tribeca Film Festival

This New York festival, begun in 2001 by actor Robert DeNiro and friends, aims to help filmmakers reach an international audience. View video clips, find out how to get tickets, and stay up-to-date on festival news.

Web: www.tribecafilmfestival.org
Facebook: Tribeca Film Festival (Page), Tribeca Film Festival Volunteer Group (Group)
Twitter: TribecaFilm
LinkedIn: Tribeca Film Festival (Company)

GAMING

IGN.com ⊛

If you're passionate about gaming, this is the site for you. Reviews, previews, news, videos, guides, cheats—it's all here, for whatever gaming platform you use. Also has sections on movies, TV, DVDs, comics, anime, music, and sports. When you register for a free account on the site, you can create your own blog, set up a wish list, and keep track of your collection. The site is comprehensive, but be warned that some of its content isn't suitable for young children.

Web: www.ign.com
Facebook: IGN blogs (Group), IGN (Page)
Twitter: IGNcom, IGNGameSite
LinkedIn: IGN Entertainment (Company)

Station.com

Owned by Sony Online Entertainment, this site offers free online games, downloadable PC games, and games for your console or hand-held device. Many of the for-purchase games have free trials so you can try before you buy. For just under 30 bucks a month, Station Access lets you play the site's premium live online games and confers other benefits, such as a newsletter, additional character slots, and bonus games.

Web: www.station.sony.com
Facebook: (None)
Twitter: (None)
LinkedIn: Sony Online Entertainment (Company)

MOVIES

CinemaNow ⑤

Get movies over the Internet by visiting this site. CinemaNow gives you three options for purchasing a movie: download-to-own (buy a movie to watch as many times as you want on your computer and up to two other devices), pay-per-view (when you download a pay-per-view movie, you have up to 24 hours to watch it), and burn-to-DVD (download a movie, watch it on your computer, and make a copy on a DVD that you can watch on just about any DVD player). You can also buy television shows.

Web: www.cinemanow.com
Facebook: (None)
Twitter: RoxioCinemaNow (Page)
LinkedIn: CinemaNow (Company)

Flixster

Flixster is a social network for movie fanatics, which shows you which movies your friends liked—and which ones they hated. Sign up for a free account and you can create a profile; write reviews; make connections and read friends' reviews; get movie recommendations; make lists of your favorite movies, actors, and photos; and a whole lot more.

Web: www.flixster.com
Facebook: Flixster (Page)
Twitter: (None)
LinkedIn: Flixster (Company)

Hollywood Elsewhere

Jeffrey Wells, a former *Entertainment Weekly* reporter and Hollywood columnist for numerous publications, writes what he calls "a daily stream-of-Hollywood-consciousness column."

Web: www.hollywood-elsewhere.com
Facebook: (None)
Twitter: wellshwood
LinkedIn: (None)

The Internet Movie Database 🏅

If you want to know anything at all about movies or actors, the Internet Movie Database (IMDb) is the place you're most likely to find it. Search for a movie or TV show episode to find its cast, trailer, still photos, and additional data such as trivia, quotes, and goofs. When you search for an actor, you get biographical information, photos, videos, trivia, and a list of roles. IMDb also has movie and celebrity news, games, and an independent film section. If you register for a free account, you can read discussion forums and join the conversation, rate movies, and submit info to the site. Movie buffs could easily spend all day poking around here.

Web: www.imdb.com
Facebook: IMDb (Page)
Twitter: IMDb
LinkedIn: IMDb.com (Company)

5

The Movie Blog

A blog about movies that's been around for more than five years, the Movie Blog features half a dozen contributors who aren't shy about giving their opinion. A well-written, informative, and entertaining blog. Also has a podcast.

Web: www.themovieblog.com
Facebook: (None)
Twitter: TMB_Tweets
LinkedIn: (None)

MTV Movies Blog

MTV updates this blog throughout the day to bring you the latest movie news and trailers, as well as interviews and the occasional celebrity blogger.

Web: http://moviesblog.mtv.com/
Facebook: (None)
Twitter: mtvmoviesblog
LinkedIn: (None)

Spill

Spill offers movie reviews and a community of nearly 7,500 other film buffs. When you join, you can post in the forums, read and write reviews, watch video reviews, and upload your own photos and videos.

Web: http://my.spill.com/
Facebook: Spill (Page)
Twitter: spillcrew
LinkedIn: (None)

Variety

The online version of *Variety* magazine is all about the entertainment industry. Get insider movie news and gossip, choose from a wide range of blogs and columns, read reviews and ratings, check out Festival Central to read what's happening at major film festivals, and view photos and videos. If you're in the biz, you can network with other entertainment-industry pros or look for a job.

Web: www.variety.com
Facebook: Variety (Page)
Twitter: (None)
LinkedIn: Variety (Company)

INDEPENDENT FILMS

IndieGoGo

IndieGoGo is an online social marketplace that hooks up filmmakers and fans. Filmmakers build a page where they pitch their idea to the world, then promote it to build an audience. Fans can respond by watching a project, rating or commenting on it, or contributing to its funding. A cool idea for helping indie filmmakers pitch their ideas and build an audience.

Web: www.indiegogo.com
Facebook: IndieGoGo.com (Page)
Twitter: IndieGoGo
LinkedIn: Indiegogo.com (Company)

Richmond Moving Image Co-op

The Richmond Moving Image Co-op (RMIC), staffed by volunteers, is based in Richmond, Virginia. RMIC strives to support independent film by providing public screenings, classes, and workshops. Filmmakers and fans can also get access to equipment, information, and resources. RMIC hosts the annual James River Film Festival and Flicker, a bimonthly screening of short films by local filmmakers. The site has a great Resources section for filmmakers.

Web: http://rmicweb.org/
Facebook: Richmond Moving Image Co-op (Page)
Twitter: (None)
LinkedIn: (None)

MOVIE REVIEWS

The Agony Booth

If you love to hate bad movies (or maybe you hate to love them), you'll like this site, which reviews and analyzes the worst that Hollywood has to offer. Contribute a brief review of your all-time least-favorite film in The Agonizer, or sound off in the forums.

Web: http://agonybooth.com/
Facebook: the agony booth (Page)
Twitter: agonybooth
LinkedIn: (None)

Filmcritic.com

This site has its own critics to provide reviews of current releases, as well as an extensive archive—more than 7,500 movie reviews in all. There's a widget you can download that puts the site's most recent reviews right on your computer's desktop.

Web: www.filmcritic.com
Facebook: Filmcritic.com (Page)
Twitter: amcfilmcritic
LinkedIn: (None)

Kids-in-Mind

Parents who worry whether a particular movie is kid-friendly will appreciate this site. Movies are rated on a scale of 0—10 for these areas of concern: sex/nudity, violence/gore, and profanity. Detailed analyses of movies explain those ratings, comment on problematic issues such as substance abuse, and note discussion topics that may come up after kids see the film. The site's clearly written reviews are invaluable for finding family-friendly films.

Web: www.kids-in-mind.com
Facebook: Kids-In-Mind.com (Page)
Twitter: (None)
LinkedIn: (None)

Metacritic

Metacritic compiles a wide range of reviews from respected sources and then averages those scores on a scale of 0—100 so you can see how critics graded the film. For any film you choose, you can read an overview and see what a particular critic had to say about it. Registered site users can also rate and review movies; users' average scores are displayed alongside the critics'. Besides movies, Metacritic compiles reviews of DVDs, TV shows, books, music, and games.

Web: www.metacritic.com
Facebook: Metacritic Fans (Page)
Twitter: metacritic
LinkedIn: (None)

Movie Review Query Engine

This site's database contains more than 68,000 movies. When you search for a movie, MRQE returns reviews for that title, as well as blogs and news stories that mention it. There's a forum where registered users can discuss movies with others.

Web: www.mrqe.com
Facebook: The Movie Review Query Engine (Page), MRQE.com, The Movie Review Query Engine (Group)
Twitter: MRQE
LinkedIn: (None)

Roger Ebert

Roger Ebert is one of the best-known film critics in the U.S., and his site is a feast for anyone who loves movies. Read reviews, ask movie-related questions, find out Ebert's picks for the greatest movies, take a look at the movie glossary, read what's happening at film festivals, and get updates on the Oscars.

Web: http://rogerebert.suntimes.com/
Facebook: roger ebert (Page), Roger Ebert (Group)
Twitter: ebertchicago
LinkedIn: (None)

5

Rotten Tomatoes 🏆

This excellent site collects reviews from critics, both professional and amateur, and averages them using the Tomatometer: Movies that get a passing grade (60% positive reviews or better) are certified Fresh; movies that don't hit the 60% mark are classified Rotten. Don't go to the movies without visiting this site first.

Web: www.rottentomatoes.com
Facebook: Rotten Tomatoes (Page)
Twitter: RottenTomatoes
LinkedIn: Rotten Tomatoes (Company)

MOVIE THEATERS

AMC Entertainment, Inc.

With more than 350 theaters and 5,000 screens, AMC is one of the largest cinema chains in the world. Most of AMC's theaters are located in the U.S. and Canada, although the company also has cinemas in France, the United Kingdom, Mexico, and Hong Kong. Use the website to find movies and showtimes, buy tickets, purchase an AMC gift card, or find out about hosting a meeting at a theater.

Web: www.amctheatres.com
Facebook: AMC Theatres (Page)
Twitter: AMCCINEMAS
LinkedIn: AMC Theatres (Company)

Carmike Cinemas

This cinema chain focuses on communities with a population of 100,000 or less. Visit its site to see current and coming attractions and special events, buy tickets and gift certificates, or enter a contest.

Web: www.carmike.com
Facebook: Carmike Cinemas (Page)
Twitter: CarmikeCinemas
LinkedIn: Carmike Cinemas (Company)

Cinemark

Cinemark has more than 3,600 screens in the United States and another 1,000-plus screens in 12 countries. Its website lets you find movies and showtimes near you, sign up to receive local showtimes by email, buy tickets and gift cards, and learn about scheduling a private event, such as a business meeting or birthday party. The site has links to CinéArts (art and independent films), IMAX, and digital and 3D locations.

Web: www.cinemark.com
Facebook: CineMark (Page)
Twitter: CinemarkXD
LinkedIn: Cinemark (Company)

Fandango

Fandango lets you find local movies and showtimes, and then buy tickets online. Choose a movie and type in your ZIP code, or just submit your ZIP code to see a selection of what's playing near you. Then use a credit card to buy tickets. There's lots more on the site besides ticketing: Play games, watch movie trailers, read reviews and the site's blog, and learn more about your favorite movie or actor.

Web: www.fandango.com
Facebook: Fandango (Page), Join for 4 Free Fandango Movie Passes! (Group)
Twitter: Fandango
LinkedIn: Fandango (Company)

Hollywood.com 🏆

Much more than a place to find out when movies are playing and buy tickets (although of course you can do that), Hollywood.com covers all things Hollywood. Here you'll find movie news and celebrity bios, interviews, and gossip. You'll also find trailers, DVD and TV info, forums, contests, and fan sites. When you search for a movie, you get a ton of results: information about the movie, but also the trailer, clips, still photos, reviews, and so on. You can create an account, which gives you your own page on the site; keep a blog; connect with other fans; review films; and participate in the forums. A great site for movie lovers.

Web: www.hollywood.com
Facebook: (None)
Twitter: Hollywood_com
LinkedIn: Hollywood (Company)

IMAX

IMAX films take your movie-watching experience to the next level, with huge images in high-definition and digital surround sound. And with IMAX 3D, images appear to leap right off the screen. This site lists current IMAX films and the theaters showing them. To get the latest IMAX news, sign up for the free eNewsletter or have updates sent to your mobile phone.

Web: www.imax.com
Facebook: IMAX (Page)
Twitter: IMAX
LinkedIn: IMAX (Company)

Moviefone

Movies, showtimes, tickets, and a bunch of other fun stuff. Moviefone covers movie news, DVD releases, and celebrity fashion and gossip. You can watch trailers and check out special features such as best and worst lists, glimpses behind the scenes, and quizzes and trivia.

Web: http://movies.aol.com/
Facebook: Moviefone (Page)
Twitter: moviefone
LinkedIn: (None)

MovieTickets.com

Find a movie near you and then buy tickets. Sign up for a free account if you want to create a list of your favorite theaters, customize the site, and get a weekly newsletter and special offers in your email inbox.

Web: www.movietickets.com
Facebook: MovieTickets.com (Page)
Twitter: _MovieTickets_
LinkedIn: MovieTickets.com (Company)

NCM Fathom Events

If you're interested in special events that go beyond the usual Saturday-night flicks, check out this site. From concerts to sports to one-time live events to simulcasts of Metropolitan Opera performances, Fathom Events lists upcoming events and helps you find a participating theater near you. Sign up for email event alerts and buy tickets in advance.

Web: www.fathomevents.com
Facebook: (None)
Twitter: fathomevents
LinkedIn: NCM Fathom (Company)

Regal Entertainment Group

The largest theater chain in the United States, Regal hosted 242 million moviegoers in 2007. Besides providing tools to find a theater and buy tickets, its website spotlights a current movie and has links to IMAX, Regal Cinema Art, and digital 3D theaters. You can also join the Regal Crown Club, which lets you earn free snacks and movies by presenting your card when you visit a Regal Cinema.

Web: www.regmovies.com
Facebook: The Official Page of Regal Entertainment Group (Page)
Twitter: RegalMovies
LinkedIn: Regal Entertainment Group (Company)

MUSIC

AllMusic

Not only is AllMusic all about music, but it makes a strong effort to cover all kinds of music. Rock, jazz, R & B, rap, country, blues, world, electronica, classical—you'll find them all on this site. The site offers more than five million music samples across these genres, as well as reviews, new releases, videos, a blog, and a featured album each day. Whatever your musical tastes, you're sure to find something of interest here.

Web: www.allmusic.com
Facebook: (None)
Twitter: allmusic
LinkedIn: (None)

GRAMMY.com

The official site of the Grammy awards, honoring the best in music each year. Find past winners, get the latest music news, and shop in the Grammy store.

Web: www.grammy.com
Facebook: The GRAMMYs (Page), Latin Grammys (Page)
Twitter: TheGRAMMYs
LinkedIn: The Recording Academy (Company)

iLike

This popular social network catalogs what you listen to through iTunes or Windows Media Player (you have to download a free program to get started). Your music library appears in your iLike profile, organized by how often and how recently you've played songs. iLike matches you up with other iLike users who have similar tastes in music. Through the site, you can buy songs or albums from Amazon and iTunes, but iLink also has free downloads from lots of independent musicians.

Web: www.ilike.com
Facebook: Music (Page), iLike this artist (Application)
Twitter: iLike
LinkedIn: iLike (Company)

vSide

Inhabitants of this 3D virtual world for teens can listen to great music, dance, chat, party, and generally hang out. You must be 13 or older to join.

Web: www.vside.com
Facebook: vSide (Page), vSide (Group)
Twitter: vside
LinkedIn: vSide (Company)

MUSIC GENRES: ALTERNATIVE

Alternative Addiction 🏅

For the latest news in alternative music, point your web browser to Alternative Addiction. The site features music news and reviews, information about up-and-coming unsigned bands, and a forum for fans, as well as lots of downloads and videos. First Listen features new music, and AA Radio broadcasts the best in alternative music, 24 hours a day. Enter contests or buy stuff in the Alternative Addiction Shop.

Web: www.alternativeaddiction.com
Facebook: Alternative Addiction… (Page)
Twitter: AddictedMusic
LinkedIn: (None)

AlternativeMusic.com ⑤

Web: http://alternativemusic.com/
Facebook: Lakeshore Record Exchange (Page), Lakeshore Record Exchange (Group)
Twitter: _lakeshore_
LinkedIn: (None)

Whether you're looking for a hot new release or a hard-to-find curio, AlternativeMusic.com is your best bet for buying it. You can search for a particular title or browse the Main and Rarities catalogs. Preview new music or sign up for a free newsletter. Has a blog and a podcast too.

Indie Rock Café

A blog about the alternative music scene. Posts are helpfully organized into categories: Artists & Bands, MP3s & Videos, Concerts & Festivals, Releases & Reviews.

Web: www.indierockcafe.com
Facebook: Indie Rock Cafe (Page)
Twitter: indierockcafe
LinkedIn: (None)

Insound $

Insound is an online store that promotes and distributes alternative and independent music. You can buy CDs, downloads, and vinyl here, as well as cool T-shirts, posters, and other gifts. Find out about upcoming releases, listen to Insound radio, and check out special offers.

Web: www.insound.com
Facebook: Insound (Page)
Twitter: Insound
LinkedIn: (None)

MUSIC GENRES: BLUEGRASS

Blistered Fingers

Each June and August, the Blistered Fingers Family Music Bluegrass Festival takes place in Maine. Visit this site to learn all about it—how to get tickets, who's playing, how to get there. View photos of past festivals and sign up for the festival mailing list.

Web: http://blisteredfingers.com/
Facebook: Blistered Fingers (People)
Twitter: (None)
LinkedIn: (None)

Bluegrass Unlimited

The home of *Bluegrass Unlimited* magazine on the Web, this site gives highlights of the current issue, including reviews and new releases. You can browse past issues, search the site's archives, or sign up for a subscription.

Web: www.bluegrassmusic.com
Facebook: Bluegrass Unlimited Magazine (Page)
Twitter: (None)
LinkedIn: (None)

Huck Finn Jubilee

This three-day California music festival features country and bluegrass. All the information you need is here: tickets, artists, schedule, nonmusic events, camping and lodging info, vendors, and directions.

Web: www.huckfinn.org
Facebook: Huck Finn Jubilee (Page)
Twitter: (None)
LinkedIn: (None)

Planet Bluegrass

Check out Planet Bluegrass to learn about its Colorado music festivals, including Telluride Bluegrass, Rocky Grass, Folks Festival, and the Wildflower Concert Series. Planet Bluegrass emphasizes sustainability with its blog, Sustainable Festivation, and a Green area of the site that lays out the Planet Bluegrass Sustainability Doctrine and offers tips and resources for keeping your festival experience green.

Web: www.bluegrass.com
Facebook: Planet Bluegrass (Page)
Twitter: planetbluegrass
LinkedIn: (None)

MUSIC GENRES: CHRISTIAN AND GOSPEL

CCM Magazine.com

Read about Christian music artists (including upcoming releases and tours) and reviews of their work. Listen to the featured release and other music samples. Join the discussions in the forum. A great site with lots of resources that will keep you up-to-date with what's happening in Christian music.

5

Web: www.ccmmagazine.com
Facebook: (None)
Twitter: ccmmagazine
LinkedIn: (None)

ChristianMusic.org

Want to know the current bestsellers in Christian music? Take a look at this site, which lists the top 12. Sign up for a newsletter (the site offers more than 30), find a Christian-music-related Facebook group, or shop in the store.

Web: www.christianmusic.org
Facebook: (None)
Twitter: 4TheSoulTunes
LinkedIn: (None)

Gospel Music Channel

The official website of the Gospel Music Channel. Find your local station and check the schedule to see what's on. Learn about news and artists, shop for your favorite music, and watch videos. The site has areas that feature different music genres: Rock, Pop, Country, and Soul.

Web: www.gospelmusicchannel.com
Facebook: gmctv (Page)
Twitter: gmctv
LinkedIn: Gospel Music Channel (Company)

MUSIC GENRES: CLASSICAL AND OPERA

Gramophone 🏅

Gramophone is one of the world's premier classical music magazines, and its companion website is bursting with information: news, features, awards, competition notices, a forum, a podcast, a free newsletter, and much more. Don't miss the Editor's Choice section, which spotlights 10 great new recordings each month. An incredible resource for classical music lovers.

Web: www.gramophone.co.uk
Facebook: Gramophone (Page)
Twitter: GramophoneMag
LinkedIn: (None)

The Metropolitan Opera

The internationally acclaimed Metropolitan Opera in New York has put together an attractive and informative website. Learn about upcoming productions and the Met's pioneering program of simulcasting select performances in high-definition into movie theaters around the world. There are sections on the history of the Met (including an archive of performance details), features and interviews, and advice for neophyte operagoers. You can buy subscriptions and tickets online.

Web: www.metoperafamily.org/metopera/
Facebook: The Metropolitan Opera (Page), The Metropolitan Opera Guild (Page), The Metropolitan Opera House (Group)
Twitter: MetOpera
LinkedIn: Metropolitan Opera (Company)

MonteVerdi

Offering music videos for the classical set, MonteVerdi covers opera, symphonic music, ballet, and more. You can also download audio clips; buy CDs, DVDs, and sheet music from the store; check out links to other classical sites; participate in discussions with other music lovers; and test your knowledge with the music quiz.

Web: http://monteverdi.tv
Facebook: MonteVerdi Media (Page)
Twitter: MonteVerdiMedia
LinkedIn: (None)

New York Philharmonic

The New York Philharmonic is the oldest symphony orchestra in the United States. On its website you'll find information about tickets, schedules, upcoming broadcasts, and recordings. Its Education section is excellent for anyone who wants to learn about classical music, from kids to adults. Visit the store to buy recordings and other merchandise.

Web: http://nyphil.org/
Facebook: New York Philharmonic (Page), New York Philharmonic (Groups)
Twitter: nyphil
LinkedIn: New York Philharmonic (Company)

OPERA America

OPERA America is "the national service organization for opera," promoting opera and supporting opera professionals. Its website has sections for Artists, Companies, and Audiences, as well as a Quick Links section to opera resources, such as a nationwide list of opera companies and a directory of new works.

Web: www.operaamerica.org
Facebook: OPERA America (Page)
Twitter: operaamerica
LinkedIn: OPERA America (Company)

Opera Chic

Opera and classical music gossip, news, and reviews (with some fashion commentary thrown in) from an anonymous American blogger living in Milan. The posts are witty, insightful, and often hilarious.

Web: http://operachic.typepad.com/
Facebook: (None)
Twitter: operachic
LinkedIn: (None)

WGBH Classical to Go!

A weekly podcast of classical music from WGBH in Boston.

Web: www.wgbh.org/classical
Facebook: WGBH (Page), TeamClassical Boston (Page), Media Access Group @ WGBH (Page), WGBH Volunteers (Group)
Twitter: wgbhradio
LinkedIn: WGBH (Company)

MUSIC GENRES: COUNTRY

CMT.com 🏅

The official website of Country Music Television, CMT.com offers a lot more than listings. Here you'll find the latest news in country music, in-depth information on artists and new music, videos, lyrics, blogs, and shows for your mobile device. Listen to CMT Radio or one of dozens of other Internet radio stations with a country twang. If you love country, you'll want to visit this site again and again.

Web: www.cmt.com
Facebook: Country Music Television (CMT) (Page), CMT (Page), CMT One Country (Page), CMT (Group)
Twitter: (None)
LinkedIn: CMT (Company), MTV Networks (Company), Turner Broadcasting (Company)

Country Music Awards

Everything you could ever want to know about the Country Music Awards: history, nominees and winners, events, news, and a database of awards. You'll also find a Games & Multimedia section and a shop where you can buy official CMA gear.

Web: http://cmaawards.com/
Facebook: Country Music Association (Page)
Twitter: Country Music
LinkedIn: (None)

5

Digital Rodeo

A terrific social site for anyone who loves country music, whether a fan, an artist, a songwriter, or someone in the music industry. Make friends, keep up with the latest news, and watch videos. If you're into country music, make this site your home on the Web.

Web: www.digitalrodeo.com
Facebook: DigitalRodeo.com (Page)
Twitter: Digital_Rodeo
LinkedIn: (None)

Great American Country

Web: www.gactv.com
Facebook: GAC - Great American Country (Page)
Twitter: gactv
LinkedIn: (None)

See what's playing on Great American Country TV. And while you're on the site, take a look at the latest videos, features, news, and sweepstakes. The Fan Zone has photos, wallpaper, trivia, and so on.

MUSIC GENRES: HIP-HOP AND RAP

AllHipHop.com

Hip-hop fans will find plenty of interest on this frequently updated site: daily news, interviews, reviews, multimedia (including music, videos, and podcasts), articles on the hip-hop lifestyle (fashion, gaming, gadgets, health, films, and sports), and an active, fast-growing community. Buy featured albums or other music, electronics, jewelry, and more in the site's store. A comprehensive and well-organized site that covers everything hip-hop.

Web: http://allhiphop.com/
Facebook: Greg Watkins (People)
Twitter: allhiphopcom
LinkedIn: (None)

HipHop DX

An online magazine covering the world of hip-hop, HipHop DX has these sections: Home, Hip Hop, Community, Media, Lifestyle, and Fashion. You'll find the latest news, lyrics, album reviews, blogs, a message board and chat room, free mixtapes, and a lot more.

Web: www.hiphopdx.com
Facebook: HipHopDX.com (Group)
Twitter: HipHopDX, @HipHopDX/news
LinkedIn: (None)

Rap Basement

In 2007, Rap Basement won Best Hip-Hop Lifestyle Site in the VH1 Hip-Hop Honors awards. It's easy to see why: Calling itself the "hip-hop lifestyle network," this site presents the latest news; release dates; tour schedules; music, movie, and game reviews; lyrics; wallpapers; artist interviews; and lots of multimedia, including audio, video, and photos.

Web: www.rapbasement.com
Facebook: Rap Basement (Page)
Twitter: rap_basement, @rap_basement/rappear
LinkedIn: (None)

MUSIC GENRES: JAZZ

All About Jazz

This site really *is* all about jazz. Whether you're looking for news, reviews, feature articles, information about a musician, or a place to talk about jazz, you'll find it here. You can download a featured MP3 each day to sample music free. The site is developing a wiki, the Open Jazz Project, to create a comprehensive, community-built resource on jazz.

Web: www.allaboutjazz.com
Facebook: All About Jazz (Page)
Twitter: AllAboutJazz
LinkedIn: (None)

JazzCorner.com

Serving as a portal to hundreds of jazz websites, JazzCorner.com links to the official sites of musicians, arrangers, management companies, record labels, and more. The Speakeasy is a members' forum with message boards. The JazzCorner Jukebox plays all jazz, all the time. JazzVision is the place to go to share and watch jazz videos. You can also read news and interviews and check the Gigs section for an events calendar.

Web: www.jazzcorner.com
Facebook: JazzCorner (Page)
Twitter: jazzcorner
LinkedIn: (None)

A Passion for Jazz!

With a focus on jazz history and education, jazz pianist D C DowDell aims to pass on his passion for jazz. The site is a potpourri of jazz information, including festivals, performance tips, how to find a teacher and get started playing jazz, a glossary, and tons more. Jazz fans and musicians can buy posters, music theory books, fake books, sheet music, CDs and records, and calendars.

Web: www.apassion4jazz.net
Facebook: (None)
Twitter: APassion4Jazz
LinkedIn: (None)

MUSIC GENRES: ROCK AND POP

The Lonely Note

This long-running blog describes itself as "music reviews and news by contributors with an eclectic appetite for all things rock and pop," and that's just what you'll find here.

Web: http://lonelynote.blogspot.com
Facebook: (None)
Twitter: LonelyNote
LinkedIn: (None)

MTV Music: Rock

Visit this site to watch videos from your favorite rock artists—what's hot now, and what's up-and-coming.

Web: www.mtv.com/music/rock
Facebook: MTV (Page), MTV (Group)
Twitter: MTV, MTV/movieblogs, MTV/mtv-talent, MTV/gossip
LinkedIn: MTV Networks (Company, Group)

Popjustice

This British site covers all things pop: daily news, videos, interviews and articles, reviews, upcoming releases, and so on. There's an online radio station, podcasts, and a forum for discussions.

Web: www.popjustice.com
Facebook: Popjustice (Page)
Twitter: popjustice, @popjustice/quickly-tiresome, @popjustice/bells-end
LinkedIn: (None)

Rock and Roll Hall of Fame and Museum

The Rock and Roll Hall of Fame is located in Cleveland, Ohio, but you can visit it on the Web from wherever you are. Here you'll find a list of inductees, information about current exhibits and items in the museum's collection, events, education, Today in Rock, an online store, and more, including tons of information about the shining stars of rock music.

Web: www.rockhall.com
Facebook: Rock and Roll Hall of Fame + Museum (Page)
Twitter: rock_hall
LinkedIn: Rock and Roll Hall of Fame and Museum (Company)

Vintage Rock

This site is dedicated to vintage rock, "music that people have been digging for 10, 20, 30, even 40 years." Read news on your favorite past and present rockers, listen to music in the Digital Lounge or watch vintagerockdotcom's YouTube videos, and check out features and artist profiles. The site offers both nostalgia and news.

5

Web: www.vintagerock.com
Facebook: Vintage Rock: Timeless Rock and Roll (Page)
Twitter: Vintage_Rock
LinkedIn: (None)

MUSIC GENRES: WORLD MUSIC

Global Rhythm

This online version of *Global Rhythm* magazine features world music festivals and concerts, world music downloads and news, and music reviews from Africa, Europe, Latin America, Asia, and the Middle East. You can subscribe to the magazine in its print or digital version. For a good sampling of music, listen to Global Beat, the site's monthly podcast.

Web: www.globalrhythm.net
Facebook: Global Rhythm Magazine (Page)
Twitter: (None)
LinkedIn: Global Rhythm Magazine (Company)

SCIENCE FICTION AND FANTASY

SFFWorld.com

There really is a world of science fiction and fantasy at SFFWorld.com: movie and book reviews, stories and poems, games, comics—and news and interviews related to all of these. You'll also find blogs, forums, and an art gallery.

Web: www.sffworld.com
Facebook: (None)
Twitter: sffworld
LinkedIn: (None)

Star Wars

In the 30-plus years since the original movie, *Star Wars* has become an institution, attracting legions of new fans every year. The official *Star Wars* site contains enough content and activities to satisfy even the most die-hard fan. Watch videos and get the latest news, play games, join a fan club or forum, read a blog or take a poll, and buy *Star Wars*—related items in the shop. There's a special section just for kids. For a fee, you can join Hyperspace, the official *Star Wars* fan club, which offers tons of extras for the serious fans.

Web: www.starwars.com
Facebook: Star Wars (Page), Star Wars (Group)
Twitter: starwars
LinkedIn: Lucasfilm, Lucasfilm Animation (Company)

Syfy.com 🏅

The online home of the Sci Fi Channel, at SciFi.com you can find information about shows, including the current schedule and full episodes of shows that have aired. Sci Fi Wire presents news related to movies, books, shows, and games; Sci Fi Weekly is an online newsletter that presents in-depth news, reviews, and interviews. There are numerous blogs, a section where you can play games, forums for discussing your favorite shows, an online store, and more. Whether you like TV shows, movies, games, or books—or all of those—you'll find a lot here to satisfy your sci-fi appetite.

Web: www.syfy.com
Facebook: Syfy - Imagine Greater (Page)
Twitter: Syfy, Syfy/destination-truth, Syfy/eureka, Syfy/sanctuary
LinkedIn: (None)

TELEVISION

American Idol

Can't get enough American Idol? Check out this site for a banquet of extras. Here you'll find news, contestant bios, video clips and downloads, photos, polls, and an insider blog. MyIDOL is a community just for fans. When you register and create a profile (it's free), you can write a blog, put together a photo gallery, talk with other fans in the forums, and create favorites lists. There's also an American Idol store where you can buy gear related to the show: books, DVDs, music, clothing, and more.

Web: www.americanidol.com
Facebook: American Idol (Page), American Idol (Group)
Twitter: AmericanIdol/
LinkedIn: Fox Television (Company)

BBC

The official site of the BBC has a customizable home page that presents news, sports, weather, radio and TV listings, and a World Service that reports the news in 33 languages.

Web: www.bbc.co.uk
Facebook: (None)
Twitter: BBC, BBC/tv, BBC/radio2, BBC/bbc6music
LinkedIn: BBC (Company)

CSI: Crime Scene Investigation

Fans of CSI should investigate this site to watch previous episodes and video clips, get recaps, view photos, read about the cast, and interact with other fans in the forums.

Web: www.cbs.com/primetime/csi/
Facebook: CSI Crime Scene Investigation (Page), CSI Crime Scene Investigation (Group), CSI Miami (Page), CSI NY (Page)
Twitter: CSI_CBS
LinkedIn: (None)

Lost

Lost fans are likely to get lost in this site—there's so much to see and do here. You can watch previous episodes, read cast biographies and episode recaps, view missing pieces and hunt for clues, play show-related games, and discuss the show with other fans. And that's just for starters. Listen to podcasts, subscribe to the official *Lost* magazine, discuss theories, even upload your own video theory. You can also buy show-related merchandise.

Web: http://abc.go.com/primetime/lost/
Facebook: Lost (Page), Lost (Group)
Twitter: Lost_on_ABC
LinkedIn: (None)

Pentagon Channel

The Pentagon Channel broadcasts military news and information, including news briefings from the Department of Defense, interviews with military personnel, and features about the work of the armed forces. Although the Pentagon Channel is intended to inform and support the 2.6 million people in the U.S. armed forces, anyone can watch. See what's on the air now (and watch it on your computer), check out the program lineup, or watch podcasts.

Web: www.pentagonchannel.mil
Facebook: Pentagon Channel (Page)
Twitter: pentagonchannel
LinkedIn: Femath Media (Company)

Public Broadcasting Service (PBS)

The interactive PBS website is rich in content, with pages that support its entertaining and educational programming. Content is divided into these areas: Arts & Drama, History, Home & Hobbies, Life & Culture, News & Views, and Science & Nature. In addition, there are sections for kids, teens, parents, and

5

teachers. You can watch videos online and check out PBS podcasts (both audio and video). Find a program or your local PBS affiliate. And you can support PBS by making a donation to your local station or shopping in the site's online store.

Web: www.pbs.org
Facebook: PBS (Page), PBS Kids (Page)
Twitter: PBS, @PBS/people, @PBS/pbs-and-station-blos
LinkedIn: (None)

Television Without Pity

TWoP features witty, tongue-in-cheek recaps of TV shows (and movies too). You'll also find listings, forums, blogs, videos and photos, and a wiki where you can share your knowledge about television shows and actors.

Web: www.televisionwithoutpity.com
Facebook: Television Without Pity: The Official TWoP Page (Page), Television Without Pity fans (Group)
Twitter: TVWithoutPity
LinkedIn: (None)

Titan TV

This television programming guide lets you see what's on for the next two weeks. Click a show to see a description. You can also tag your favorites, sign up for reminders, and view videos.

Web: http://video.titantv.com/
Facebook: (None)
Twitter: TitanTV
LinkedIn: (None)

TiVo

TiVo revolutionized television viewing by letting people watch the shows they want, when they want. This site explains how TiVo works and where to buy a TiVo DVR (digital video recorder). Click the Find TV Shows link to go to TiVo Central Online to search television listings, get recommendations, and see a list of the most-recorded shows.

Web: www.tivo.com
Facebook: TiVo (Page), TiVo (Group)
Twitter: TiVo
LinkedIn: TiVo (Company)

TV Guide 🏅

TV Guide's online site offers a whole lot more than television listings. The site is jampacked with news, features, photos, movie and DVD info, blogs, and videos. Interactive features for registered users include message boards, community blogs, and fan groups.

Web: www.tvguide.com
Facebook: TV Guide (Page)
Twitter: TVGuide
LinkedIn: TV Guide, TV Guide Channel, TV Guide Online (Company)

Yahoo! TV

Yahoo! TV provides local listings and a what-to-watch guide of today's recommended shows. There's ample news, gossip, photos, and videos to satisfy any TV fan. Best of all, you can watch full episodes of dozens of your favorite shows, from today's hits to the blasts from the past.

Web: http://tv.yahoo.com/
Facebook: (None)
Twitter: YahooTV, YahooTV/Stars
LinkedIn: (None)

Zap2It

Don't just sit on the couch flipping channels; find out which shows are worth your time to watch. This site doesn't just provide listings; it reviews shows, so you can get the scoop on both new and existing shows. You also get news and reviews of movies and DVDs, videos and full-show episodes, a bunch of blogs, and celebrity gossip.

Web: www.zap2it.com
Facebook: Zap2it (Page), Zap2It's Guide to Lost (Group)
Twitter: Zap2it
LinkedIn: Zap2it.com, Tribune Media Services (Company)

THEATER AND MUSICALS

League of Chicago Theatres

This organization is a group of Chicago-area theaters that promotes, supports, and advocates Chicago's theater industry—in Chicago and around the world. Its site has a directory of theaters, a search engine to find shows, Hot Tix (half-price tickets for select performances), listings for theater jobs and auditions, and opportunities to buy tickets, gift certificates, or make a donation to the organization.

Web: www.chicagoplays.com
Facebook: League of Chicago Theatres (Page)
Twitter: (None)
LinkedIn: (None)

London Theatre Guide

London is one of the world's theater capitals, and this site tells you what's on, what's coming, and what's good. Read rumors and theater-related news, check out critics' ratings and review highlights, see theaters' seating plans (so you'll know whether you're getting a good seat), and find out how to buy tickets. You can browse listings by location (West End, Fringe, Festivals) and type of show.

Web: www.londontheatre.co.uk
Facebook: London Theatre (Page)
Twitter: LDN_Theatre
LinkedIn: (None)

Playbill ⭐

Playbill offers an almost-overwhelming amount of information and features related to the world of theater. The site focuses on theater in New York City, but there's theater news and information from around the world: listings and tickets, theater news, celebrity buzz, multimedia clips and images, seating charts, Playbill Radio, and audition announcements. A top-notch site.

Web: www.playbill.com
Facebook: Playbill (Page), PLAYBILL (Group)
Twitter: (None)
LinkedIn: Playbill (Company)

Theater Mania

Here you'll find comprehensive listings, news, reviews, interviews, video content, and ticketing for plays in New York City and across the country. Theater Mania covers 40 cities across the United States, as well as London, Canada, and South Africa. A free subscription gets you the site's newsletter and periodic special offers. Has special sections for kids and nightlife, as well as an online store.

Web: www.theatermania.com
Facebook: TheaterMania.com (Page)
Twitter: theatermania
LinkedIn: TheaterMania (Company)

5

FAMILY/PARENTING

The Internet offers a variety of information for the bewildered parent looking for advice in dealing with every stage of a child's development. This chapter focuses more on social media outlets offering assistance to parents than on material suitable for children. There are a few references that are popular with children and teens as an aid for parents seeking material that is appropriate for young users.

ADOPTION

Adoption Support Forum

This private forum gives adoptive parents a sense of community and support. Users must contact the forum owner for admission. Threads are not visible to nonregistered users.

Web: http://forums.foreverparents.com/
Facebook: Forever Parents (Page), Adoption Support at Forever Parents (Group)
Twitter: (None)
LinkedIn: (None)

Adoptive Families Magazine

The online component of Adoptive Families Magazine, this site provides access to articles sorted by topic and includes guides and directories.

Web: www.adoptivefamilies.com
Facebook: Adoptive Families (Group)
Twitter: (None)
LinkedIn: (None)

Dave Thomas Foundation for Adoption

Dave Thomas, founder of Wendy's, established this nonprofit organization dedicated to increasing the number of adoptions for children in the foster-care system.

Web: www.davethomasfoundation.org
Facebook: Dave Thomas Foundation for Adoption (Page), Dave Thomas Foundation for Adoption (Group)
Twitter: DTFA
LinkedIn: Dave Thomas Foundation for Adoption (Group)

Foster Parenting Podcast

Tim and Wendy are foster parents who share their wisdom in weekly podcasts aimed at demystifying the foster-care system.

Web: http://fosterpodcast.com/
Facebook: Foster Parenting Podcast (Page)
Twitter: (None)
LinkedIn: (None)

A New Beginning Adoption Agency

This non-profit group provides assistance with unplanned pregnancy services and is licensed in Idaho, Oregon, and Utah. Also offers home studies, adoption education and support, infant waiting list, foster/adopt, international home studies, cultural activities, and parenting classes.

Web: http://adoptanewbeginning.org/
Facebook: A New Beginning Adoption Agency (Page)
Twitter: (None)
LinkedIn: (None)

Open Adoption

This site is a comprehensive resource for families considering open adoption. The site hosts links, a directory of adoption professionals, and websites for prospective parents seeking birth mothers contemplating open adoption as an option for their children.

Web: www.openadoption.com
Facebook: (None)
Twitter: Open Adoption
LinkedIn: (None)

This Woman's Work

Writer Dawn Friedman keeps her fans at thiswomanswork.com abreast of her movements via Twitter, recounting moods and stories about raising two children and participating in an open adoption with her daughter's birth mother.

Web: www.thiswomanswork.com/
Facebook: Dawn Friedman (Page)
Twitter: Moominmama, thiswomanswork
LinkedIn: Dawn Friedman (People)

BABIES/TODDLERS

Baby Center 🏅

Many readers consider BabyCenter.com a web pioneer, one of the best websites. The site consistently receives Best Blog nominations, and its "Your Pregnancy, Week By Week" email newsletters are treasured by web-savvy expectant mothers. In addition to newsletters, the site offers articles, features, and an active discussion board.

Web: www.babycenter.com
Facebook: BabyCenter (Page), BabyCenter (Group)
Twitter: babycenter, BCLatino
LinkedIn: BabyCenter (Company)

BabySpot.com

BabySpot.com helps parents share photos and videos with friends and relatives for free. In addition to providing easy-to-use uploading software, the site allows members to blog about their children and share advice with other BabySpot.com members.

Web: www.babyspot.com
Facebook: (None)
Twitter: babyspot
LinkedIn: Babyspot.com (Company)

Celebrity Baby Blog

A *People* magazine blog devoted to news about celebrities and their children, the site is irresistible and offers product reviews and information on baby clothing and accessories spotted on celebrity offspring.

Web: http://celebritybabies.people.com/
Facebook: Celebrity Baby Blog (Page)
Twitter: CBBvips
LinkedIn: (None)

The Cradle

The Cradle is a social network for new parents, offering them articles and advice on getting through the first months with their baby. Parents can also establish their own websites showcasing photo galleries, blogs, and gift registry links. The site's sensibility is focused on eco-living.

Web: www.thecradle.com
Facebook: The Cradle (Page)
Twitter: TheCradle
LinkedIn: (None)

Diaper Free Baby

A network of support groups for parents who practice natural infant hygiene through elimination communication. Site visitors can obtain information, product reviews, and directories for local groups in their areas.

Web: www.diaperfreebaby.org
Facebook: Diaper Free Baby/ Elimination Communication (Group)
Twitter: (None)
LinkedIn: (None)

Facebook: My Babybook

My Babybook is a Facebook application that helps parents launch a page for their babies on Facebook. Parents can share photos and videos with only a select group of friends on their Facebook accounts.

Web: http://apps.facebook.com/baby_book/
Facebook: My Babybook (Application)
Twitter: (None)
LinkedIn: (None)

JumpStart World

Preschoolers and their parents can purchase monthly subscriptions to a 3D virtual world that accompanies all JumpStart educational software. The site encourages children's learning skills through interactive games. The online world also enables parents to upload photos, personalize avatars for their kids, and send them text messages inside their virtual domain.

Web: http://shop.knowledgeadventure.com/Departments/New-JumpStart-World.aspx
Facebook: (None)
Twitter: (None)
LinkedIn: Knowledge Adventure (Company)

Mothering

This discussion forum from mothering.com offers families with natural-living lifestyles a place to share tips about alternative child-rearing practices and products. The forum is no longer active, but the archived materials might be of interest to you.

Web: www.mothering.com/discussions/
Facebook: Mothering Magazine (Page)
Twitter: MotheringMag
LinkedIn: (None)

The Poop—SF Chronicle Baby Blog

This is a group blog written for the San Francisco Chronicle, featuring a mixture of wry posts about raising children in the San Francisco Bay Area.

Web: www.sfgate.com/cgi-bin/blogs/parenting/index
Facebook: Fans of The Poop parenting blog (Page)
Twitter: (None)
LinkedIn: (None)

TotSpot

Still in the beta phase of development, TotSpot is a social network for babies. Yep, babies. Parents can create profiles for their offspring and update them with video and photos. The concept is closer to an electronic scrapbook than Facebook for babies, so don't fret.

Web: http://blog.totspot.com/
Facebook: TotSpot (Group)
Twitter: totspot
LinkedIn: TotSpot (Company)

Zero to Three Website

Zero to Three is a nonprofit organization that supports healthy child development for infants and toddlers. The site provides parents with science-based articles and tools to help them nurture their little ones.

Web: www.zerotothree.org/site/PageServer
Facebook: ZERO TO THREE Policy Network (Page)
Twitter: (None)
LinkedIn: ZERO TO THREE (Company)

BOYS

Boys Life Magazine

This companion website to the *Boy's Life* magazine provides handy information, games, and jokes to entertain the boys in your life.

Web: www.boyslife.org
Facebook: Boys' Life magazine (Page)
Twitter: BoysLife
LinkedIn: (None)

6

Club Penguin

One of the most popular virtual worlds for children, this virtual world lets users interact with one another as penguins, exploring a snow-covered terrain while playing games or decorating their personal spaces, called igloos. The Disney-owned site is designed for 6- to 14-year-olds. Players can roam the site free but must purchase memberships to establish igloos or acquire accessories.

Web: www.clubpenguin.com
Facebook: Club Penguin (Page) Club Penguin!!!!!! (Group)
Twitter: Disney_CP
LinkedIn: (None)

Full of Boys

Authored by a Christian stay-at-home mother of three boys, this blog is easy to follow and regularly updated.

Web: http://fullofboys.wordpress.com/
Facebook: (None)
Twitter: jenngarton (Visitors must first submit request for acceptance to follow author.)
LinkedIn: (None)

My Lego Network

My Lego Network is a multiplayer online game that boys and their fathers can bond over while building Lego structures and figures.

Web: http://mln.lego.com/en-us/Network/default.aspx
Facebook: My LEGO Network (Group)
Twitter: (None)
LinkedIn: (None)

Webkinz World

Webkinz World is the online supplement to the popular plush toy pets called Webkinz. Using a secret code that comes with each toy, users can enter the world in the guise of their new pet and interact with others by playing games, competing in contests, and visiting virtual neighbors.

Web: www.webkinz.com/us_en/
Facebook: Webkinz (Page)
Twitter: webkinz
LinkedIn: Webkinz (Company)

CAREGIVERS/ NANNIES/ BABYSITTERS

The Nanny Doctor

Operated by Lindsay Heller, a licensed clinical psychologist and former nanny of 10 years, this blog offers nannies and their employers support in balancing the emotions inherent in raising a child with the help of a third-party professional.

Web: http://thenannydoctor.blogspot.com/
Facebook: The Nanny Doctor: Consulting for Families & Nannies (Page)
Twitter: TheNannyDoctor
LinkedIn: (None)

VickyandJen.com—What Really Matters

Vicky and Jen are ordinary moms who share tips and insights on organizing one's family with simplicity and calm.

Web: www.vickyandjen.com
Facebook: Vicky Hall Thornton (Page)
Twitter: VickyandJencom
LinkedIn: (None)

CHILD ABUSE AND MISSING CHILDREN

ChildHelp

Childhelp.org is a national nonprofit organization focused on treating abused and neglected children. The group operates a 24-hour national hotline offering treatment, prevention, and intervention options, as well as local treatment centers and educational programs.

Web: www.childhelp.org
Facebook: Childhelp (Page, Group)
Twitter: Childhelp
LinkedIn: Childhelp DC Area Chapter (Group)

Committed to Freedom

Committed to Freedom is a website and community designed to provide spiritual tools for abuse survivors. The organization's president hosts a weekly podcast, discussing coping mechanisms for people who use faith to move beyond abuse.

Web: http://committedtofreedom.org/podcast.html
Facebook: Committed to Freedom (Group)
Twitter: (None)
LinkedIn: (None)

Prevent Child Abuse America

Prevent Child Abuse America is a national organization composed of local chapters devoted to building awareness about child-abuse prevention and helping abused or neglected children at the local level.

Web: www.preventchildabuse.org
Facebook: Prevent Child Abuse America (Page, Group)
Twitter: PCAAmerica
LinkedIn: Prevent Child Abuse America (Company, Group)

CHILD CUSTODY

Get Your Justice Live

This is an interactive Internet radio program hosted by Larry Holland, who maintains the Family Court Report Blog. Mr. Holland is a pro-father's-rights advocate.

Web: www.getyourjusticelive.com
Facebook: Get Your Justice Live: Broadcasting Live Every Wed. & Sun. Night @ 8PM EST (Page) Get Your Justice Live (Group)
Twitter: (None)
LinkedIn: (None)

DIVORCE

Divorce Care for Kids

This site is a clearinghouse for local faith-based support groups aiding divorced parents and their children. The organization provides Christian-related tools for ministers and pastors who are helping people overcome the negative emotions of separation and divorce.

Web: www.divorcecare.org/dc4k/
Facebook: DivorceCare for Kids (DC4K) (Page), DC4K-Divorce Care for Kids (Group)
Twitter: (None)
LinkedIn: (None)

Divorce Dating

This website was created to introduce adults who have been divorced, are going through a divorce, or wouldn't mind dating someone who is divorced.

Web: www.divorcedating.com
Facebook: Divorce Dating (Group)
Twitter: vikkiziegler
LinkedIn: Vikki Ziegler (People)

Divorce 360

Divorce360 is a community network site for people coping with divorce, separation, and custody issues. The site offers expert advice as well as group chat functions. The site is well organized and offers features on every phase of ending a marriage.

Web: www.divorce360.com
Facebook: (None)
Twitter: d360
LinkedIn: (None)

The Modern Woman's Divorce Guide

An official honoree at the 2008 Webby Awards, this well-designed site provides information and advice for women contemplating divorce. The Toolbox section of the site includes comprehensive divorce checklists.

6

Web: http://themodernwomansdivorceguide.com/
Facebook: The Modern Woman's Divorce Guide (Page)
Twitter: (None)
LinkedIn: The Modern Woman's Divorce Guide (Group)

Twitter: Calvero's Depot

Follow the micro musings of Kim, the web mistress of several popular sites, as she deals with a divorce and caring for her children.

Web: http://twitter.com/Calvero
Facebook: (None)
Twitter: Calvero
LinkedIn: (None)

Wikivorce.com

Wikivorce.com is a British divorce site that provides content, community, and support for Britons undergoing divorce.

Web: www.wikivorce.com
Facebook: Wikivorce (Page)
Twitter: Wikivorce
LinkedIn: (None)

FATHERS

Dadstayshome.com Forum

Dadstayshome.com is a discussion forum for fathers who raise their children on a full-time basis.

Web: www.dadstayshome.com
Facebook: Dad Stays Home (Group)
Twitter: (None)
LinkedIn: (None)

DIY Father

This is a New Zealand—based site devoted to guiding fathers through all aspects of parenting. The site is easy to navigate and features useful Q&As from members.

Web: www.diyfather.com
Facebook: DIYFather.com (Page)
Twitter: diyfather
LinkedIn: (None)

The Father Life

The Father Life site provides fathers with articles, discussion boards, and resource links.

Web: www.thefatherlife.com
Facebook: TheFatherLife.com (Page)
Twitter: thefatherlife
LinkedIn: (None)

Geek Dad

Geek Dad is a group blog by the editors of *Wired* magazine. The posts are wide ranging and offer a variety of perspectives on parenting, but still fall into a "boys and their toys" category. There are more entries on Sea Monkeys, Legos, and camping gear than bibs, sippy cups, and diaper bags, for example.

Web: http://blog.wired.com/geekdad/
Facebook: Wired (Page)
Twitter: WIRED
LinkedIn: Wired Magazine (Company)

Twitter: Joegerstandt

With more than 7500 followers on Twitter, this stay-at-home dad must be doing something right.

Web: http://twitter.com/joegerstandt
Facebook: (None)
Twitter: joegerstandt
LinkedIn: (None)

GIRLS

BarbieGirls.com

Barbie now has a virtual world where her fans can join her, packed with games, avatar fashion, and zones that allow users to mingle and explore.

Web: www.barbiegirls.com
Facebook: (None)
Twitter: bgirlscentral
LinkedIn: Mattel (Company)

Black Belt Mama

This is a blog authored by a mother raising two daughters who takes up martial arts.

Web: www.blackbeltmama.com
Facebook: (None)
Twitter: blackbeltmama
LinkedIn: (None)

The Dad Man

The Dad Man provides fathers with advice and support on how to maintain healthy bonds with their daughters. The site features a daily blog, tips, and quizzes, as well as resources for adult daughters eager to strengthen relationships with their own fathers.

Web: www.thedadman.com
Facebook: (None)
Twitter: (None)
LinkedIn: The Dad Man (Company)

GirlSense

GirlSense is a social network for teen fashion. Members can create and post outfits for their virtual character, interact with other members through chat and group forums, and decorate their own living spaces, called boutiques.

Web: www.girlsense.com/premium/
Facebook: GirlSense (Page), girlsense (Group)
Twitter: girlsense
LinkedIn: Girlsense Lovers (Group)

Mom of Three Girls

A working mother of three girls frequently updates this blog, sharing tales about her children or new household cleaning tips.

Web: www.momof3girls.net
Facebook: (None)
Twitter: DebMom0f3
LinkedIn: (None)

Pixie Hollow

Disney created this virtual world to highlight the Tinkerbell movie and line of products. Visitors can create their own fairy avatar and inhabit a fairy forest filled with games and messaging options. Who needs Disneyland now?

Web: http://pixiehollow.go.com/
Facebook: Welcome to Pixie Hollow (Group)
Twitter: (None)
LinkedIn: Walt Disney Internet Group (Company)

Stardoll.com

Stardoll.com is a virtual world for paper-doll fans. Visitors, both young and adult, create electronic paper dolls to dress and show off to new friends in the social network.

Web: www.stardoll.com
Facebook: Dad Stays Home (Group)
Twitter: Stardoll, stardoll_
LinkedIn: (None)

Walt's Girls

This is a podcast site created by two friends devoted to Disney World and everything Disney. This site is also part of the Disney Podcast Network.

Web: http://waltsgirls.com/
Facebook: Walt's Girl (Page)
Twitter: (None)
LinkedIn: (None)

Webkinz World

Webkinz World is the online supplement to the popular plush toy pets called Webkinz. Using a secret code that comes with each toy, users can enter the world in the guise of their new pet and interact with others by playing games, competing in contests, and visiting virtual neighbors.

Web: www.webkinz.com/us_en/
Facebook: Webkinz (Page)
Twitter: webkinz
LinkedIn: Webkinz (Company)

6

MOTHERS

Cool Mom Picks

Cool Mom Picks is a site devoted to product reviews for busy parents. Run by a collective of volunteers, the site tracks new or nonmainstream products and services created by emerging designers or mom-run companies. Cool Mom Picks provides readers with info on intriguing child-related items such as products, websites, or causes.

Web: www.coolmompicks.com
Facebook: Cool Mom Picks (Page)
Twitter: coolmompicks
LinkedIn: (None)

The Mac Mommy

Follow the adventures of Melissa Davis, a computer consultant and mother to a toddler.

Web: http://themacmommy.blogspot.com/
Facebook: (None)
Twitter: TheMacMommy
LinkedIn: (None)

Mamasource.com

Mamasource is a private website for mothers to share mothering tips, product reviews, and opinions. Mamasource is unique in that it establishes an instant community via email blasts and bulletin boards. Members can post questions and receive immediate answers without having to trawl archives. All members are available to respond to each new question or query.

Web: www.mamasource.com/join/welcome
Facebook: (None)
Twitter: mamasource
LinkedIn: (None)

Mombian

Mombian is a website for lesbian mothers. The site has a video blog section featuring an amusing vlog series called "She Got Me Pregnant." Shot in weekly episodes, Dana and her partner, Helen, star in the series, which explores what it's like to be a lesbian mom. The site features product reviews, contests, kid-friendly project demos, interviews, and zany antics like re-creating the Dinah Shore PGA golf tournament in their living room.

Web: www.mombian.com/category/video-blog/
Facebook: Mombian (Page)
Twitter: mombian
LinkedIn: (None)

MomLogic.com

Launched by Warner Bros. Television Group in 2007, Momlogic.com is a slick community site for women who also happen to be parents. The site offers editorial features such as video, articles, and interviews, but the site's main thrust is its community boards. Its content is the most similar in style to mainstream women's magazines like *In Style*, *People*, and *Elle*, with celebrity-related fashion news and personal essays.

Web: www.momlogic.com
Facebook: MomLogic (Page)
Twitter: momlogic
LinkedIn: (None)

The Mom Salon

The Mom Salon is a directory of smart-mom blogs, organized by topic and state. The main site provides articles, product reviews, and tips on improving one's blog. There is also a daily blog that features the best posts found on current mom blogs. The site has also added a Mom Blogging Wiki and a social networking component so that mom bloggers can befriend one another.

Web: www.themomsalon.com/index.htm
Facebook: (None)
Twitter: themomsalon
LinkedIn: (None)

Moms Group Manual

This blog is a resource for parents looking to connect with other parents for play dates or friendship. Created by Jessica Smith, the blog not only offers local mom-group resources but also provides sensible advice on how to make friends with other time-starved caregivers. Jessica also provides the latest information on websites devoted to fostering community among parents.

Web: www.momsgroupmanual.com
Facebook: (None)
Twitter: JessicaKnows
LinkedIn: (None)

MomShare

MomShare is more of a community news filter than a discussion board, but the site does provide a place to discuss mother-related news and stories with other mothers. Members can post links to news found on other sites or in newspapers or contribute user-generated articles and essays.

Web: http://momshare.net/
Facebook: (None)
Twitter: momshare
LinkedIn: (None)

MotherhoodLater.com

Motherhoodlater.com is a support group for mothers who started families at the age of 35 or older. The group offers online and offline support. Mothers can network at local chapter meetings in the New York area; Anchorage; Fairfield County, Connecticut; Los Angeles; and Cedar Rapids, Iowa. Mothers can also interact online at the website, coordinate "Mothers Night Out" events and play dates, or commiserate on the blog.

Web: www.motherhoodlater.com
Facebook: Motherhood Later...Than Sooner (Page, Group)
Twitter: (None)
LinkedIn: Motherhood Later....Than Sooner (Group)

Motherhood Uncensored

Kristen Chase interviews authors, teachers, and popular bloggers on a weekly podcast that offers frank and unsentimental discussions about parenting, pregnancy, and culture.

Web: www.blogtalkradio.com/motherhooduncensored
Facebook: BlogTalkRadio (Page, Group)
Twitter: blogtalkradio
LinkedIn: Blog Talk Radio (Company)

Mothers Click

Mothers Click is a social networking version of local mothers' groups in real life. The site offers organizing functions such as mass email group settings, FAQ posts, and other community building tools. Mothers Click replicates the local mothers' groups in a social network setting. The site features menu planning and recipe tips, resource links, classifieds, and activity announcements.

Web: www.mothersclick.com
Facebook: MothersClick (Page)
Twitter: mothersclick
LinkedIn: (None)

Secret Agent Mama

Mishelle Lane is a photographer and blogger who regularly posts photos along with her entries. She captures everyday events and lovely landscapes in your Midwestern town.

Web: www.secretagentmama.com/
Facebook: Mishelle Lane Photography (Page)
Twitter: secretagentmama
LinkedIn: (None)

PARENTS

Babble

Babblepedia bills itself as the encyclopedia of parenting knowledge. An offshoot of *Babble—The Magazine*, babblepedia offers parents peer-generated information about all aspects of child rearing.

6

Entry categories are organized alphabetically and are extremely literate.

Web: www.babble.com/babblepedia/
Facebook: Babble.com (Page)
Twitter: BabbleEditors, BabbleCelebrity, BabbleFood !
LinkedIn: Babble Media | Babble.com (Company)

Handipoints

Handipoints is a virtual world for children that encourages them to perform chores in the real world to earn points in this virtual world. Parents can use the site to track a child's progress in completing chores and reward them with points for finished tasks.

Web: www.handipoints.com
Facebook: Handipoints (Page)
Twitter: handipoints
LinkedIn: (None)

IParenting

Disney owns this site for parents, offering content and community. Members can establish their own blogs, post birth or parenting stories, or participate in the myriad of bulletin boards on the site.

Web: www.iparenting.com
Facebook: (None)
Twitter: iparenting
LinkedIn: (None)

Microblog—lil'Grams

The baby book for modern parents, lil'Grams enables users to electronically capture, organize and share baby milestones with friends and family.

Web: www.lilgrams.com
Facebook: lilgrams (Page)
Twitter: lilgrams
LinkedIn: (None)

Shaping Youth

This site's goal is to offer parents resources for combating the overinfluence of marketing and media over today's youth and children. Visitors can access articles, audio and video clips, and other tools for teaching media literacy to their children.

Web: www.shapingyouth.org/blog/index.php
Facebook: (None)
Twitter: ShapingYouth
LinkedIn: (None)

PREGNANCY AND CHILDBIRTH

Café Mom

Café Mom provides mothers with an online space to network, exchange information, and find tools to make their lives easier. Mothers can start and share journals and share photos. The site even has a photo Showdown section that lets them playfully compare photos of their children.

Web: www.cafemom.com
Facebook: CafeMom (Page, Group), Cafemom Friends (Group)
Twitter: cafemom
LinkedIn: CafeMom (Company)

InterNational Council on Infertility Information Dissemination

The InterNational Council on Infertility Information Dissemination (INCIID, pronounced "inside") is a nonprofit clearinghouse on infertility-treatment information and support. The site hosts professional and peer-moderated chat and discussion forums for people considering or undergoing infertility treatment or pregnancy loss. INCIID also offers information for individuals considering adoption or child-free lifestyles.

Web: www.inciid.org/index.php?page=forums
Facebook: INCIID Inc. (Group), InterNational Council on Infertility Information Dissemination Inc (INCIID) (Page)
Twitter: INCIID
LinkedIn: (None)

iVillage Pregnancy and Parenting

The Pregnancy and Parenting sector on iVillage.com is a robust area offering loads of content and resources for expectant parents. Visitors will find health tools, quizzes, instructional video from child-care experts and features for user contributions. For example, the Who's in Your Momtourage area asks visitors to post stories about the support team in their lives.

Web: http://parenting.ivillage.com/
Facebook: iVillage (Page, Group)
Twitter: iVillage
LinkedIn: iVillage (Company)

Mums & Tots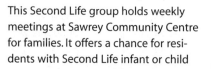

This Second Life group holds weekly meetings at Sawrey Community Centre for families. It offers a chance for residents with Second Life infant or child avatars to interact and form playgroups.

Web: http://slurl.com/secondlife/Sawrey/121/79/35/
Facebook: Second Life (Page, Group)
Twitter: SecondLife
LinkedIn: (None)

NewBaby.com

NewBaby.com is a social networking site where members can connect via video. The site has one of the largest online libraries of mom-made videos. In addition, members can also access advice from experts, product reviews, and features. Here is a network perfect for moms who are too busy (or sleep-deprived) to spend much time on the computer—she can express herself and interact with her peers by uploading and watching video through the site.

Web: www.newbaby.com
Facebook: NewBaby.com (Page)
Twitter: NewBaby Team, NewBaby VADO
LinkedIn: (None)

PregTASTIC Online Radio

Pregtastic is a weekly podcast celebrating the good and bad aspects of pregnancy and childbirth with humor and enthusiasm. Anchored by two moms, the show features interviews and discussions about medical news, birth stories, rumors, and advice.

Web: www.pregtastic.com
Facebook: PregTASTIC Pregnancy Radio (Page)
Twitter: pregtastic
LinkedIn: (None)

SCHOOLS

Bella Online School Reform Discussion Group

Members of the Bella Online Voice of Women opine about ways to improve U.S. education and share the latest news on the topic. Click School Reform in the Education section to access this area of the forum.

Web: http://forums.bellaonline.com/
Facebook: (None)
Twitter: bellaonline
LinkedIn: (None)

Classroom 2.0

Classroom 2.0 is a social networking site for educators interested in using collaborative tech tools to improve student performance and skills.

Web: www.classroom20.com
Facebook: Classroom 2.0 (Group), Classroom 2.0 LIVE! (Group)
Twitter: classroom20, liveclass20
LinkedIn: Classroom 2.0 (Group)

Elluminate

This site lets teachers interact with students in a virtual classroom. Students can interact with the instructor and peers using webcams, IM, and chat functions.

6

Web: www.elluminate.com
Facebook: Elluminate (Page)
Twitter: elluminateweb, elluminate
LinkedIn: (None)

Parent Teacher Association

The PTA established this website for parents to remain connected with teachers and school administrations. The site offers child-raising resources and education advocacy tools.

Web: www.pta.org
Facebook: Parent Teacher Association (Page)
Twitter: (None)
LinkedIn: PTA (Group)

SINGLE PARENTS

DaddyBlogger.com

Robert Pederson's blog focuses on child custody laws. Pederson has previously launched the Equal Parenting Bike Trek, vowing to ride his bike from Michigan to Washington, D.C., in order to bring attention to joint custody law reform.

Web: www.daddy.typepad.com
Facebook: (None)
Twitter: daddyblogger
LinkedIn: (None)

Divorcing Daze

Two single moms dish about divorces, dating, and life in New York.

Web: www.divorcingdaze.com
Facebook: DivorcingDaze (Page)
Twitter: DivorcingDaze
LinkedIn: (None)

OmniDate

OmniDate is a virtual world designed for singles who want to interact safely with new acquaintances in a low-pressure environment.

Web: www.omnidate.com
Facebook: OmniDate, Virtual Dating (Page)
Twitter: OmniDate
LinkedIn: (None)

Single Mom Seeking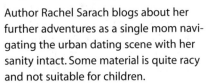

Author Rachel Sarach blogs about her further adventures as a single mom navigating the urban dating scene with her sanity intact. Some material is quite racy and not suitable for children.

Web: http://singlemomseeking.com/blog/
Facebook: (None)
Twitter: singlemomseekin
LinkedIn: Rachel Sarah (People)

SPECIAL-NEEDS CHILDREN

Cape Able

This is a section of Second Life that showcases the presence of people with disabilities in the virtual world. There is a large deaf community on this sim.

Web:
http://slurl.com/secondlife/Cape%20Able/167/162/28/
Facebook: Second Life (Page, Group)
Twitter: SecondLife
LinkedIn: (None)

Gimp Girl

Gimpgirl.com, an online community for women with disabilities, has established a presence in Second Life. The group owns an amphitheater where it hosts workshops, lectures, and in-world gatherings.

Web: http://gimpgirl.com/
Facebook: GimpGirl Community (Group)
Twitter: gimpgirl
LinkedIn: GimpGirl Community (Group)

STAY-AT-HOME PARENTS

AlexCaseyBaby

Trained as a professional journalist, this stay at home mom blogs opinions on a wide variety of topics.

Web: http://workathomemom.typepad.com/
Facebook: Alex Casey Baby (Group)
Twitter: AlexCaseyBaby
LinkedIn: (None)

The Bitterest Pill

Dan Klass broadcasts a monthly show from his home in Los Angeles, where he's a stay-at-home dad trying, as he says, "to make sense of being a man in a traditional woman's role."

Web: www.thebitterestpill.com
Facebook: Dan Klass of The Bitterest Pill (Page)
Twitter: danklass
LinkedIn: (None)

Shannon Gurney Photoblog

This stay-at-home mom is a photographer who regularly uploads photos documenting her photography business and family.

Web: http://www.shannongurneyphoto.com/blog/
Facebook: Shannon Gurney Photography (Page)
Twitter: shan4osu
LinkedIn: (None)

TEENS

gURL.com

gURL.com is one of the leading online communities for teenage girls that has no affiliation with a corporate media company. The site offers young women discussion boards, quizzes, and chat functions.

Web: www.gurl.com
Facebook: gURL.com (Page)
Twitter: (None)
LinkedIn: (None)

Habbo

Habbo is a virtual world for teens. Users create avatars that inhabit a virtual hotel and interact with one another from their own rooms or common areas or chat rooms.

Web: www.habbo.com
Facebook: Habbo (Page), habbo (Page)
Twitter: HabboUS
LinkedIn: (None)

TeenAids PeerCorps Vlog

You can view the vlogs prepared by Dr. John and his teen volunteers, documenting their work teaching teens about the dangers of AIDS and unprotected sex.

Web: www.teenaids.org
Facebook: TeenAIDS Peer-Corps (Group)
Twitter: MetroTeenAIDS
LinkedIn: (None)

WORKING MOTHERS

The Domestic Diva

The Domestic Diva authors a personal blog, touting her unique insight on life, love, and housework.

Web: http://thedomesticdiva.org/
Facebook: (None)
Twitter: thedomesticdiva
LinkedIn: (None)

Manic Mommies

Erin and Kristin juggle family and full-time jobs and still have time to share this entertaining and resonant podcast.

Web: http://manicmommies.com/
Facebook: Manic Mommies (Page)
Twitter: manicmommies
LinkedIn: Manic Mommies Media, Inc. (Company), Manic Mommies (Group)

6

This Mommy Gig

This Mommy Gig is a group blog for working parents, especially mothers. Contributors share opinions, advice, and stories about handling family and work obligations.

Web: http://thismommygig.org/
Facebook: This Mommy Gig (Group)
Twitter: thismommygig
LinkedIn: (None)

Work It, Mom

Work It, Mom brings working mothers together in this social networking site. Users can create their own profiles, read articles written by other members, or join other users in group chat on discussion boards and groups.

Web: www.workitmom.com
Facebook: Work It! Mom (Group)
Twitter: Workitmom
LinkedIn: (None)

FOOD AND DRINK

A virtual feast awaits you on the Internet, a delicious array of sites that will tempt your taste buds and set your mouth watering. Of thousands of baking, cooking, and recipe sites, this chapter lists some of the very best and provides the social media connections you can make to ensure you're up to speed 24/7. You'll also find sites for wine and beer lovers, restaurants and bakeries, gourmet food, and groceries. Special diets are also covered. Bon appétit!

BAKERIES

Collin Street Bakery

Started in 1896, this Texas bakery offers a variety of products for sale online: pecan pies and cakes, deluxe fruitcake, cheesecakes and other cakes, breads and muffins, and more.

Web: www.collinstreet.com
Facebook: (None)
Twitter: CollinStreet
LinkedIn: Collin Street Bakery, Inc. (Company)

Mrs. Fields

Mrs. Fields is known for decadent gourmet cookies, and that's what you'll find on this site. You can shop by gift occasion, product, or price.

Web: www.mrsfields.com
Facebook: Mrs. Fields (Page), Mrs. Fields (Group)
Twitter: (None)
LinkedIn: Mrs. Fields Famous Brands (Company), Mrs. Fields Cookies (Company), Mrs. Fields Famous Brands Network (Group)

Stony Brook Cookie Company

Stony Brook's bakers craft their cookies by hand in small batches using only the finest ingredients—no preservatives, trans fats, artificial flavors, or artificial colors. (You can read their ingredient lists on the site.) Order cookies by the dozen, in two-cookie party-favor packs, in gift boxes, or in party trays.

Web: www.stonybrookcookie.com
Facebook: Stony Brook Cookie Company (Group)
Twitter: (None)
LinkedIn: (None)

BAKING

About.com: Desserts/Baking

Since 1997, Guide Carroll Pellegrinelli has shared her favorite recipes and baking tips in this well-organized site that covers everything from the top-10 brownie recipes to baking with kids to how to send baked goods through the mail.

Web: http://baking.about.com
Facebook: (None)
Twitter: (None)
LinkedIn: About.com (Company)

Bake Space

"Come for the food, stay for the conversation," invites this social network for bakers. When you join, you create your own virtual kitchen on the site and can swap recipes, create a blog, upload videos, join in forum discussions, and make friends with others who love good food as much as you do.

Web: www.bakespace.com
Facebook: BakeSpace.com (Page, Group)
Twitter: bakespace
LinkedIn: Friends of BakeSpace (Group)

Baking Bites

Nicole Weston writes about food news, gives baking tips and advice, reviews products, and offers lots of yummy recipes.

Web: http://bakingbites.com
Facebook: Baking Bites (Page)
Twitter: (None)
Linkedin: (None)

Betty Crocker Baking Recipes, Tips, and Ideas

This site has lots of baking recipes, most featuring Betty Crocker products, as well as videos that demonstrate baking tips. When you sign up for a free account, you also get your own personal recipe box to save your favorites, grocery lists, online coupons, recipe reviews, the ability to participate in the site's forums, and other perks.

Web: www.bettycrocker.com/baking/
Facebook: Betty Crocker (Page), Betty Crocker (Group)
Twitter: BettyCrocker
LinkedIn: General Mills (Company)

Betty Crocker Baking Videos

Learn baking techniques by watching this site's professionally produced, easy-to-follow videos.

Web: www.bettycrocker.com/baking/baking-videos
Facebook: Betty Crocker (Page), Betty Crocker (Group)
Twitter: BettyCrocker
LinkedIn: General Mills (Company)

Breadtopia

"For the love of bread," this site has a great range of videos for making all kinds of bread and pizza dough. Sign up for notification of new videos.

Web: www.breadtopia.com
Facebook: (None)
Twitter: breadtopia
LinkedIn: (None)

FoodNetwork.com Cooking Demos: Baking

It's not surprising that the Food Network has lots of great videos to help you master baking techniques.

Web: www.foodnetwork.com/how-to/index.html
Facebook: Food Network (Page), Food Network (Group)
Twitter: FoodNetwork
LinkedIn: (None)

JoyofBaking.com 🏅

The recipes on this scrumptious site feature mouthwatering photos of the final result. See what's new, browse the recipe index, or look for a specific kind of baked good, from biscotti and cookies to pies, tarts, and cakes. There are also recipes for various holidays. Each recipe has interesting commentary and helpful tips, and there are sections on substitutions, ingredients, conversions, and baking terms.

Web: www.joyofbaking.com
Facebook: Joyofbaking.com (Page)
Twitter: joyofbaking
LinkedIn: (None)

MyRecipes.com Baking Videos

Watch-and-learn videos demonstrate basic baking techniques. Requires Flash.

Web: www.myrecipes.com/recipes/howto/
Facebook: MyRecipes.com (Page)
Twitter: My_Recipes
LinkedIn: (None)

Nestle VeryBestBaking.com

Get recipes and baking tips, learn about Nestle products and promotions, register for a free account, and participate in the site's Baker-to-Baker community.

Web: www.verybestbaking.com
Facebook: NESTLE® TOLL HOUSE®
Twitter: NestleUSA
LinkedIn: Nestle USA (Company)

Nosh with Me

Nominated for Best Food Blog in the 2007 Blogger's Choice awards, Nosh with Me documents "one girl's love affair with her KitchenAid mixer." Tons of recipes with plenty of commentary.

Web: http://noshwithme.com/
Facebook: Nosh With Me (Page)
Twitter: noshwithme
LinkedIn: (None)

Pillsbury Baking

A site for bakers that features Pillsbury products. Here you'll find recipes, baking basics, tips, and ideas; products and promotions; and information about the Pillsbury company, including its history. Sign up for a free account to keep recipes in your recipe box, get grocery lists, find products, and receive the Pillsbury newsletter.

Web: www.pillsburybaking.com
Facebook: Pillsbury (Page)
Twitter: PillsburyTreats
LinkedIn: General Mills (Company)

Real Baking with Rose Levy Beranbaum

Internationally renowned cookbook writer and baking expert Rose Levy Beranbaum writes about baking in this blog sponsored by Gold Medal flour. In addition to Rose's blog, there are reader forums and a newsletter.

Web: www.realbakingwithrose.com
Facebook: Rose Levy Beranbaum (Page)
Twitter: FlourRose
LinkedIn: (None)

BEER

All About Beer 🍴

The companion website to *All About Beer* magazine features articles, reviews, interviews, beer news, a travel section, and more. Use its Brew Pub finder to locate a brew pub near home or when you're traveling; there's also a beer-store finder and beer-events calendar. You can subscribe to the magazine online.

Web: www.allaboutbeer.com
Facebook: ALL ABOUT BEER (Page), All About Beer! (Group)
Twitter: allaboutbeer
LinkedIn: (None)

Basic Brewing 🍴

Basic Brewing offers audio and video podcasts about home-brewing, including interviews, stories, and advice.

Web: http://basicbrewing.com/
Facebook: Basic Brewing Radio (Page), Basic Brewing Video (Page)
Twitter: basicbrewing
LinkedIn: (None)

Beer Advocate 🍴 ⭐

This popular and comprehensive beer-lovers' site is a good place to go to learn about beer: its Beer 101 section explains the basics of beer, its varieties, beer history, home brewing, and more. Beer aficionados will appreciate the database of more than 40,000 beers, complete with 600,000-plus reviews submitted by the site's users. Has beer news; tips on how to taste beer; a travel section so you can find great breweries, beer stores, and brew pubs on the road; events listings; and a community of more than 150,000 beer enthusiasts to connect with.

Web: http://beeradvocate.com/
Facebook: Beer Adovcate (Page), Beer Advocate (Group)
Twitter: BeerAdvocate
LinkedIn: (None)

7

Beer Advocate Beer Forum ✿

If you're a beer lover, what could be better than discussing your favorite beverage with like-minded people around the world? Lots of discussions take place on this lively board.

Web: http://beeradvocate.com/forum
Facebook: Beer Advocate (Page), Beer Advocate (Group)
Twitter: BeerAdvocate
LinkedIn: (None)

Beer Me! ✿

The ultimate guide to breweries all over the world—more than 10,000 of them. You can check out the latest listings on the What's New? page or use the Regional Guide to find breweries in a specific location. Check out the Beer List or Hall of Fame to find great beers.

Web: http://beerme.com/
Facebook: Beer Me! (Page)
Twitter: (None)
LinkedIn: (None)

Brewers Association ✿

If you like craft beers, you should know about this organization, which aims to "promote and protect American craft beer and American craft brewers and the community of brewing enthusiasts." The site explains what the Brewers Association does and offers resources for learning about beer (styles, history, matching beer with food, and more), home-brewing, craft brewing, and beer-related events. The online store sells beer-related merchandise such as books, pint glasses, and beer-themed clothing.

Web: www.beertown.org
Facebook: (None)
Twitter: BrewersAssoc
LinkedIn: Brewers Association (Company)

Brew Pub Zone ✿

This directory will help you find not only brew pubs but also microbreweries, craft beers, home-brewing supplies, and beer festivals and other events. You can browse by state or search for brew pubs and microbreweries in a specific city.

Web: www.brewpubzone.com
Facebook: Brew Pub Zone (Page)
Twitter: (None)
LinkedIn: (None)

Brew Your Own (BYO) ✿

Brew Your Own is a magazine dedicated to home-brewing beer. The website has featured stories from the magazine, step-by-step recipes, a home-brewing reference guide, an introduction to home-brewing for first-timers, podcasts, and a blog. You can order back issues, request a free trial issue, or subscribe.

Web: http://byo.com/
Facebook: Brew Your Own magazine (Page)
Twitter: BrewYourOwn
LinkedIn: (None)

Budweiser.com ✿

If this Bud's for you, so is this site (as long as you're 21 or older). Watch Budweiser commercials and learn fun facts; read about the famous Clydesdale horses; download ringtones, wallpaper, and graphics; and trace the history of Budweiser from its beginnings in 1852 to the present. The Bud Shop sells beer-related and Budweiser-themed gear.

Web: www.budweiser.com
Facebook: Budweiser (Page), Budweiser (Group)
Twitter: budweiser
LinkedIn: Anheuser-Busch (Company)

Craft Beer Radio ✿

Craft Beer Radio is an Internet talk show about craft and microbrewed beers. There's also a forum and a wiki.

Web: www.craftbeerradio.com
Facebook: Craft Beer Radio (Page)
Twitter: (None)
LinkedIn: (None)

Dogfish Head 🍺

Dogfish Head Brewings & Eats, Delaware's first brew pub, opened in 1995. Since then, Dogfish Head has grown into a popular brewery offering 18 styles of beer (as well as a few varieties of distilled spirits). This site tells you about current releases and where you can find a distributor, as well as the brew pub in Rehoboth Beach and brewery tours. The online store has hats, tees, books, glasses, and more.

Web: www.dogfish.com
Facebook: Dogfish Head Beer (Page), Dogfish Head (Group)
Twitter: dogfishbeer
LinkedIn: Dogfish Head Craft Brewery (Company)

Guinness 🍺

Learn where and how Guinness stout is brewed; read about the company's history; watch commercials or view Guinness ads going back to the 1930s; download wallpaper, screensavers, and posters; send an e-card. Has an online store. You must be 21 or older to enter the site.

Web: www.guinness.com
Facebook: Guinness (Page), Guinness (Group)
Twitter: guinnesspours
LinkedIn: Guinness (Company)

Hail the Ale! 🍺

A blog about the pleasures of beer.

Web: www.hailtheale.com
Facebook: (None)
Twitter: hailtheale
LinkedIn: (None)

Magic Hat Brewing Company 🍺

The South Burlington, Vermont–based brewery has put together a colorful and imaginative website where you can read about the brewery's beers (or "elixirs" as the site calls them), find a place to buy Magic Hat beers, read the Grog Blog, or plan a visit to the brewery.

Web: www.magichat.net
Facebook: Magic Hat Brewing Company (Page), Magic Hat (Group)
Twitter: magichat
LinkedIn: Magic Hat Brewing Company (Company)

MoreBeer 🍺

If you need home-brew supplies, take a look at this site. Product categories are helpfully organized: New to Brewing, All Ingredients, Brew Day Equipment, Fermentation Equipment, Bottling & Kegging, Draft Beer Dispensing, All Grain & Hardware, Cleaning & Sanitizing, and BrewWear & Fun Items. Has a lot of free info and instructions, including podcasts, to help you brew right.

Web: http://morebeer.com/
Facebook: (None)
Twitter: MoreBeer
LinkedIn: (None)

RateBeer 🍺

RateBeer features consumer-supplied beer ratings, as well as articles on beer culture and events, weekly beer-related editorials, and a semiannual RateBeer Best competition. The site has thousands of members from more than 60 countries who have rated tens of thousands of beers from around the world. Find the world's best beers, as well as beer events, places, and references. Has information on home-brewing, as well as resources for professional brewers and beer retailers. A great site for serious beer lovers.

Web: www.ratebeer.com
Facebook: RateBeer (Group)
Twitter: ratebeer
LinkedIn: RateBeer (Group)

Realbeer.com 🍺

A wonderful resource for beer lovers, Realbeer.com features news about beer and the brewing industry, links to retail sites, a searchable directory of breweries and pubs, city and regional guides with a focus on beer, other beer-related links, and events. Its Beer.edu section contains a staggering amount of information about beer: cooking with beer, beer and health, beer guides for many countries, home-brewing, and just about anything else you might want to know. Check out the forums for lively conversation.

Web: www.realbeer.com
Facebook: RealBeer.com (Page)
Twitter: RealBeer
LinkedIn: (None)

Sierra Nevada Brewing Company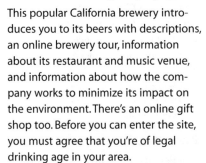

This popular California brewery introduces you to its beers with descriptions, an online brewery tour, information about its restaurant and music venue, and information about how the company works to minimize its impact on the environment. There's an online gift shop too. Before you can enter the site, you must agree that you're of legal drinking age in your area.

Web: www.sierranevada.com
Facebook: Sierra Nevada (Page)
Twitter: SierraNevadaCA
LinkedIn: (None)

BEVERAGES

BevNET.com

BevNET reviews ready-to-drink, nonalcoholic beverages. Here you'll find all kinds of information about the beverage industry, including companies, news, job posts, and classifieds. Those who work in the industry can subscribe to *Beverage Spectrum* magazine.

Web: www.bevnet.com
Facebook: BevNET.com (Page)
Twitter: BevNetcom
LinkedIn: Bevnet.com Inc (Company), BevNet.com (Group)

Coca-Cola

The website of this popular soft drink company features music, sports, and "The Coke Side of Life," where you can create Coca-Cola–themed artwork, watch commercials, and download such goodies as screensavers and wallpaper. There's information about the company, an online store, and a rewards program in which you can enter codes found on Coke products for points that can be redeemed for merchandise.

Web: www.coca-cola.com
Facebook: Coca-Cola (Page)
Twitter: CocaCola
LinkedIn: The Coca-Cola Company (Company), The Coca-Cola Company (Group)

Dr. Pepper

Learn about Dr. Pepper products and history, and find out about the Dr. Pepper Museum (yep, there is one—it's in Waco, Texas). Here you'll also find ads to watch, games and downloads, promotions, and a Dr. Pepper store.

Web: www.drpepper.com
Facebook: Dr Pepper (Page), Dr. Pepper (Group)
Twitter: drpepper
LinkedIn: Dr Pepper Snapple Group (Company)

Jones Soda

Jones Soda is known for its far-out flavors (like Fufu Berry and Blue Bubblegum) and the ever-changing photos on its labels, and this site reflects the company's fun attitude. Here you can learn more about the company, see current and retired flavors, play games and get downloads, view a photo gallery of labels, listen to music, watch videos, and participate in the community forum.

Web: www.jonessoda.com
Facebook: Jones Soda (Page), Jones Soda (Group)
Twiiter: jonessodaco
LinkedIn: Jones Soda Co. (Company)

Pepsi

This is the place to go to learn about Pepsi products, the company, and some of the causes it supports. For your entertainment, there's music, sports, games, commercials, downloads, and a shop to buy Pepsi stuff.

Web: www.pepsi.com
Facebook: Pepsi-Refresh Everything (Page)
Twitter: pepsi
LinkedIn: Pepsi Bottling Group (Company)

Perrier

The site for this fizzy French mineral water tells you all about Perrier and where it comes from. You'll also find drink recipes, party planning advice, a newsletter sign-up, and photos of celebrities drinking Perrier.

Web: www.usa.perrier.com
Facebook: Perrier
Twitter: (None)
LinkedIn: (None)

Snapple

Snapple makes iced teas, juice drinks, and "enhanced water beverages." On this site you can read about Snapple beverages and their health benefits, find stores that sell Snapple, check out current promotions and fun facts, and subscribe to the Snapple newsletter.

Web: www.snapple.com
Facebook: Snapple (Page)
Twitter: Snapple
LinkedIn: Dr Pepper Snapple Group (Company)

BEVERAGES: ALCOHOLIC

Absolut 🕸

The website of this popular vodka features an archive of ad campaigns, drink recipes, company information, and a blog. Visitors must be at least 21 years old to enter.

Web: www.absolut.com
Facebook: ABSOLUT VODKA (Page), ABSOLUT VODKA (Group)
Twitter: AbsolutFans
LinkedIn: (None)

Bacardi 🕸

After you've entered your date of birth (to prove you're 21 or older), you can get cocktail recipes that feature Bacardi rums, watch music videos and get downloads, and listen to Bacardi Internet radio. There's even a Bacardi Widget you can download to your cellphone to find the nearest bar, club, liquor store, hotel, or taxi based on ZIP code.

Web: www.bacardi.com
Facebook: BACARDI® (Page), Bacardi (Group)
Twitter: BACARDI
LinkedIn: Bacardi (Company)

Bar None Drinks 🕸

This site is all about cocktails, with drink recipes, drinking games, news from the alcoholic-beverage industry, bartending tips, a drinks dictionary, a newsletter, and forums. There's also a store so you can stock your bar with supplies.

Web: www.barnonedrinks.com
Facebook: (None)
Twitter: BNDrinks
LinkedIn: Bar None Drinks (Company)

Bombay Sapphire 🕸

This top-shelf gin has an attractive and highly interactive website that's organized into three main sections: Inspired Drinks (recipes for gin-based cocktails), Inspired Design (advertising and the Bombay Sapphire Foundation), and Inspired Taste (tasting notes and more). For visitors who are 21 or older.

Facebook: Bombay Sapphire (Page)
Twitter: sapphiredrinks
LinkedIn: (None)

7

Drinkhacker.com

Lifestyle, entertainment, and tech writer Christopher Null reviews and rates cocktails, wine, and beer.

Web: www.drinkhacker.com
Facebook: Drinkhacker.com (Page)
Twitter: drinkhacker
LinkedIn: Drinkhacker.com (Company)

Drinks Mixer

With more than 16,200 drink recipes, this site will help you find just about any drink you want—and a whole bunch you've probably never heard of, like Motor Oil or Bacon and Tomato Sandwich. Recipes are organized by categories—cocktails, shots, punches, non-alcoholic, coffee and tea, beer and ale, and liqueurs—and you can rate and comment on any recipe. There's also a forum, a glossary and bartender guide, and drinking games.

Web: www.drinksmixer.com
Facebook: (None)
Twitter: DrinksMixer
LinkedIn: (None)

Intoximeters Drink Wheel

This site is hosted by Intoximeters, Inc., which makes breath alcohol analyzers. To encourage responsible drinking, the Drink Wheel helps you find out how much is too much for your gender and body weight. Enter the number of drinks, type of drink, time period, gender, and body weight, and find the blood/breath alcohol concentration for that data. The results page also tells you legal levels for more states. There's even HTML code you can copy and paste to add the Drink Wheel to your own website.

Web: www.intox.com/wheel/drinkwheel.asp
Facebook: (None)
Twitter: (None)
LinkedIn: Intoximeters (Company)

Jack Daniels

Take a virtual tour of the Tennessee distillery and learn how this famous whiskey is crafted. Learn about the history of Jack Daniels, including the man himself. Try cocktail and food recipes, download wallpaper and screensavers, and find Jack Daniels–sponsored events. You need to enter your date of birth before you can view the site—under 21s need not apply.

Web: www.jackdaniels.com
Facebook: Jack Daniel's Tennessee Whiskey (Page), Jack Daniels Appreciation Fan Club (Group)
Twitter: JackDanielsFans
LinkedIn: (None)

Jose Cuervo

People of legal drinking age who enjoy tequila can visit this site to learn about Jose Cuervo products and history, find out how tequila is made, and try food and drink recipes. The Virtual Blender lets you drag and drop ingredients into a blender, blend them, and get a cocktail recipe.

Web: www.cuervo.com
Facebook: Jose Cuervo Tequila (Page)
Twitter: jcuervogold
LinkedIn: Jose Cuervo (Company)

Malt Madness

This encyclopedic site contains hundreds of pages about single-malt whiskey, and whether you're new to single malts or a connoisseur, you'll find interesting information here. There's a Beginner's Guide, information about distilleries, a Hit List of favorites, tasting notes, and a blog.

Web: www.maltmadness.com
Facebook: Malt Maniacs & Friends (Group)
Twitter: Maltmaniacs
LinkedIn: (None)

Webtender ⊛

The Webtender is your online bartender, with tons of drink recipes, lists of the most popular drinks, active forums, a bartender's handbook, and stores where you can buy books and supplies. Want to try a new cocktail but not sure what to make? Try the "In My Bar" section, where you specify the supplies you have on hand and get drink recipes that use those ingredients.

Web: www.webtender.com
Facebook: The Webtender (Page, Group)
Twitter: (None)
LinkedIn: The Webtender (Company)

BEVERAGES: COFFEE AND TEA

Brewed Coffee

News, opinions, and musings about coffee.

Web: www.brewed-coffee.com
Facebook: Brewed Coffee Blog (Page)
Twitter: (None)
LinkedIn: (None)

Coffee @ NationalGeographic.com

From bean to brew, National Geographic explores the history, production, and varieties of coffee on this educational site.

Web: www.nationalgeographic.com/coffee/
Facebook: National Geographic (Page)
Twitter: NatGeoSociety
LinkedIn: National Geographic Society (Company)

Coffee Review

If you're on a quest to find the perfect cup of coffee, take some time to explore this informative site, which reviews all kinds of coffee and rates them on a 100-point scale. The Coffee Reference section covers the basics of coffee: varieties, history, production, regions, a glossary, coffee and health, and coffee culture. You can subscribe to the site's free newsletter or shop for its top-rated coffees.

Web: www.coffeereview.com
Facebook: (None)
Twitter: coffeereview
LinkedIn: (None)

Oregon Chai

Chai is a creamy blend of tea, honey, vanilla, spices, and milk. This site gives news and information about Oregon Chai products and recipes for lots of chai-based drinks, such as Caramel Chai Latte and Raspberry Chai Mocha. Cafe owners will find information about how to order Oregon Chai products for their business.

Web: www.oregonchai.com
Facebook: Oregon Chai (Page), I Love Oregon Chai (Group)
Twitter: OregonChai
LinkedIn: (None)

Peets Coffee & Tea

Peets hand-roasts coffee in small batches and delivers it fresh to you. On this site, you can take an online tour of the company's artisan roastery and learn how it's made. You can also shop in the online store (coffees, teas, samplers, equipment, gifts, and other products), find a physical store, sign up for Peetniks to have Peets coffee delivered on a regular schedule, or send an ecup (an email gift certificate for one beverage redeemable at any Peets store).

Web: www.peets.com
Facebook: Peet's Coffee & Tea (Page, Group)
Twitter: Peets_Tweets
LinkedIn: (None)

7

The Republic of Tea

This site sells hundreds of premium teas and blends: black, green, white, herbal, organic, decaf, and many more. Read about the company's many products, see what's new, and check out special offers.

Web: www.republicoftea.com
Facebook: Addicts of The Republic of Tea (Group)
Twitter: (None)
LinkedIn: The Republic of Tea (Company)

Starbucks

Starbucks fans can learn all about the company on this site. Read about featured coffees and other Starbucks products, find a store, purchase or reload a Starbucks card, and shop online.

Web: www.starbucks.com
Facebook: Starbucks (Page), Addicted to Starbucks (Group)
Twitter: Starbucks
LinkedIn: Starbucks Coffee Company (Company), Starbucks' Enthusiasts (Group)

Stash Tea

Begun in 1972, Stash Tea sells all kinds of specialty teas, offering more than 200 blends, as well as teapots, tea accessories, gifts, and baked goods and other food items. This website answers all your questions about tea, from varieties of tea to the history of the teapot, and offers recipes, a print catalog, and products for sale. Watch tea-related videos and read customer-submitted recipes, quotes, beauty secrets, and other tips.

Web: www.stashtea.com
Facebook: Stash Tea (Page), Stash Tea Lovers Unite (Group)
Twitter: stashtea
LinkedIn: (None)

COOKING AND RECIPES

All Recipes

As its name suggests, this site is all about recipes. Find yummy recipes by type of food (appetizers and snacks, main dishes, desserts, and so on), ingredients/cooking method (such as pasta or barbeque), or occasion/cooking style (such as holidays or world cuisine). Of course, you can also search for a particular dish. There's a featured recipe each day, lots of food photos to whet your appetite, and plenty of tips and product reviews.

Web: http://allrecipes.com/
Facebook: All Recipes (Group)
Twitter: AllrecipesNews
LinkedIn: Allrecipes.com (Company)

ChefTalk

Billing itself as "a food lover's link to professional chefs," ChefTalk features discussion forums where you can interact with chefs and ask advice on food-related matters, as well as read cookbook reviews and view a food photo gallery. Here you'll find chef-created recipes, cooking articles, and a glossary of cooking terms. Professional chefs can check out job opportunities on the job board.

Web: www.cheftalk.com
Facebook: ChefTalk.com (Page)
Twitter: ChefTalk
LinkedIn: (None)

Chef Tom Cooks

Chef Tom blogs from New York City, sharing great recipes.

Web: http://cheftomcooks.com/
Facebook: Chef Tom Cooks ! (Page)
Twitter: cheftom
LinkedIn: (None)

Chile Pepper Magazine

Some like it hot—and if that's you, check out this site's chili pepper recipes and articles. You can subscribe online.

Web: http://site.chilepepper.com/
Facebook: Chile Pepper Magazine (Page)
Twitter: (None)
LinkedIn: (None)

Cooking Light

Cooking Light is the biggest food magazine in the United States, and its companion website shows how to make meals both light and delicious. Sections include Food, Menus & Planning, Cooking 101, Healthy Life, and Community.

Web: www.cookinglight.com
Facebook: Cooking Light magazine (Page)
Twitter: Cooking_Light
LinkedIn: (None)

Cooking 101

The iVillage cooking forum has lively discussions about recipes and cooking basics. A good place to get menu ideas and make friends.

Web: http://messageboards.ivillage.com/iv-fdpantry
Facebook: (None)
Twitter: iVillageBuzz
LinkedIn: (None)

Cook's Illustrated Ⓢ

This site has some free recipes and product reviews, but most of its content is for members who pay a subscription fee. Subscribers get access to 15 years' worth of recipes from *Cook's Illustrated* magazine, cooking videos, menus and shopping lists, full access to the Tasting Lab (which rates different brands of food products) and Equipment reviews, Quick Tips, and forums. With a 14-day free trial membership, you can look around before you decide to subscribe.

Web: www.cooksillustrated.com
Facebook: Cook's Illustrated Magazine (Group)
Twitter: (None)
LinkedIn: (None)

Cooks Recipes

Thousands of free recipes (including video recipes), reviews, tons of tips, a cooking dictionary, and lots more make this site well worth a visit.

Web: www.cooksrecipes.com
Facebook: CooksRecipes.com - Recipes for Every Cook! (Page)
Twitter: (None)
LinkedIn: (None)

Discuss Cooking

This site has dozens of forums for discussing all aspects of cooking: get tips, post and find recipes, and discuss your favorites.

Web: www.discusscooking.com
Facebook: Discuss Cooking (Group) (Must submit request to join)
Twitter: (None)
LinkedIn: (None)

Epicurious 🏅

If you love to eat, this site is for you. You'll find delicious recipes, including some from the pages of *Gourmet, Bon Appétit,* and *SELF* magazines; video instruction; articles and guides; a blog; podcasts; and a community area with forums, user pages, a chat area, and user-submitted recipes and videos. The site is well designed and full of recipes and tips.

Web: www.epicurious.com
Facebook: Epicurious (Page)
Twitter: epicurious
LinkedIn: (None)

7

Fabulous Foods

Here you'll find thousands of recipes, covering everything from soup to nuts. There are tips, seasonal features, recipes for campers, tutorials from guest chefs, a cooking school to teach the basics, cookbook reviews, a section to help you stay fit while you're eating all that fabulous food, and more.

Web: www.fabulousfoods.com
Facebook: FabulousFoods.com (Group)
Twitter: (None)
LinkedIn: (None)

Food Network

All your favorite Food Network shows are here, with videos, recipes, and advice. Check out the tips for holidays and parties, quick-and-easy cooking, and healthy eating, as well as the current Top 10 recipes. The Video Center has streaming broadband channels such as Daily Menu Ideas and Bobby Flay.

Web: www.foodnetwork.com
Facebook: Food Network (Page), Food Network (Group)
Twitter: FoodNetwork
LinkedIn: (None)

FoodNetwork.com Video Center

A great resource for learning great new recipes by watching them prepared, this site offers daily menu ideas, seasonal specials, cooking tips, and more.

Web: www.foodnetwork.com/food/video_guide
Facebook: Food Network (Page), Food Network (Group)
Twitter: FoodNetwork
LinkedIn: (None)

iFoods.tv

Watch and learn with free online recipe videos and cooking tutorials. When you register, you can upload your own videos and recipes, rate and comment on videos, and participate in the forum. The site awards "brownie points" for participating. You get 10 points, for example,

when you upload a video recipe and 5 points for every text recipe. Each month, the five members with the most brownie points win prizes.

Web: www.ifoods.tv
Facebook: Look and Taste (Page), Look and Taste (Group)
Twitter: lookandtaste
LinkedIn: (None)

The Italian Chef

Italy is home to some of the world's greatest cuisine, and this site helps you cook it like a pro. The site has the recipes, features, and cookbook reviews you'd expect; it also has restaurant reviews and advice about traveling to Italy. Mangia!

Web: www.italianchef.com
Facebook: The Italian Chef (Page)
Twitter: theitalianchef
LinkedIn: (None)

Kraft Foods Recipes

Known for its wide variety of food products, Kraft also offers an array of recipes by category and meal, plus how-to video demonstrations and an online Recipe Box.

Facebook: Kraft Foods (Page), Kraft Foods (Group)
Web: www.kraftrecipes.com/recipes/main.aspx
Twitter: kraftfoods
LinkedIn: Kraft Foods (Company)

MyRecipes.com

MyRecipes.com features thousands of recipes in 150 categories, as well as menus from magazines such as *Cooking Light, Southern Living, Sunset, Coastal Living, Cottage Living, Real Simple,* and *Health.* When you create an account, you can create a recipe file to save your favorite recipes and menus and generate shopping lists.

Web: www.myrecipes.com
Facebook: MyRecipes.com (Page)
Twitter: My_Recipes
LinkedIn: (None)

Recipe Source

This site has 70,000 recipes in two main sections: International cuisine is organized by region and ethnic group; other recipes are organized by kind of dish, from soups and appetizers to sweets and desserts.

Web: www.recipesource.com
Facebook: (None)
Twitter: recipesource
LinkedIn:(None)

Recipes Wiki

With nearly 50,000 entries about recipes, cooking, and ingredients, this wiki is a foodie's paradise. Contribute, edit, and discuss food-related articles here.

Web: http://recipes.wikia.com/
Facebook: Recipes Wiki (Page)
Twitter: RecipesWiki
LinkedIn: (None)

RecipeZaar

RecipeZaar members have shared nearly 300,000 recipes on this site, so you'll find lots of yummy ideas here. You'll also find cookbooks, menus, community forums, and the Eater's Digest blog. Premium membership, available for $24.95 per year, lets you personalize recipes and create your own custom cookbook, build shopping lists, and contact other members individually.

Web: www.recipezaar.com
Facebook: RecipeZaar (Page)
Twitter: recipezaar
LinkedIn: Recipezaar (Company)

The Secret Recipe Blog

If you've ever wished you could make your favorite restaurant dish at home, check out this blog, which specializes in copycat recipes. Recipes are rated by the blog's readers.

Web: www.recipesecrets.net/blog/
Facebook: RecipeSecrets.net (Page)
Twitter: recipesecrets
LinkedIn: (None)

Top Secret Recipes

Cookbook author Todd Wilbur specializes in "cloning" recipes for some of the most popular foods in the United States, from supermarket products to restaurant-chain favorites. Most of the recipes are for sale, but many are available free. Site visitors can rate and comment on recipes, so you know whether others thought Wilbur got a recipe right before you buy or try it.

Web: www.topsecretrecipes.com
Facebook: Todd Wilbur (Page)
Twitter: topsecretrecipe
LinkedIn: (None)

Weight Watchers Food and Recipes

Watching your weight is no reason to give up great food, and the Food & Recipes area of the Weight Watchers website has plenty of suggestions for delicious meals. Learn how the Weight Watchers food plan works, and get recipes and ideas for healthy eating (at home or at a restaurant). Find out about joining a support group, either in your area or online (online support is available by subscription).

Web: www.weightwatchers.com/food/index.aspx
Facebook: Weight Watchers (Page), Weight Watchers (Group)
Twitter: WeightWatchers
LinkedIn: Weight Watchers (Company), Weight Watchers Members (Group)

7

FOOD: GENERAL

Amateur Gourmet

Author Adam D. Roberts provides food news, recipes, restaurant reviews, how-to tips, and other writings on this fun, well-written blog.

Web: www.amateurgourmet.com
Facebook: The Amateur Gourmet (Page), The Amateur Gourmet (Group)
Twitter: amateurgourmet
LinkedIn: (None)

Foodies!

Food-related news and articles from worldwide sources.

Web: http://foodies.newsvine.com/
Facebook: Newsvine (Page)
Twitter: newsvine
LinkedIn: Newsvine (Company), Newsvine (Group)

FriendsEAT.com

A social network for those who are passionate about food. After you join, you become a "Foodie" and can create a profile and blog; upload recipes, restaurant reviews, and videos; and interact with other Foodies.

Web: http://friendseat.com/
Facebook: FriendsEAT.com (Page)
Twitter: FriendsEAT
LinkedIn: (None)

Global Gourmet

This site's motto is "We bring you the world on a plate," and there's lots of info here about delicious food from around the world. Departments include Kate's Global Kitchen, Cookbook Profiles, Holiday & Party Recipes, I Love Desserts, On Wine, Green Basics, Cooking with Kids, and more.

Web: www.globalgourmet.com
Facebook: (None)
Twitter: GlobalGourmet
LinkedIn: (None)

Gourmet Food Mall

This site offers a directory of online stores where you can buy gourmet and specialty food items, gift baskets, and cooking accessories, as well as everyday favorites.

Web: www.gourmetfoodmall.com
Facebook: GourmetFoodMall (Page)
Twitter: gourmetfoodmall
LinkedIn: (None)

Harry & David

For delicious gourmet gifts—fresh fruits, decadent chocolates, yummy desserts, Harry & David's famous Moose Munch, and more—visit this site. Shop by occasion, price, or customer favorites. You can also join the Fruit-of-the-Month Club.

Web: www.harryanddavid.com
Facebook: Harry and David Murfreesboro (Page), Harry and David (Group)
Twitter: harryanddavid
LinkedIn: Harry and David (Company)

Hickory Farms

Shop here for sausages, cheese, fruit, nuts, and other snacks, as well as meats/seafood and desserts/sweets. If you're looking for a gift, check out the gift baskets, boxes, and towers.

Web: www.hickoryfarms.com
Facebook: Hickory Farms (Page), Hickory Farms (Group)
Twitter: HickoryFarms
LinkedIn: Hickory Farms (Company)

Omaha Steaks

Omaha Steaks sells steaks, of course, but also other meats and side dishes, pasta, appetizers, desserts, complete meals, and more. Check out current specials and bestsellers, try recipes, shop for gifts, or find a bricks-and-mortar store near you.

Web: www.omahasteaks.com
Facebook: Omaha Steaks (Page)
Twitter: OmahaSteaks
LinkedIn: Omaha Steaks (Company)

Slashfood

Multiple bloggers talk about food—from cooking it to eating it—along with food-related news.

Web: www.slashfood.com
Facebook: Slashfood (Page)
Twitter: slashfood
LinkedIn: (None)

GROCERIES

Amazon.com

Is there anything this online megaretailer *doesn't* sell? Amazon.com lists more than 22,000 nonperishable grocery items, including natural and organic items, delivered straight to your door. Orders may qualify for free Super Saver or Amazon Prime shipping.

Web: www.amazon.com/grocery/
Facebook: Amazon.com (Page), Amazon.com (Group)
Twitter: amazon
LinkedIn: Amazon.com (Company)

Coupon Mom

The Coupon Mom presents a directory of coupons you can print out and take to the store. You'll also find grocery deals by state, a database of coupons, restaurant coupons, free samples and offers, a blog, and more. When you join the site, you get a free eBook that gives strategies for cutting your grocery bill in half.

Web: www.couponmom.com
Facebook: Coupon Mom (Page)
Twitter: couponmom
LinkedIn: Coupon Mom Inc (Company)

Groceries Express

When you visit this site, enter your ZIP code so that Groceries Express can fill its virtual aisles with the products, specials, and delivery options available for your area. As you select products, they appear in your shopping cart on the right side of the screen, which keeps a running total of your purchase (including shipping).

Web: http://groceries-express.com/
Facebook: (None)
Twitter: (None)
LinkedIn: Groceries-Express.com (Company)

Kroger

The Kroger Company owns more than a dozen supermarket chains and other stores throughout the United States. This site offers recipes and party-planning tips, ideas for healthy living, gift suggestions, and the like. You can find a store near you, order a prescription refill, and view weekly specials.

Web: www.kroger.com
Facebook: Kroger (Page), Kroger (Group)
Twitter: KrogerDeals
LinkedIn: Kroger (Company), The Kroger Co (Group)

NetGrocer

NetGrocer offers all the grocery items you'd find at your local supermarket, including deli, dairy, kosher, and organic products, as well as health and beauty products. The company has more than 3,500 refrigerated, frozen, and perishable items that it can ship right to your door.

Web: http://netgrocer.com/
Facebook: Netgrocer (Page)
Twitter: Netgrocer
LinkedIn: (None)

Peapod

Choose the products you want on this site; Peapod does your shopping for you and, within hours, delivers them straight to your home or business.

Web: www.peapod.com
Facebook: Peapod Delivers (Page), Peapod (Group)
Twitter: PeapodDelivers
LinkedIn: Peapod (Company)

7

Piggly Wiggly

Piggly Wiggly was the first self-service grocery store in Memphis, Tennessee, in 1916. Today, it has stores in 16 states. Its website provides kitchen tips, menu suggestions, recipes, and printable shopping lists. You can also shop for Piggly Wiggly collectibles and find store locations.

Facebook: Piggly Wiggly (Page)
Twitter: (None)
LinkedIn: Piggly Wiggly Carolina (Company), Piggly Wiggly Carolina (Group)

Safeway

With 1,775 stores across the United States and Canada, Safeway is one of the largest supermarket chains in North America. In certain areas, you can shop online and have your groceries delivered to you at home (enter your ZIP code to learn whether this service is available in your area). The website also has information about Safeway stores, a Wellness Center (articles about health and nutrition), and a Recipe Center.

Web: http://shop.safeway.com/
Facebook: Safeway (Page), Safeway (Group)
Twitter: Safeway
LinkedIn: Safeway (Company)

Trader Joe's

This fun, funky chain features gourmet, organic, vegetarian, and unusual foods. The website has the company's history, store locations, product info (including lists of gluten-free, low-sodium, and vegan foods), recipes, and more.

Web: www.traderjoes.com
Facebook: Trader Joe's (Page), Trader Joe's (Group)
Twitter: TraderJoesList
LinkedIn: Trader Joe's (Company), Trader Joe's Specialty Store (Group)

Whole Foods Market

Whole Foods has more than 270 locations in the United States, Canada, and the United Kingdom. Its focus is on natural and organic foods. Here you can learn about the company, its stores, and its products; find nutrition and health information; and try out some delicious recipes. Has blogs and a podcast.

Web: www.wholefoodsmarket.com
Facebook: Whole Foods Market (Page), WHOLE FOODS MARKET (Group)
Twitter: WholeFoods
LinkedIn: Whole Foods Market (Company)

ORGANIC FOODS

The Daily Table

With a focus on organic food and sustainable agriculture, this blog is of interest to those who want to eat healthier and protect the planet.

Web: http://sustainabletable.org/blog/
Facebook: Sustainable Table (Page), Sustainable Table (Group)
Twitter: eatsustainable
LinkedIn: (None)

Eden Foods

This family-owned natural food company, begun in 1968, aims to bring clean, natural, organic food to its customers. It offers food-related articles and recipes, as well as a wide range of organic food for purchase.

Web: www.edenfoods.com
Facebook: Eden Foods (Page)
Twitter: edenfoods
LinkedIn: Eden Foods, Inc. (Company)

Local Harvest

As Local Harvest points out, "the best organic food is what's grown closest to you." This website offers a directory of farmers' markets, farms, and restaurants, so you can find an organic food source that's close to home. There's an online store for products you can't find elsewhere.

Web: www.localharvest.org
Facebook: LocalHarvest (Page)
Twitter: LocalHarvestorg
LinkedIn: (None)

Organic Authority

"Get hip, go organic!" proclaims this site's motto, and here you'll find everything you need to do just that: information about organic food, organic recipes, tips on organic living and gardening, feature articles, a blog, and more. Has an online store.

Web: www.organicauthority.com
Facebook: Organic Authority (Page)
Twitter: OrganicAuthorit
LinkedIn: (None)

Organic Consumers Association

The OCA estimates that 50 million American consumers buy organic products, and the group's focus includes food safety, industrial agriculture, and genetic engineering, among other issues. Visit this website to learn about the group's work and current issues, as well as find trusted sources of organic food.

Web: www.organicconsumers.org
Facebook: Organic Consumers Association (Page), Organic Consumers Association on Facebook (Group)
Twitter: OrganicConsumer
LinkedIn: (None)

Organic To Go

Organic To Go cafes are located in California and Washington. The company also does corporate catering. Check out the current menu and find a location.

Web: www.organictogo.com
Facebook: Organic To Go (Page)
Twitter: (None)
LinkedIn: Organic To Go (Company)

Organic Trade Assocation

The mission of this business association is to "promote and protect the growth of organic trade to benefit the environment, farmers, the public, and the economy."

Organic businesses and farmers can join the OTA; consumers can find educational materials and directories of organic businesses.

Web: www.ota.com
Facebook: Organic Trade Association (Page)
Twitter: OrganicTrade
LinkedIn: (None)

RESTAURANTS

A&W Restaurants

Web: www.awrestaurants.com
Facebook: A&W Restaurants (Page)
Twitter: AW_Restaurants
LinkedIn: Yum! Restaurants International (Company)

Applebee's

Web: www.applebees.com
Facebook: Applebee's (Page)
Twitter: Applebeeing
LinkedIn: Applebee's (Company)

Arby's

Web: www.arbys.com
Facebook: Arby's (Page)
Twitter: ColoradoArbys
LinkedIn: Arby's Restaurant Group (Company)

Bahama Breeze

Web: www.bahamabreeze.com
Facebook: Bahama Breeze Island Grille (Page)
Twitter: (None)
LinkedIn: (None)

Benihana

Web: www.benihana.com
Facebook: Benihana (Page)
Twitter: Benihana_
LinkedIn: Benihana (Company)

Bennigan's

Web: www.bennigans.com
Facebook: Bennigan's (Page)
Twitter: (None)
LinkedIn: Bennigans (Company)

Black Angus Steakhouse

Web: www.blackangus.com
Facebook: (None)
Twitter: (None)
LinkedIn: Black Angus Steakhouses (Company)

7

Blimpie Subs and Salads
Web: www.blimpie.com
Facebook: Blimpie (Page)
Twitter: BlimpieSandwich
LinkedIn: Blimpie International (Company)

Bob Evans
Web: www.bobevans.com
Facebook: Bob Evans (Page)
Twitter: BobEvansFarms
LinkedIn: Bob Evans (Company)

Bojangles' Famous Chicken 'n Biscuits
Web: www.bojangles.com
Facebook: Bojangles' (Page), BOJANGLES (Group)
Twitter: (None)
LinkedIn: Bojangles' Restaurants, Inc. (Company)

Bonefish Grill
Web: www.bonefishgrill.com
Facebook: Bonefish Grill (Page), Bonefish Grill (Group)
Twitter: BonefishGrill
LinkedIn: Bonefish Grill (Company)

Border Café
Web: www.bordercafe.com
Facebook: Border Cafe (Page)
Twitter: (None)
LinkedIn: (None)

Boston Market
Web: www.bostonmarket.com
Facebook: Boston Market (Page)
Twitter: bostmarket
LinkedIn: Boston Market (Company)

Bugaboo Creek Steak House
Web: www.bugaboocreek.com
Facebook: Bugaboo Creek Steak House (Group)
Twitter: Bugaboo_Creek
LinkedIn: (None)

Burger King
Web: www.burgerking.com
Facebook: Burger King ! (Page)
Twitter: theBKlounge
LinkedIn: Burger King Corporation (Company)

Carrabba's Italian Grill
Web: www.carrabbas.com
Facebook: Carrabba's Italian Grill (Page), Carrabba's Italian Grill (Group)
Twitter: Carrabbas
LinkedIn: Carrabba's Italian Grill (Company)

Cheesecake Factory
Web: www.cheesecakefactory.com
Facebook: The Cheesecake Factory (Page), The Cheesecake Factory (Group)
Twitter: Cheesecake
LinkedIn: The Cheesecake Factory (Company)

Chevy's Fresh Mex
Web: www.chevys.com
Facebook: Chevy's Fresh Mex (Page), Chevy's Fresh Mex Fan Club (Group)
Twitter: FreshMexCoMo
LinkedIn: (None)

Chick-fil-A
Web: www.chick-fil-a.com
Facebook: Chick-fil-A (Page), Chick-fil-a (Group)
Twitter: ChickfilA
LinkedIn: Chick-fil-A (Company), Chick-fil-A Lovers (Group)

Chili's Grill & Bar
Web: www.chilis.com
Facebook: Chili's Grill & Bar (Page)
Twitter: Chilis
LinkedIn: Chili's (Company)

Cracker Barrel Old Country Store & Restaurant
Web: www.crackerbarrel.com
Facebook: Cracker Barrel (Page), Cracker Barrel (Group)
Twitter: (None)
LinkedIn: Cracker Barrel (Company)

Dairy Queen
Web: www.dairyqueen.com
Facebook: Dairy Queen (Page)
Twitter: DairyQueen
LinkedIn: Fourteen Foods (Company)

Denny's
Web: www.dennys.com
Facebook: Denny's (Page)
Twitter: DennysGrandSlam
LinkedIn: Denny's (Company)

Friendly's
Web: www.friendlys.com
Facebook: Friendly's (Page)
Twitter: EatAtFriendlys
LinkedIn: Friendly Ice Cream Corporation (Company)

Fuddruckers
Web: www.fuddruckers.com
Facebook: Fuddruckers (Page)
Twitter: fuddsprime
LinkedIn: Fuddruckers (Company)

Godfather's Pizza
Web: www.godfathers.com
Facebook: Godfather's Pizza (Page)
Twitter: (None)
LinkedIn: Godfather's Pizza (Company)

The Ground Round
Web: www.groundround.com
Facebook: Ground Round (Page)
Twitter: (None)
LinkedIn: Ground Round IOC, LLC (Company)

Hard Rock Café
Web: www.hardrock.com
Facebook: Hard Rock Café (Page)
Twitter: hardrockdotcom
LinkedIn: Hard Rock Café (Company), Hard Rock Café
Fans - "Love All, Serve All" (Group)

Hops Grill and Brewery
Web: www.hopsrestaurants.com
Facebook: Hops Restaurant, Bar, & Brewery (Page)
Twitter: (None)
LinkedIn: (None)

Houlihan's
Web: www.houlihans.com
Facebook: Houlihan's Restaurant (Page)
Twitter: (None)
LinkedIn: Houlihan's Restaurants, Inc. (Company)

IHOP
Web: www.ihop.com
Facebook: IHOP (Page)
Twitter: (None)
LinkedIn: DineEquity, Inc. (Company)

KFC
Web: www.kfc.com
Facebook: KFC - Kentucky Fried Chicken (Page)
Twitter: kfc_colonel
LinkedIn: Yum! Restaurants International (Company)

Lone Star Steakhouse & Saloon
Web: www.lonestarsteakhouse.com
Facebook: (None)
Twitter: LoneStarSteak
LinkedIn: (None)

Long John Silver's
Web: www.ljsilvers.com
Facebook: Long John Silver's (Page)
Twitter: longjohnslvrs
LinkedIn: Yum! Brands (Company)

McDonald's
Web: www.mcdonalds.com
Facebook: McDonald's (Page)
Twitter: McDonalds
LinkedIn: McDonald's Corporation (Company)

Moe's Southwest Grill
Web: www.moes.com
Facebook: Moe's Southwest Grill (Page), Moe's
Southwest Grill (Group)
Twitter: Moes_HQ
LinkedIn: National Restaurant Development, Inc
(Company)

O'Charleys
Web: www.ocharleys.com
Facebook: O'Charley's (Page)
Twitter: (None)
LinkedIn: O'Charley's (Company)

Old Country Buffet
Web: www.oldcountrybuffet.com
Facebook: (None)
Twitter: (None)
LinkedIn: Buffets, Inc. (Company)

The Old Spaghetti Factory
Web: www.osf.com
Facebook: The Old Spaghetti Factory (Page)
Twitter: (None)
LinkedIn: (None)

Olive Garden Italian Restaurant
Web: www.olivegarden.com
Facebook: Olive Garden Italian Restaurant (Page)
Twitter: The_OliveGarden
LinkedIn: (None)

On The Border
Web: www.ontheborder.com
Facebook: On the Border (Page), On The Border (Group)
Twitter: OnTheBorderLBK
LinkedIn: On The Border (Company)

7

Outback Steakhouse

Web: www.outbacksteakhouse.com
Facebook: Outback Steakhouse (Page)
Twitter: outback_tonight
LinkedIn: Outback Steakhouse (Company), Outback Steakhouse International (Company)

Panera Bread

Web: www.panerabread.com
Facebook: Panera Bread (Page), Panera Bread (Group)
Twitter: panerabread
LinkedIn: Panera Bread (Company)

Paradise Bakery & Café

Web: www.paradisebakery.com
Facebook: Paradise Bakery & Café (Page)
Twitter: Paradise_Bakery
LinkedIn: (None)

Perkins Restaurant and Bakery

Web: www.perkinsrestaurants.com
Facebook: Perkins Restaurant and Bakery (Page)
Twitter: (None)
LinkedIn: (None)

Pizza Hut

Web: www.pizzahut.com
Facebook: Pizza Hut (Page)
Twitter: pizzahut
LinkedIn: Pizza Hut (Company), Yum! Restaurants International (Company)

Popeyes Chicken and Biscuits

Web: www.popeyes.com
Facebook: Popeyes Louisiana Kitchen (Page)
Twitter: PopeyesChicken
LinkedIn: Popeyes Louisiana Kitchen (Company)

Quiznos Sub Sandwich Shop

Web: www.quiznos.com
Facebook: Quiznos (Page), Quiznos (Group)
Twitter: Quiznos
LinkedIn: Quiznos (Company)

Rainforest Cafe

Web: www.rainforestcafe.com
Facebook: Rainforest Café (Page)
Twitter: RainforestMGM
LinkedIn: (None)

Red Lobster Seafood Restaurants

Web: www.redlobster.com
Facebook: Red Lobster (Page)
Twitter: redlobster
LinkedIn: (None)

Red Robin

Web: www.redrobin.com
Facebook: Red Robin Gourmet Burgers Official Page (Page)
Twitter: redrobinburgers
LinkedIn: Red Robin (Company)

Romano's Macaroni Grill

Web: www.macaronigrill.com
Facebook: Romano's Macaroni Grill (Page)
Twitter: MacaroniGrill
LinkedIn: Romano's Macaroni Grill (Company)

Roy Rogers Restaurants

Web: www.royrogersrestaurants.com
Facebook: Roy Rogers Restaurants (Page)
Twitter: RoysRestaurants
LinkedIn: (None)

Ruby Tuesday

Web: www.rubytuesday.com
Facebook: Ruby Tuesday (Page), Ruby Tuesday (Group)
Twitter: (None)
LinkedIn: Ruby Tuesday (Company)

Ruth's Chris Steak House

Web: www.ruthschris.com
Facebook: RUTH'S CHRIS STEAKHOUSE (Page)
Twitter: (None)
LinkedIn: Ruth's Chris Steak House (Company)

Schlotzsky's

Web: www.schlotzskys.com
Facebook: Official Schlotzsky's (Page)
Twitter: Schlotzskys
LinkedIn: Schlotzsky's, Inc. (Company)

Shoney's Restaurant

Web: www.shoneys.com
Facebook: Shoney's Restaurant (Page)
Twitter: ShoneysLetsEat
LinkedIn: (None)

Sizzler USA

Web: www.sizzler.com
Facebook: Sizzler (Page)
Twitter: Sizzler_USA
LinkedIn: Sizzler USA (Company)

Sonic

Web: www.sonicdrivein.com
Facebook: Sonic Drive-In (Page)
Twitter: sonicdrive_in
LinkedIn: Sonic Drive-In (Company)

Souplantation & Sweet Tomatoes
Web: www.sweettomatoes.com
Facebook: Souplantation/Sweet Tomatoes (Page)
Twitter: Souplantation
LinkedIn: Garden Fresh Restaurant Corp. (dba Souplantation & Sweet Tomatoes Restaurants) (Company)

Steak 'n Shake
Web: www.steaknshake.com
Facebook: Steak 'n Shake (Page)
Twitter: (None)
LinkedIn: Steak n Shake (Company)

Subway
Web: www.subway.com
Facebook: SUBWAY (Page), Addicted to SUBWAY! (Group)
Twitter: subwayfreshbuzz
LinkedIn: Subway (Company)

Taco Bell
Web: www.tacobell.com
Facebook: Taco Bell (Page)
Twitter: TacoBell
LinkedIn: Taco Bell (Company)

T.G.I. Friday's Worldwide
Web: www.fridays.com
Facebook: T.G.I. Friday's (Page)
Twitter: TGIFridaysCorp
LinkedIn: TGI Fridays (Company)

Tony Roma's
Web: www.tonyromas.com
Facebook: Tony Roma's (Page)
Twitter: (None)
LinkedIn: International Trading Franchises, LLC (Company)

Trader Vic's
Web: www.tradervics.com
Facebook: (None)
Twitter: TraderVics
LinkedIn: (None)

Uno Chicago Grill
Web: www.unos.com
Facebook: Uno Chicago Grill (Page)
Twitter: UnoChicagoGrill
LinkedIn: Uno Chicago Grill (Company)

Waffle House
Web: www.wafflehouse.com
Facebook: Waffle House (Page)
Twitter: WHRegulars
LinkedIn: Waffle House (Company)

Wendy's Old-Fashioned Hamburgers
Web: www.wendys.com
Facebook: Wendy's (Page)
Twitter: Wendys
LinkedIn: Wendy's/Arby's Group, Inc. (Company)

White Castle
Web: www.whitecastle.com
Facebook: White Castle (Page)
Twitter: OfficialWC
LinkedIn: White Castle (Company)

SPECIAL DIETS: GLUTEN FREE

7

GlutenFree.com

This site sells gluten-free products and provides free recipes, information, and resources related to celiac disease and autism.

Web: www.glutenfree.com
Facebook: (None)
Twitter: GlutenFree_com
LinkedIn: (None)

Gluten-Free Girl

Shauna James Ahern, an author who has celiac disease, blogs about gluten-free living and cooking. Lots of yummy recipes.

Web: http://glutenfreegirl.blogspot.com/
Facebook: Gluten-Free Girl (Page), Shauna James Ahern (People)
Twitter: glutenfreegirl
LinkedIn: (None)

The Gluten-Free Mall

An online store with a wide selection of gluten-free, wheat-free, and casein-free foods.

Web: www.glutenfreemall.com
Facebook: Gluten-Free Mall (Page)
Twitter: celiac_disease
LinkedIn: (None)

Gluten Free Mommy

Natalie Naramor offers gluten-free recipes the whole family will love, as well as tips on gluten-free living and eating.

Web: http://glutenfreemommy.com/
Facebook: (None)
Twitter: glutenfreemommy
LinkedIn: (None)

Karina's Kitchen

Cookbook author and artist Karina Allrich offers a kitchenful of delicious gluten-free, casein-free, soy-free recipes, accompanied by mouthwatering photos.

Web: http://glutenfreegoddess.blogspot.com/
Facebook: Karina's Kitchen - Recipes from a Gluten-Free Goddess (Page)
Twitter: KarinaAllrich
LinkedIn: (None)

Tom Sawyer Gluten-Free Products

Tom Sawyer has developed a gluten-free flour that the company claims can be substituted for regular flour in your favorite recipes, no adjustments needed. On this site you can learn about and buy Tom Sawyer products, get baking hints and recipes, and find information about gluten intolerance and celiac disease.

Web: www.glutenfreeflour.com
Facebook: Tom Sawyer (Page)
Twitter: tomsawyergf
LinkedIn: (None)

SPECIAL DIETS: KOSHER

The Jew and the Carrot

This blog's name was inspired by these words of artist Paul Cézanne: "There will come a day when a carrot, freshly observed, will spark a revolution." Here, several writers blog about the Jewish community, food, and contemporary issues.

Web: http://jcarrot.org/
Facebook: The Jew & The Carrot (Page), The Jew & The Carrot Blog (Group)
Twitter: jcarrot
LinkedIn: (None)

Kosher.com

"Your one-stop kosher superstore" sells kosher foods (including gluten-free and organic) and Judaica. You'll also find free recipes, articles, cartoons, and a blog.

Web: www.kosher.com
Facebook: Kosher.com! (Group)
Twitter: kosherdotcom
LinkedIn: Kosher.com (Company)

OU (Orthodox Union)

The Orthodox Union certifies more than 400,000 products using strict standards of kosher supervision. Its site provides educational resources, a restaurant locator, and more than 2,300 recipes.

Web: www.oukosher.org
Facebook: (None)
Twitter: (None)
LinkedIn: Orthodox Union (Company)

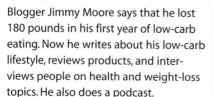

SPECIAL DIETS: LOW CARB

Healthy Low-Carb Living

Amy Dungan has been living low-carb since 2001 and posting about it on this blog since 2006.

Web: http://lovinglowcarblife.blogspot.com/
Facebook: (None)
Twitter: AmyDungan
LinkedIn: (None)

Jimmy Moore's Livin' la Vida Low-Carb 🏅

Blogger Jimmy Moore says that he lost 180 pounds in his first year of low-carb eating. Now he writes about his low-carb lifestyle, reviews products, and interviews people on health and weight-loss topics. He also does a podcast.

Web: http://livinlavidalowcarb.com/blog/
Facebook: Jimmy Moore's Livin' la Vida Low-Carb (Page)
Twitter: livinlowcarbman
LinkedIn: (None)

Netrition: Low Carb Foods

This online nutrition store has an excellent selection of low-carb foods, nutrition bars, mixes, and products. Registered shoppers can read and submit ratings and reviews for individual products.

Web:
www26.netrition.com/low_carb_products_page.html
Facebook: Netrition.com (Page)
Twitter: (None)
LinkedIn: (None)

SPECIAL DIETS: VEGETARIAN AND VEGAN

Groovy Vegetarian

This vegetarian lifestyle blog highlights news and items of interest to vegetarians.

Web: www.groovyvegetarian.com
Facebook: Groovy Vegetarian (Page) Groovy Vegetarians (Group)
Twitter: m38967
LinkedIn: (None)

Vegan Outreach 🚫

This nonprofit organization describes its mission as being "dedicated to reducing animal suffering by promoting informed, ethical eating." It aims to educate consumers about food-industry practices and promote vegan-style eating. Its Vegan Starter Guide tells you what vegans eat and offers recipes, a glossary, and featured products. Some of the images and text on the site may be upsetting to children and others.

Web: www.veganoutreach.org
Facebook: Vegan Outreach (Page)
Twitter: veganoutreach
LinkedIn: Compassionate Action for Animals (Group)

VegCooking

This PETA-sponsored site features vegetarian menus and recipes, cookbook reviews and cooking tips, a guide for eating out and buying vegan products, and an introduction to vegetarianism.

Web: www.vegcooking.com
Facebook: PETA (People for the Ethical Treatment of Animals) (Page)
Twitter: peta
LinkedIn: PETA (Company), PETA (Group)

7

Vegetarian and Vegan Information

This encyclopedic site gives information about vegetarianism and veganism, from defining terms to nutrition information to recipes and resources.

Web: www.vegetarianvegan.com
Facebook: (None)
Twitter: vegetarianvegan
LinkedIn: (None)

Vegetarian Resource Group

The website of the nonprofit Vegetarian Resource Group, publisher of *Vegetarian Journal*, features online articles from the magazine. You'll also find a restaurant guide; information about veganism, nutrition, and food ingredients; lots of recipes; and more.

Web: www.vrg.org
Facebook: The Vegetarian Resource Group (Page)
Twitter: VegResourceGrp
LinkedIn: (None)

VegWeb.com 🏅

This site offers vegetarian recipes and articles, a shopping directory, a directory of links to other vegetarian resources, and a social area called VegFriends. When you register, you can create a profile, connect with other vegetarians, write your own blog, participate in chats and forum discussions, and create recipe and grocery lists.

Web: http://vegweb.com/
Facebook: VegWeb (Page)
Twitter: VegWeb
LinkedIn: (None)

WINE

Ambrosia Wine

This online retailer says it sells "only memorable wines." You can shop by type of wine, browse weekly specials, or find bargain-priced wines under $20. Each wine has a full description (often with tasting notes). You can join a wine club and try a new wine each month, plus receive discounts on your purchases on the site. Ambrosia Wine can ship only to certain states, so check to make sure yours is one of them.

Web: www.ambrosiawine.com
Facebook: (None)
Twitter: AmbrosiaWine
LinkedIn: (None)

Bordeaux 🕏

This site tells you all about the wines produced in the Bordeaux region of France: varieties, vintages, classifications, how wines are made, and how to taste wine and pair it with food. You can also take a virtual tour of Bordeaux, "the wine capital of the world."

Web: www.bordeaux.com
Facebook: Bordeaux Wine (Page)
Twitter: BordeauxLovers
LinkedIn: (None)

CorkSavvy 🕏

Get savvy about wine at this site, which features news and reviews, a wine of the week, searchable wine and vineyard lists, interviews, advice about matching wine to food, and other wine resources.

Web: www.corksavvy.com
Facebook: Corksavvy.com (Page)
Twitter: CorkSavvy
LinkedIn: (None)

E. & J. Gallo Winery

The largest wine producer in the United States (and second largest in the world), Gallo has made wine for 75 years. On this site you'll find information about the Gallo family and the winery's history, how the wines are made, and the varieties available. Use the wine-pairing tool to find the perfect wine to complement a particular food. There's also a wine store and wine clubs you can join. You must be of legal drinking age to enter some areas of the site.

Web: www.gallo.com
Facebook: E & J Gallo Winery (Page)
Twitter: (None)
LinkedIn: Giglio Distributing Co. (Company), Gallo Wine Co. (Group)

Fetzer Vineyards

After you've entered your birth date (to prove you're 21 or older), you can enter the site to learn about this northern California vineyard and its wines. Use the wine compass to match your taste preferences to a type of wine. Find recipes and wine–food pairing suggestions.

Web: www.fetzer.com
Facebook: Fetzer (Page)
Twitter: (None)
LinkedIn: (None)

Food & Wine Magazine

Food & Wine magazine's companion website is full of features that highlight good food and good wine. You'll find plenty of recipes, advice on finding a great wine, and entertaining tips, as well as news, videos, and more. The site's wine blog is called The Tasting Room.

Web: www.foodandwine.com
Facebook: Food & Wine (Page)
Twitter: fandw
LinkedIn: (None)

Geerlings & Wade

This wine merchant ships fine wines to 32 states. You can browse by price range, region, type of wine, or food pairing. You can also buy wine accessories, such as bottle openers and chillers. There are also free recipes and articles about different winemaking regions.

Web: www.geerwade.com
Facebook: Francis Sanders (Page)
Twitter: FrancisSanders
LinkedIn: Geerlings & Wade (Company)

International Wine Review

Subscribers to this site receive bimonthly reports that focus on a particular wine region, with tasting notes and ratings of hundreds of wines and suggestions for matching wine with food. Subscribers also have access to previous reports and the site's archive of wine notes and ratings. Nonsubscribers can read the free articles in the site's Education area and blog.

Facebook: International Wine Review (Page)
Twitter: iWineReview
LinkedIn: (None)

Into Wine

Here, "wine experts and enthusiasts share their unique wine experiences." Various bloggers write about regions, kinds of wine, food and wine pairing, storing wine, and more. Into Wine TV presents video wine tastings.

Web: www.intowine.com
Facebook: IntoWine.com (Page)
Twitter: IntoWinecom
LinkedIn: (None)

7

K&L Wine Merchants

Recently named one of the top-10 online wine shops by *Food & Wine* magazine, K&L features both new and vintage wines from all over the world. Check out the staff's current top picks or find a great wine for less than $25. You'll find lots of information about winemaking regions, varieties, vintages, and individual wines. Also sells distilled spirits, accessories, gift certificates, and wine-club memberships. There's a blog and a free newsletter.

Web: www.klwines.com
Facebook: K&L Wine Merchants (Page), Fans of K&L Wine Merchants (Group)
Twitter: (None)
LinkedIn: K&L Wine Merchants (Company)

Kendall Jackson Vineyards

Learn about the wines made by this California winery, including the foods they best complement. Here you'll find advice on serving wine and entertaining, and upcoming events featuring Kendall Jackson wines. Join a wine club for monthly wine shipments, buy gifts, or plan a visit to the winery.

Web: www.kj.com
Facebook: Kendall-Jackson (Page), Kendall Jackson Wines (Group)
Twitter: KJWines
LinkedIn: Kendall-Jackson Wine Estates (Company)

Robert Mondavi Winery

Pay a virtual visit to this California winery and read about its history, vineyards, winemaking, and wines. See the winery's art collection and learn about upcoming events and concerts. Shop in the wine shop or join a wine club to receive a shipment of wine each month.

Web: www.robertmondaviwinery.com
Facebook: Robert Mondavi Winery (Page)
Twitter: RMondavi_Winery
LinkedIn: Opus One (Company)

Robert Parker Online

Robert Parker, founder of *The Wine Advocate*, has created "the independent consumer's guide to fine wines" in this site. Most of the site's content is reserved for paying subscribers, but there's plenty of free information too, such as a wine glossary and a retailer search engine. Subscribers get access to a huge database with more than 100,000 *Wine Advocate* tasting notes, wine and food reviews, an archive of articles from the magazine, and more.

Web: http://erobertparker.com/
Facebook: Robert M. Parker (Page)
Twitter: RobertMParkerJr
LinkedIn: (None)

Vinfolio

Vinfolio believes in "fine wine, finer service." Its site offers a wine shop, a virtual wine cellar, services for the wine collector, and blogs and forums for wine lovers.

Web: www.vinfolio.com
Facebook: Vinfolio (Page)
Twitter: Vinfolio
LinkedIn: Vinfolio (Company)

Vinography

Founded by Alder Yarrow in 2003, this blog now features several contributors who write about wine and food, offering wine-related news and reviews from around the world. Received a 2008 American Wine Blog Award for best overall blog.

Web: www.vinography.com
Facebook: (None)
Twitter: vinography
LinkedIn: (None)

West Coast Wine Network 🌿

Here, a community of wine enthusiasts discuss their passion: good wine. Whether you're a newbie or a connoisseur, you're welcome to join the conversation.

Web: www.westcoastwine.net
Facebook: westcoastwine.net (Brad Harrington's West Coast Wine Network) (Group)
Twitter: (None)
LinkedIn: (None)

Winecast 🌿

A podcast and blog featuring wine notes, quick picks, wine-related news, and more.

Web: http://winecast.net/
Facebook: Winecast (Page)
Twitter: winecast
LinkedIn: (None)

Wine.com 🌿

Wine.com is primarily an online store where you can search for and buy wine, as well as gift baskets and other wine-related gifts, or join a monthly wine club. The site's other resources include a Wine Basics section, where you can learn about wine by type or region and get advice about food pairings, serving wine, and entertaining. There's also a Community section where wine lovers can publish reviews and create their own wine lists.

Web: www.wine.com
Facebook: Wine.com (Page)
Twitter: Wine_com
LinkedIn: Wine.com (Company)

Wine Enthusiast Magazine 🌿

The online home of *Wine Enthusiast* has featured articles from the magazine, as well as its own unique content. Check out the wine and spirits ratings and database of award-winning restaurants.

Web: www.winemag.com
Facebook: Wine Enthusiast (Page)
Twitter: WineEnthusiast
LinkedIn: (None)

Wine for Newbies 🌿

A series of more than 75 audio lessons that compose a complete course in wine: tasting, varieties and regions, and other info for anyone who wants to learn how to appreciate wine. There's also a wine blog, a directory of other wine education sites, and a bookstore.

Web: http://winefornewbies.net/
Facebook: Wine For Newbies (Page)
Twitter: WineForNewbies
LinkedIn: (None)

WineLoversPage.com 🌿

The Wine Lover's Page is all about wine appreciation. There's a self-paced wine-tasting course, hundreds of tasting notes, and the *30-Second Wine Advisor*, a free newsletter. Here you'll also find podcasts, forums, and videos.

Web: www.wineloverspage.com
Facebook: WineLoversPage.com (Group)
Twitter: (None)
LinkedIn: (None)

Wine Societies 🌿

This site combines a wine marketplace (where you can auction or sell wine to wholesale or retail buyers) with a social network that lets you connect with other wine lovers; create a profile; post reviews, wine lists, photos, and videos; set up groups; and more.

Web: www.winesocieties.com
Facebook: Wine Societies, Inc. - A unique marketplace and community (Group)
Twitter: WineSocieties
LinkedIn: Wine Societies, Inc. (Company), Wine Societies, Inc. (Group)

7

Wines of Germany 🚫

This site, maintained by the U.S. office of the Deutsches Weininstitut, aims to promote and educate about German wines. Basics include information about the kinds of grapes grown in Germany, how to read a wine label, tasting, wine and health, and so on. There's also travel information, including visiting German wineries and wine festivals.

Web: www.germanwineusa.org
Facebook: (None)
Twitter: WinesofGermany, GermanWineUSA
LinkedIn: (None)

Wine Spectator 🚫

The website of this respected wine magazine offers wine news and ratings, educational resources, blogs, videos, and forums. There are also sections on wine collecting, food and travel, and wine trade news. Much of the site is available only to paying subscribers, but free content includes a daily wine pick, wine basics, and the most recent Top 100 list.

Web: www.winespectator.com
Facebook: Wine Spectator (Page)
Twitter: winespeconline
LinkedIn: (None)

WineZap 🚫

This site says its purpose is to help you "find, price, and compare wines." And that's true. But WineZap is also a place to connect with other wine enthusiasts. When you join, you can create a profile; make friends and send them messages; post reviews, photos, and videos; leave comments on others' posts; join or create a group; and stock your virtual wine cellar.

Web: http://winezap.com/
Facebook: WineZap (Page)
Twitter: WineZap
LinkedIn: (None)

GOING GREEN/ENVIRONMENT

More and more people are realizing that we need to take care of the Earth so that it can sustain our communities, future generations, and the amazing diversity of life that occupies the planet. This chapter provides resources devoted to protecting and preserving the environment. In particular, the big three social media websites—Facebook, Twitter, and LinkedIn—offer access to an untold number of people-supported resources designed to keep this planet alive and healthy.

ANIMAL RESCUE

Animal Rescue, Inc.

Animal Rescue, Inc. finds homes for stray animals in the Baltimore, Maryland–York, Pennsylvania, region. Its website tells you about its facilities and how to volunteer or adopt a pet.

Web: www.animalrescueinc.org
Facebook: Animal Rescue Incorporated (Page), Rescue Me Incorporated (Group), Pets Incorporated (Group)
Twitter: (None)
LinkedIn: SPCA of the Triad, Inc. (Group)

Farm Sanctuary

Farm Sanctuary has two facilities for abused farm animals: one in New York and one in California. The organization works to expose cruel farming practices; it rescues animals and educates people about factory farming and other abusive practices. Read rescue stories, plan a visit, or get involved.

Web: www.farmsanctuary.org
Facebook: All Groups Unite to Stop Animal Cruelty (Group), Farm Sanctuary's Advocacy Campaign Team (Group)
Twitter: FarmSanctuary
LinkedIn: Farm Sanctuary (Group)

Flint Creek Wildlife Rehabilitation

Flint Creek Wildlife Rehabilitation is an Illinois organization that cares for injured and orphaned wildlife, with the goal of returning healthy animals to the wild. Its blog gives news and patient updates.

Web: http://blog.flintcreekwildlife.org/
Facebook: Flint Creek Wildlife Rehabilitation (Page)
Twitter: flintcreek
LinkedIn: (None)

Happy Trails Farm Animal Sanctuary

This Ohio-based organization rescues, cares for, and finds homes for farm animals that have been abandoned, neglected, or abused. Read about featured animals, find an animal to adopt, or learn how you can support Happy Trails.

Web: www.happytrailsfarm.org
Facebook: Happy Trails Farm Animal Sanctuary, Inc. (Page)
Twitter: (None)
LinkedIn: (None)

North Shore Animal League America

North Shore Animal League America, located in Port Washington, New York, claims to be the world's largest no-kill animal shelter, saving an animal's life every 27 minutes. Here you can learn about and support the shelter's work, view animals up for adoption, and get tips on how to care for your pet. Has an online store.

Web: www.nsalamerica.org
Facebook: Stop Cruelty to All Animals NOW! Be a Voice for the Voiceless! (Group)
Twitter: (None)
LinkedIn: (None)

Performing Animal Welfare Society

PAWS protects and offers sanctuary to performing animals, exotic pets, and other wildlife. Its website describes the organization's three sanctuaries, presents news and events, and educates visitors about captive wildlife. Shop in the PAWS shop or support its work with a donation.

Web: www.pawsweb.org
Facebook: No Animals in the Circus (Group)
Twitter: CatWelfareSG
LinkedIn: (None)

BIODIVERSITY

African Biodiversity Network

This organization seeks to protect and promote African biodiversity and traditional cultural practices in the face of growing industrialization. Here you'll find news and information about the organization's priorities, programs, resources, and partners.

Web: www.africanbiodiversity.org
Facebook: Campaign Against Canned Hunting (Group)
Twitter: (None)
LinkedIn: (None)

Biodiversity Economics

This field of study uses economic tools to promote ecology and conservation. The main feature here is a searchable library of biodiversity economics papers; there's also a directory of biodiversity economists and a list of events and conferences.

Web: www.biodiversityeconomics.org
Facebook: 999 It's Time (Group), Green Party (Group)
Twitter: (None)
LinkedIn: Biodiversity Economics and Finance (Group)

Biodiversity Hotspots

Conservation International has created this site to call attention to places around the world where biodiversity is threatened. In addition to news and featured hot spots, the site has these sections: Hotspots Science, Hotspots by Region, and Resources.

Web: www.biodiversityhotspots.org
Facebook: Atlas Atlantic Mediterranean Space (Group), Eco Ventures (Group)
Twitter: (None)
LinkedIn: (None)

Biodiversity Project

With a focus on North America, the Biodiversity Project works to protect, restore, and conserve ecosystems. Read up on biodiversity basics and get information about the project's programs, services, and publications.

Web: www.biodiverse.org
Facebook: Biodiversity Project (Group)
Twitter: (None)
LinkedIn: Biodiversity Heritage Library (Group), National Trust for Nature Conservation (Group), Fauna and Flora International (Group)

Biodiversity Support Program

A program of the World Wildlife Fund, BSP promotes caring for the world's biological diversity. Here you'll find information about BSP's programs and publications.

Web: www.worldwildlife.org/bsp/
Facebook: Strawberry Creek Restoration Program
(Group)
Twitter: (None)
LinkedIn: (None)

Explore Biodiversity

This site was designed by scientist-educators to teach about biodiversity. Watch videos that explain and explore biodiversity, from bacteria and plants to fish and birds to mammals. Also has video podcasts.

Web: www.explorebiodiversity.com
Facebook: Save the Indonesian Forest! (Group)
Twitter: (None)
LinkedIn: (None)

Tropical Biodiversity: The Amazon

Steven Alexander and his wife manage the 261-acre Bosque Santa Lúcia forest reserve in Brazil. On this site, Alexander blogs about the plants and animals of the forest. Lots of good photos.

Web: http://bosque-santa.blogspot.com
Facebook: Save the Amazon (Group)
Twitter: (None)
LinkedIn: Fauna Forever Tambopata (Group)

World Atlas of Biodiversity

This interactive map gives information about endangered and extinct species and shows where biodiversity is at risk.

Web: http://stort.unep-wcmc.org/
imaps/gb2002/book/viewer.htm
Facebook: (None)
Twitter: BIODIVERSITYgrp
LinkedIn: (None)

CONSERVATION AND PRESERVATION

The Conservation Fund

Since 1985, this nonprofit's mission has been "to [protect] America's most important landscapes and waterways for future generations," focusing on wildlife habitats, working farms and forests, community green spaces, and historic sites—more than six million acres in all. Learn about the fund's work, current issues, and how to help.

Web: www.conservationfund.org
Facebook: The Conservation Fund (Page), The Access Fund (Group)
Twitter: (None)
LinkedIn: The Dian Fossey Gorilla Fund International (Group)

Conservation International

Conservation International aims "to protect life on Earth and to demonstrate that human societies will thrive when in balance with nature." The site's Discover section explains about CI and what it does. The Learn section covers important issues such as climate change, land use, protecting oceans, and more; Explore acquaints you with priority areas and conservation regions. Check out the Act and Give sections to get involved.

Web: www.conservation.org/Pages/default.aspx
Facebook: Conservation International (Page), Bat Conservation International (Page), International Water Conservation Day (Group)
Twitter: (None)
LinkedIn: Society for Conservation Biology (Group)

8

Conservation Magazine

Published by the Society for Conservation Biology, *Conservation* magazine reports on current topics and controversies. Read featured stories, browse the archive of past issues, subscribe, and take a virtual tour of the current issue.

Web: www.conservationmagazine.org/
Facebook: Conservation Magazine (Page), Lifescape Magazine (Group), Gabon Magazine (Group), Oceans Magazine (Group)
Twitter: conservationmag
LinkedIn: Water Efficiency Magazine (Group)

Conservation Value Notes

Conservation biologist Jonathan L. Gelbard is founder of the Conservation Value Institute, "whose mission focuses on researching and educating the public in ways to simultaneously solve environmental problems, save money, and improve our health and quality of life." His blog looks at the ways in which a healthier environment can benefit people and communities.

Web: http://conservationvalue.blogspot.com
Facebook: Conservation Value Institute (Group)
Twitter: jongelbard
LinkedIn: Wetlands Watch (Group)

Defenders of Wildlife

As its name suggests, Defenders of Wildlife works to protect wildlife, particularly endangered species. You can read wildlife-related news and fact sheets about wildlife and habitats, as well as information about programs and policies. Learn how to defend wildlife through activism and supporting the organization.

Web: www.defenders.org
Facebook: Defenders of Wildlife (Page), Defenders of Wildlife (Group)
Twitter: (None)
LinkedIn: Defenders of Wildlife (Group)

Earth Day Network

Make every day Earth Day by visiting the Earth Day Network, which promotes environmentalism and year-round action to protect the Earth. Watch environmental videos on Earth Day TV (requires Flash); find out about news, current issues, and events; and get involved as a volunteer or donor.

Web: www.earthday.org
Facebook: Earth Day Network (Page), Earth Day Network (Group)
Twitter: EarthDayNetwork
LinkedIn: (None)

Earth Island Institute

This organization supports grass-roots efforts to conserve, preserve, and protect the environment. Here you can learn about current projects or launch your own. Check out the current issue of *Earth Island Journal*, read the editor's blog, or subscribe online.

Web: www.earthisland.org
Facebook: Earth Island Institute (Group)
Twitter: (None)
LinkedIn: (None)

Earthjustice

Earthjustice believes that "the Earth needs a good lawyer," and this nonprofit, public-interest law firm is providing it. Founded in 1971 as the Sierra Club Legal Defense Fund, Earthjustice works to strengthen and enforce environmental laws. This site explains how Earthjustice works and how you can help.

Web: www.earthjustice.org
Facebook: Earthjustice (Page), Save the Gray Wolves (Group)
Twitter: Earthjustice
LinkedIn: Earthjustice (Group)

Earth-Touch.com

Watch high-definition wildlife videos from around the world. Also has a podcast and blog.

Web: www.earth-touch.com
Facebook: Earth-Touch.com (Group)
Twitter: (None)
LinkedIn: (None)

Ecological Society of America

The ESA is a scientists' organization that promotes ecology, the study of relationships between organisms and their environments. This site offers science and education resources, certification and job information, a directory of certified ecologists, and more.

Web: http://esa.org
Facebook: The Ecological Society of America (Group)
Twitter: Esa_org
LinkedIn: The Ecological Society of America (ESA) (Group)

EcologyFund.com

When you visit EcologyFund.com and click a button, you contribute to preserving land or reducing pollution—and it doesn't cost you a cent. The site's sponsors contribute money to these causes for each click. Come back each day and click again to save more land. Or contribute even more by setting up a free email account (funded through ads) or shopping with the site's sponsors.

Web: www.ecologyfund.com/ecology/_ecology.html
Facebook: Feed a Child with a Click (Group)
Twitter: (None)
LinkedIn: (None)

Ecology Project International

EPI offers field-based educational programs that bring students and scientists together to learn about the environment and promote conservation. Programs exist in Baja California, Costa Rica, the Galapagos Islands, and Montana. Find upcoming courses and download an application.

Web: www.ecologyproject.org
Facebook: Ecology Project International (Group)
Twitter: ecologyproject
LinkedIn: Create Value in Projects (Group)

Environmental Defense Fund

This organization works with businesses, governments, and communities to protect and sustain the environment. Learn about the EDF's work and current projects and find out how you can contribute. Areas of interest include global warming; land, water, and wildlife; oceans; and health.

Web: www.edf.org
Facebook: Environmental Defense Fund (Page), Environmental Defense Fund (Group)
Twitter: EnvDefenseFund
LinkedIn: Environmental Defense Fund (Group)

Environmental Media Fund

The EMF calls itself "a catalyst for solutions." Its mission is to promote environmental issues using film, video, digital and interactive media, media-based educational teaching tools, and special events. Learn about current projects, request EMF assistance with your own project, or make a donation.

Web: www.environmentalmediafund.org
Facebook: EROS Student Organization and Media (Group)
Twitter: acumenfund, World_Wildlife
LinkedIn: Sustainable Industries (Group)

Forest Protection Portal

This site's goal is to protect and conserve forests, working to end deforestation and promote sustainable forest management. Here you'll find news, links, action alerts, and a blog—all related to forest protection.

Web: http://forests.org
Facebook: Ecological Internet (Page)
Twitter: ecointernet
LinkedIn: (None)

8

Invasive Species Blog

If you're concerned about the effects that invasive species have on their non-native environments, check out this blog by Jennifer Forman Orth, Ph.D.

Web: http://invasivespecies.blogspot.com
Facebook: Networkedblogs invasive species weblog (Group)
Twitter: invasivespecies
LinkedIn: (None)

IUCN Red List

The International Union for Conservation of Nature and Natural Resources has put together a list of threatened species around the world. Visit this site to learn about endangered species (including photos) and how to help save them.

Web: www.iucnredlist.org
Facebook: IUCN Red List of Threatened, Endangered, and Extinct Species (Group)
Twitter: (None)
LinkedIn: IUCN Red List Global Amphibian Assessment 1998-Present (Group)

LandScope America

An online guide to natural places in the United States, this site has interactive maps, data, success stories, and plenty of opportunities to get involved.

Web: www.landscope.org
Facebook: LandScope America (Page)
Twitter: (None)
LinkedIn: (None)

Living on Earth

Hosted by Steve Curwood, *Living on Earth* is a weekly radio-show broadcast on more than 300 public radio stations. It features environmental news, interviews, and commentary. On this site you can find out where to tune in or listen to a podcast of the show.

Web: www.loe.org
Facebook: Living on Earth (Page), Living on Earth (Group)
Twitter: (None)
LinkedIn: (None)

Marine Conservation Blog

Multiple contributors from the Marine Conservation Biology Institute write about issues related to protecting our oceans and their creatures.

Web: www.marineconservationblog.blogspot.com
Facebook: Marine Conservation Biology Institute (Page)
Twitter: (None)
LinkedIn: (None)

Mongabay.com

This site gathers conservation and environmental science news, presenting relevant articles in one place. You can read news related to particular topics, such as rainforests; view photos; or explore the kids' pages. Has a blog.

Web: http://news.mongabay.com
Facebook: Mongabay.com (Page)
Twitter: (None)
LinkedIn: (None)

National Audubon Society

The Audubon Society maintains a nationwide network of local chapters and nature centers, promoting scientific and educational programs and advocating for the conservation of natural ecosystems and wildlife habitats, with a focus on birds. Learn about birds and the environment, take action on urgent environmental issues, and find an Audubon chapter or nature center near you.

Web: www.audubon.org
Facebook: National Audubon Society (Group)
Twitter: audubonsociety
LinkedIn: Audubon Society (Group)

National Wildlife Federation

Animals in the wild cannot speak for themselves, and the NWF provides a voice for them, to protect wildlife for future generations. Visit this website to explore the sections Wildlife, Global Warming, Outside in Nature, Magazines, and Shop, or make a donation online.

Web: www.nwf.org
Facebook: National Wildlife Federation (Page), National Wildlife Federation (Group)
Twitter: NWF
LinkedIn: National Wildlife Federation (Group)

Natural Resources Defense Council

The NRDC "works to protect wildlife and wild places and to ensure a healthy environment for all life on earth." Its informative website presents news, current issues, and policy information. There are sections on Green Living and Green Business, as well as videos, podcasts, interactive features, and a blog.

Web: www.nrdc.org
Facebook: NRDC (National Resources Defense Council) (Page), NRDC (National Resources Defense Council) (Group)
Twitter: NRDC
LinkedIn: National Resources Defense Council (NRDC) (Group)

Nature Canada

More than 40,000 individuals and 350 nature organizations belong to Nature Canada. The sections of its site are Connect with Nature, Endangered Species, Bird Conservation, Parks & Protected Areas, and Nature Network.

Web: www.naturecanada.ca
Facebook: Nature Conservancy of Canada (Group)
Twitter: NatureCanada
LinkedIn: (None)

The Nature Conservancy ⬢

Founded in 1951, this conservation group has more than one million members and projects across the United States and around the world. Here you'll find nature-related news and features, information about regions and habitats, podcasts, book reviews, a carbon-footprint calculator, *Nature Conservancy* magazine, an online store, and much more.

Web: www.nature.org
Facebook: Nature Conservancy of Canada (Group)
Twitter: nature_org
LinkedIn: (None)

NatureServe

NatureServe is a network of natural-heritage programs that provide information about rare and endangered species and ecosystems under threat. Visit its site to learn more about its projects and local programs; get animal, ecology, and plant data; or make a donation (join NWF or adopt an animal).

Web: www.natureserve.org
Facebook: (None)
Twitter: natureserve
LinkedIn: (None)

The Ohio Nature Blog

Ecologist and nature photographer Tom Arbour blogs about the natural landscape of Ohio. Lots of photos.

Web: http://hiramtom.blogspot.com
Facebook: Tom Arbour
Twitter: naturedad
LinkedIn: (None)

Save the Whales

Since 1977, this organization has worked to protect whales and other marine mammals through educational programs. You'll find lots of resources about whales, as well as action alerts, membership info, and an online store where you can adopt a whale and buy merchandise.

Web: http://savethewhales.org
Facebook: Save the Whales (Group)
Twitter: savethewhales7
LinkedIn: Pacific Whale Foundation (Group)

8

Sierra Club

From its beginnings in 1892, the Sierra Club has aimed to help people explore and protect the Earth and its wild places. The site offers blogs, up-to-the-minute environmental news, a radio show, and a newsletter. You can learn about the Sierra Club's current environmental initiatives and how to do your part. Join the Sierra Club, book an environmentally friendly trip, or buy merchandise in its online store.

Web: www.sierraclub.org
Facebook: The Sierra Club (Page)
Twitter: sierra_club
LinkedIn: Sierra Club (Group)

Society for Conservation Biology

The SCB is an international professional organization whose mission is to advance the science and practice of conserving the Earth's biological diversity.

Web: www.conbio.org
Facebook: Society for Conservation Biology (Group)
Twitter: (None)
LinkedIn: Society for Conservation Biology (Group)

Student Conservation Association

Creating the next generation of community and conservation leaders, the SCA aims to "inspire lifelong stewardship of our environment and communities by engaging young people in hands-on service to the land." Learn about the SCA's programs, internship opportunities, and how to request help in the field.

Web: www.thesca.org
Facebook: Student Conservation Association (Page), The Student Conservation Association (Group)
Twitter: the_sca
LinkedIn: Student Conservation Association Alumni (Group)

Together Green

Together Green offers an Audubon program designed to provide opportunities that inspire people to help improve environmental health.

Web: www.togethergreen.org
Facebook: Living Green Together (Group)
Twitter: (None)
LinkedIn: Lean and Green (Group)

Wildlife Conservation Society

The Wildlife Conservation Society promotes science, conservation, and education to save wildlife and its habitats. Explore its site to find out about its conservation efforts around the world, educational programs, and publications.

Web: www.wcs.org
Facebook: Wildlife Conservation Society (WCS) (Group)
Twitter: (None)
LinkedIn: The Wildlife Society (Group), Wildlife Conservation Society (Group)

The Wildlife Society

This nonprofit organization focuses on science and education to protect wildlife and its habitats, emphasizing biodiversity, sustainability, and benefits to society. You can learn more about what the Wildlife Society does, check out its publications, and search for a wildlife-related job.

Web: http://joomla.wildlife.org
Facebook: The Wildlife Society (Page), The Wildlife Society (Group)
Twitter: wildlifesociety
LinkedIn: The Wildlife Society (Group)

World Land Trust

This international conservation group preserves the rainforest and other habitats by buying acreage—more than 350,000 acres so far. Learn about current projects and how you can help.

Web: www.worldlandtrust.org
Facebook: World Land Trust-US (Page), Save Rainforest with World Land Trust (Group)
Twitter: worldlandtrust, rainforestforever
LinkedIn: World Land Trust (Wildlife Conservation Organisation) (Group)

World Wildlife Fund

The World Wildlife Fund, with nearly five million international members, works to protect wildlife in 100 countries. This site is packed with resources about wildlife, nature, and conservation, including a searchable database of more than 26,000 species. Read the latest environmental news, view wildlife photos, or get fun stuff like wallpaper, e-cards, and games. Support the WWF by making a donation, shopping in its online store, or booking a trip.

Web: www.worldwildlife.org
Facebook: World Wildlife Fund (Page), World Wildlife Fund (Group)
Twitter: world_wildlife
LinkedIn: World Wildlife Fund (Group)

FAIR TRADE

Co-op America

Co-op America's mission is to "harness economic power…to create a socially just and environmentally sustainable society." Here you can learn about Fair Trade products. The Responsible Shopper guide reveals environmental and employee abuses by companies and makes suggestions on how you can act to curb such abuses.

Web: www.greenamericatoday.org/
Facebook: Co-op America (Group)
Twitter: (None)
LinkedIn: Co-op America (Group)

Fair Trade Certified

TransFair USA certifies fair-trade products, so you can be sure your shopping dollars support earth- and community-friendly businesses. Learn about fair-trade certification and where you can find fair-trade products.

Web: www.transfairusa.org
Facebook: Fair Trade Certified (Page)
Twitter: fairtradeusa
LinkedIn: Friends of Fair Trade Certified (Group)

Fair Trade Federation

A group of businesses and organizations committed to fair trade, this federation promotes fair trade and public awareness of its importance. Here you'll find these sections: Explore Fair Trade, Find Members, Get Involved, and Join Us.

Web: www.fairtradefederation.org
Facebook: Fair Trade Federation (Page)
Twitter: (None)
LinkedIn: The Fair Trade Federation (Group)

Fair Trade Resource Network

Dedicated to promoting the fair-trade movement, this site spells out fair-trade basics, lists news and events, and makes suggestions for taking action. You can also watch videos about fair-trade communities and products.

Web: www.fairtraderesource.org
Facebook: Fair Trade Resource Network (Page), FTRN :::—-> Fair Trade Resource Network (Group)
Twitter: (None)
LinkedIn: (None)

World of Good

In partnership with eBay, World of Good, Inc., has created a community whose members have a shared commitment to socially and environmentally responsible products and shopping. Members can create blogs, contribute articles, and start forum discussions.

Web: http://community.worldofgood.com
Facebook: (None)
Twitter: world_of_good
LinkedIn: (None)

8

GLOBAL WARMING AND CLIMATE CHANGE

DeSmogBlog

The goal of this blog is to convince readers about the reality of climate change and the science that points to it. Here you'll find news and opinions about global warming.

Web: www.desmogblog.com
Facebook: DeSmogBlog (Page)
Twitter: desmogblog
LinkedIn: (None)

Fight Global Warming

This site, sponsored by the Environmental Defense Fund, presents the science behind global warming and examines its impact on the planet. Find out how much your daily habits affect climate change and how you can make a difference. Has a blog, Climate 411.

Web: www.fightglobalwarming.com
Facebook: Fight Global Warming (Group)
Twitter: (None)
LinkedIn: Global Sustainability (Group)

GlobalWarming.org

This site takes a skeptical view of global warming, scrutinizing economics, science, and public debate. You can read news, research, and the Cooler Heads blog.

Web: www.globalwarming.org
Facebook: (None)
Twitter: cooler_heads
LinkedIn: (None)

Global Warming Videos

View videos about global warming, or register to upload your own. The site also has news, articles, and forums on the topic.

Web: www.globalwarmingvideos.org
Facebook: Say No to Global Warming (Group)
Twitter: (None)
LinkedIn: (None)

An Inconvenient Truth

If you saw—or didn't see—Al Gore's 2006 movie about the effects of global warming, take a look at the film's official website. You can learn more about the movie and the DVD, read about the science behind the film, and find out how to take action. There's an educational guide and other goodies to download.

Web: www.climatecrisis.net
Facebook: An Inconvenient Truth (Group)
Twitter: (None)
LinkedIn: Climate Project Canada (Group)

NASA Earth Observatory

View satellite images of Earth and learn about changes to climate and the environment. Sections include Data & Images, Features, News, Reference, Missions, and Experiments. There's also an interactive glossary of science terms.

Web: http://earthobservatory.nasa.gov
Facebook: NASA Earth Observatory (Page, Application)
Twitter: NASA_EO
LinkedIn: (None)

RealClimate

On this blog, working climate scientists write about news and developments in their field. Posts relate strictly to science, steering clear of politics and economics.

Web: www.realclimate.org
Facebook: (None)
Twitter: RealClimate
LinkedIn: (None)

Skeptical Science

This site examines and refutes the arguments of global warming skeptics, based on science.

Web: www.skepticalscience.com
Facebook: Skeptical Science (Page)
Twitter: scepticscience
LinkedIn: (None)

StopGlobalWarming.org

This site offers tips and articles about what you can do to decrease global warming, as well as news, video features, and other resources. You can join more than a million other concerned people in the Stop Global Warming Virtual March, an online petition to reduce carbon emissions.

Web: www.stopglobalwarming.org
Facebook: StopGlobalWarming.org (Page), StopGlobalWarming.org (Group)
Twitter: stopglobalwarm
LinkedIn: (None)

We Can Solve It

This site's philosophy is that by working together, people can put a stop to global warming. Sponsored by the Alliance for Climate Protection, the site presents news, solutions, action alerts, and success stories.

Web: www.wecansolveit.org
Facebook: We Can Solve It (Group, Application)
Twitter: (None)
LinkedIn: Global Economic Crisis (Group)

GOVERNMENT AGENCIES

National Park Service

If you're yearning for open green spaces, consider visiting a national park. The website of the National Park Service lists and profiles parks in all 50 states. You can also learn what the NPS is doing to protect natural resources and ecosystems.

Web: www.nps.gov
Facebook: National Park Service (Page), National Park Service (Group)
Twitter: (None)
LinkedIn: (None)

U.S. Department of Agriculture

Environmentalists will be interested in the section of the USDA's site that's devoted to Natural Resources and the Environment, which has a plants database, a water management center, a live webcam on Mount St. Helens, and more.

Web: www.usda.gov/wps/portal/usdahome
Facebook: U.S. Department of Agriculture (Page)
Twitter: USDAgov
LinkedIn: (None)

U.S. Department of Energy

The Department of Energy's website offers energy-saving tips, news and special features, and information about the DOE and what it does. Sections include Science & Technology, Energy Sources, Energy Efficiency, The Environment, Prices & Trends, National Security, and Safety & Health.

Web: www.energy.gov/
Facebook: Steven Chu (Page)
Twitter: Steven Chu
LinkedIn: (None)

U.S. Environmental Protection Agency

The EPA is charged with protecting both the environment and people's health. The agency's website contains a lot of information: news, programs, and features about environmental issues such as acid rain, climate change, recycling, and wetlands. Read the site's blog or submit a question for an EPA official.

Web: www.epa.gov
Facebook: U.S. Environmental Protection Agency (Page)
Twitter: EPAgov
LinkedIn: (None)

8

U.S. Fish & Wildlife Service

The mission of the Fish & Wildlife Service is to work with others to "conserve, protect, and enhance fish, wildlife, and plants and their habitats for the continuing benefit of the American people." Read about the service's programs, including wildlife refuges and protecting coastal ecosystems.

Web: www.fws.gov
Facebook: U.S. Fish and Wildlife Service (Page), U.S. Fish and Wildlife Service (Group)
Twitter: USFWSHQ
LinkedIn: (None)

GREEN LIVING

Campaign Earth

This site offers a monthly challenge that will help you reduce your ecological footprint for the good of the planet. You can register to receive the monthly challenge via email, read information about global warming and other issues, or make a donation.

Web: www.campaignearth.org
Facebook: Campaign Earth (Group)
Twitter: (None)
LinkedIn: (None)

Care2

When you join this site, you join more than nine million like-minded individuals who want to make the world a better place. Make connections, join environmental groups, sign or start a petition, view and share photos, and get tips on healthy and green living. Visit the Click to Donate section to support your favorite causes with a daily click—for free.

Web: www.care2.com
Facebook: Care2 (Page)
Twitter: Care2
LinkedIn: (None)

EcoMall

This directory lists hundreds of sites with thousands of products for environmentally conscious consumers. Search for a specific product or browse dozens of categories.

Web: www.ecomall.com
Facebook: (None)
Twitter: ecomall
LinkedIn: (None)

GenGreen

GenGreen promotes green living at the local level, helping you find recycling centers, green events and businesses, cooperatives, and Earth-loving people in your area. It also has general tips for green living. When you join GenGreen, you can make connections, create a blog, contribute news and events, join in discussions, and more.

Web: www.gengreenlife.com/
Facebook: GenGreen (Page)
Twitter: GenGreen
LinkedIn: (None)

GreenBiz.com

If you're interested in making your business greener, spend some time on this site, which features articles and how-tos about going green while keeping an eye on the bottom line.

Web: www.greenbiz.com
Facebook: GreenBiz.Com (Page)
Twitter: (None)
LinkedIn: GreenBiz.com—Green Business Professionals (Group)

The Green Guide

Sponsored by the National Geographic Society, the Green Guide offers tips for green living: home, health, fashion, cooking, gardening—it's all here. Check out the buying guide, blogs, and *Green Guide* magazine.

Web: www.thegreenguide.com
Facebook: (None)
Twitter: (None)
LinkedIn: The Gardening Seeds Guide (Group)

Green Home: The Environmental Store

This online retailer specializes in environmentally friendly products, from all-natural clothing and home furnishings to appliances, pest control, and restaurant supplies. If you're looking for green products, start here.

Web: www.greenhome.com
Facebook: Green Home (Page)
Twitter: greenhomey
LinkedIn: Go Green (at home and at work) (Group)

Green Living

Here's an online store specializing in products to make your life greener. Search for a particular product or browse categories such as fair trade, green building, pets, and for the home.

Web: www.green-living.com
Facebook: Green Living (Page)
Twitter: grnlvg
LinkedIn: The-Green-Group.com (Group), Go Green (at home and at work) (Group)

Green Living Ideas

As its name suggests, this site is packed with ideas for environmentally responsible living. Here you'll find articles, GreenTalk Radio podcasts, newsletters, and an online store.

Web: http://greenlivingideas.com
Facebook: Green Living Ideas (Page)
Twitter: GreenLivingIdea
LinkedIn: (None)

Green Living Tips

Articles here offer a wealth of tips for living an Earth-friendly life. Categories include building, business, cleaning, clothing, energy, family, food, gadgets, garden, health, home, pets, repairs, transportation, and water. Read current tips

and submit your own. Has a blog and a newsletter.

Web: www.greenlivingtips.com
Facebook: Green Living Tips (Page)
Twitter: greenlivingtips
LinkedIn: Go Green (at home and at work) (Group)

Grist

Specializing in environmental news and commentary, this site keeps you informed about what's happening with the environment and provides tips and suggestions for going green. The site's blog is called Gristmill.

Web: http://grist.org
Facebook: Grist.org (Page)
Twitter: grist
LinkedIn: Grist (Group)

Planet Green

Planet Green is a television network that provides 24-hour programming on living in an Earth-friendly way. See what's on, watch video clips, play games, or participate in the forums. The site's sections offer green-living tips in these areas: Fashion & Beauty, Food & Health, Home & Garden, Tech & Transport, Travel & Outdoors, and Work & Connect.

Web: http://planetgreen.discovery.com
Facebook: Planet Green (Page), Planet Green (Group)
Twitter: PlanetGreen
LinkedIn: (None)

TreeHugger

There's tons of information here for anyone who wants to take responsibility for a greener, healthier Earth. You'll find news and articles on all aspects of green living, how-to guides, tips on buying green products and gifts, audio and video podcasts, forums, and a whole lot more.

Web: www.treehugger.com
Facebook: TreeHugger (Page), TreeHugger (Group)
Twitter: TreeHugger
LinkedIn: (None)

8

White Apricot

Those who want to be trendy, stylish, and eco-friendly should like this site, which sells fashion, beauty, and lifestyle products.

Web: www.whiteapricot.com
Facebook: White Apricot (Group), White Apricot—Eco & Green Fashion! (Group)
Twitter: (None)
LinkedIn: (None)

NUCLEAR ENERGY AND NUCLEAR WASTE

American Nuclear Society

This society promotes the awareness and understanding of the application of nuclear science and technology.

Web: www.ans.org
Facebook: American Nuclear Society (Page)
Twitter: (None)
LinkedIn: American Nuclear Society (Group)

Nuclear Energy Institute

The NEI is the industry organization for nuclear energy/technology companies. Its site promotes nuclear energy by examining these key issues: Protecting the Environment, Reliable and Affordable Energy, New Plants, Safety and Security, and Nuclear Waste Disposal. Has resources and statistics, as well as breaking news and policy updates.

Web: www.nei.org
Facebook: (None)
Twitter: N_E_I
LinkedIn: (None)

RAINFORESTS

The Nature Conservancy

The Nature Conservancy has gathered video clips and movies that transport you to the world's great rainforests.

Web: www.nature.org/rainforests/explore/video.html
Facebook: The Nature Conservancy (Page)
Twitter: nature_org
LinkedIn: (None)

Rainforest Foundation U.S.

The Rainforest Foundation supports the indigenous people who live in rainforests in their efforts to protect their environment. This site has action alerts, rainforest facts and figures, a section for kids, an online store, and other resources.

Web: www.rainforestfoundation.org
Facebook: Rainforest Foundation US (Page)
Twitter: RainforestUS
LinkedIn: (None)

The Rainforest Site

Help save the world's rainforests with a free daily click. Thanks to the site's sponsors, each click preserves several square feet of rainforest land, with nearly a million square feet protected so far. Buying from sponsors saves even more land.

Web: www.therainforestsite.com/clickToGive/home.faces?siteId=4
Facebook: The Rainforest Site (Page)
Twitter: (None)
LinkedIn: (None)

Rainforest2Reef

The mission of this nonprofit is to protect Mexico's Selva Maya rainforest. Here you can read about the group's current research and projects, join its mailing list, or make a donation.

Web: www.rainforest2reef.org
Facebook: Rainforest2Reef, Inc. (Page)
Twitter: Rainforest2Reef
LinkedIn: Rainforest2Reef: Protecting Standing Forests to Protect Climate Change (Group)

World Rainforest Information Portal

Sponsored by the Rainforest Action Network, this site is an excellent starting point for learning about the world's rainforests. Sections are listed as questions: Why are rainforests important? What's happening in the rainforests? Why are rainforests being destroyed? How are rainforests protected? How can I help?

Web: http://ran.org/
Facebook: Rainforest Action Network (Page)
Twitter: RAN
LinkedIn: (None)

RECYCLING

Californians Against Waste

Founded in 1977, this group is "a non-profit environmental research and advocacy organization that identifies, develops, promotes and monitors policy solutions to pollution and conservation problems posing a threat to public health and the environment." Its site isn't just for Californians—read news, get involved, and learn how to live green. Has a blog.

Web: www.cawrecycles.org
Facebook: Californians Against Waste (Page)
Twitter: cawrecycles
LinkedIn: (None)

Freecycle

Freecycle operates on the idea that one person's junk is another's treasure. When you've got something you want to get rid of, list it on Freecycle, and someone will take it off your hands. Membership is free, and all items posted must be free.

Freecycle has more than 4,500 local groups, so you're sure to find one near you.

Web: www.freecycle.org
Facebook: Freecycle (Group)
Twitter: Freecycle
LinkedIn: Freecycle.org (Group)

Master Composter

Everything you ever wanted to know about composting, from the basics to how to use finished compost. Also has educational resources, a message board, a glossary, and links to local resources.

Web: www.mastercomposter.com
Facebook: (None)
Twitter: MasterComposter
LinkedIn: Master Composter (Group)

RENEWABLE AND ALTERNATIVE ENERGY

AlternativeEnergy.com

There's a world of information here about alternative and renewable energy: news and features, announcements, videos, photos, products, jobs, and more. AlternativeEnergy.com is also a social network of people working to save the planet. When you join, you can create a blog, upload photos and videos, join or create groups, posts stories and announcements, and more.

Web: www.alternativeenergy.com
Facebook: AltEnergy Talk Radio (Group)
Twitter: Alternative Energy.com
LinkedIn: Energy Talk Radio LIVE Networks (Group)

8

Alternative Energy News

Focusing on news and information about renewable energy, this site offers these sections: News, Events, Forums, Photos, DIY (do-it-yourself projects), and a directory of websites for further information.

Web: www.alternative-energy-news.info
Facebook: Alternative Energy (Page)
Twitter: AENews
LinkedIn: (None)

Alternative Energy Store

This site's motto is "making renewable do-able," and it offers the materials and resources to do just that. The store sells renewable-energy merchandise. Beyond that, the site's Learn section offers alternative-energy resources, including articles and how-to videos, and its Community section lets you connect with and learn from others making the switch to alternative energy sources.

Web: http://home.altenergystore.com
Facebook: AltE (Page)
Twitter: AltEStore
LinkedIn: (None)

EnergyPlanet

This directory has links to renewable-energy sites and resources in dozens of categories, from biodiesel and electric cars to hydrogen, solar power, and wind energy.

Web: www.energyplanet.info
Facebook: Energy Planet (Page)
Twitter: (None)
LinkedIn: Renewable Energy Network (Group)

National Center for Appropriate Technology

With projects both local and national in scope, NCAT aims to help people "by championing small-scale, local, and sustainable solutions to reduce poverty, promote healthy communities, and protect natural resources." Learn about NCAT's current and past projects, see what events are coming up at its six regional offices, and check out sustainability resources.

Web: www.ncat.org
Facebook: (None)
Twitter: (None)
LinkedIn: Appropriate Technology (Group)

National Renewable Energy Laboratory

NREL is committed to renewable energy—it even powers its website with electricity from renewable sources. There are lots of resources here: a primer on renewable energy, the science behind emerging technologies, and applying those technologies in the real world.

Web: www.nrel.gov
Facebook: National Renewable Energy Laboratory (Group)
Twitter: NREL
LinkedIn: (None)

8

HEALTH

The Internet is a rich source of health information. Not all of it is accurate or up-to-date, so you will need to use a little critical thinking when analyzing what you find. There are, however, many sites with doctor-approved data on a wide variety of illnesses, injuries, and ailments, as well as information on proactively maintaining health and wellness. And the social media outlets help you connect with those who share in your particular health interests.

ALTERNATIVE MEDICINE

American Botanical Council

News and information for herbalists and the general public. You can sample articles from *HerbalGram*, the American Botanical Council's journal; search for articles (HerbClips) on specific topics; research various herbs (by clicking Healthy Ingredients); and much more.

Web: http://abc.herbalgram.org
Facebook: American Botanical Council (Group)
Twitter: (None)
LinkedIn: (None)

Mayo Clinic: Alternative Medicine

Mayo Clinic offers competent medical advice on complementary and alternative medical treatments. You can explore alternative and complementary treatments by disease, discover the potential benefits of massage and other manipulation and touch therapies, and get the straight story on herbs.

Web: www.mayoclinic.com/health/consumer-health/MY00434/DSECTION=alternative-medicine
Facebook: Mayo Clinic (Page, Group)
Twitter: (None)
LinkedIn: Mayo Clinic (Company), Mayo Clinic Users Group (Group)

Metroactive 🖳

This community is for practitioners of alternative health and medicine, and also for people looking for alternative treatments to help with their health conditions.

Web: www.metroactive.org
Facebook: Healers, Healthcare Providers and Practitioners (Group)
Twitter: (None)
LinkedIn: (None)

CANCER

American Cancer Society

At this site you can choose a cancer type or topic, learn about treatment options, find help and support, access research information and other resources, and learn how to donate and volunteer.

Web: www.cancer.org
Facebook: American Cancer Society (Page, Group)
Twitter: (None)
LinkedIn: American Cancer Society (Company), American Cancer Society Supporter (Group), American Cancer Society Relay For Life (Group), American Cancer Society Group (Group)

Blog for a Cure

At this site, people with cancer can create a free blog to keep their friends and families updated on their treatment and recovery progress.

Web: www.blogforacure.com
Facebook: Blog for a Cure (Page)
Twitter: BlogForaCure
LinkedIn: (None)

CancerCare.org

CancerCare.org is a not-for-profit organization dedicated to dispersing information and providing support services for all those affected by cancer. Learn where to go for financial assistance, drug assistance programs, home care, and hospice alternatives. Discussion forums help you connect with others who are dealing with similar issues and concerns.

Web: www.cancercare.org
Facebook: CancerCare (Page)
Twitter: CancerCare
LinkedIn: CancerCare (Company)

CancerKids

Exceptional electronic support for kids with cancer and their families through personal websites and mailing lists. Provides a place where kids who have cancer can post their own web pages.

Web: www.cancerkids.org
Facebook: Cancerkids (Group)
Twitter: cancerkids_org
LinkedIn: (None)

National Cancer Institute

The National Cancer Institute (NCI) coordinates the U.S. government's cancer research program. NCI's website is for cancer patients, the public, and the mass media; on it, you will find news and information on many of its programs and resources, general cancer information, and news about clinical trials.

Web: www.cancer.gov
Facebook: National Cancer Institute (NCI) (Group)
Twitter: (None)
LinkedIn: National Cancer Institute (Company)

Susan G. Komen for the Cure

A site from the Susan G. Komen Foundation dedicated to detailing research, community projects, and news about breast cancer prevention and control. Find out more about the foundation's popular Race for the Cure running event at this user-friendly site.

Web: www.komen.org
Facebook: Susan G. Komen for the Cure (Page), Susan G. Komen (Group)
Twitter: (None)
LinkedIn: Susan G. Komen for the Cure (Company), Susan G. Komen (For the Cure) (Group)

CHILDREN'S HEALTH

American Academy of Pediatrics

Home of the American Academy of Pediatrics, this site is primarily designed for pediatricians, parents, and child-care workers to keep them informed of the latest healthcare issues related to children.

Web: www.aap.org
Facebook: American Academy of Pediatrics (Page)
Twitter: AmerAcadPeds
LinkedIn: American Academy of Pediatrics (Company, Group)

KidsHealth

Created by the medical experts at the Nemours Foundation, KidsHealth has train loads of information on infections, behavior and emotions, food and fitness, and growing up healthy, as well as cool games and animations! This site is sectioned into three areas for Parents, Kids, and Teens.

Web: http://kidshealth.org
Facebook: KidsHealth (Page)
Twitter: KidsHealth
LinkedIn: Nemours (Company)

Riley Hospital for Children

Located in Indianapolis, Indiana, Riley Hospital for Children is consistently ranked as one of the top children's healthcare facilities in the United States. At this site, you can learn more about the hospital and its pediatricians, find general information about child-care and common childhood diseases, email a patient, and take a virtual tour of the hospital.

Web: www.rileyhospital.org
Facebook: Riley Hospital for Children (Page)
Twitter: RileyHospital
LinkedIn: Clarian Health Partners (Company), Clarian Health (Group)

DEATH AND DYING

Beyond Indigo

Beyond Indigo is a company in Minnesota that provides "grief support, products, and services to individuals and companies who assist people who are grieving." You can share your grief and hardships with others and obtain valuable advice on the message boards, take online quizzes, submit your story of loss, and even post a memorial to your loved one.

Web: www.beyondindigo.com
Facebook: Beyond Indigo (Page)
Twitter: beyondindigo
LinkedIn: (None)

GriefNet 🏅

GriefNet is an Internet community of persons dealing with grief, death, and major loss providing an integrated approach to online grief support. GriefNet is supervised by Cendra Lynn, Ph.D., a clinical grief psychologist, death educator, and traumatologist. The site has a special area for kids who are dealing with the death of a loved one.

Web: http://griefnet.org
Facebook: GriefNet (Page)
Twitter: (None)
LinkedIn: (None)

DENTAL CARE

American Academy of Cosmetic Dentistry

Patients can locate a cosmetic dentist, learn the basics of cosmetic dentistry, and submit a before-and-after image of their smile in the photo gallery. Professionals can learn more about the professional organization's research credentialing information. Reporters can find all the information they need to write their next feature article on cosmetic dentistry.

Web: www.aacd.com
Facebook: American Academy of Cosmetic Dentistry (Page), AACD (American Academy of Cosmetic Dentistry (Group)
Twitter: TheAACD
LinkedIn: American Academy of Cosmetic Dentistry (Company), American Academy of Cosmetic Dentistry (Group)

American Dental Association

This site features a host of resources for dental professionals, including information on DAT (Dental Admissions Testing), a discussion forum, and a calendar of events and meetings. Patients will find a search tool for tracking down an ADA member dentist, games and animations for kids, oral-health education videos, and so on.

Web: www.ada.org
Facebook: American Dental Association (Page)
Twitter: (None)
LinkedIn: American Dental Association (Company, Group)

9

American Dental Hygienists' Association

ADHA is "the largest professional organization representing the interests of dental hygienists," and most of the content at this site is specifically for hygienists, including information about education, careers, continuing education, and membership. Consumers can click the Oral Health Information link in the navigation bar to access articles on oral health. A special area is featured just for kids.

Web: www.adha.org
Facebook: American Dental Hygienists' Association (Page)
Twitter: (None)
LinkedIn: (None)

American Student Dental Association

ASDA is a student organization that more than 87% of all dental students belong to. This group is for networking and sharing of information among its members and the public.

Web: www.asdanet.org
Facebook: American Student Dental Association (ASDA) (Group)
Twitter: (None)
LinkedIn: American Student Dental Association (Group)

DIABETES

ADA: American Diabetes Association

The American Diabetes Association website offers the latest information on diabetes and living with the disease. If you or a loved one suffers from diabetes, make this site your first stop to learning more about the disease and available treatments.

Web: www.diabetes.org
Facebook: American Diabetes Association (Page)
Twitter: (None)
LinkedIn: American Diabetes Association (Company)

Centers for Disease Control and Prevention Diabetes FAQ

The Centers for Disease Control presents this diabetes question-and-answer area, where you can learn what diabetes is, the types of diabetes, common causes, successful treatments, and more. The site also features links to other diabetes pages at CDC and other websites.

Web: www.cdc.gov/diabetes/faq/basics.htm
Facebook: Centers for Disease Control and Prevention (CDC) (Group)
Twitter: (None)
LinkedIn: Centers for Disease Control and Prevention (Company)

Children with Diabetes Online Community

An online community for kids, families, and adults with diabetes, featuring message boards, chat rooms, and questions and answers from medical professionals. Site features a family support network, an area for parents that includes parental humor, a separate section for grandparents, an online booklet on how to deal with diabetes at school, and information on scholarships and financial aid.

Web: www.childrenwithdiabetes.com
Facebook: Children with Diabetes (Page)
Twitter: (None)
LinkedIn: (None)

Diabetes Mine

A "gold mine" of straight talk and encouragement for people living with diabetes, this blog covers a wide range of topics such as drug safety, blood testing, and diet.

Web: www.diabetesmine.com
Facebook: DiabetesMine.com (Page)
Twitter: DiabetesMine
LinkedIn: (None)

Diabetic Gourmet Magazine

Search the recipe archives of *Diabetic Gourmet Magazine* for all diabetic recipes. The site also provides a great resource for additional information on diabetes, including the Diabetes 101 tutorial, tips on healthful living and exercise, and forums where you can communicate with others who suffer from diabetes and related conditions.

Web: http://diabeticgourmet.com/
Facebook: (None)
Twitter: diabeticgourmet
LinkedIn: (None)

dLife Podcasts

These podcasts provide information, inspiration, and connection for people with diabetes, through interviews, advice, and how-tos.

Web: www.dlife.com/dLife/do/ShowContent/dlife_media/downloads/podcasts.html
Facebook: (None)
Twitter: dLife
LinkedIn: dLife (Company), dLife - For Your Diabetes Life (Group)

DIET AND NUTRITION

Diet Blog

This site posts articles from various contributors, all relating to diet and nutrition. Their premise is that the basis of weight management is good nutrition and exercise, and that different things work for different people, so they seek to present a variety of techniques and information. They have a great motto: "The best diet is the one you don't know you're on."

Web: www.diet-blog.com
Facebook: Diet Blog (Page)
Twitter: dietblog
LinkedIn: (None)

Discovery Health Podcasts

From this site you will find links to podcasts of some of the most popular health-related radio shows from the Discovery Health satellite radio channel.

Web: http://health.discovery.com/podcasts/podcast.html
Facebook: Discovery Health (Page)
Twitter: Disc_Health
LinkedIn: (None)

eDiets 🏅

eDiets has a goal of "building a global online diet, fitness, and motivation destination to provide consumers with solutions that help them realize life's full potential." This is an excellent site for learning the basics of popular diets, including the Glycemic Diet, the Eating for Life Plan, and the Mediterranean Diet. Site features a tabbed navigation bar that provides quick access to News, Diet, Fitness, Recipes, Community (support groups, mentors, experts, chat rooms, and success stories), and Help & Support.

Web: www.ediets.com
Facebook: (None)
Twitter: eDiets
LinkedIn: (None)

Nutrition.gov

A new federal resource, this site provides easy access to all online federal government information on nutrition. Obtain government information on nutrition, healthful eating, physical activity, and food safety. Provides accurate scientific information on nutrition and dietary guidance.

Web: www.nutrition.gov
Facebook: (None)
Twitter: Nutrition_gov
LinkedIn: (None)

9

DISABILITIES

DisabilityInfo.gov

Disability.gov is the U. S. government site that functions as a gateway to all information and resources that the government provides on the subject of disabilities.

Web: www.disability.gov
Facebook: Disability.gov (Page)
Twitter: Disabilitygov
LinkedIn: Disability.gov (Group)

LD Online

A source for parents, teachers, and others to obtain information and resources relating to learning disabilities. Learn the basics, go into more depth, or view Dr. Silver's Q&A list. Features a Kids area with some fun activities, as well as a discussion forum and a list of agencies and organizations where you can go for help.

Web: www.ldonline.org
Facebook: LD OnLine (Page)
Twitter: ldonline
LinkedIn: LD OnLine (Group)

Social Security Administration: Disability Benefits

If you have a disability and are a U.S. citizen, you have rights to certain Social Security benefits, including potential disability pay, Medicare, and Medicaid. Here you can find information on the various benefits and links to the forms you need to fill out. If you know someone who's scamming the Social Security Administration, you can visit this site to report them.

Web: www.ssa.gov/disability
Facebook: (None)
Twitter: 1SocialSecurity
LinkedIn: SSA (Company)

Thru Our Eyes

This series of podcasts profiles people from all over the United States on topics specifically of interest to the blind and visually impaired.

Web: www.podcastdirectory.com/podcasts/17541
Facebook: Thru Our Eyes Group (Group)
Twitter: (None)
LinkedIn: (None)

DRUG INFORMATION

FDA: U.S. Food and Drug Administration

The FDA is in charge of testing and approving the manufacture, distribution, and use of pharmaceuticals. Here you can look up information on any medications that have come under the FDA's scrutiny. This is an excellent site to research drug alerts and get the facts about potentially harmful or rumored-to-be-harmful medications and counterfeit medications.

Web: www.fda.gov
Facebook: (None)
Twitter: FDA_Drug_Info
LinkedIn: (None)

The People's Pharmacy Health News Podcasts

Health News Update, with Joe and Terry Graedon, brings you this week's news on home remedies, drugs and pharmacy, the FDA, and general health issues.

Web: www.peoplespharmacy.org/podcast/
Facebook: The People's Pharmacy with Joe and Terry Graedon (Page)
Twitter: PeoplesPharmacy
LinkedIn: (None)

9

EXERCISE AND FITNESS

American Council on Exercise

The American Council on Exercise is the world's largest nonprofit fitness certification and education provider. This site features Health and Fitness Information, including Fit Facts, Health & Fitness Tips, a Fitness Q&A, an Exercise Library, and Healthy Recipes for nutritious meals and snacks. You can also track down local trainers who are ACE certified and shop for ACE apparel, videos, and other merchandise online.

Web: www.acefitness.org
Facebook: American Council on Exercise (Page), American Council on Exercise: Certified Professionals (Group)
Twitter: acefitness
LinkedIn: American Council on Exercise (Company), American Council on Exercise: Certified Professionals (Group)

Fitness Online 🏅

The online home of Weider Productions, Inc., publisher of *Flex*, *Men's Fitness*, *Natural Health*, and other magazines, this site features an incredible wealth of information organized in an easy-to-navigate format. Links to exercise, nutrition, and health lead to articles on each subject. An online trainer, fitness calculators, and forums make this one of the best fitness sites.

Web: www.fitnessonline.com
Facebook: (None)
Twitter: (None)
LinkedIn: Weider Publications (Company)

Kids Walk to School

This site, created by the U. S. Centers for Disease Control and Prevention, encourages kids to walk to school and ride their bikes as part of an exercise program to keep our kids fit. In a time when kids are becoming more and more sedentary, this is just the approach we need.

Web: www.cdc.gov/nccdphp/dnpa/kidswalk
Facebook: (None)
Twitter: (None)
LinkedIn: Centers for Disease Control and Prevention (Company)

Pedestrian and Bicycle Information Center

The Pedestrian and Bicycle Information Center (PBIC) is "a clearinghouse for information about health and safety, engineering, advocacy, education, enforcement, access, and mobility for pedestrians (including transit users) and bicyclists. The PBIC serves anyone interested in pedestrian and bicycle issues, including planners, engineers, private citizens, advocates, educators, police enforcement and the health community." Community leaders and interested citizens can learn specific steps to take to make their communities safe places to walk and bicycle.

Web: www.walkinginfo.org
Facebook: Pedestrian and Bicycle Information Center (Page)
Twitter: (None)
LinkedIn: (None)

9

FIRST AID AND SAFETY

American College of Emergency Physicians

Everything you need to know about preventing emergencies and responding to emergencies when they happen. Find out what you need to pack in a first-aid kit for your home and learn how to prepare an emergency-response plan. The site features a special area for patients and consumers.

Web: www.acep.org
Facebook: American College of Emergency Physicians (Page), American College of Emergency Physicians (ACEP) (Group)
Twitter: (None)
LinkedIn: American College of Emergency Physicians (Company), American College of Emergency Physicians (ACEP) (Group)

First Aid Advice

At this page you can view and listen to various podcasts that explain how to deal with injury and other emergency situations such as heart attacks, shock, wounds and bleeding, and burns and scalds.

Web: www.sja.org.uk/sja/first-aid-advice.aspx
Facebook: St. John Ambulance (Page), FIRST AID (Group)
Twitter: (None)
LinkedIn: St. John Ambulance (Group)

National Safety Council

Information at this site is focused on preventing accidents, such as those involving cars and other machinery. You'll find a phone number you can call to report someone who routinely lets his or her children ride without a seat belt. And you can learn more about preventing injuries from everyday situations, such as using sunblock to reduce the chance of skin cancer.

Web: www.nsc.org
Facebook: National Safety Council (Page, Group)
Twitter: NSCsafety
LinkedIn: National Safety Council (Group)

HEALTHCARE ADMINISTRATION AND MANAGEMENT

American Association of Healthcare Administrative Management

The American Association of Healthcare Administrative Management (AAHAM) is "the premier professional organization in healthcare administrative management," dedicated to the professional development of healthcare administrators. This site offers information about the association and its member benefits, certification programs, job openings, advocacy and networking, and local chapters. If you're in the field of healthcare administration and management, definitely check out this site.

Web: www.aaham.org
Facebook: AAHAM - American Association of Healthcare Administrative Management (Page)
Twitter: (None)
LinkedIn: AAHAM (Group)

American Physical Therapy Association

A national professional organization representing more than 66,000 physical therapists across the nation, this group's goal is "to foster advancements in physical therapy practice, research, and education." A calendar of events, continuing education resources, information about practicing physical therapy, a list of FAQs, and much more make this a valuable site for any physical therapist. Also provides some job leads.

9

Web: www.apta.org
Facebook: American Physical Therapy Association (APTA)
Twitter: (None)
LinkedIn: American Physical Therapy Association
(Company), American Physical Therapy Association (Group)

Institute for Healthcare Improvement

IHI is dedicated to improving healthcare
around the world. This site features
information about IHI's programs, a collection of articles on the hot topics in
the world of healthcare, discussion
groups, tools for connecting with other
healthcare professionals, and tools for
helping you track improvement in your
healthcare business or organization.

Web: www.ihi.org/ihi
Facebook: Institute for Healthcare Improvement (Group)
Twitter: (None)
LinkedIn: IHI (Company), Institute for Healthcare
Improvement (IHI) & Quality Innovators (Group)

Modern Healthcare

Modern Healthcare "is the industry's leading source of healthcare business news."
This service works hard to keep healthcare professionals, especially hospital
administrators, informed about the latest
developments and trends in the healthcare industry so that they can stay ahead
of the curve.

Web: www.modernhealthcare.com
Facebook: Institute for Healthcare Improvement (Group)
Twitter: modrnhealthcr
LinkedIn: Modern Healthcare Magazine (Group)

HEALTH INSURANCE

America's Health Insurance Plans

America's Health Insurance Plans is a
trade organization that represents
approximately 1,300 health-insurance
companies responsible for insuring more
than 200 million Americans. Here you
can learn more about the organization
and access information for members and
consumers.

Web: www.ahip.org
Facebook: (None)
Twitter: (None)
LinkedIn: America's Health Insurance Plans (Company)

eHealthInsurance

When you need to find affordable health
insurance, this is a great place to start
looking. Enter a few pieces of information about where you live and the number of people in your family that you
want to insure, click a button, and imme-
diately receive a long list of quotes from
various health-insurance companies. If
you find a quote that looks like it's in the
ballpark, you can enter additional details
to apply.

Web: www.ehealthinsurance.com
Facebook: eHealthInsurance (Page)
Twitter: HealthInsurnce
LinkedIn: eHealthInsurancePlans (Company)

Facebook: Universal Health Care (Group)

This group is for proponents of a universal healthcare system in the United
States. Members are encouraged to post
news articles, events, and links relating
to progress toward that goal.

Facebook: Universal Health Care (Group)
Twitter: (None)
LinkedIn: (None)

9

HIV/AIDS

Centers for Disease Control and Prevention: HIV

The CDC provides "leadership in helping control the HIV/AIDS epidemic by working with community, state, national, and international partners in surveillance, research, and prevention and evaluation activities." This site acts as an information kiosk for a variety of topics on HIV and AIDS. You can check out the A–Z Index to find information on a specific issue or navigate by categories, such as African Americans, Basic Information, Statistics & Surveillance, Testing, Prevention Programs, Research, Funding, and Women. The site also features questions and answers, brochures, slideshows, software, journal articles, and reports. The home page lists links to the most current articles.

Web: www.cdc.gov/hiv/dhap.htm
Facebook: Centers for Disease Control and Prevention (CDC) (Group)
Twitter: (None)
LinkedIn: Centers for Disease Control and Prevention (Company)

Children with AIDS Project

Children with AIDS Project of America is a publicly supported 501(3) nonprofit organization, providing support, care, and adoption programs for children infected with HIV/AIDS. Find details on services and fees, register to become an adoptive parent, and learn how to help the cause.

Web: www.aidskids.org
Facebook: (None)
Twitter: (None)
LinkedIn: Centers for Disease Control and Prevention (Company)

HIV InSite: Gateway to HIV and AIDS Knowledge

InSite features one of the most comprehensive collections of medical information about HIV/AIDS on the Web. Directed more to healthcare professionals than to the ordinary person, this site is packed with the most current articles and research about HIV/AIDS, including testing and treatments. Healthcare professionals who deal with HIV/AIDS will want to bookmark this site for repeat visits. If you're an HIV/AIDS patient or your loved one has been diagnosed with HIV/AIDS and you want to learn as much about available testing and treatments as possible, you'll find just what you need to begin your in-depth research at this site.

Web: http://hivinsite.ucsf.edu
Facebook: (None)
Twitter: HIVInSite
LinkedIn: (None)

UNAIDS

UNAIDS is the United Nation's AIDS site, where you can learn about AIDS hot spots and find out what the UN is doing to combat the spread of AIDS and assist AIDS survivors. This site features valuable statistics about AIDS around the world.

Web: www.unaids.org
Facebook: UNAIDS (Page)
Twitter: UNAIDS
LinkedIn: UNAIDS (Company), UNAIDS (Group)

9

MEDICAL EDUCATION AND PROFESSIONS

The AAMC's Academic Medicine Website

The Association of American Medical Colleges site lists and provides links to accredited U.S. and Canadian medical schools, major teaching hospitals, and academic and professional societies. It provides the latest information on news and events, includes AAMC publications and information, and presents research and government-relations resources. It also includes information and links to education, research, and healthcare.

Web: www.aamc.org
Facebook: Association of American Medical Colleges (Page)
Twitter: (None)
LinkedIn: AAMC (Company)

BBC Science & Nature: Human Body & Mind

This site takes you on a virtual tour of the human body and mind. You can build your own skeleton, stretch muscles, arrange internal organs, take the senses challenge, play the nervous system game, and much more. The site also explores issues dealing with psychology and the functioning of the human brain.

Web: www.bbc.co.uk/science/humanbody
Facebook: (None)
Twitter: (None)
LinkedIn: BBC Worldwide (Company)

Student Doctor Network

The Student Doctor Network (SDN) is "a nonprofit website, dedicated to the pre-health and health professional student community," whose mission it is to help students select and prepare for various professional careers in health. The site includes plenty of useful resources, but also acts as a forum where professionals and students can meet to exchange information.

Web: www.studentdoctor.net
Facebook: (None)
Twitter: (None)
LinkedIn: The Student Doctor Network (Group)

MEDICAL HISTORY

History of Medicine

Click on the History of Medicine link on the left at this site to get to the goodies. There are nearly 60,000 images, including portraits, pictures of institutions, caricatures, genre scenes, and graphic art in a variety of media, illustrating the social and historical aspects of medicine.

Web: www.nlm.nih.gov
Facebook: National Library of Medicine (NLM) (Page, Group)
Twitter: nlm_newsroom
LinkedIn: National Library of Medicine (Company), Friends of the National Library of Medicine (Group)

Indiana Medical History Museum

The Indiana Medical History Museum, on the campus of Central State Hospital, is where you'll find cool stuff like brains in jars, headless skeletons, and lots of information about medical history into the early twentieth century.

Web: www.imhm.org/
Facebook: Indiana Medical History Museum (Page)
Twitter: imhm
LinkedIn: (None)

9

MEDICAL REFERENCE AND DIAGNOSIS TOOLS

FamilyDoctor.org

Created and maintained by the American Academy of Family Physicians, this site has the basic information you and your doctor need to know about all aspects of adult and child health. There are separate sections for men's and women's health, seniors, healthy living, and parents and kids. Much of the content is also available in Spanish.

Web: http://familydoctor.org
Facebook: familydoctor.org (Page)
Twitter: (None)
LinkedIn: (None)

HealthBoards

This site offers a unique one-stop peer support community with more than 150 message boards on various diseases, conditions, and health topics.

Web: www.healthboards.com
Facebook: (None)
Twitter: healthboards
LinkedIn: (None)

MayoClinic.com

This is the website of the famed Mayo Clinic in Rochester, Minnesota. The site opens with an index of health conditions, a symptom checker, and a first-aid guide to place a virtual medical bag full of tools at your fingertips. Or you can begin your search using the navigation bar at the top of the page, which contains links for Diseases & Conditions, Drugs & Supplements, Treatment Decisions, Healthy Living (articles and tips), Ask a Specialist (Q&A area), and Health Tools (BMI calculator, calorie calculator, self-assessments, and quizzes).

Web: www.mayoclinic.com
Facebook: Mayo Clinic (Page)
Twitter: MayoClinic
LinkedIn: Mayo Clinic (Company)

Medline Plus

Brought to you by the U.S. National Library of Medicine and National Institutes of Health, Medline Plus features articles on more than 700 health-related topics, information on prescription and over-the-counter medications, a health encyclopedia, a medical dictionary, current news stories, a searchable directory of doctors and dentists, interactive tutorials, information on clinical trials, and other information and resources. An excellent site!

Web: www.nlm.nih.gov/medlineplus
Facebook: (None)
Twitter: medlineplus4you
LinkedIn: (None)

National Institutes of Health

The U.S. Department of Health and Human Services National Institutes of Health provides an often-overlooked goldmine of health information for healthcare providers and consumers alike. Here you can find information on the latest proven treatments for various conditions, learn about clinical trials and alternative treatment options, and find health hot lines and prescription-drug information. This site also features information about grants, the latest news and events, scientific resources, and visitor information.

Web: www.nih.gov
Facebook: National Institutes of Health (NIH) (Page)
Twitter: NIHforHealth
LinkedIn: NIH (Company), National Institutes of Health (Company)

NPR: On Health Podcast

From National Public Radio: in-depth reports on medicine, staying healthy, and the major issues surrounding healthcare. The best of *Morning Edition*, *All Things Considered*, and other award-winning NPR programs.

Web: www.npr.org/health
Facebook: (None)
Twitter: NPRHealth
LinkedIn: National Public Radio (Company), NPR Supporters & Listeners (Group)

Sound Medicine Podcast

This is the weekly talk radio show sponsored by the IU School of Medicine and WFYI, the NPR affiliate in Indianapolis, Indiana. It covers various medical and scientific topics, focusing on educating the public.

Web: www.soundmedicine.iu.edu
Facebook: WFYI Indianapolis Public Broadcasting (Page)
Twitter: wfyi
LinkedIn: WFYI (Company)

WebMD 🏅

You'll find articles, news, and tips for improving your health and well-being. Searchable database packed with information, including definitions of diseases, prescription information, and treatments. A comprehensive encyclopedia of health and medicine.

Web: www.webmd.com
Facebook: WebMD (Page)
Twitter: WebMD, WebMD_News, WebMD_Blogs
LinkedIn: WebMD (Company)

MEN'S HEALTH AND ISSUES

CDC: Men's Health

The Centers for Disease Control sponsors this site specifically devoted to men's health and related issues. The site covers men's health issues from A to Z, tips for establishing a healthy lifestyle, a quiz to test your health IQ, statistics, and links to related sites. The What's New area keeps visitors posted concerning the latest developments in the health field that address the most persistent and serious health issues affecting men. Excellent information in a format that makes it easy to find just the information you need.

Web: www.cdc.gov/men/
Facebook: Centers for Disease Control and Prevention (CDC) (Group)
Twitter: (None)
LinkedIn: Centers for Disease Control and Prevention (Company)

Men's Health Network

Men's Health Network (MHN) is a non-profit organization dedicated to keeping men, boys, and families informed about various health issues related to the male population. Physicians, researchers, public-health workers, and other individuals and health professionals contribute to the site. You can find out more about the organization, subscribe to its newsletter, and find links to other helpful sites.

Web: www.menshealthnetwork.org
Facebook: Men's Health Network (Page)
Twitter: MensHlthNetwork
LinkedIn: (None)

9

Men Stuff

An educational website with information on more than 100 topics related to men's issues, such as circumcision, divorce, fathers, and sexuality. Provides a non-judgmental environment where men can learn more about becoming better fathers, husbands, and human beings; find out more about male health issues, including testicular cancer and sexual dysfunction; and stay informed about other current issues relating to male health and well-being. When dealing with just about any issue related to being a man, there's no better site in this category.

Web: www.menstuff.org
Facebook: (None)
Twitter: menstuff
LinkedIn: (None)

MENTAL HEALTH

All in the Mind

This podcast delves into all things mental, including the latest research and expert commentary on our brains and behavior.

Web: www.abc.net.au/rn/allinthemind/default.htm
Facebook: ABC Radio National (Page)
Twitter: RadioNational
LinkedIn: Australian Broadcasting Corporation (Company)

Anxiety Panic Internet Resource

A self-help guide for those suffering from anxiety and/or panic disorders. This site addresses the causes of and treatments for panic attacks, phobias, extreme shyness, obsessive-compulsive behaviors, and generalized anxiety that disrupt the lives of an estimated 15% of the population. If you or someone you love suffers from an anxiety or panic disorder, visit this site for relief and help.

Web: www.algy.com/anxiety
Facebook: tAPir (Group)
Twitter: (None)
LinkedIn: (None)

Asperger and Autism Information

More advanced individuals with Autism, Asperger syndrome, and Pervasive developmental disorder (MAAP) "is a non-profit organization dedicated to providing information and advice to families." You can find the latest information about autism and Asperger's syndrome, locate additional resources near you, check out some free publications, and learn more about your legal rights or the rights of a loved one.

Web: http://aspergersyndrome.org/
Facebook: AspergerSyndrome.org / OASIS @ MAAP
Twitter: (None)
LinkedIn: (None)

Attention Deficit Disorder Association

This extremely comprehensive site on the topic of ADD features a great collection of articles and fact sheets on ADD and attention deficit hyperactivity disorder (ADHD), suggestions on organization and time management, insights and tips on how to deal with workplace issues, specific details about coaching, help with legal issues, and the latest information on current treatments.

Web: www.add.org
Facebook: (None)
Twitter: adultadhd
LinkedIn: (None)

Autism.tv

Cutting-edge site features a collection of podcasts and webcasts dealing with autism, including channels from the DAN! conference, Autism Technology, and Autism Today. Some channels are pay-per-view.

Web: www.autism.tv
Facebook: (None)
Twitter: AutismTV
LinkedIn: (None)

Bipolar World

Bipolar World is dedicated to those who are living with bipolar disorder. This site provides information about bipolar disorder and its treatment and enables visitors to communicate with others who are living with the disorder. Visit this site regularly to obtain late-breaking news about discoveries and treatments, read personal stories, find community support, and learn about legislation that can protect your rights. The site also features chat rooms and discussion forums.

Web: www.bipolarworld.net
Facebook: (None)
Twitter: Bipolarworld
LinkedIn: (None)

International Obsessive-Compulsive Foundation

Learn about the different classifications of OCD and the treatments that have been effective. Find out the causes and symptoms of the disease, as well as how to get help. Find out whom to contact for more information.

Web: www.ocfoundation.org
Facebook: International OCD Foundation (Page)
Twitter: IOCDF
LinkedIn: (None)

National Center for Post-Traumatic Stress Disorder

The National Center for Post-Traumatic Stress Disorder (PTSD) has a mission: "To advance the clinical care and social welfare of U.S. veterans through research, education, and training on PTSD and stress-related disorders." Even if you're not a veteran, you can pick up plenty of useful and current information about traumatic stress disorder.

Web: www.ptsd.va.gov/
Facebook: (None)
Twitter: VA_PTSD_Info
LinkedIn: (None)

National Eating Disorder Association

This site, created and maintained by the National Eating Disorders Association (NEDA), offers information, help, and referrals for those suffering from a wide range of eating disorders, including anorexia, bulimia, and binge eating. It also provides information for those concerned with body image and weight issues. NEDA is the largest nonprofit organization in the United States that focuses on eating disorders.

Web: www.nationaleatingdisorders.org
Facebook: National Eating Disorders Awareness Week (Page)
Twitter: (None)
LinkedIn: (None)

National Institute of Mental Health

The NIMH site provides news about mental health research, reports, and clinical trials, for both mental health professionals and members of the public. Excellent place to visit for late-breaking news and discoveries related to a wide range of mental health issues. Valuable offerings on this site include the publications, which you can download free. Each brochure is packaged as a PDF file that contains the bare essentials of what you need to know to understand a specific mental health disorder, effective treatment options, and the prognosis.

Web: www.nimh.nih.gov
Facebook: National Institute of Mental Health (Page)
Twitter: NIMHgov
LinkedIn: National Institute of Mental Health (Company)

9

National Mental Health Information Center

The SAMHSA National Mental Health Information Center provides information about mental health via toll-free telephone services, an electronic bulletin board, and publications. You can get information about mental health programs including children and family services, suicide prevention, and protection/advocacy programs; check the Newsroom for recent press releases; and explore the Publications library full of free online articles on everything from health administration to youth violence prevention.

Web: http://mentalhealth.samhsa.gov/
Facebook: (None)
Twitter: (None)
LinkedIn: the Friends of SAMHSA (Company)

Obsessive-Compulsive Disorder for Kids

Excellent overview of OCD written specifically to help children understand the disorder. Article describes obsessions and compulsions in an easily digestible format and goes on to explain various available treatments.

Web: http://kidshealth.org/kid/health_problems/learning_problem/ocd.html
Facebook: (None)
Twitter: (None)
LinkedIn: Nemours (Company)

Psych Central

A comprehensive list of mental health disorders along with quizzes, medications, book reviews, and other helpful resources. An excellent place to learn the signs, symptoms, and treatments for a wide range of mental health disorders.

Web: http://psychcentral.com/disorders
Facebook: PsychCentral.com (Page)
Twitter: psychcentral
LinkedIn: (None)

PAIN MANAGEMENT

American Academy of Pain Management

A site for healthcare professionals and consumers suffering from chronic pain, providing both with the opportunity to connect and learn more about pain-management techniques. Consumers can click the Patients link to search the database for a qualified pain-management professional and access a directory of links to other sites that provide more specific information about pain management.

Web: www.aapainmanage.org
Facebook: (None)
Twitter: (None)
LinkedIn: American Academy of Pain Management (Company)

Pain.com

This site offers a world of information on pain, including information about pain products and the companies that make them, pain resources, a collection of original full-text articles on pain and its management by noted pain professionals, and much more. Site offers CME/CPE/CE credit for healthcare professionals.

Web: www.pain.com
Facebook: Pain.com (Page)
Twitter: paindotcom
LinkedIn: (None)

StopPain.org

StopPain.org is dedicated to helping patients alleviate their chronic, nonmalignant pain through all available and effective means, including pain medication, palliative care (in a home, hospital, or hospice setting), psychological interventions (including hypnosis, biofeedback, and psychotherapy), rehabilitative therapies (including physical and occupational therapy), injections, implants, and complementary therapies (including acupuncture and massage). Finding the information you need at this site can be a bit of a challenge, but the site features quality content, including a multimedia library.

Web: www.stoppain.org
Facebook: Beth Israel Deaconess Medical Center (Page)
Twitter: (None)
LinkedIn: Beth Israel Deaconess Medical Center (Company)

SEXUALITY

Kinsey Confidential Podcast 🕸

This podcast provides an opportunity to ask questions and have them answered by experts in sexual health and behavior from the Kinsey Institute at Indiana University.

Web: www.kinseyconfidential.org/podcast/
Facebook: Kinsey Confidential (Page)
Twitter: kinseycon
LinkedIn: (None)

Kinsey Institute

Visit Indiana University, home of the Kinsey Institute, where the sexual revolution of the 1960s found fuel, or at least permission, to begin. Here you can learn about the Kinsey Institute and its services and events, tour the library catalog and the gallery, view publications and other resources, and learn about educational opportunities at the institute.

Web: www.kinseyinstitute.org/index.html
Facebook: The Kinsey Institute for Research in Sex, Gender and Reproduction (Page)
Twitter: kinseyinstitute
LinkedIn: (None)

Nerve.com 🕸

Online magazine that celebrates the beauty and absurdity of sex through thought-provoking and funny articles on various topics relating to human relationships and sexuality. View photographs, read personal essays, check out *Nerve*'s fiction and poetry, check out the personals, get advice, or visit the message boards to view questions and opinions from other fans of *Nerve*.

Web: www.nerve.com
Facebook: Nerve.com (Page)
Twitter: (None)
LinkedIn: Nerve.Com (Company)

Scarleteen

Billed as "sex education for the real world," Scarleteen functions as an information kiosk and sexual myth-buster all in one. Site covers anatomy, safe sex practices, reproduction, infections, sexual politics, and more. The Crisis Hotline area provides excellent information on how to deal with abuse and other crises, and you can shop online for a few essentials, such as Scarleteen T-shirts and undies. Site also features discussion forums.

Web: www.scarleteen.com
Facebook: Scarleteen (Page)
Twitter: Scarleteen
LinkedIn: (None)

SUBSTANCE ABUSE AND RECOVERY

9

Al-Anon

Al-Anon is a self-help recovery program for family and friends of alcoholics. Included here is a program overview and a list of contacts and events. Subscribe to *The Forum*, Al-Anon's monthly magazine, at this site.

Web: www.al-anon.org
Facebook: Al-Anon Blog (Page)
Twitter: (None)
LinkedIn: (None)

Alcoholics Anonymous

From the home page, choose the English, Spanish, or French version of the text, and continue. You'll find 12 questions you can answer to help determine whether AA might be helpful. You'll also find local contact information and a special section for professionals.

Web: www.aa.org
Facebook: (None)
Twitter: AlcoholicsAnony
LinkedIn: (None)

Assistance in Recovery

When someone you love is on the road to self-destruction, you don't have to simply stand by and watch. You can stage an intervention in the hopes of convincing your loved one to get help. Addiction Intervention Resources is "a national organization of professional intervention specialists, counselors, and consultants that provide fast and effective crisis management services through a proven protocol of education, action, and healing." Here you can find out more about the organization and learn how it can help you stage an effective intervention.

Web: www.addictionintervention.com
Facebook: AiR: Assistance in Recovery (Page)
Twitter: (None)
LinkedIn: (None)

Campaign for Tobacco-Free Kids

Information on antitobacco campaigns, including up-to-date special reports on the dangers associated with teen smoking. The site also presents press releases and news items, fact sheets, and information on each state's efforts in the fight against tobacco.

Web: http://tobaccofreekids.org
Facebook: Campaign for Tobacco-Free Kids (Page)
Twitter: (None)
LinkedIn: (None)

D.A.R.E.

This is the home page of the Drug Abuse Resistance Education (D.A.R.E.) organization. It offers information for kids, parents, and educators. Find out how law enforcement is cooperating in your community and elsewhere to stop drug use. This is a family-friendly site.

Web: www.dare.org
Facebook: D.A.R.E. America (Page)
Twitter: DAREAMERICA
LinkedIn: (None)

MUSC Alcohol and Drug Dependency Podcasts

Brought to you by the Medical University of South Carolina, these podcasts deal with issues of alcohol and drug dependency. Topics include the latest alcoholism treatments and marijuana abuse and treatment. From the main page, click By Health Topic and then click Alcohol and Drug Dependency.

Web: www.muschealth.com/multimedia/Podcasts/index.aspx
Facebook: Medical University of South Carolina (MUSC) (Page)
Twitter: (None)
LinkedIn: Medical University of South Carolina (Company)

MySpace: Friends of Bill W.

This group of more than 10,000 members provides support for those who struggle with alcohol addiction.

Web: http://groups.myspace.com/info
Facebook: Gifts for Friends of Bill W. (Application)
Twitter: (None)
LinkedIn: Friends of Bill (Group)

Partnership for a Drug-Free America

A searchable database of drug information makes this site one of the best places to start researching addictions to specific drugs. It also includes answers to frequently asked questions about drugs, a section of advice for parents, and a page specifically directed at teens.

Web: www.drugfree.org
Facebook: The Partnership for a Drug-Free America (Page)
Twitter: (None)
LinkedIn: (None)

Substance Abuse & Mental Health Services Administration

A division of the United States Department of Health and Human Services, SAMHSA offers help for those who are struggling with an addiction or a mental health problem. Upon reaching the opening page, click the I Need Help With… link. This opens a page with links to several tools and resources, including a Treatment Facility Locator, self-tests to determine whether you have a problem, and SAMHSA's National Clearinghouse for Alcohol and Drug Information.

Web: www.samhsa.gov
Facebook: SAMHSA (Page)
Twitter: samhsagov
LinkedIn: (None)

TRAVEL HEALTH

Centers for Disease Control and Prevention: Travelers' Health

Are you planning a trip abroad? Then check out this site before you go, to determine whether you need to be aware of any diseases you may encounter on your trip and recommended vaccines or medicines you should obtain before you leave. Visit the CDC travel site a few months before your planned departure. Some vaccinations require a series of shots over a long period of time to be effective.

Web: www.cdc.gov/travel/
Facebook: Centers for Disease Control and Prevention (CDC) (Group)
Twitter: (None)
LinkedIn: Centers for Disease Control and Prevention (Company)

VITAMINS AND SUPPLEMENTS

MotherNature.com

This site offers a plethora of "natural" products and services aimed at helping you have a healthier lifestyle. You can research health issues, use a Supplement Planner to determine what vitamins are best for you, read customer reviews of products, and purchase vitamins and supplements online. Organic and kosher items are also available, as is information on homeopathy, aromatherapy, sexual health, and pet care. With its huge product line, excellent search tools, and simplified order forms, this site earns its place in the Best of the Best club.

Web: www.mothernature.com
Facebook: MotherNature.com (Page, Group)
Twitter: MotherNatureInc
LinkedIn: (None)

Nature Made

Nature Made is a large manufacturer of vitamin, mineral, and herbal supplements. You can learn about its products, shop online, research various wellness topics, and check out the wellness profile for your sex and age group. You can search products by name, category, and common needs. Find retail stores that carry Nature Made products in your area, and Ask an Expert for advice on health, wellness, nutrition, and vitamins and supplements.

Web: www.naturemade.com
Facebook: Nature Made (Page)
Twitter: NatureMadeVita
Linkedin: (None)

9

WOMEN'S HEALTH

Feminist Women's Health Center

Feminist Women's Health Center is dedicated to building "a world where all women freely make their own decisions regarding their bodies, reproduction, and sexuality—a world where all women can fulfill their own unique potential and live healthy whole lives." This site features information on birth control, abortion, menstrual cycles, breast care, menopause, and other issues specifically related to women's health. Site also features special content for teenagers, a list of clinics and resources, a collection of inspirational poetry and stories, a news and views area, and Q&As.

Web: www.feministcenter.org
Facebook: Feminist Women's Health Center (Page)
Twitter: FWHC
Linkedin: (None)

HealthyWomen

The National Women's Health Resource Center (NWHRC), a nonprofit organization, is "the leading independent health information source for women. NWHRC develops and distributes up-to-date and objective women's health information based on the latest advances in medical research and practice." At this site you will find tool kits for common conditions, nutrition, health, and fitness tips, and many other resources.

Web: www.healthywomen.org
Facebook: HealthyWomen (Page, Group)
Twitter: HealthyWomen
Linkedin: (None)

YOGA

ABC of Yoga

ABC of Yoga "covers a wide range of topics about the different aspects of Yoga such as the various yoga styles, postures, poses, and techniques." The opening page presents sections on Learn Yoga, Travel (yoga vacations), News, Shop, and Community. You can use the tabs that run across the top of the site to navigate to the desired section or use the links below that for more precise navigation. Site covers basics, getting started, different styles, exercises and postures, and much more. You can also find a directory of links to other yoga sites. Very complete and attractively designed site.

Web: www.abc-of-yoga.com
Facebook: Abcof Yoga (Page)
Twitter: abcyoga
Linkedin: (None)

Sivananda Yoga "Om" Page

A clearinghouse for information on yoga and Vedanta. The site has yoga exercise tips, a guide to higher consciousness, and biographies of Swami Vishnu and his guru, Swami Sivananda. From the home page, you can access the Five Points of Yoga and the Four Paths of Yoga for a fairly extensive illustrated guide to positions, exercises, and philosophy.

Web: www.sivananda.org
Facebook: Sivananda Ashram Yoga Ranch (Page)
Twitter: swami_sivananda
Linkedin: (None)

9

Yoga Journal ⬡

Yoga Journal is a magazine, and you can subscribe to it at this site, but this site offers a lot of excellent information free, even if you're not a subscriber. The opening page features a collection of articles from the current issue along with a photo gallery, expert advice, an online poll, and a calendar of events. Near the top of the page is a navigation bar that provides quick access to the many areas of the site, including Basics, Poses, Practice, Health, Wisdom, and Lifestyle. The opening page also offers a Pose Finder, Expert Advice, and a tool for finding yoga classes near you. The site has an attractive design, is easy to navigate, and features excellent content, making it an easy choice for Best of the Best in the Yoga category.

Web: www.yogajournal.com
Facebook: Yoga Journal (Page)
Twitter: Yoga_Journal
Linkedin: Yoga Journal (Company)

9

HOBBIES

No matter how odd or obscure your hobby, you'll find others on the Internet who share it. This chapter lists some of the best sites for some of the more popular/mainstream hobbies, from arts and crafts to creative writing as well as the social media avenues to connect to them.

AMATEUR RADIO

AmateurLogic.TV

This blog and accompanying video clips provide a great source of practical information about amateur radio. There also are interviews, factory tours, and how-to demonstrations.

Web: www.amateurlogic.com/blog/
Facebook: AmateurLogic (Group)
Twitter: amateurlogic
LinkedIn: (None)

ARRL: National Association for Amateur Radio

ARRL is a national association for amateur radio operators, representing more than 150,000 members. You can visit this site to learn more about the organization, access information about classes and exams, and find out about local clubs and hamfests. Site also features news and bulletins, a list of services provided by ARRL, licensing information, and an online store.

Web: www.arrl.org
Facebook: ARRL: National Association for Amateur Radio (Page)
Twitter: arrl
LinkedIn: ARRL (Company)

The DX Zone Forums List

A huge list of amateur radio discussion forums all over the Web.

Web: www.dxzone.com/catalog/Internet_and_Radio/Forums/
Facebook: DXZone.com (Page, Group)
Twitter: dxzone
LinkedIn: (None)

This Week in Amateur Radio

Where better to find podcasts than in a community devoted to amateur audio broadcasting? This site's main feature is a link to a weekly 60-minute podcast on the state of the ham radio community.

Web: www.twiar.org
Facebook: (None)
Twitter: TWIAR
LinkedIn: (None)

ANTIQUES

Antiques Roadshow

Even if you're an inexperienced antiquer, PBS's *Antiques Roadshow* is a great show and website to visit to learn from the experts. The show comes to cities around the country to meet with the locals and appraise their items. The show's experts not only spot the real antiques but also make a point to appraise fake items so that you, the viewer, learn what to look for in your antiquing jaunts. Check out the appraisal contest. You can buy books and videos about antiques through the online store.

Web: www.pbs.org/wgbh/pages/roadshow
Facebook: Antiques Roadshow (Page)
Twitter: RoadshowPBS
LinkedIn: (None)

Beckett Collectibles Online

Specializing in sports cards and memorabilia, this site claims more than 10 million items for sale through a network of dealers. In addition to making purchases and trades, you can learn more about the value of cards and purchase related products, such as binders and books. This site also features a wiki called Beckettpedia, which serves as a free collaborative encyclopedia featuring sports and nonsports collectibles information, created and maintained by site visitors from around the world.

Web: www.beckett.com
Facebook: Beckett Media (Page)
Twitter: beckettmedia
LinkedIn: (None)

GoAntiques

GoAntiques.com offers a searchable index of more than 3,000 quality antiques and collectibles dealers in the United States and other countries. Search by state or country.

Web: www.goantiques.com
Facebook: GoAntiques (Page, Group)
Twitter: (None)
LinkedIn: GoAntiques (Company)

iCollector.com

Bid on items from more than 350 auction houses and dealers worldwide, or search auction-house catalogs for upcoming sales around the world. Search a selection of archived catalogs from auction-house sales since 1994 and find out about dealers and galleries, related associations, and publications.

Web: www.icollector.com
Facebook: iCollector (Page)
Twitter: iCollector
LinkedIn: iCollector.com

TreasureNet

A discussion forum for all aspects of treasure hunting, identification, and restoration. There are sections where you can post snapshots of your finds for others to admire and help identify; learn about clubs in your area; find out how to select and use metal detectors, radar, magnetometers, and other devices; and discuss how to clean and preserve artifacts.

Web: http://forum.treasurenet.com
Facebook: TreasureNet Forums (Page)
Twitter: (None)
LinkedIn: (None)

ART

Absolutearts.com

Absolutearts.com is a blog where you can find criticism and discussions related to contemporary art and philosophy.

Web: http://blog.absolutearts.com
Facebook: absolutearts.com (Page)
Twitter: (None)
LinkedIn: (None)

Facebook: Digital Art, Illustration, Painting, Graphic Design

A place to share your digital illustrations and artistic creations. Both digital and traditional art is welcomed.

Web: www.facebook.com/group.php?gid=2212111981
Facebook: Digital Art, Illustration, Painting, Graphic Design (Group)
Twitter: (None)
LinkedIn: (None)

10

How Magazine's HowDesign.com

This website is the graphic design industry's "trusted source for creative inspiration, business advice, and tools of the trade." Designed with the graphic artist in mind, it is visually appealing and offers a wide range of content, including feature articles and information on design conferences and competitions. There's even an online forum for connecting with other graphic artists, a job bank, and a store where you can subscribe to the magazine.

Web: www.howdesign.com
Facebook: HOW Magazine (Page)
Twitter: HOWBrand
LinkedIn: (None)

BOATING

American Sailing Association

Aspiring sailors will likely find a school near them—no matter where they live—that is staffed by instructors who have earned ASA certification through rigorous training and studies. This site includes a nice forum and information for prospective members.

Web: www.american-sailing.com
Facebook: american sailing association members ONLY (Group)
Twitter: _ASA_
LinkedIn: (None)

Boating Magazine

Boating Magazine provides this website for its subscribers and visitors who are looking for the latest reliable information and advice on purchasing, repairing, and getting the most out of their boats. The site features several sections, including Tests, Boat Doctor, Gear Head, Web Exclusives, and Ultimate Angler. It also features discussion forums and sweepstakes.

Web: www.boatingmag.com
Facebook: Boating Magazine (Page)
Twitter: (None)
LinkedIn: (None)

Boats.com

Looking to buy or sell a boat? Boats.com features tabbed navigation to provide quick access to buying and selling boats, both new and used. You can even apply for financing and insurance online and locate a marina to dock and store your boat. But Boats.com is much more than an online boat store. It also provides news articles, features, reviews, and boating tips, so you can fully enjoy your boating experience.

Web: www.boats.com
Facebook: Boats.com (Page)
Twitter: (None)
LinkedIn: boats.com (Company)

Discover Boating

Discover Boating programs "focus on increasing participation and creating interest in recreational boating by demonstrating the benefits, affordability, and accessibility of the boating lifestyle while helping to educate potential boaters and offering opportunities to experience the fun and togetherness of being on the water on a boat." Content is presented in six sections: Getting Started, Why Boating, Buying a Boat, Activities and Locations, Owning and Operating, and Resources. This site introduces visitors to safe boating practices while showing how to get the most out of your boating adventures. You can also order a free DVD online that introduces you to boating and provides video footage that you can't get at the site.

Web: www.discoverboating.com
Facebook: Discover Boating (Page)
Twitter: discoverboating
LinkedIn: (None)

10

Facebook: Boating and Water Sports Group 📖

Join this group if you are a boater or like watersports such as wakeboarding, tubing, water-skiing, kneeboarding, and so on. A great place to post your pictures!

Web: www.facebook.com/group.php?gid=2204871453
Facebook: Boating and Water Sports Group (Group)
Twitter: (None)
LinkedIn: (None)

Facebook: Sailing Networks

Sailing Networks connects sailors and boaters worldwide. Build your sailing profile, add your boats, and find a crew or a boat to crew on. Keep a logbook of your boating activities and organize your crew for racing or cruising. In this community you can chat and share pictures in the sailing and boating-specific forums and join hundreds of specialist groups.

Web: http://apps.facebook.com/sailingnetworks/
Facebook: Sailing Networks (Application)
Twitter: (None)
LinkedIn: (None)

Yachting Videos

This collection of boat-related videos includes how-tos, explanations of boating rules and regulations, and reviews of new boats and accessories.

Web: www.yachtingmagazine.com/videos.jsp
Facebook: Yachting Magazine (Page)
Twitter: YachtingMag
LinkedIn: (None)

BOOKS

ABE Books

If you're looking for hard-to-find books or collectible books, visit ABE Books online. This site is designed to make it easy to browse or to search for specific titles and authors in the inventories of hundreds of small used booksellers. ABE Books also provides tools for those who have rare books that they want to sell.

Web: www.abebooks.com
Facebook: ABE Books (Page)
Twitter: AbeBooks
LinkedIn: (None)

Audible

If you like to listen to books being read to you as you travel, exercise, or relax, but you don't like to mess with tapes or CDs, check out Audible's collection of downloadable audiobooks. You can download the audio file to your computer and then burn it to a CD, transfer it to an MP3 player or Pocket PC, and then carry the book with you wherever you go. If you become a member, you can download a set number of books every month for a monthly fee. You have 18,000 books to choose from.

Web: www.audible.com
Facebook: Audible.com (Page)
Twitter: (None)
LinkedIn: Audible, Inc. (Company)

BookCrossing

Do you like to share books with others and meet people who love the same books? Then check out BookCrossing, where you can review your favorite books, tag them, release them into the wild, and track their journeys to readers in your community or around the world. When someone finds a book you released, by leaving it somewhere or donating it to a library or another organization, the person can sign on to BookCrossing and report finding the book. If the person enters a journal entry about the book, BookCrossing notifies you by email so that you can read the entry. BookCrossing's goal is to turn the whole world into a great big library.

Web: www.bookcrossing.com
Facebook: Bookcrossing (Page)
Twitter: (None)
LinkedIn: (None)

BookHive

BookHive is designed to help teachers, parents, and kids from reading age to about 12 years old to find quality books and literature. This site is attractive, especially for kids, and includes several valuable features, such as a recommended book list, Zinger Tales (audiobooks), Find a Book (which helps you search for books by category), and Fun Activities (where you can play games online).

Web: www.bookhive.org
Facebook: Charlotte Mecklenburg Library (Page)
Twitter: cmlibrary
LinkedIn: (None)

The Millions

The Millions is a blog that has offered coverage on books, arts, and culture since 2003. It has been featured on NPR and noted by the *New York Times* and the *Village Voice*. Many people contribute book reviews here, and you can search the archives to find out whether a particular book has been reviewed.

Web: www.themillionsblog.com
Facebook: The Official Millions Fan Club (Group)
Twitter: The_Millions
LinkedIn: (None)

NetLibrary

NetLibrary is a collection of electronic versions of books, some of which are available to read free and others of which are available for purchase. After locating an eBook at NetLibrary, visitors have the option of either purchasing or borrowing the eBook. By borrowing an eBook, users have exclusive access to the book during the checkout period. (No one else can borrow the same book unless there are multiple copies.) eBooks are automatically checked back in to the NetLibrary collection when the checkout period expires. Some free eBooks are available in the Reading Room.

Web: www.netlibrary.com
Facebook: NetLibrary EBooks (People)
Twitter: (None)
LinkedIn: (None)

Project Gutenberg

Search the archives of Project Gutenberg to find the 18,000 electronic texts in the public domain that are available free for download. Great collection of classic literature and reference books free!

Web: www.gutenberg.net
Facebook: Project Gutenberg (Page)
Twitter: (None)
LinkedIn: (None)

Readers Read

This blog contains the latest book news, plus excerpts, bestseller lists, and author essays and interviews. You'll find everything here from news about bookstore mergers to reviews and excerpts from newly published bestsellers.

Web: www.readersread.com
Facebook: Readers Read (Page)
Twitter: books
LinkedIn: (None)

CAMPING

American Park Network—Camping

Planning a camping trip to a national park? Check here first for site availability, park activities, fees, and much more. Camping in some national parks requires reservations, and you'll find contact information here. Some park campgrounds are available on a first-come, first-served basis, and this site provides information on how to make sure you get a spot.

Web: www.ohranger.com
Facebook: (None)
Twitter: OhRanger
LinkedIn: (None)

10

Visit Your National Parks

This is an official National Park Service page. Learn about U.S. national parks, pick one that is right for your camping needs, find out what the fees are, and make reservations. This site features a Park Spotlight and a guide to lesser-known parks, along with lots of useful and up-to-date information.

Web: www.nps.gov/parks.html
Facebook: National Park Service (Page)
Twitter: NatlParkService
LinkedIn: (None)

COINS

American Numismatic Association

The ANA, a nonprofit, educational organization chartered by Congress, is dedicated to the collection and study of coins, paper money, tokens, and medals, and was created for the benefit of its members and the numismatic community. The association provides this comprehensive site with links, articles, online exhibits, educational programs, and much more. A special area for young collectors is available, too.

Web: www.money.org
Facebook: American Numismatic Association (Page)
Twitter: (None)
LinkedIn: American Numismatic Association (Company, Group)

CoinLink Numismatic and Rare Coins Index

Large rare-coin index with links to more than 800 numismatic sites. Piles of links to sites dealing with currency exchange, gold prices, ancient coins, statehood quarters, and exonumia (coinlike objects, such as tokens and medals). Sites are rated, providing links to only the best resources.

Web: www.coinlink.com
Facebook: (None)
Twitter: CoinLink
LinkedIn: (None)

CRAFTS

Craftster.org

If you're creative, but paint-by-numbers doesn't do anything for you, check out Craftster.org. Here you can pick up ideas from other craft outlaws who like to think up projects on their own. Most of the projects are accompanied by photographs, so you can get a good look at the finished product. A robust online forum allows you to connect with others who are not inspired by cross-stitched "home sweet home" plaques and wooden boxes with ducks in bonnets painted on them.

Web: www.craftster.org
Facebook: Craftster.org (Group)
Twitter: (None)
LinkedIn: (None)

Craftzine Blog

This blog features craft projects you can do at home with minimal investment, everything from pincushions to baby shoes to sketchbooks to jewelry.

Web: http://blog.craftzine.com/
Facebook: CRAFT Magazine (Page)
Twitter: craft
LinkedIn: (None)

Do-It-Yourself Network

A huge collection of projects complete with step-by-step instructions for the do-it-yourselfer. Projects include everything from creating your own party favors to weatherproofing your home. If you're handy around the house or you just enjoy doing creative projects on your own, you'll find plenty to keep you busy. Click the Crafts link for more information.

Web: www.diynetwork.com
Facebook: DIY Network (Page)
Twitter: DIYNetwork
LinkedIn: (None)

Michael's: The Arts and Crafts Store

At this site, you can get craft tips and new project ideas, find out about upcoming store activities, have fun on the Kids pages, join in the online activities and interactive crafts, find the Michael's store nearest you, or even find investor information. The Kids/Teachers tab features activities, crafts, events, and games that appeal to younger kids.

Web: www.michaels.com
Facebook: (None)
Twitter: (None)
LinkedIn: Michaels Arts and Crafts (Company)

ReadyMade

This site is "for people who like to make stuff." You can find articles from *Ready Made* magazine, along with a store where you can buy plans and kits for many of the projects. ReadyMade can show you how to make everything from posters to your own modular dwelling! Subscribe online, sample the current issue, dig through the archives, read and post messages in the forums, and much more.

Web: www.readymademag.com
Facebook: ReadyMade (Page)
Twitter: ReadyMade Tweets
LinkedIn: (None)

CROCHETING

The Art of Crochet

This YouTube channel features more than 300 videos that show in detail how to perform various crocheting stitches and techniques. Very helpful!

Web: www.youtube.com/user/tjw1963
Facebook: The Art of Crochet by Teresa
Twitter: tjw1963
LinkedIn: (None)

HIKING AND BACKPACKING

American Hiking Society

News and information from an organization dedicated to promoting hiking and establishing, protecting, and maintaining foot trails throughout North America. Sign up to volunteer to help maintain trails, and learn how to take kid-friendly hikes and adventures. All of this and more can be found on this site, which boasts thousands of members nationwide.

Web: www.americanhiking.org
Facebook: American Hiking Society (Page)
Twitter: (None)
LinkedIn: (None)

American Volkssport Association

The American Volkssport Association is a nonprofit group that encourages people to "walk scenic trails at your own pace for fun, fitness, and friendship." AVA has a network of 350 walking clubs that collectively organize more than 3,000 annual walking events in all 50 states. They occasionally organize biking, skiing, and swimming events too.

Web: www.ava.org
Facebook: American Volkssport Association (Group)
Twitter: (None)
LinkedIn: (None)

The Backpacker.com

TheBackpacker.com caters to all levels of backpackers, from those just thinking about it to seasoned veterans. Here, you can find reviews of the latest gear, search for trail reviews by state, learn basic backpacking techniques, find out what you need to pack, and hook up with other backpackers in your area.

10

Web: www.thebackpacker.com
Facebook: The Backpacker.com Forum Facebook Group (Group)
Twitter: (None)
LinkedIn: (None)

Facebook: Mountaineering, Mountain Climbing, Alpine Trekking, Backpacking, and Hiking 📖

For friends of all outdoor activities taking place in the mountains. Here you can exchange experiences, tips, ideas for new destinations and routes, and gear reviews. You can also post pictures and videos of your trips.

Web: www.facebook.com/group.php?gid=2343408030
Facebook: Mountaineering, Mountain Climbing, Alpine Trekking, Backpacking, and Hiking (Group)
Twitter: (None)
LinkedIn: (None)

Trails.com

Founded in 1999, Trails.com is a comprehensive "online planning resource for self-guided outdoor and adventure travel throughout North America." As a result of its partnerships with leading guidebook publishers, this site gives you access—for a small fee—to more than 30,000 trail descriptions covering more than 20 outdoor activities. Additional website features include USGS topographical maps, GPS tools, aerial photos, and much more.

Web: www.trails.com
Facebook: Trails.com (Page)
Twitter: (None)
LinkedIn: (None)

HUNTING

Ducks Unlimited

Home base for the world's leading organization for conserving wetlands and promoting duck hunting.

Web: www.ducks.org
Facebook: Ducks Unlimited, Inc. (Page)
Twitter: DucksUnlimited
LinkedIn: Ducks Unlimited (Company)

Hunting Footage

This site contains more than 1,000 video clips with hunting themes. You can upload your own hunting videos and comment on those uploaded by others.

Web: www.huntingfootage.com
Facebook: HuntingFootage (Group)
Twitter: (None)
LinkedIn: (None)

HuntingLife.com

This blog summarizes hunting- and conservation-related press releases and has guest articles and essays about hunting.

Web: www.huntinglife.com
Facebook: HuntingLife.com (Page)
Twitter: HuntingLife
LinkedIn: (None)

U.S. Fish and Wildlife Service

Dedicated to conserving nature in the United States, this site helps hunters get appropriate permits and learn more about safe hunting. It also aims to teach kids what it means when a species is endangered. Click the Hunting link for a list of frequently asked questions about hunting and how hunters can benefit conservation efforts.

Web: www.fws.gov
Facebook: U.S. Fish and Wildlife Service (Page)
Twitter: USFWSHQ
LinkedIn: US Fish and Wildlife Service (Company)

10

U.S. Sportsmen's Alliance

This is the place to go if you want to get serious about wildlife management and the future of hunting, fishing, and trapping. This is the only organization whose sole mission is the conservation of natural resources. Learn about its mission and how to join.

Web: www.ussportsmen.org
Facebook: U.S. Sportsmen's Alliance (Page)
Twitter: (None)
LinkedIn: (None)

KNITTING

Knitting Help

Grab your knitting needles and yarn and learn a new knitting skill the easy way: by watching! This free series of videos starts you off at the basic level and takes you well into advanced topics. There is an online knitting forum here as well.

Web: www.knittinghelp.com
Facebook: KnittingHelp.com (Page)
Twitter: KnittingHelp
LinkedIn: (None)

Vogue Knitting

Whether you're a novice knitter or an experienced pro who yearns to move beyond knitting stodgy old sweaters and scarves, this site offers everything you need. Click the How To tab for excellent illustrated instructions on how to knit. Click the Magazine tab to learn what the latest edition of *Vogue Knitting* has to offer. Click the Store tab to check out a large selection of books for sale. Site also features links to other knitting sites, Web Exclusives (printable PDF files with instructions and charts for knitting projects), and Corrections (for any erroneous information that happens to end up in one of the books or magazines).

Web: www.vogueknitting.com
Facebook: Vogue Knitting (Page)
Twitter: (None)
LinkedIn: (None)

MODEL TRAINS

Model Railroad Podcast Show

A podcast featuring model train news and reviews, covering everything from model numbers and naming schemes to DVD reviews and historical trivia.

Web: www.modelrailcast.com
Facebook: The Model Railcast Show (Group)
Twitter: (None)
LinkedIn: (None)

National Model Railroad Association

NMRA members built and maintain this site as a service to the model railroading community. Here, you can find a beginner's guide, a railroad track maintenance guide, a robust collection of photographs and illustrations, a scratch-built showcase, NMRA news and calendar, a free screensaver, information about national and regional conventions, a directory of links to other model railroad sites, and much more. The directory of links is impressive and well organized, helping you find just about anything a model railroad enthusiast might need, including manufacturers, layout tours, modeling clubs, and hobby shops.

Web: www.nmra.org
Facebook: National Model Railroad Association (NMRA) (Page)
Twitter: (None)
LinkedIn: (None)

10

PHOTOGRAPHY

Apogee Photo

Dedicated to entertaining and informing photographers of all ages, this site offers high-quality articles and columns about photography. Features basic instructions on taking pictures, techniques for novice and advanced photographers, information about digital imaging, and more. Also provides links to workshops, books, and schools that may be of interest to readers.

Web: www.apogeephoto.com
Facebook: (None)
Twitter: (None)
LinkedIn: Apogee Photo Magazine (Company)

BetterPhoto.com

This excellent source for novice photographers features scads of information about photography basics, plus online workshops that lead you step-by-step through the process of learning new techniques. Created and maintained by Jim Miotke, author of *Absolute Beginner's Guide to Taking Great Pho*tos, this site also provides a Q&A section, discussion forums, and a buyer's guide.

Web: www.betterphoto.com/home.asp
Facebook: BetterPhoto.com (Page, Group)
Twitter: (None)
LinkedIn: BetterPhoto.com (Company)

Luminous Landscape

The Luminous Landscape is the self-proclaimed "most comprehensive site devoted to the art of landscape, nature and documentary photography using digital as well as traditional image processing techniques." It's not commercial, so you won't be inundated with ads. Instead, the site provides more than 2,000 pages of articles, tutorials, product reviews, and actual photographs. This site features excellent information from experienced photographers around the world.

Web: www.luminous-landscape.com
Facebook: The Luminous Landscape (Group)
Twitter: (None)
LinkedIn: (None)

Photography Review

Learn photography skills from fellow photographers, check out product reviews of cameras by consumers and professionals, as well as other photography equipment, and then scan the online swap sheet to find good used gear. The site is "by photographers for photographers," leaning more toward an advanced audience. Content is organized into several areas: Reviews, Shop, Share, and Learn. The Learn area features buying guides, photo lessons, how-tos, and additional links.

Web: www.photographyreview.com
Facebook: PhotographyREVIEW.com (Page)
Twitter: Camera_Review
LinkedIn: (None)

Shutterfly

A picture-management site, where you can upload and share your digital pictures. You can also get prints made of your photos, which you can pick up at any Target store or have them emailed to you; order photo albums, collages, and posters; and enjoy unlimited free picture storage and sharing.

Web: www.shutterfly.com
Facebook: Shutterfly (Page)
Twitter: Shutterfly
LinkedIn: Shutterfly (Company)

QUILTING

McCall's Quilting Magazine

McCall's Quilting is one of the top quilting magazines around. A few minutes at this site proves why. Here you can find settings and a huge collection of tips, current articles, back issues, lessons, bonus patterns, a kids corner, vintage quilt patterns, patterns and instructions for quick quilts, a newsletter you can register to receive via email, and much more. The site also features discussion forums and chat rooms where you can gather with other quilting enthusiasts to share your interests, get help, and ask and answer questions.

Web: www.mccallsquilting.com
Facebook: McCall's Quilting (Page, Group)
Twitter: (None)
LinkedIn: (None)

Planet Patchwork

This comprehensive site for quilters includes reviews of quilting software, books, and products, plus links and excellence awards. Running down the center of the page are links to feature stories. Along the left side of the page is a navigation bar that provides access to specific areas of the site, including Block of the Month, Quilt Gallery, Quilters, Essays, For Beginners, and Techniques. You can also find discussion forums and plenty of links to additional quilting sites.

Web: http://planetpatchwork.com
Facebook: Planet Patchwork (Page)
Twitter: planetpatchwork
LinkedIn: (None)

SEWING

Joann Communities

Joann Fabric and Craft Stores sponsors this online community discussion area. Membership is free, and you can get a variety of information about topics such as fabrics, sewing, quilting, and needle crafts.

Web: http://my.joann.com/
Facebook: Jo-Ann Fabric and Craft Stores (Page)
Twitter: Joanndotcom
LinkedIn: JoAnn(fabric and craft) Stores (Company)

Material Mama Fashion Sewing Podcast

This podcast is about fashion sewing—that is, sewing clothing for your family. It discusses fabrics, ideas, inspiration, machines, and tips.

Web:
www.podcastalley.com/podcast_details.php?pod_id=36798
Facebook: Material Mama Podcast (Page)
Twitter: (None)
LinkedIn: (None)

Threads Videos

An extensive list of free video clips showing how to do various sewing-related activities such as pressing and using decorative stitches, along with reviews of the latest sewing machines and equipment and other interesting news.

Web: www.threadsmagazine.com/videos
Facebook: Threads Magazine (Page)
Twitter: (None)
LinkedIn: (None)

10

STAMPS

American Philatelic Society ⬟

This well-designed site features the American Philatelic Society's journal, a dealer locator, a searchable library catalog, a printable membership application, extensive information on the basics of stamp collecting, and details on its expert service. If you're interested in stamp collecting, whether you are a novice or an expert, bookmark this site and visit it often. This site is packed with the most useful information you'll find on the subject of stamp collecting, making it a sure winner of the Best of the Best designation. There's even a special area where kids can learn the basics of stamp collecting.

Web: www.stamps.org
Facebook: American Philatelic Society (Page)
Twitter: (None)
LinkedIn: (None)

Champion Stamp Company

When you're looking for the latest news and information about the world of stamp collecting, turn to Champion Stamp Company. The opening page has headline news, and you can use the navigation bar on the left to access stamp-collecting basics, show dates and locations, information for clubs, and links to other sites. A solid site for stamp collectors, especially the seasoned veteran.

Web: www.championstamp.com
Facebook: Champion Stamp Co, Inc. (Page)
Twitter: (None)
LinkedIn: (None)

WOODWORKING

Home Construction Improvement

This blog reviews home improvement products including lighting devices, baby room preparation, basement finishing and waterproofing, building a staircase, buying blinds online, and much more.

Web: www.homeconstructionimprovement.com
Facebook: Home Construction Improvement (Page)
Twitter: tfratzel
LinkedIn: (None)

Popular Woodworking

This site is the Internet home of *Popular Woodworking* magazine. Use the navigation bar at the top to jump to your desired area of interest: Articles, Tools & Techniques, Project Plans, Article Index, Blogs, Store, Finishing, and Video. The site also features conference information and other valuable resources.

Web: www.popularwoodworking.com
Facebook: Popular Woodworking (Page), Popular Woodworking Magazine (Group)
Twitter: (None)
LinkedIn: (None)

Rockler Woodworking Blog

The Rockler Woodworking blog is updated regularly with information on Rockler demos and special events, woodworking tips and insights, tool advice, and news on the latest innovations in woodworking equipment and supplies.

Web: www.rockler.com/blog/
Facebook: Rockler Woodworking and Hardware (Page)
Twitter: Rockler
LinkedIn: (None)

WoodNet

This site features woodworking tips, techniques, tool reviews, plans and supplies for woodworkers as provided by the editors of three of the most respected woodworking magazines around: *Woodsmith*, *ShopNotes*, and *Workbench*.

Web: www.woodnet.net
Facebook: WoodNet Forum (Group)
Twitter: (None)
LinkedIn: (None)

WoodWeb

An excellent directory of woodworking websites; it provides links to woodworking information, resources, and products. Everything from adhesives and tools to software is available.

Web: www.woodweb.com
Facebook: WoodWeb - Woodworking Industry Information (Page)
Twitter: (None)
LinkedIn: (None)

WRITING

Authorlink

Authorlink, an award-winning Internet news/information/marketing service for the publishing industry, has been around for several years, which proves its viability. The service provides editors and agents fast access to prescreened professional fiction and nonfiction manuscripts that have been submitted by authors. Readers and writers can quickly order any titles from the secure e-store. These titles are available at major bookstores and online bookstores such as Amazon.com. Authorlink also has its own publishing imprint, Authorlink Press, which offers all the standard services, including electronic press, short-run publishing services, and other services. If you are a writer or just interested in reading a good book, this is the site for you.

Web: www.authorlink.com
Facebook: Authorlink (Group)
Twitter: AuthorInk
LinkedIn: (None)

Children's Writing Supersite

Articles and recommendations for becoming a successful writer for children. Chat with other children's writers and illustrators.

Web: www.write4kids.com
Facebook: Write4Kids.com, The Children's Writing SuperSite (Page)
Twitter: (None)
LinkedIn: (None)

The Write News

This site presents everything you ever wanted to know about the publishing business. An online industry newsletter with more than 1,000 links for writers, agents, and publishers.

Web: http://writenews.com
Facebook: Write News (Page)
Twitter: writenews
LinkedIn: (None)

Writers Write

Find writing jobs, improve your craft, and mingle with fellow authors here.

Web: www.writerswrite.com
Facebook: Writers Write (Page)
Twitter: writerwrite
LinkedIn: (None)

10

HOME

This chapter looks at social media resources for things you might research, buy, sell, or create for your home life. That includes your car, home, gardens, pets, and everything having to do with those things, such as real estate sales, redecorating, remodeling, and maintenance. You will also find resources for managing your financial life here, with sections for taxes, insurance, financial planning, and investing.

AUTOMOBILES

Carfax ⑤

An essential resource for anyone thinking of buying a used car. Enter the car's vehicle identification number (VIN) at the site and find out whether the car has been labeled a lemon, or one with repeated problems. If you like the service, you can look up additional VINs for $34.99 (or $44.99 for five reports).

Web: www.carfax.com
Facebook: CARFAX (Page)
Twitter: (None)
LinkedIn: CARFAX (Company)

CarsDirect.com 🏅

CarsDirect provides essential information for negotiating deals on new cars. It tells you the invoice and retail prices for all new vehicles and all available combinations of options, and recommends a target price based on what cars are selling for in your area. You can also find out about rebates and special offers, and look up used cars in your area.

Web: www.carsdirect.com
Facebook: CarsDirect.com (Page)
Twitter: CarsDirect
LinkedIn: CarsDirect.com (Company)

Edmund's Automobile Buying Guides

The place to go when you're thinking of buying a new or used car. A multitude of information is available, including price guides, dealer cost information, buyer advice and recommendations, recall information, and much more.

Web: www.edmunds.com
Facebook: Edmunds.com (Page)
Twitter: edmunds
LinkedIn: Edmunds.com (Company)

Facebook: Best Cars Around the World 📧

This just-for-fun group is where you can post pictures of cool and exotic cars from around the world and drool over the pictures that others post.

Web: www.facebook.com/group.php?gid=5606196470
Facebook: Best Cars Around the World (Group)
Twitter: (None)
LinkedIn: (None)

Hemmings Motor News

Hemmings Motor News is the authority on classic collector cars. Check out this site for classifieds, upcoming events, and links to museums, dealers, parts locators, and much more.

Web: www.hmn.com
Facebook: Hemmings Motor News (Page)
Twitter: (None)
LinkedIn: Hemmings Motor News (Company)

Howcast Car Maintenance

This series of videos explains how to diagnose basic problems, how to improve your gas mileage, how to find vehicle leaks with an ultraviolet light, and more.

Web: www.howcast.com/categories/218-Car-Maintenance
Facebook: Howcast (Page)
Twitter: (None)
LinkedIn: Howcast Media (Company)

Kelley Blue Book

Before you sell a car or purchase a used car, you should check its "blue book" value, and Kelley Blue Book is the standard nearly all auto dealers use to determine the value of a used car. At this site, you can plug in a few details, including the make, model, and year of the car and its condition, to see the blue book value for yourself. This site is packed with information and tips about buying new and used cars and provides all the tools you need in order to finance and purchase a car online.

Web: www.kbb.com
Facebook: Kelley Blue Book's kbb.com (Page)
Twitter: (None)
LinkedIn: Kelley Blue Book (Company)

BANKING AND PERSONAL FINANCES

Bankrate.com

Whatever financial services you are seeking, you can look here for rate comparisons. You can search for rates on mortgages, auto loans, credit cards, savings accounts, home equity loans, retirement funds, and so on.

Web: www.bankrate.com
Facebook: Bankrate.com (Page)
Twitter: Bankrate
LinkedIn: Bankrate, Inc. (Company)

CNNMoney ⬥BEST⬥

A combined service of CNN and the magazines *Fortune* and *Money*, this site is full of articles, columns, and advice about managing personal wealth, including investments, banking, lending, and borrowing.

Web: http://money.cnn.com/pf/
Facebook: CNNMoney.com (Page)
Twitter: CNNMoney
LinkedIn: CNNMoney.com (Company)

CLEANING AND HOUSEKEEPING

Housekeeping Channel

This site offers a wealth of tips and articles about housekeeping, including a stain-removal wizard, a home and cleaning services finder, and reviews of popular cleaning products.

Web: www.housekeepingchannel.com
Facebook: The Housekeeping Channel (Page)
Twitter: hkchannel
LinkedIn: (None)

DECORATING AND INTERIOR DESIGN

American Society of Interior Designers

An online referral service for the largest organization of professional interior designers in the world. Find information about the organization that has more than 30,000 designers, educators, and media members; more than 7,000 student members; and 3,500 industry foundation members. Learn how designers work, or find the right designer for your project.

Web: www.interiors.org
Facebook: American Society of Interior Designers (Page, Group)
Twitter: ASID
LinkedIn: American Society of Interior Designers (Company, Group)

Better Homes and Gardens

Better Homes and Gardens is much more than simply the online version of the magazine. This site features a huge collection of articles on decorating your home and establishing a beautiful garden, along with an entire box of free tools that can help you select colors and furnishings for a room, settle on a floor plan for your new house or renovation, and design your garden. You'll find slideshows, short video clips, and plenty of photos to spark your imagination and invigorate your enthusiasm for improving your home. The site also features blogs, message boards, and more tips than you can possibly pursue.

Web: www.bhg.com
Facebook: Better Homes and Gardens (Page, Group)
Twitter: BHG
LinkedIn: (None)

The Decorating Diva

This blog covers a variety of decorating and design topics, including trends, colors, environmental health in the home, decorating for holidays, and being eco-friendly.

Web: http://thedecoratingdiva.com
Facebook: The Decorating Diva LLC (Page)
Twitter: Decorating Diva
LinkedIn: (None)

DoItYourself Interior Design

This site helps the do-it-yourselfer get up to speed on interior design by focusing on a room and offering ideas and tips. Site includes several areas, including Decorating for Kids, Design by Room, Designers and Ideas, Holiday Decorating, and Home Accents.

Web: www.doityourself.com/scat/interiordesign
Facebook: Doityourself.com (Page)
Twitter: DoitYourselfcom
LinkedIn: (None)

Facebook: Home Decorating Ideas

Decorating your home can be a very personal and creative experience with the great decorating ideas found in this group. It is open to everyone who loves decor.

Web: www.facebook.com/group.php?gid=4026714670
Facebook: Home Decorating Ideas (Group)
Twitter: (None)
LinkedIn: (None)

ELECTRICAL

DoItYourself.com Electrical Wiring

DoItYourself.com provides useful information on all aspects of home ownership and maintenance. This particular page contains dozens of links to very informative how-to articles on electrical wiring inside your home. Here you can learn the basics and find specific instructions for wiring ceiling fans, dimmer switches, and track lighting. Learn how to use an electrical meter, and much more.

Web: http://doityourself.com/electric/
Facebook: DoItYourself.com (Page)
Twitter: DoitYourselfcom
LinkedIn: (None)

EZ DIY Electricity

This blog answers reader questions about residential electrical wiring projects—everything from dryer connections to ceiling-fan troubleshooting—from a licensed electrical contractor and master electrician.

Web: www.ezdiyelectricity.com
Facebook: EZ DIY Electricity - Residential electrical wiring projects made easy (Page)
Twitter: DIY_Electricity
LinkedIn: Wayne Gilchrist (People)

11

Facebook: How to Buy Green Energy (Electricity) in Your State 📖

Green-energy options exist in many states. By adding what is often a very small surcharge of just a few dollars a month to your utility bill, you can support the alternative-energy industry. This group is targeted at ensuring that everyone is aware that these green-energy options exist.

Web: www.facebook.com/group.php?gid=3489309240
Facebook: How to Buy Green Energy (Electricity) in Your State (Page)
Twitter: (None)
LinkedIn: (None)

HOME BUILDING/ CONSTRUCTION

Construction Resource

Construction-Resource.com provides construction and remodeling information for home owners and sellers, realtors, and builders. You can find articles on construction and remodeling, discussion forums, construction calculators, and other information, tools, and resources to help you with your home-construction and home-improvement projects.

Web: www.construction-resource.com
Facebook: Home Construction Resource (Page)
Twitter: (None)
LinkedIn: (None)

Down Home Radio Show

This radio podcast reports on the newest tips, trends, and topics in the construction industry, in a simple and sincere way. The host invites local and national authorities on home-building products and remodeling topics to join him in sharing their knowledge.

Web: www.downhomeradio.com
Facebook: Down Home Radio Show (Page)
Twitter: (None)
LinkedIn: (None)

HOME REPAIRS AND REMODELING

AC Doctor

AC Doctor is a referral service that can help you track down a qualified heating and air-conditioning technician in your area. However, this site goes far beyond helping you find a qualified technician. It provides beginner's guides that teach you how an air-conditioning or heating system works, includes tips for keeping your heating-and-cooling system running most efficiently, and has articles on how to improve your system's ventilation and filtering. Special area on Energy Savers can help you trim your heating and air-conditioning bills.

Web: www.acdoctor.com
Facebook: AC Doctor (Page)
Twitter: ACDoctor
LinkedIn: (None)

BobVila.com

Bob Vila, host of the popular TV show *This Old House* and *Bob Vila's Home Again,* is almost synonymous with home restoration and improvement projects. Here you can visit Bob and his crew online, check out the TV shows, peruse his how-to library, sample his software design tools, post a question, and even shop for home-improvement tools and products.

Web: www.bobvila.com
Facebook: (None)
Twitter: BobVilacom
LinkedIn: BobVila.com (Company)

DoItYourself.com 🏅

If you know your way around a toolbox and prefer doing your home repairs and remodeling yourself, bookmark DoItYourself.com. Here, you can find all the information you need in order to deal with plumbing, electricity, home decor, and exterior remodeling. This site has an attractive design, plenty of tools to help you find the information you want, and an outstanding collection of instructions, tips, and advice.

Web: www.doityourself.com
Facebook: DoItYourself.com (Page)
Twitter: DoItYourselfcom
LinkedIn: (None)

Home Construction Improvement

This blog reviews home-improvement products, including lighting devices, baby room preparation, basement finishing and waterproofing, building a staircase, buying blinds online, and much more.

Web: www.homeconstructionimprovement.com
Facebook: Home Construction Improvement (Page)
Twitter: tfratzel
LinkedIn: (None)

The Old House

If you've purchased an older fixer-upper, the very first step you should take is to visit The Old House website, where you can find products and suppliers, do-it-yourself guides, feature articles, online forums, and much more. If you're looking for something more in-depth, check out the store for books and how-to videos.

Web: www.oldhouseweb.com
Facebook: OldHouseWeb.com (Page)
Twitter: OldHouseWeb
LinkedIn: (None)

INSURANCE

Insurance Journal

This page links to many video clips and archived broadcasts dealing with insurance and the insurance industry. It is primarily for insurance professionals, but interesting to the consumer as well.

Web: www.insurancejournal.com/broadcasts/
Facebook: Insurance Journal (Page)
Twitter: (None)
LinkedIn: Wells Publishing (Company)

Insure.com

If you're trying to decide which insurer to go with, visit this site first. Insure.com provides free ratings from Standard & Poor's and Duff & Phelps Credit Rating Co. Their ratings will help you evaluate the quality and financial soundness of the insurers you are considering. You'll also find in-depth articles, and insurance tips on auto, homeowners, health, life, and business insurance. Perhaps best of all, this site does not sell insurance and is not owned or operated by an insurance company.

Web: www.insure.com
Facebook: Insure.com (Page)
Twitter: InsureCom
LinkedIn: (None)

InsWeb

Online insurance shopping service. You provide input and receive quotes from various insurers. Comparison shop and choose what suits your needs best. InsWeb compares quotes from more than 15,000 insurance companies to find the most affordable insurance options for you. The site also features a Learning Center that can help you become a more educated shopper.

Web: www.insweb.com
Facebook: InsWeb Corporation (Page)
Twitter: InsWeb
LinkedIn: InsWeb (Company)

11

INVESTING AND RETIREMENT PLANNING

E*Trade

E*Trade is an online trading service geared toward the individual investor. With E*Trade, you can buy and sell securities online for NYSE, AMEX, and NASDAQ. Stock-performance information and company information are available.

Web: www.etrade.com
Facebook: E*TRADE FINANCIAL (Page)
Twitter: (None)
LinkedIn: E*TRADE Financial (Company)

Facebook: Investing, Investments, Investors, and More 🔲

This group is for people who are interested in creating a balanced, diversified portfolio of investments.

Web: www.facebook.com/group.php?gid=15994422059
Facebook: Investing, Investments, Investors, and More… (Page)
Twitter: LaderaFinancial
LinkedIn: (None)

Financial Times

This site is packed with late-breaking business news from around the world. Get the scoop on what OPEC is up to, how the dollar stacks up against the euro, and how business is doing in the Pacific Rim. Excellent reports, commentary, and analysis!

Web: http://news.ft.com/home/us
Facebook: Financial Times (Page, Group)
Twitter: (None)
LinkedIn: Financial Times (Company)

FOLIOfn

FOLIOfn is an online broker that uses a slightly different model for its investors, enabling investors to create a diversified portfolio for less in trading costs. Ready-to-go portfolios allow you to purchase a collection of securities (typically 30 to 50 different securities) for the price of a single trade.

Web: www.folioinvesting.com
Facebook: FOLIOfn (Page)
Twitter: (None)
LinkedIn: FOLIOfn (Company)

Investopedia

Are you thinking about investing? Have you started investing but you really don't feel very comfortable yet? Then check out Investopedia, the online encyclopedia where you can take a tutorial on the basics, move up to more advanced topics, peruse an assortment of investment information and tips, access free tools and calculators, play an investment game, test your knowledge with quizzes, and much more.

Web: www.investopedia.com
Facebook: Investopedia (Page), Investopedia Community (Group)
Twitter: (None)
LinkedIn: Investopedia ULC (Company)

Motley Fool 🅱️

The Motley Fool is a well-known online financial forum originating on America Online. This is the Motley Fool's home on the Web. The Fool provides individual investors with investment tips and advice. The Motley Fool website offers The Fool's School, an online investment guide that is subtitled "13 Steps to Investing Foolishly." When you're ready to start investing "foolishly," visit this Best of the Best site.

Web: www.fool.com
Facebook: The Motley Fool (Page, Group)
Twitter: (None)
LinkedIn: The Motley Fool (Company)

LAWN CARE AND LANDSCAPING

American Lawns

This site is a great resource for anyone looking to improve his or her own lawn. You will find information on the different types of turf, how to deal with weeds, and feature-length articles on all sorts of lawn-care–related topics.

Web: www.american-lawns.com
Facebook: American Lawns (Page)
Twitter: (None)
LinkedIn: (None)

Facebook: I'd Rather Be Gardening 🗐

This group is for the amateur to connoisseur gardener. Members discuss topics such as plants, flowers, shrubs, trees, herbs, vegetables, fruits, and composting.

Web: www.facebook.com/group.php?gid=2894360012
Facebook: I'd rather be gardening! (Page)
Twitter: (None)
LinkedIn: (None)

Facebook: Organic Gardening 101 🗐

This group provides a community for people who are interested in learning about or teaching organic gardening skills. There are also videos available to group members.

Web: www.facebook.com/group.php?gid=2224133069
Facebook: Organic Gardening 101 (Page)
Twitter: (None)
LinkedIn: (None)

Focus on Flowers

Master gardener Moya Andrews shares gardening tips and her fervor for the esthetic of gardens.

Web: http://indianapublicmedia.org/focusonflowers
Facebook: Focus on Flowers (Page)
Twitter: focusonflowers
LinkedIn: (None)

The Gestalt Gardener

Each week gardening expert Felder Rushing talks with professionals and amateurs alike about all aspects of gardening; he shares stories and answers listeners' garden-related questions.

Web: www.mpbonline.org/radio/programs/GestaltGardener/index.htm
Facebook: Mississippi Public Broadcasting (Page)
Twitter: (None)
LinkedIn: (None)

Growing Wisdom

This website has lots of gardening-related video clips, everything from how to plant perennials to how to dress up your home decor with colorful potted plants.

Web: www.growingwisdom.com
Facebook: Growing Wisdom (Page)
Twitter: growingwisdom
LinkedIn: (None)

Landscaping for Energy Efficiency

Are you looking for cost-effective yet eye-pleasing ways to lower your energy bills? This site gives advice on how to plant trees, shrubs, vines, grasses, and hedges for reducing heating and cooling costs, while also bringing other improvements to your community. Reader tips are included.

Web: www.pioneerthinking.com/landscape.html
Facebook: Pioneer Thinking (Page)
Twitter: pioneerthinking
LinkedIn: (None)

11

MORTGAGES AND REAL ESTATE

The Appraisal Institute

This highly regarded group represents real estate appraisers and produces the professionally oriented *Appraisal Journal*. The site provides a number of services to its members and the public, such as the yearly curriculum of courses and seminars, a section on industry news, a bulletin board service, and an online library featuring real estate papers, articles, and publications.

Web: www.appraisalinstitute.org
Facebook: (None)
Twitter: (None)
LinkedIn: Appraisal Institute (Company), Appraisal Institute Membership (Group)

Facebook: Real Estate Investing Network 📖

This group is for people who either currently invest in real estate or have an interest in doing so but don't know how to get started. Many group members are advisors to investors, such as lawyers, accountants, and tax professionals.

Web: www.facebook.com/group.php?gid=4039783099
Facebook: Real Estate Investing Network
Twitter: (None)
LinkedIn: (None)

LendingTree.com

LendingTree.com can fix you up with a great deal on a loan, whether you need money to finance a mortgage, purchase a car, pay tuition, consolidate your debt, or start a business. Just fill out a brief application online, and LendingTree.com provides you with offers from four lenders. LendingTree.com can also help you find homeowner's insurance, an automobile warranty, or a real estate agent. Features some resources that can help make you a more well-informed borrower.

Web: www.lendingtree.com
Facebook: LendingTree (Page)
Twitter: LendingTree
LinkedIn: LendingTree (Company)

MOVING AND RELOCATION SERVICES

ABF U-Pack

This blog, sponsored by www.UPack.com, covers topics such as how to do a self-move, how to rent storage space, how to ship a motorcycle, and how to avoid moving scams.

Web: http://blog.upack.com/
Facebook: ABF U-Pack Moving (Page)
Twitter: ABFUPackMoving
LinkedIn: (None)

Move.com

This multipurpose moving/relocation referral site can help you search for real estate for sale and rental properties, as well as help you find a mortgage, a moving company (self-service, full-service, or truck rental), and more.

Web: www.move.com
Facebook: Move.com (Page)
Twitter: (None)
LinkedIn: Move.com (Company)

PETS

American Kennel Club

Find out more about this organization, read about different breeds, and locate an AKC near you. You'll also enjoy the informational brochures covering everything from boarding your dog to showing your dog. Besides the great graphics layout, the ease of use, and all the information, the site enables you to purchase everything concerning dogs, from books, videos, and apparel to artwork.

Web: www.akc.org
Facebook: American Kennel Club (Page), (AKC) American Kennel Club (Page), American Kennel Club (Group)
Twitter: (None)
LinkedIn: American Kennel Club (Company)

AnimalNetwork

Looking for a magazine about your favorite pet? Check out this site to find magazines for every pet imaginable, from dogs and cats to fish and reptiles. You can even find magazines about horses. Free trial subscriptions available if you subscribe online.

Web: www.animalnetwork.com
Facebook: Animal Network (Group)
Twitter: (None)
LinkedIn: (None)

The AVMA Network

The American Veterinary Medical Association answers questions on pet care, selection, and loss, and how your veterinarian helps you enjoy your pet. The Kids' Korner includes pictures you can print out for your kids to color. Each picture includes an activity or advice on feeding, training, or basic care. This site is extremely attractive, is well organized, and offers a wealth of information.

Web: www.avma.org
Facebook: American Veterinary Medical Association (Page)
Twitter: (None)
LinkedIn: (None)

Cat Fanciers Association

The world's largest purebred cat registry features its top award-winning felines and information on each recognized breed. This site encourages responsible cat ownership and advises how you can show purebred and household pet felines and participate in local CFA cat clubs and shows throughout the world.

Web: www.cfainc.org
Facebook: Cat Fanciers Association (Group)
Twitter: CFAcatlover
LinkedIn: (None)

Dr. Jungle's Pets and Animals Speak

This blog focuses on many types of animals, including exotic birds, fish, reptiles, and amphibians, as well as dogs and cats. There are many pictures and anecdotes on this folksy, personal site—not many press releases or official reports.

Web: http://animal-world.com/newsfeed/
Facebook: (None)
Twitter: drjungle
LinkedIn: (None)

Facebook: Picture Perfect Pets

Want to show off a picture of your pet? Join this group and post it here so others can admire your little darling.

Web: www.facebook.com/group.php?gid=19380163944
Facebook: ~Picture Perfect Pets~ (Page)
Twitter: (None)
LinkedIn: (None)

11

HealthyPet.com

This site, sponsored by the American Animal Hospital Association, enables you to search for an accredited animal hospital; you can also look up conditions and concerns in the Pet Care Library.

Web: www.healthypet.com
Facebook: American Animal Hospital Association (AAHA) (Page)
Twitter: HealthyPet
LinkedIn: (None)

Pet Connection Blog

This blog reports on news and information of interest to veterinary professionals and pet owners, such as dog-food recalls, vaccination studies, infection types, behavior-modification techniques, and animal shelters.

Web: www.petconnection.com/blog/
Facebook: (None)
Twitter: petconnection
LinkedIn: (None)

PetFinder

A large searchable database of animals available for adoption via rescue groups from all over the United States. You can find dogs, cats, and other pets by breed, age, size, gender, and/or location (by ZIP code).

Web: www.petfinder.com
Facebook: Petfinder.com (Page)
Twitter: (None)
LinkedIn: (None)

Pets Need Dental Care, Too

This site, sponsored by Hill's, advises you of dental problems your pet might be experiencing. Dental problems can cause serious health problems in addition to painful tooth loss or gum disease. If your pet is acting strangely or seems to be ill for no apparent reason, you should check out this site.

Web: www.petdental.com
Facebook: Hill's Pet Nutirtion (Page)
Twitter: (None)
LinkedIn: Hill's Pet Nutirtion (Company)

TAXES

H&R Block

Although you'll find plenty of information here to help you get better rates on credit cards, mortgages, and loans, the tax information is the most helpful. Use the Withholding Calculator to figure out how much you should be having taken out of your paycheck. Or find out the status of your refund check. Features tax news and tips, a year-round tax planning guide, a tax calendar, information about new tax laws, a well-stocked library of tax forms and IRS publications, and hundreds of tax-saving tips. Very attractive site, easy to navigate, and packed with great tax information.

Web: www.hrblock.com
Facebook: H&R Block (Page, Group)
Twitter: (None)
LinkedIn: H&R Block Financial Advisors (Company)

IRS: Internal Revenue Service

The IRS site provides everything you need in order to become an informed taxpayer. Search the site for specific information or for downloadable, printable tax forms you might have trouble finding at your local post office or library. The site also provides news about the IRS and tax legislation, along with information specifically for individuals, businesses, nonprofit organizations, and tax professionals. Learn about the earned income tax credit, tax scams and frauds, and your rights as a taxpayer.

Web: www.irs.gov
Facebook: (None)
Twitter: IRSnews
LinkedIn: (None)

11

TaxFoundation.org

Dedicated to translating the overly complex and cryptic income tax code into something the ordinary taxpayer can understand, TaxFoundation.org publishes reports that explain in plain English what taxpayers need to know. The foundation also answers tax questions from individuals and the media and features headline tax news and commentary.

Web: www.taxfoundation.org
Facebook: Tax Foundation (Page)
Twitter: taxfoundation
LinkedIn: (None)

Tax Policy Blog

This blog is sponsored by the Tax Foundation, a nonpartisan, nonprofit research organization that monitors tax policy. They regularly post links and press releases from authoritative sources, including the *Wall Street Journal*, and often provide expert commentary on the stories to explain what they mean to the taxpayer.

Web: www.taxfoundation.org/blog
Facebook: (None)
Twitter: taxfoundation
LinkedIn: (None)

11

RELIGION/PHILOSOPHY

Whether you are a spiritual seeker or are firm in your current beliefs, social media is a rich source of information and community. This chapter points you to social media resources for many of the most popular world religions, including explanations of their core tenets, discussion groups and communities for people who have questions.

RELIGION AND SPIRITUALITY: GENERAL

Beliefnet 🏆

Nonsectarian religious site devoted to keeping believers and nonbelievers informed about their beliefs. Covers everything from atheism and Christianity to earth-based (pagan) religions. Additional sections explore the link between religions and marriage, sexuality, politics, and the like. Take online quizzes, check out the message boards, or join a meditation or prayer group online.

Web: http://beliefnet.com/
Facebook: beliefnet (Page)
Twitter: beliefnet
LinkedIn: (None)

Heroes of Faith

This site, which promotes no specific religion, features founders of the world's great religions along with individuals whose words and deeds qualify them to be considered heroes of faith.

Web: www.myhero.com/faith/faith_content.asp
Facebook: The MY HERO Project (Group)
Twitter: myhero
LinkedIn: The MY HERO Project (Company)

Learn Out Loud: Religion and Spirituality Free Audio and Video

At this site you can download free audio and video recordings of various spiritual leaders and messages, including Billy Graham sermons, the Bhagavad Gita, the King James Bible, Jewish History lectures, and New Age guided meditations.

Web: www.learnoutloud.com/Free-Audio-Video/Religion-and-Spirituality
Facebook: learnOutLoud.com (Page)
Twitter: (None)
LinkedIn: (None)

Religion in American History

This is a group blog to foster discussion and share research, insights, reviews, observations, syllabi, links, new books, project information, grant opportunities, seminars, lectures, and thoughts about religion in American history and American religious history.

Web: http://usreligion.blogspot.com/
Facebook: Religion in American History (Page)
Twitter: (None)
LinkedIn: (None)

Religion News Service

The Religion News Service provides a daily newsletter featuring unbiased coverage of religion, ethics, and spiritual issues from a secular viewpoint.

Web: www.religionnews.com
Facebook: Religion News Service (Page)
Twitter: (None)
LinkedIn: (None)

The Revealer

This blog is a well-written daily review of religion and the press. It has three sections: Today (news that is relevant right now), Timely (news that has a short shelf life), and Timeless (news that doesn't go out-of-date).

Web: www.therevealer.org
Facebook: The Revealer (Page)
Twitter: the_revealer
LinkedIn: (None)

ATHEISM AND HUMANISM

American Atheists

Information about atheism, separation of church and state, legal battles, school prayer, and biblical contradictions. Features an online store, a magazine, and plenty of up-to-date news articles on legislation and events related to atheism in the United States.

Web: www.atheists.org
Facebook: American Atheists (Page)
Twitter: American Atheists, atheists_org
LinkedIn: (None)

Atheist Alliance International

Reach out to other atheists through this site, which aims to educate the public about the dangers of authoritarian religions through articles, books, links to other websites, and reference material.

Web: www.atheistalliance.org
Facebook: Atheist Alliance International (Page, Group)
Twitter: (None)
LinkedIn: (None)

Atheist Revolution

This blog's motto is "breaking free from irrational belief and opposing Christian extremism in America." The author reports atheist-positive news stories, provides commentary on current events, and critiques religious activity in the public sphere as it affects United States citizens.

Web: www.atheistrev.com
Facebook: (none)
Twitter: vjack
LinkedIn: (None)

ExChristian.net

This online community, which includes blogs, galleries, chat, and forums, offers commentary and support for people who are currently atheist but were formerly Christian.

Web: http://exchristian.net/
Facebook: ExChristian.net (Page), ExChristian.net - encouraging ex-christians (Group)
Twitter: exchristian_net
LinkedIn: (None)

Freethought & Rationalism Discussion Board

A well-run, popular discussion board with sections such as the existence of God, biblical criticism, evolution, science, moral foundations, social theory, and church/state separation.

Web: http://www.freeratio.org/
Facebook: FRDB (Freethought & Rationalism) (Group)
Twitter: FRDB
LinkedIn: (None)

Humanist Network News Podcast

The Humanist Network News podcast is the official podcast of the American Humanist Association, the oldest and largest humanist association in the United States.

Web: http://www.americanhumanist.org/hnn/podcast/
Facebook: (None)
Twitter: americnhumanist
LinkedIn: American Humanist Association (Company, Group)

12

BAHA'I

The Baha'i Faith

This is the official site of the Baha'i International Community. You can access a Baha'i news service, download materials from a media bank, and access selected writings and discussions about Baha'i.

Web: www.bahai.org
Facebook: Bahai Forums (Page)
Twitter: (None)
LinkedIn: (None)

Baha'i Faith: Religion Renewed for a Changing World

This site is focused primarily on the United States Baha'i faith community. It provides a clear explanation of Baha'i beliefs and describes social action and education opportunities available to the Baha'i community.

Web: www.bahai.us
Facebook: Bahai Forums (Page)
Twitter: BahaiUS
LinkedIn: (None)

BUDDHISM

Feringhee: the India Diaries

The word *feringhee* is Hindi/Urdu meaning foreigner, outsider, or westerner. In this blog, an American dancer trained in the ancient Buddhist temple dance style of Bharatanatyam follows the Dalai Lama throughout India. "Why do people go to India to find themselves? India is where you go to lose yourself."

Web: www.sirensongs.blogspot.com
Facebook: (None)
Twitter: sirensongs
LinkedIn: (None)

Tricycle: The Buddhist Review

Tricycle: The Buddhist Review is America's leading Buddhist magazine, a publication intended to express Buddhist perspectives and practices to Western cultures. Here you can find an excellent collection of articles from the magazine, along with blogs, audio teachings, discussion forums, personals, classifieds, and links to related sites.

Web: www.tricycle.com
Facebook: Tricycle: The Buddhist Review (Page)
Twitter: tricyclemag
LinkedIn: Tricycle Magazine (Company)

CHRISTIANITY

Bible Gateway

This award-winning site provides a search form for the Bible and handles many common translations. You can conduct searches and output verses in French, German, Swedish, Spanish, Tagalog, Latin, English, among others. Also features audio versions of the Bible and its many passages, both Old and New Testaments.

Web: www.biblegateway.com
Facebook: Bible Gateway (Page)
Twitter: biblegateway
LinkedIn: (None)

Catholic Online

Bills itself as the "world's largest and most comprehensive Roman Catholic information service," and upon visiting this site, we would have to agree. This site provides a huge collection of current articles, along with message centers, forums, and research materials related to Roman Catholicism. You'll also find information about Catholic organizations, dioceses and archdioceses, publications, software, and doctrines.

12

Web: www.catholic.org
Facebook: Catholic Online (Page)
Twitter: catholiconline
LinkedIn: (None)

Christian Articles Archive

Contains articles for Christian newsletters, religious periodicals, brochures, and sermon illustrations. Also provides information about using Internet email conferencing for Christian teaching and discipleship.

Web: www.joyfulheart.com
Facebook: Joyful Heart Renewal Ministries (Page)
Twitter: PastorRalph
LinkedIn: (None)

Crosswalk.com 🏅

Crosswalk offers Christians access to a directory of more than 20,000 Christian sites, news, information, Bible study tools, chat and discussion forums, a Bible search directory, and much more. But there's also a community to join and entertainment to be had here through the learning and sharing that takes place.

Web: www.crosswalk.com
Facebook: Crosswalk.com (Page)
Twitter: crosswalk_com
LinkedIn: (None)

89.7 Power FM: The Christian Rock Station

You can listen to this Dallas-based FM radio station free on the Web and discuss Christian music on the accompanying bulletin board/forum.

Web: www.897powerfm.com
Facebook: Power FM (Page)
Twitter: powerfm
LinkedIn: (None)

Glide Memorial Church

San Francisco's "church without walls" has a long history of serving the downtrodden outcasts of our society, from the hippies and Black Panthers in the 1960s,

Vietnam protestors in the 1970s, AIDS victims in the 1980s, crack addicts in the 1990s, and all people suffering from socioeconomic problems into the twenty-first century. Here, you can learn more about Glide and how you can help.

Web: www.glide.org
Facebook: Glide (Page)
Twitter: glidesf
LinkedIn: Glide Foundation (Company)

Greek Orthodox Archdiocese of America

Provides information about Orthodox Christianity, the Greek Orthodox Archdiocese, the online chapel, Orthodox Christian resources, Orthodox Christian organizations, the Ministry Outreach Program, and more.

Web: www.goarch.org/en/resources/
Facebook: Greek Orthodox Archdiocese of America (Page)
Twitter: (None)
LinkedIn: Greek Orthodox Archdiocese of America (Company)

Premier.tv

A very large, comprehensive Christian web television archive, with many video clips playable via their own web-based TV player interface.

Web: www.premier.tv
Facebook: PREMIER TV (Group)
Twitter: (None)
LinkedIn: (None)

Religious Society of Friends

Offers a large directory of links about Quakers on the Web. Includes links to sites focusing on Quaker schools, journals, the American Friends Service Committee, genealogy sites, Quaker history, newsgroups, and more.

Web: www.quaker.org
Facebook: The Religious Society of Friends (Quakers) (Page)
Twitter: (None)
LinkedIn: (None)

Serving in Mission

This site offers the Great Commission Search Engine, which enables you to search for Christian missions all over the world. The site also features a SIM for Kids area.

Web: www.sim.org
Facebook: SIM (Serving in Mission) (Page), SIM USA (Serving in Mission) (Group)
Twitter: simintl
LinkedIn: SIM International (Company)

The Spurgeon Archive

This award-winning site is a collection of resources by and about Charles H. Spurgeon, English preacher and theologian. Contains information on his personal library, the full text of his sermons, his writings, and excerpts from *The Sword and the Trowel* and *The Treasury of David*.

Web: www.spurgeon.org
Facebook: Phil Johnson (Page)
Twitter: Phil_Johnson_
LinkedIn: (None)

Vatican

Online home of the Roman Catholic Church, this site takes you on a virtual tour of the Vatican, where you can access the latest news, perform research in the Vatican library and secret archives, tour the Vatican museums, read about past popes, and much more.

Web: www.vatican.va
Facebook: The Vatican-The Holy See (Group)
Twitter: (None)
LinkedIn: (None)

HINDUISM

Hindu Blog

The India-based author of this blog states, "For me, Hinduism is not a religion in the conventional sense. I find it more interesting without the religious tag or when it is in its pure form, the Sanatana Dharma." He writes in English, but with a decidedly Indian flair and style, and talks about various festivals going on in India as well as his own personal musings.

Web: www.hindu-blog.com
Facebook: Hindu Blog (Page)
Twitter: hindublog
LinkedIn: (None)

Kauai's Hindu Monastery

Created and maintained by the Himalayan Academy, this site provides a basic introduction to Hinduism, plus links to *Hinduism Today* magazine, Hindu books and art, the Hawaii Ashram, and other resources.

Web: www.himalayanacademy.com
Facebook: Kauai's Hindu Monastery (Page)
Twitter: KauaiMonastery
LinkedIn: (None)

Ramakrishnananda Tape Ministry

Satsangs and live lectures given by His Holiness Bhaktivedanta Ramakrishnananda Swami on yoga and spirituality.

Web: www.ramakrishnananda.com
Facebook: Fan of Vishwa Dharma Mandalam (Group)
Twitter: (None)
LinkedIn: (None)

ISLAM

The American Muslim

This blog from an American Muslim individual contains personal expressions based on religion, politics, and social issues.

Web: http://salaamsblog.wordpress.com
Facebook: American Muslim Blog and Radio (Page)
Twitter: rsalaam
LinkedIn: (None)

IslamiCity.com

Includes overview of doctrine and the Quran; news, culture, education, and political information; downloadable radio/TV broadcasts (free software download); online shopping; a chat room; a virtual mosque tour; web links; and a matrimonial service. Heavy coverage of Middle East politics. The site also features excellent information on understanding Islam.

Web: www.islamicity.com
Facebook: (none)
Twitter: IslamiCity
LinkedIn: (None)

Muxlim TV

This video-based site collects video clips dealing with Islam and religion, as well as clips of interest to Muslims but not directly connected to Islamic practice.

Web: http://tv.muxlim.com/
Facebook: muxlim (Page), Muxlim.tv (Group)
Twitter: MuslimLifestyle
LinkedIn: Muxlim Inc. (Company)

Progressive Islam

This site is a group blog written by Islamic progressives. They are open to hearing from contributors who reflect the North American Muslim community

from Salafi to Neo-Traditionalist, from Secular to Religiously Committed, from the Wacky to the Regular. There is an area where readers can start their own blogs as well.

Web: http://progressiveislam.org/
Facebook: (none)
Twitter: progislam
LinkedIn: (None)

Virtually Islamic

This blog offers news, commentary, information, and speculation about Islam in the digital age, and is part of virtuallyislamic.com.

Web: http://virtuallyislamic.blogspot.com/
Facebook: Gary R Bunt (Page)
Twitter: garybunt
LinkedIn: (None)

JUDAISM

Chabad Lubavitch: Torah, Judaism, and Jewish Info

Offers information pertaining to Chabad philosophy and Chassidic Judaism. Includes kosher recipes and children's links, multimedia, a LISTSERV, and Gopher resources.

Web: www.chabad.org
Facebook: chabad.org (Page)
Twitter: Chabad
LinkedIn: (None)

Jewish Theological Seminary

Represents this conservative seminary online. Provides a wealth of resources and links to conservative Jewish synagogues and institutions.

Web: www.jtsa.edu
Facebook: Jewish Theological Seminary (Page)
Twitter: (None)
LinkedIn: The Jewish Theological Seminary (JTS) (Group)

12

Jews for Judaism

Through education and community, this site is working to counter attempts by Christians to convert Jewish believers. It provides resources, links, and information about local groups and counseling for those who might be interested.

Web: www.jewsforjudaism.org
Facebook: Jews for Judaism (Page, Group)
Twitter: jewsforjudaism
LinkedIn: Jews for Judaism (Group)

Judaism 101

This site is an online encyclopedia of Judaism, covering "Jewish beliefs, people, places, things, language, scripture, holidays, practices and customs." The purpose is to inform and educate Jews and non-Jews about the religion by answering frequently asked questions.

Web: www.jewfaq.org
Facebook: Judaism 101 (Group)
Twitter: (None)
LinkedIn: (None)

MavenSearch

Searchable directory for links to all things Jewish. Type a keyword or phrase to search the directory or browse by category. Categories include Communities, Travel and Tourism, Israel, Holocaust, and Shopping & Gifts.

Web: www.maven.co.il
Facebook: (None)
Twitter: MavenSearch
LinkedIn: (None)

Shamash

This award-winning site run by the Jewish Internet Consortium offers links to various Jewish religious organizations ranging from Hillel to the World Zionist Organization. Includes FAQs pertaining to various facets of Judaism.

Web: http://shamash.org/
Facebook: Shamash: The Jewish Network (Page, Group)
Twitter: ShamashNetwork
LinkedIn: (None)

Torah.org

This site provides Jewish educational material through article and reference archives, program and speaker information, and popular email classes.

Web: www.torah.org
Facebook: Torah.org (Page)
Twitter: TorahDotOrg
LinkedIn: (None)

Virtual Jerusalem

Virtual Jerusalem offers updated news and information about Judaism and Israeli life, with departments for news, travel, technology, holidays, and entertainment. Site also features bulletin boards, live chat, and a Jewish email directory.

Web: www.virtualjerusalem.com
Facebook: VirtualJerusalem.com (Page)
Twitter: VJerusalem
LinkedIn: (None)

NEW THOUGHT

Center for Inner Awareness: A New Thought University

The Center for Inner Awareness is a "seminary" for New Thought. It is a nonprofit religious-education institution that offers classes and certificates and ordains ministers in the Church of Truth that are recognized by most New Thought churches and metaphysical organizations. You can find out about their academic program here and read the staff blog.

Web: www.centerforinnerawareness.org
Facebook: The Center for Inner Awareness (Group)
Twitter: (None)
LinkedIn: (None)

12

SHOPPING/FASHION

Since the advent of the Internet, it has become easier than ever to make a fashion statement. The Web yields so much choice with respect to shopping and style. This chapter covers all aspects of fashion: shopping sites, accessories, beauty, street style, home furnishings, high fashion, and career clothing. However, we've opted to include more new sites and concepts rather than sites promoting well-established brands. After you've selected an outfit, Web 2.0 now offers the opportunity to share your style with others through social networking sites, user video channels, and blogs.

ACCESSORIES

Bag Bliss

Bag Bliss reviews the latest bags from high-end retailers such as Neiman Marcus. Visitors can also purchase handbags from this blog site.

Web: http://bagbliss.com
Facebook: (None)
Twitter: BagBliss, BagBliss/vibrant-peacock-network
LinkedIn: (None)

Bag Borrow or Steal 📖

This premium membership website lets members rent designer handbags, jewelry, and sunglasses on a short-term or long-term basis. The site also sells new and used items at a discount to members.

Web: www.bagborroworsteal.com
Facebook: Bag Borrow or Steal (Pages), Avelle | Bag Borrow or Steal (Groups)
Twitter: bagborroworsteal
LinkedIn: Bag Borrow or Steal (Company)

The Bag Snob

This blog focuses on designer handbags with an emphasis on the latest "It Bags" from Louis Vuitton, Marc Jacobs, Dior, Hermés, and Chanel. The site also has an email newsletter and a newsfeed.

Web: http://bagsnob.com
Facebook: The Bag Snob (Page)
Twitter: BagSnob, BagSnob/web-snob, BagSnob/snob-sites, BagSnob/fave-blogs
LinkedIn: (None)

Etsy.com $

Etsy.com is a website featuring hand-crafted merchandise from artisans all over the world.

Web: www.etsy.com
Facebook: Etsy (Pages), Etsy (Groups), Etsy Sellers (Groups), We Love Etsy (Groups)
Twitter: Etsy, Etsy/handmade-weddings, Etsy/crafting
LinkedIn: Etsy (Company)

Framesdirect.com Video Gallery

Framesdirect.com, the online eyewear retailer, offers video updates on eyewear trends and optical safety tips.

Web: www.framesdirect.com/eyewear-blog/videos/
Facebook: FramesDirect.com (Pages)
Twitter: framesdirect, framesdirect/framesdirect-com-peeps
LinkedIn: (None)

The Gloss

This blog covers hats, handbags, belts, lingerie, eyewear, and electronic accessories.

Web: www.thegloss.com
Facebook: The Gloss (Page)
Twitter: theglossdotcom
LinkedIn: (None)

Handbags.com

Handbags.com is a comprehensive site offering bags for sale; it features new content on a daily basis, a blog, a celebrity style watch, and a lively forum.

Web: www.handbags.com
Facebook: (None)
Twitter: handbagsdotcom
LinkedIn: (None)

The Purse Forum

The Purse Forum has more than 120,000 members who gather to discuss their latest finds, celebrity style, and new deals.

Web: http://forum.purseblog.com/
Facebook: Purse Blog and Forum (Page)
Twitter: PurseBlog
LinkedIn: (None)

PursePage.com

Founded in 2006, The Purse Page is a fashion blog that reviews an eclectic mix of designer purses, celebrity fashion and provides information on designer sales events.

Web: www.pursepage.com
Facebook: The Purse Page (Page)
Twitter: pursepage
LinkedIn: (None)

Thirty-One Gifts

Thirty-One Gifts, one of America's fastest-growing direct selling companies, offers handbags and other accessories as well as stylish storage solutions at amazingly affordable prices. From signature purses and totes to kid's items and accents for the home, you'll find something to fit every personality and situation. Check out the Skirt Purse, one of the most innovative purse designs on the market today!

Web: www.thirtyonegifts.com
Facebook: Thirty-One Gifts (Page)
Twitter: _thirtyonegifts
LinkedIn: Thirty-One Gifts (Company)

BARGAIN HUNTING

The Bargainist

This website provides discount information and coupon codes for merchandise purchased from major retailers and chain stores.

Web: www.bargainist.com
Facebook: The Bargainist (Page)
Twitter: bargainist, bargainist/readers, bargainist/mens-bargains, bargainist/kids-bargains, bargainist/beauty-bargains, bargainist/life-bargains, bargainist/home-bargains
LinkedIn: (None)

The Budget Fashionista

This blog provides excellent coverage of fashion news and deals for looking your best on less. The blog also has an active community forum, coupons, a men's section, and podcasts.

Web: www.thebudgetfashionista.com
Facebook: Kathryn Finney - The Budget Fashionista (Page)
Twitter: KathrynFinney
LinkedIn: (None)

Chicsteals

Carly J. Cais posts tips on finding fashionable clothes that cost a fraction of the designer outfits featured in magazines. She also posts weekly roundups of designer-style steals that are under $100.

Web: http://chicsteals.blogspot.com/
Facebook: (None)
Twitter: carlyjcais
LinkedIn: (none)

FatWallet.com Forums

FatWallet.com's discussion forums drive the popularity of this shopping bargain site. Members can also earn cash back in an awards program that pays commission on recommendations that result in purchases.

13

Web: www.fatwallet.com/forums/
Facebook: Fatwallet.com (Page)
Twitter: FatWallet, fatwalletdeals, todaystopdeals, freestuffROCKS, blackfridayfw
LinkedIn: (None)

Overstock.com

Overstock.com offers shoppers name-brand merchandise at discounted prices by purchasing a supplier's excess inventory. Visitors can find deals in every category, including automobiles, home furnishings, bedding, clothing, sports equipment, accessories, entertainment, and electronics. The site characterizes itself as an Internet outlet mall.

Web: www.overstock.com
Facebook: Overstock.com (Page)
Twitter: Overstock, Overstock/overstock-com-folks
LinkedIn: Overstock.com (Company)

Pricegrabber.com

This comparison-shopping site offers a full spectrum of merchandise in every category, allowing visitors to find the best price for an item from several vendors instead of just one manufacturer.

Web: www.pricegrabber.com
Facebook: PriceGrabber.com (Page)
Twitter: (None)
LinkedIn: PriceGrabber.com (Company)

Sierra Trading Post

Sierra Trading Post purchases name-brand overstocks and closeouts and passes savings on to its customers. This online and brick-and-mortar retailer sells dress, casual, and outdoor clothing, footwear, home furnishings, accessories, and gear at savings of 35 to 70 percent. Today the company has four retail stores in Boise, Idaho, Reno, Nevada, Cheyenne and Cody, Wyoming, and two customer service call centers in Cheyenne and Cody.

Web: www.sierratradingpost.com
Facebook: Sierra Trading Post (Page)
Twitter: (None)
LinkedIn: Sierra Trading Post

SlickDeals.net

Members of the SlickDeals.net forum trade information on the latest deals and promotions, guaranteeing participants a chance to obtain merchandise at low rates or to acquire discounts before the stock runs out. As with FatWallet.com, reliable forum contributors are rewarded with perks and access to private areas on the site.

Web: http://forums.slickdeals.net/
Facebook: Slickdeals (Page, Group)
Twitter: slickdeals
LinkedIn: Slickdeals, Inc. (Company)

Stylehive

This bright pink blog shares bargain finds with mothers looking for tips on finding deals. The site posts info on current markdowns at online retailers, coupons, and freebies.

Web: http://stylehive.com/
Facebook: Stylehive (Page)
Twitter: stylehivebuzz, stylehive
LinkedIn: Stylehive.com (Company)

Woot.com

Woot.com is an online store and community that focuses on selling cool stuff cheap. It started as an employee-store slash market-testing type of place for an electronics distributor, but it's taken on a life of its own. Each day, Woot.com offers one item (from clothing to electronics to toys and everything in between), generally at far below retail price, and the item remains for sale until it's sold out. Be sure to watch for a Woot-Off where many items are offered throughout the day.

Web: www.woot.com
Facebook: Woot (Page)
Twitter: Woot
LinkedIn: Woot (Company)

13

BEAUTY

Afrobella.com

Afrobella explores fashion for women of color. She provides information about beauty trends and cosmetics formulated for specific skin problems affecting people with more skin pigmentation.

Web: http://afrobella.com/
Facebook: afrobella (Page)
Twitter: afrobella
LinkedIn: (None)

The Beauty Brains

The brains behind thebeautybrains.com are real cosmetic scientists who make you a smarter beauty-product consumer by offering information about how chemicals in beauty products really work on your skin or debunking misleading claims spread by the cosmetics industry. The site is well-designed, offering daily blog entries and a forum, and highlighting reader questions in its Q&A section.

Web: http://thebeautybrains.com/
Facebook: The Beauty Brains (Page)
Twitter: thebeautybrains
LinkedIn: (None)

Daily Makeover

Makeover Solutions is a fee-based community that gives members virtual makeovers using their uploaded photographs. Paying members can save and share their new looks with friends on the network and receive free email newsletters containing makeup and hairstyling tips. The site also has a free option, letting standard members try on but not save their new looks.

Web: www.dailymakeover.com
Facebook: Daily Makeover (Pages)
Twitter: DailyMakeover, DailyMakeover/beauty-brands, DailyMakeover/beauty-bloggerati
LinkedIn: (None)

E.L.F. Ⓢ

E.L.F. is an online discount beauty-product retailer that offers the basics for the eyes, lips, and face (E.L.F.).

Web: www.eyeslipsface.com
Facebook: e.l.f. Cosmetics (Page), E.L.F. (Eyes Lips Face) (Group)
Twitter: askelf, askelf/i-vlogged-blogged-e-l-f
LinkedIn: (None)

Home Spa Goddess

The Home Spa Goddess shares bath and beauty finds on this blog.

Web: http://homespagoddess.blogspot.com/
Facebook: Home Spagoddess (People), HomeSpaGoddess.com (Pages)
Twitter: HomeSpaGoddess, HomeSpaGoddess/lovely-lacquer-junkies, HomeSpaGoddess/budget-beauty-junkies
LinkedIn: (None)

CAREER DRESSING

Career Bags Ⓢ

This site offers laptop accessories and briefcases for stylish career women.

Web: http://careerbags.com/catalog/
Facebook: www.careerbags.com (Page)
Twitter: careerbags
LinkedIn: (None)

Wardrobe 911 Blog

Wardrobe 911 is authored by Teresa Morisco, a professional image consultant. Her blog offers practical fixes for all fashion emergencies.

Web: http://blog.wardrobe911.com/
Facebook: Wardrobe 911 (Page)
Twitter: wardrobe911
LinkedIn: (None)

What Not to Wear

These videos of the popular cable TV show often cover career wardrobes and business style.

13

Web: http://tlc.discovery.com/videos/what-not-to-wear/
Facebook: What Not To Wear (Page), What NOT To Wear (Group)
Twitter: (None)
LinkedIn: (None)

What to Wear for Work

Marieclaire.com offers practical advice on work wardrobe dilemmas.

Web: www.marieclaire.com/archive/life/career/dress/
Facebook: Marie Claire (Page, Group)
Twitter: marieclaire
LinkedIn: Hearst Magazines (Company)

The Working Closet Discussion Group

This discussion group on the Work It, Mom website offers practical solutions and support for finding the right wardrobe for work.

Web: www.workitmom.com/1273_1371_0.html
Facebook: (None)
Twitter: Work_It_Mom
LinkedIn: (None)

Works by Nicole Williams

Nicole Williams is a career advice expert who has authored books and hosted a TV show on Oxygen. She relaunched this site in 2007 with the idea of providing comprehensive information and support for women in the workplace. She offers work wardrobe tips in the Style section of the site.

Web: www.nicolewilliams.com/style/
Facebook: WORKS by Nicole Williams (Page)
Twitter: (None)
LinkedIn: Nicole Williams (People)

INTERIOR DESIGN

Decorati

This site is an interior designer community that lets members browse designer catalogs and showrooms and purchase items for sale and for exchange.

Web: http://decorati.com/
Facebook: Decorati (Page)
Twitter: decorati
LinkedIn: Decorati Inc. (Company)

Furniture Fashion

Furniture Fashion is an interior design and furniture blog that tracks recent trends in the marketplace.

Web: www.furniturestoreblog.com
Facebook: Furniture Fashion (Page)
Twitter: FurnitureFashio
LinkedIn: (None)

HGTV.com

The official website for the HGTV cable network provides plenty of home decorating information in video shorts, podcasts, slide shows, and articles. The site just debuted a new feature called "Rate My Space," in which site readers submit photos of their own home decoration projects and subject them to group rating. HGTV producers offer makeovers to owners with the lowest scored photos and broadcast the results on TV.

Web: www.hgtv.com
Facebook: HGTV (Page)
Twitter: hgtv
LinkedIn: (None)

Home Decoration Forum at iVillage.com

The Home Decoration Forum provides comprehensive discussion boards for every aspect of interior design and home decoration. Members trade ideas, shopping bargains, and suggestions for improving one's environment.

Web: http://ths.gardenweb.com/forums/decor/
Facebook: (None)
Twitter: gardenweb
LinkedIn: (None)

ome-furnishings retailer, may
___ ucts from this site, but it also
offers loads of design tips using easy-to-
follow directions. However, the graphics-
heavy website design may load slowly
for visitors with slow Internet connections.

Web: www.ikea.com
Facebook: IKEA (Page)
Twitter: (None)
LinkedIn: IKEA (Company)

Phasing Grace: Social Spaces and Virtual Worlds

Writer Grace McDunnough explores the
intellectual side of creating social archi-
tecture, including structures and design,
in this blog.

Web: http://phasinggrace.blogspot.com/
Facebook: Grace McDunnough (Page)
Twitter: GraceMcDunnough
LinkedIn: (None)

What Is This Crap?

Second Life gives residents an opportunity to build and decorate their own
environments, an option many players
enjoy with verve and creativity. One
Second Lifer, Crap Mariner, uses this blog
to update readers on his or her clock-
work tower in the virtual world. The blog
gives readers insight into how to build
and maintain Second Life structures.

Web: http://firstlife.isfullofcrap.com/index.html
Facebook: Laurence Simon (People)
Twitter: isfullofcrap
LinkedIn: (None)

JEANS

Denimology

Based in Britain, Denimology tracks the
latest news on jeans trends across
Europe and the UK. The site offers
reviews and well-written interviews with
denim designers, store owners, and
other fans obsessed with jeans.

Web: www.denimology.co.uk
Facebook: Denimology.com (Page)
Twitter: denimology
LinkedIn: Denimology.com (Company)

Fanpop!.com Designer Jeans

Fanpop!.com is a new social networking
site for fan-club communities. There is a
community of designer-jeans fans who
can upload photos, share info, and write
personal rants about their favorite jeans.

Web: www.fanpop.com/spots/designer-jeans
Facebook: Fanpop (Page)
Twitter: fanpop
LinkedIn: (None)

Joes Jeans $

This jeans retailer provides jeans in all
styles and shapes, including petite sizes.

Web: www.joesjeans.com
Facebook: Joe's Jeans (Page)
Twitter: (None)
LinkedIn: Joe's Jeans (Company)

LINGERIE

Armidi

Armidi's shop in Second Life sells lingerie
that's favored by many fashionable
avatars in the SL world.

Web: http://slurl.com/secondlife/Armidi/136/128/26
Facebook: Second Life (Pages), Second Life (Groups)
Twitter: SecondLife, SecondLife/second-life-accounts
LinkedIn: (None)

The Lingerie Post

The Lingerie Post features articles and interviews with lingerie and corset designers.

Web: www.the-lingerie-post.com
Facebook: The Lingerie Post (Page)
Twitter: TheLingeriePost
LinkedIn: (None)

TeamSugar

TeamSugar, the social networking component of PopSugar website network, has a channel covering intimate apparel.

Web: http://teamsugar.com/tags/underwear
Facebook: PopSugar (Page)
Twitter: heypopsugar
LinkedIn: (None)

Twitter: LingerieDiva

The LingerieDiva microblogs about her life and passion selling lingerie on the Internet.

Web: http://twitter.com/LingerieDiva
Facebook: (None)
Twitter: LingerieDiva
LinkedIn: (None)

MEN'S FASHION

Nylon for Guys Magazine

This site is the online component to the print magazine devoted to promoting men's style.

Web: www.nylonguysmag.com
Facebook: Nylon Guys Magazine (Page)
Twitter: (None)
LinkedIn: (None)

Slmen—How Men Dress in Second Life

This blog examines men's style in Second Life, highlighting interesting body modifications, clothing design, and skin facades.

Web: www.slmen.com
Facebook: Second Life (Pages), Second Life (Groups)
Twitter: SecondLife, SecondLife/second-life-accounts
LinkedIn: (None)

A Suitable Wardrobe

This blog focuses on classic suit tailoring.

Web: http://asuitablewardrobe.dynend.com/
Facebook: A Suitable Wardrobe (Page)
Twitter: (None)
LinkedIn: (None)

PETITES

Model Talk

Isobella Jade is a petite-size model who hosts this weekly Internet radio show about breaking into the modeling business.

Web: www.blogtalkradio.com/isobellajade
Facebook: Isobella Jade (Page), BlogTalkRadio (Page)
Twitter: IsobellaJade, blogtalkradio
LinkedIn: BlogTalkRadio (Company)

Petite Fashionista

Christa, a stylist, founded Petitefashionista.com in order to share her passion for discovering attractive clothing tailored to fit petite frames. She offers styling advice, news, video, and discussion groups on her blog. This site offers the most comprehensive blogroll of other petite fashion sites and resources.

Web: www.petitefashionista.com
Facebook: Petite Fashionista (Page)
Twitter: (None)
LinkedIn: (None)

Shorty Stories

The Shorty Stories website documents the allure and frustrations of petiteness. The site features interviews, product reviews, and video celebrating the petite lifestyle.

Web: http://blog.shorty-stories.com/
Facebook: Shorty Stories (Page)
Twitter: (None)
LinkedIn: (None)

13

You Look Fab Forum

You Look Fab is a website maintained by a fashion buyer and consultant. The site's discussion boards include several topics on petite dressing.

Web: www.youlookfab.com/welookfab/
Facebook: youlookfab (Page)
Twitter: youlookfab
LinkedIn: (None)

PLUS SIZE

Fatsecret.com

Fatsecret.com is an Australian site providing community to obese people eager to lose weight with the support of their peers. Members join and bond with other members through chat, games, and forums.

Web: www.fatsecret.com
Facebook: Fatsecret (Page)
Twitter: FatSecret
LinkedIn: (None)

OneStopPlus.com ⑤

This site bills itself as the "online fashion mall for sizes 12W to 44W." Shoppers can find all the name-brand plus-size lines here, along with channels specializing in lingerie, shoes and accessories, and clothing for big and tall men.

Web: www.onestopplus.com
Facebook: OneStopPlus.com (Page)
Twitter: onestopplus
LinkedIn: (None)

RELATED SITES

Chadwicks

In 1983, Chadwicks became the first company to offer woman the innovative concept of a fashion catalog with the same high-quality apparel found in department stores at a fraction of the price. Now, over 25 years later, Chadwicks is still one of America's favorite shopping destination for stylish women's fashion at an unsurpassed value.

Web: www.chadwicks.com
Facebook: Chadwicks (Page)
Twitter: ChadwicksDotCom
LinkedIn: (None)

Jessica London

Jessica London offers quality career, casual and special occasion fashion, plus classic, easy-to-wear separates, comfortable lingerie, and sleepwear to women sizes 12 to 32, plus shoes to size 12.

Web: www.jessicalondon.com
Facebook: Jessica London (Page)
Twitter: Jessica_London_
LinkedIn: (None)

Plus Model Radio

Editors of *Plus Model Magazine* host a weekly Internet radio show discussing body image and trends in plus-size fashion.

Web: www.plusmodelmag.com/General/plus-model-radio.asp
Facebook: Plus Model Magazine (Page)
Twitter: plusmodelmag
LinkedIn: (None)

Roaman's

A plus-size fashion leader for over 100 years, Roaman's was created for the woman who appreciates style and true value. Roaman's experienced buyers travel the world in search of exciting new looks that you can wear for every occasion.

Web: www.roamans.com
Facebook: Roaman's (Page)
Twitter: Roamans
LinkedIn: (None)

13

Trendy Plus Size Clothes

This site provides information and guides for finding and wearing the latest fashions cut to flatter full-figured women.

Web: www.trendy-plus-size-clothes.com/index.html
Facebook: Trendy Plus Size Clothes (Page)
Twitter: TrendyPlusSizeC
LinkedIn: (None)

SHOES

Endless.com Ⓢ

Amazon.com created this shoe and handbag site, providing name-brand leather goods at discounted prices. Endless.com ships merchandise overnight free to instantly gratify the cravings of shoeaholics and alleviate the fears of risk-averse shoppers.

Web: www.endless.com
Facebook: Endless.com (Page)
Twitter: Endless_com
LinkedIn: (None)

Juicy Shoe Shop in Second Life

Elven Dreamscape crafts colorful and well-sculpted shoes for Second Life residents. The current inventory includes sling-back pumps.

Web: http://slurl.com/secondlife/Juicy/116/140/23
Facebook: Second Life (Pages), Second Life (Groups)
Twitter: SecondLife, SecondLife/second-life-accounts
LinkedIn: (None)

Manolo Shoe Blog

Manolo Shoe Blog is an anonymous blog written in the voice of shoe designer Manolo Blahnik. Each post is a mishmash of shoe advice and broad jokes about the fashion industry.

Web: www.shoeblogs.com
Facebook: Manolo Shoeblogger (Page)
Twitter: ShoeBlogger
LinkedIn: (None)

Obsessive Sneaker Disorder

Dee Wells hosts this weekly Internet radio show devoted to sneaker collectors. Wells fields calls from listeners while sharing bits of history about the popular athletic shoe.

Web: www.obsessivesneakerdisorder.com
Facebook: Obsessive Sneaker Disorder (Application)
Twitter: (None)
LinkedIn: (None)

Shoe Blitz

Shoe Blitz is a shopping blog covering the designer end of the shoe market. Each post includes a photo of the shoe in question.

Web: www.shoeblitz.com
Facebook: The Gloss (Pages)
Twitter: theglossdotcom
LinkedIn: (None)

Sneaker Freaker

This forum attracts folks who collect and decorate sneakers.

Web: www.sneakerfreaker.com/forum/
Facebook: (None)
Twitter: snkrfrkrmag
LinkedIn: (None)

Sneaker Obsession

Sneaker Obsession posts entries about the latest news in the shoe-design industry.

Web: www.sneakerobsession.com
Facebook: Sneaker Obsession (People, Page)
Twitter: SneakObsession
LinkedIn: (None)

Sole Collector

This site focuses on collectible sneakers, offering fans a blog, a discussion forum, shopping, product reviews, and content displayed in a magazine-type format.

Web: http://solecollector.com/
Facebook: SoleCollector
Twitter: SoleCollector
LinkedIn: (None)

13

Zappos.com BEST ⑤

Zappos is an excellent shoe site beloved by many Internet shoppers. The site has a full selection of shoes in every size and style and provides free shipping and returns.

Web: www.zappos.com
Facebook: Zappos.com (Page)
Twitter: (None)
LinkedIn: Zappos.com (Company)

SHOPPING

Amazon.com ⑤

Amazon.com has expanded from its beginnings as an online bookseller into a global shopping site. One can purchase groceries, books, electronics, home furnishings, and clothing all in one session.

Web: www.amazon.com
Facebook: Amazon (Page), Amazon Kindle (Page)
Twitter: amazonseattle
LinkedIn: Amazon.com (Company)

Buy.com ⑤

Buy.com is the ultimate shopping portal, selling movies, books, home furnishings, luggage, sports equipment, toys, and electronics. The site offers name-brand merchandise at discounted prices.

Web: www.buy.com
Facebook: Buy.com (Page)
Twitter: Buy_com, buycomdeals
LinkedIn: Buy.com (Company)

Fashion Consolidated

FashCon is the largest general fashion and avatar-related group on Second Life. Hundreds of designers distribute information about new releases via FashCon so that shoppers can stay abreast of the latest style finds.

Web: http://fashcon.com/
Facebook: Second Life (Page), Second Life (Group)
Twitter: SecondLife, SecondLife/second-life-accounts
LinkedIn: (None)

Fashion Heaven

Fashion Heaven blog covers the latest fashions and trends happening in Second Life. It's an excellent introduction into the virtual world's shops and vendors.

Web: http://fashionangels.wordpress.com/
Facebook: Second Life (Pages), Second Life (Groups)
Twitter: SecondLife, SecondLife/second-life-accounts
LinkedIn: (None)

Net-a-Porter.com ⑤

Net-a-Porter.com is an Internet fashion pioneer, providing designer clothing in an e-commerce setting. This is the site to shop if you are looking for designer threads.

Web: www.net-a-porter.com/am/Home.ice
Facebook: NET-A-PORTER.COM (Page)
Twitter: NETAPORTER
LinkedIn: NET-A-PORTER.COM (Company)

New York Magazine Look Book

The Look Book feature in *New York* magazine selects random New Yorkers off the street to pose for a photograph and explain their style.

Web: http://nymag.com/nymag/strategist/look/archive/
Facebook: New York Magazine (Page)
Twitter: NewYorkMag
LinkedIn: New York Magazine (Company)

SheFinds.com

The discussion board for this popular shopping site features forums on bargain shopping as well as advice on how or when to wear an outfit.

Web: http://shefinds.com/talk/
Facebook: SheFinds.com (Page)
Twitter: shefinds, shefinds/brands, shefinds/fashion
LinkedIn: Shefinds.com (Company)

Shopaholics Daily

The Shopaholics Daily posts interesting garments, accessories, and beauty items from around the Web, as well as an excellent roundup of the other style sites.

Web: www.shopaholicsdaily.com
Facebook: The Gloss (Page)
Twitter: theglossdotcom
LinkedIn: (None)

ShopStyle

ShopStyle is another social networking and shopping site that lets you create your own "stylebook" of merchandise and coordinate outfits to display on the social network or to your friends via email. The clothes are limited to the items sold through selected merchants and vendors. There is also a home-decorating and kid's retail component.

Web: www.shopstyle.com
Facebook: ShopStyle (Page)
Twitter: ShopStyle_US
LinkedIn: ShopStyle, Inc. (Company)

Starley.com

Second Life provides plenty of shopping opportunities for fashion fans. There are plenty of vendors offering clothing, accessories, and makeup to suit every resident's style. Starley operates the Celestial Studios in Second Life and offers both clothing and makeup/skins.

Web: www.starley.com
Facebook: Second Life (Page), Second Life (Group)
Twitter: SecondLife, SecondLife/second-life-accounts
LinkedIn: (None)

StyleHive.com

Style-obsessed netizens can find cool items and clothing by watching the choices selected by other members on this social network. Members can post items that catch their eye anywhere on the Web and let other members vote on their find.

Web: http://stylehive.com/
Facebook: Stylehive (Page)
Twitter: stylehive, stylehivebuzz
LinkedIn: stylehive.com (Company)

STYLE

Electric Catwalk

These short video podcasts highlight the fashion business in Los Angeles, including runway shows and interviews.

Web: www.mefeedia.com/feeds/4209/
Facebook: Mefeedia (Page)
Twitter: MeFeedia, MeFeedia/news, MeFeedia/video business
LinkedIn: (None)

Fashionista.com

Fashionista.com is whip smart and tells it like it is. Whether citing mass merchandisers like Forever 21 for ripping off designers or calling other fashion blogs cheesy, this blog does not pull any punches.

Web: www.fashionista.com
Facebook: fashionista.com (Page)
Twitter: Fashionista_com
LinkedIn: (None)

Fashion Net

Fashion Net is a stylized guide to sophisticated fashion resources, including access to avant-garde designers, stylists, insiders, and shopping sites.

Web: www.fashion.net
Facebook: fashion.net (Page)
Twitter: (None)
LinkedIn: (None)

The Fashion Spot

The Fashion Spot is an online community for fashion devotees. The site has the most comprehensive discussion forums for fans devoted to specific designers and models. In addition, visitors can peruse articles, photo galleries, and party pictures.

Web: www.thefashionspot.com
Facebook: The Fashion Spot (Page)
Twitter: fashion_spot, fashion_spot/tfs-writers
LinkedIn: (None)

13

Fashion Television

This is a very polished broadband channel, featuring runway video, interviews, and the latest fashion news and trends.

Web: www.fashiontelevision.com
Facebook: Fashion Television (Page)
Twitter: (None)
LinkedIn: (None)

Fashion Week Daily

This site is a combo blog and larger website featuring video and trend reports on the worlds of high fashion and the party circuit.

Web: www.dailyfrontrow.com
Facebook: Daily Front Row/DailyFrontRow.com (Group)
Twitter: (None)
LinkedIn: (None)

Go Fug Yourself

Go Fug Yourself is the celebrity snark site that evaluates celebrity outfits on a scale of one to fugly. The writing is so acute and witty that you will laugh despite yourself.

Web: http://gofugyourself.celebuzz.com/
Facebook: Go Fug Yourself: The Fug Girls (Page)
Twitter: fuggirls, fuggirls/fashion, fuggirls/magazines
LinkedIn: (None)

High Fashion Girl Blog

A freelance fashion journalist keeps this site. The blog is a playful mix of high fashion, craft items, and personal reflections.

Web: http://highfashiongirl.com/
Facebook: High Fashion Girl Blog (Page)
Twitter: (None)
LinkedIn: (None)

Iconique.com Vlog

Iconique.com provides video versions of their fashion editorials in short web episodes.

Web: www.iconique.com/flash/podcast.php
Facebook: IconiQue (Page)
Twitter: (None)
LinkedIn: (None)

Independent Fashion Bloggers

This group blog is a compendium of all the independent fashion bloggers working in the industry. The site gives full access to the latest fashion shows and press events.

Web: http://independentfashionbloggers.org/
Facebook: Independent Fashion Bloggers (Page)
Twitter: (None)
LinkedIn: (None)

Men's Second Style

This site highlights the variety of fashion choices for male Second Life residents. Ryan Darragh reports on the latest fashions, avatar skin and facial textures, and body-modification vendors.

Web: www.second-man.com
Facebook: Second Life (Pages), Second Life (Groups)
Twitter: SecondLife, SecondLife/second-life-accounts
LinkedIn: (None)

My Virtual Model

Using the "Brand Me" trademark, this personalized shopping avatar expands the online shopping experience by giving a shopper the chance to try on a manufacturer's clothing. The program lets users upload a face picture that is merged with a standard template body, which the user adjusts to reflect her body type and coloring. Users can store their items in a virtual closet or send their dressed avatars to friends via email for a second opinion. The virtual model appears on more than 50 websites, including H&M, Glam.com, Glamour, Lands End, and Sears.

Web: www.mvm.com
Facebook: My Virtual Model (Page)
Twitter: (None)
LinkedIn: My Virtual Model (Company)

13

Polyvore

This is a new social network that lets users assemble outfits from images culled from online stores all over the Internet to create the perfect outfit. Users can share their looks with other members of the site and interact on discussion boards.

Web: www.polyvore.com/cgi/home
Facebook: Polyvore (Page)
Twitter: polyvore, PolyvoreDesigns
LinkedIn: Polyvore (Company)

The Sartorialist

This is a consistently excellent blog that covers street fashion as seen in Manhattan, London, and Paris.

Web: http://thesartorialist.blogspot.com/
Facebook: The Sartorialist (Page)
Twitter: (None)
LinkedIn: (None)

Second Style Fashionista

Second Style Fashionista is the blog component of Second Style magazine, a Second Life publication that highlights the best in fashion, hair, and makeup for avatars on Second Life. The site is a helpful shopping guide to Second Life artisans selling their creations.

Web: http://blog.secondstyle.com/
Facebook: Second Life (Page), Second Life (Group)
Twitter: SecondLife, SecondLife/second-life-accounts
LinkedIn: (None)

Shefinds.com Discussion Board

Members of the Shefinds.com shopping community can share information on their favorite designers.

Web: http://shefinds.com/talk
Facebook: SheFinds.com (Page)
Twitter: shefinds, shefinds/brands, shefinds/fashion
LinkedIn: Shefinds.com (Company)

Splendora BFF Lounge

Splendora.com members can create and post their own diaries in the style site's BFF Lounge. Splendora.com highlights a new diary each week across the entire Splendora.com network as the Member of the Moment.

Web: www.splendora.com/bff
Facebook: Splendora.com (Page)
Twitter: SplendoraHQ, SplendoraHQ/sale-sites
LinkedIn: Splendora (Company)

StyleBakery.com

Run by three fashion journalists, this polished site offers the latest looks and suggestions for adapting each season's offerings to the user's lifestyle and budget.

Web: www.stylebakery.com
Facebook: StyleBakery.com (Page)
Twitter: stylebakery
LinkedIn: (None)

Style.com 🏅

As the fashion hub for Vogue magazine and other titles in the Condé Nast magazine stable, Style.com is the most comprehensive website for fashion. It features original content, editorials from Vogue, and photographs and videos. It provides the best coverage of all the fashion shows each season.

Web: www.style.com
Facebook: Style (Page)
Twitter: Style_com
LinkedIn: Conde Nast (Company)

TeamSugar.com

TeamSugar.com is the community component of the fashion and gossip network of sites collected under the Sugar, Inc., banner. Fans of PopSugar and FabSugar blogs can congregate here for games, live chat, and discussion boards.

Web: http://teamsugar.com/groups/Fashion_and_Beauty
Facebook: PopSugar (Page)
Twitter: heypopsugar
LinkedIn: (None)

13

360° Fashion Network

This social networking site caters to high-level fashion insiders. Members can create their own blogs and connect with one another for collaborations, marketing campaigns, and cross-promotional opportunities.

Web: http://360fashion.net/
Facebook: 360Fashion (Page)
Twitter: 360fashion
LinkedIn: (None)

Twitter: The Diva

The Diva runs the Second Life Fashion Police blog and posts brief entries about her adventures on and offline.

Web: http://twitter.com/TheDiva
Facebook: Second Life (Page), Second Life (Group)
Twitter: SecondLife, SecondLife/second-life-accounts
LinkedIn: (None)

Twitter: Fashionstock

Fans of fashion can follow Fashionstock on Twitter and get micro video upload notices.

Web: http://twitter.com/fashionstock
Facebook: (None)
Twitter: fashionstock
LinkedIn: (None)

Twitter: Gabby Panacek

Gabby Panacek of the Couture Conundrum blog shares her every thought about life and fashion on Twitter.

Web: http://twitter.com/GabbyPanacek
Facebook: (None)
Twitter: GabbyPanacek
LinkedIn: (None)

WhoWhatWear Daily

This website posts photos of celebrities and tracks down what they are wearing and where readers can obtain the fashions or an affordable substitute.

Web: http://whowhatweardaily.com/
Facebook: Who What Wear (Page)
Twitter: WhoWhatWear
LinkedIn: (None)

WhoWhatWearDaily TV

The broadband TV supplement to the WhoWhatWearDaily.com site, this site provides informative and polished episodes with two hosts who model clothing to support their advice.

Web: http://whowhatweardaily.com/website/wwwtv.php
Facebook: Who What Wear (Page)
Twitter: WhoWhatWear
LinkedIn: (None)

TALL

Long Legs.com

This Canadian-based site is an online catalog of items for tall women.

Web: www.longlegs.ca
Facebook: Long Legs Fashion for Tall Women Ltd. (Page)
Twitter: LongLegsFashion
LinkedIn: (None)

Tall Club.com

Tall Club of Toronto is a community for tall people.

Web: www.tallclub.com
Facebook: Tall Club of Toronto (Page)
Twitter: (None)
LinkedIn: (None)

Tall Couture.com

Tall Couture.com provides fashion advice and clothing to tall women.

Web: www.tallcouture.com
Facebook: Tall Couture (Page)
Twitter: TallCouture
LinkedIn: (None)

VINTAGE

Antiquity Gazette

Vintage enthusiasts will enjoy exploring the Antiquity worlds established on Second Life. The Antiquity Gazette covers all the news and events in the Antiquity neighborhood.

Web: www.antiquitygazette.blogspot.com
Facebook: Second Life (Page), Second Life (Group)
Twitter: SecondLife, SecondLife/second-life-accounts
LinkedIn: (None)

C. Madeleine's Vintage Clothes

This site sells designer vintage clothing. It is informative and well designed. The prices are high-end.

Web: http://shop.cmadeleines.com/
Facebook: C. Madeleines (Page)
Twitter: CMadeleines
LinkedIn: (None)

Crafty Vixens Discussion Board

The Crafty Vixens forum on Tribe.net shares advice on ways to find thrift-store bargains and styling outfits out of secondhand clothing.

Web: http://craftyvixens.tribe.net/
Facebook: Crafty Vixens (Group)
Twitter: CraftyVixens
LinkedIn: (None)

Enokiworld Vintage Retailer

This website sells vintage clothing from the 1930s through the 1970s. Vintage enthusiasts comb through the site listings, looking for rare deals.

Web: www.enokiworld.com/frontpage.htm
Facebook: enokiworld (Page)
Twitter: enokiworld
LinkedIn: (None)

The Insatiable Zoe Connolly

Zoe Connolly blogs about her adventures in the steampunk lifestyle on Second Life. She builds and flies Victorian aircraft in the sim and interviews other Second Lifers engaged in antiquity lifestyles.

Web: http://zoeconnolly.blogspot.com/
Facebook: Second Life (Page), Second Life (Group)
Twitter: SecondLife, SecondLife/second-life-accounts, Zoe Connolly
LinkedIn: (None)

Thrift Eye

This young blogger posts photos of herself in her many thrift outfits. She has an engaging writing style and a good eye for photography.

Web: http://thrifteye.blogspot.com/
Facebook: (None)
Twitter: thrifteye
LinkedIn: (None)

Vintage Costumes on SL Exchange

Vintage enthusiasts can find all manner of retro and vintage wear in Second Life. The SL Exchange marketplace is the best place to review most of the vintage outfits available for purchase.

Web: www.slexchange.com/modules.php?name=Marketplace&CategoryID=324
Facebook: Second Life (Page), Second Life (Group)
Twitter: SecondLife, SecondLife/second-life-accounts
LinkedIn: (None)

13

14

SPORTS

Whether you're looking for the latest cricket scores, training for a hot dog–eating contest, trying to attend a hockey game, or simply looking to find the best place for hang gliding near your home, you can find plenty of social media fans who share in your sports passions online.

AEROBATICS

Red Bull Air Race

At this official site of the Red Bull Air Race, you can find information about the big event in the sport of competitive aerobatics, including where a race is held near you. Read about pilots and their aircraft, view photos and videos from the competition, and find out the latest race results.

Web: www.redbullairrace.com
Facebook: Red Bull Air Race (Page)
Twitter: Redbullairrace
LinkedIn: (None)

AUTO RACING

Courant.com

Find some very nice racing blogs on this site, from IndyCar racing to the National Hot Rod Association and motor speedways around the nation.

Web: http://blogs.courant.com/autoracing
Facebook: The Backstretch: Hartford Courant Auto Racing Blog (Page)
Twitter: (None)
LinkedIn: (None)

Demolition Derby Drivers Association

A good starting point for anyone looking for the latest news and info about demolition derby events. The URL sums it up! The site offers message boards, a chat room, and mechanic tips and techniques.

Web: www.wecrash.com
Facebook: WeCrash Demo DVDs (Page)
Twitter: WeCrashCrew
LinkedIn: (None)

DragTimes.com

Looking for drag-racing news, videos, and forums? Start with this site, an excellent source of information, including blogs, classified ads, and drag-racing timeslips.

Web: www.dragtimes.com
Facebook: DragTimes.com (Page)
Twitter: DragTimes
LinkedIn: (None)

Formula Drift

The official website of the Formula Drift Professional Drifting Championship Series. Find driver profiles, race schedules, merchandise, a blog, an e-newsletter, and more.

Web: www.formulad.com
Facebook: Formula Drift (Page)
Twitter: FormulaDrift
LinkedIn: (None)

Formula 1

If Formula One racing is more your speed, this official website is the best place to check in for news, races, team and driver info, photo galleries, and so on.

Web: www.formula1.com
Facebook: Formula 1 (Page)
Twitter: (None)
LinkedIn: (None)

Full Throttle 🏅

This guy's blog has been a finalist in several Weblog Awards, and fellow NASCAR fans are sure to find some interesting news and opinions here.

Web: http://fullthrottle.cranialcavity.net
Facebook: (None)
Twitter: FThrottle
LinkedIn: (None)

IndyCar Racing

This is the official website of the IndyCar racing series. You'll find podcasts, videos, RSS feeds, stats, race schedules, blogs, and so much more.

Web: www.indycar.com
Facebook: IndyCar Racing (Page), The Official Indy Racing League ® Fan Group (Group)
Twitter: IndyCarNation
LinkedIn: (None)

International Hot Rod Association

Here's the global home of the International Hot Road Association promoting professional, semiprofessional, and local-level racing around the world. View results and stats, video clips, and buy tickets.

Web: www.ihra.com
Facebook: IHRA/Nitro Jam Drag Racing (Page)
Twitter: (None)
LinkedIn: (None)

International Ice Racing Association

As if auto racing isn't fast enough, how about racing on ice? Visit this site to view the latest race results and point standings.

Web: http://iira-icerace.org/
Facebook: IIRA Ice Racing (Group)
Twitter: (None)
LinkedIn: (None)

NASCAR

Enter the popular world of NASCAR (National Association for Stock Car Auto Racing) through this official website. View driver profiles, standings, race schedules, photos, and videos. You'll also find forums, blogs, chat, merchandising, and ticket sales.

Web: www.nascar.com
Facebook: NASCAR (Page), NASCAR! (Group)
Twitter: (None)
LinkedIn: NASCAR (Company)

National Hot Rod Association

This site offers up all kinds of information for drag-racing fans, including details and news about events across the country, ticket info, rules, and stats. For a fee, you can become a member and access additional features on the site.

Web: www.nhra.com
Facebook: NHRA (Group)
Twitter: NHRA
LinkedIn: (None)

SpeedTV.com

When it comes to going fast, SpeedTV channel has it all, and its website is great, too. Here you'll find podcasts on auto racing, including IRL, F1, and Champ Car.

Web: www.speedtv.com/podcenter
Facebook: SPEEDtv.com (Page)
Twitter: (None)
LinkedIn: (None)

World Racing Forum 📰

This site plays host for dozens of racing forums, so you're bound to find your favorite racing forum, whether it's open-wheel racing, world racing arena, or others.

Web: www.worldracingforum.com
Facebook: World Racing Forum (Page)
Twitter: (None)
LinkedIn: (None)

BASEBALL

Baseball Almanac

Here's a site dedicated to preserving the history of baseball. It's almost like an encyclopedia with thousands upon thousands of pages filled with every fact and figure about baseball imaginable. It's the go-to source for any baseball questions you may have.

Web: www.baseball-almanac.com
Facebook: Baseball Almanac (Page)
Twitter: (None)
LinkedIn: (None)

Baseball America

You can find lots of baseball podcasts to subscribe to on this site. Coverage includes major and minor leagues, and college and high-school teams.

Web: www.baseballamerica.com/today/media/podcasts/
Facebook: Baseball America (Page)
Twitter: BaseballAmerica
LinkedIn: (None)

Major League Baseball

If the great American pastime of baseball is your sport, the best place to start is the official Major League Baseball website. Here, you'll find links to all your favorite teams across the country, as well as team standings, stats, players, sched-

ules, and news. You can also participate in a fantasy league, shop for team memorabilia, and connect with fans from around the world in the blogging and message boards.

Web: www.mlb.com
Facebook: Major League Baseball (Page, Group)
Twitter: (None)
LinkedIn: Major League Baseball (Company)

Minor League Baseball

Check in here to see how the minor-league baseball teams are doing. See who's up-and-coming, and get the latest scores.

Web: www.minorleaguebaseball.com
Facebook: Minor League Baseball (Page)
Twitter: (None)
LinkedIn: Minor League Baseball (Company)

BASE JUMPING

BLiNC 📰

This site offers some very nice forums for BASE-jumping enthusiasts, from the beginner to the experienced. The forums also include classifieds for parachuting gear.

Web: www.blincmagazine.com/forum
Facebook: BLiNC Magazine (Group)
Twitter: (None)
LinkedIn: (None)

BASKETBALL

The Basketball Jones

This lively and entertaining NBA podcast is recorded weekly. Be sure to check out their blog as well.

Web: http://thebasketballjones.net/
Facebook: The Basketball Jones | NBA Podcast (Page)
Twitter: (None)
LinkedIn: (None)

14

Basketball Statistics Blog

Here's an interesting blog site about basketball, specifically from a statistician's and coach's perspectives. The blogger examines rules, game play, and more.

Web: www.ebablogs.com
Facebook: (None)
Twitter: eBAstatsGroup
LinkedIn: (None)

ESPN

Every real sports fan knows to make ESPN a priority stop when surfing the Web for sports information, including basketball news and scores. Be sure to check out the NBA video clips.

Web: http://espn.go.com
Facebook: ESPN (Page, Group)
Twitter: (None)
LinkedIn: ESPN (Company)

NBA

The official site of the National Basketball Association; you'll find up-to-date news on everything related to professional basketball. Find links to all the team sites, player bios, scores, standings, and stats. View upcoming schedules, purchase tickets, and view video clips.

Web: www.nba.com
Facebook: NBA (Page)
Twitter: (None)
LinkedIn: National Basketball Association (Company)

NCAA

Log on to the National Collegiate Athletic Association's fan site to view various college sports, including men's and women's basketball. You can find news about your favorite college teams, including scores and rankings.

Web: www.ncaa.com
Facebook: NCAA (Page)
Twitter: (None)
LinkedIn: NCAA (Company)

BILLIARDS

AZBilliards.com

Truly the A-to-Z site for billiards and pool. You'll find pages on tours and tournaments, players, columns, forums, and online shopping. View TV listings for upcoming tournaments, read interviews with the major players, and sign up for RSS feeds.

Web: www.azbilliards.com
Facebook: (None)
Twitter: AzBilliards
LinkedIn: (None)

Billiards Digest

At this great site for billiards fans, you'll find blogs and columns from the magazine's editors as well as top players in the sport.

Web: www.billiardsdigest.com/blogs.php
Facebook: Billiards Digest (Page)
Twitter: (None)
LinkedIn: (None)

World Snooker Association

A very nice site dedicated to the game of snooker, a popular cue sport. The site features news, tournament information, player information, and a video gallery.

Web: www.worldsnooker.com
Facebook: World Snooker (Page)
Twitter: WorldSnooker1
LinkedIn: (None)

BOWLING

Bowl.com

Home of the United States Bowling Congress, this site is dedicated to the sport of bowling, from youth leagues to collegiate leagues to adult leagues. You'll find tons of information about bowling records and stats, explanations of rules, news reports, and shopping for equipment and apparel.

Web: www.bowl.com
Facebook: USBC (Page)
Twitter: USBC
LinkedIn: (None)

BowlingFans.com

The perfect site for bowling fans, offering tips on techniques, a glossary of bowling terms, and a calendar of events. Be sure to check out the community forums and online chat.

Web: www.bowlingfans.com
Facebook: BowlingFans.com (Group)
Twitter: (None)
LinkedIn: (None)

National Duckpin Bowling Congress

If you're serious about duckpin bowling, mark this site, the official site of the National Duckpin Bowling Congress, as a favorite. You'll find information about tournaments, hall of fame bowlers, world-record stats, and links to other duckpin bowling sites.

Web: www.ndbc.org
Facebook: National Duckpin Bowling Congress (Page)
Twitter: (None)
LinkedIn: (None)

Professional Bowlers Association

The official site of the Professional Bowlers Association, this website is bursting at the seams with bowling info, including the PBA tours and tickets.

Web: www.pba.com
Facebook: Professional Bowlers Association (PBA) (Page)
Twitter: (None)
LinkedIn: (None)

BOXING

East Side Boxing

If you want to talk boxing, stop by this site and join in on the conversations. Discuss recent fights or relive classic matchups from the past.

Web: www.eastsideboxing.com/forum
Facebook: East Side Boxing (Page)
Twitter: (None)
LinkedIn: (None)

BUNGEE JUMPING

Bungee.com

This site is an excellent source for the nitty-gritty aspects of bungee jumping, including where to find good insurance for this radical sport. This site also offers a mailing list so you can keep abreast of the latest bungee-jumping news.

Web: www.bungee.com
Facebook: Bungee.com (Page)
Twitter: (None)
LinkedIn: (None)

CLIMBING

All Climbing

A fantastic blog about climbing, covering bouldering, climbing areas, and mountaineering.

Web: www.allclimbing.com
Facebook: All Climbing (Page)
Twitter: (None)
LinkedIn: (None)

14

Rock and Ice Magazine

There's plenty of coverage of both rock- and ice-climbing sports on this site. The site offers news, forums, a guide directory, job listings, and a retail store.

Web: www.rockandice.com
Facebook: Rock and Ice Magazine (Page)
Twitter: (None)
LinkedIn: (None)

COMPETITIVE EATING

International Federation of Competitive Eating

The official governing body of stomach-centric sports, this site keeps track of contests, records and rankings, eater profiles, and safety tips.

Web: www.ifoce.com
Facebook: International Federation of Competitive Eating (Page)
Twitter: (None)
LinkedIn: (None)

Major League Eating

Find out about the hottest eating contests, from hot dogs to pizza and beyond. The site features clips from the latest competitions.

Web: www.ifoce.com
Facebook: Major League Eating (Page)
Twitter: (None)
LinkedIn: (None)

CRICKET

Cricket World

You can find numerous podcasts about cricket here, as well as a well-rounded website focusing on the world of cricket playing.

Web: www.cricketworld.com/radio/
Facebook: CRICKET WORLD (Group), Cricket World (Page)
Twitter: (None)
LinkedIn: (None)

ESPN Cricinfo

Are you a jolly good cricket fan? Check out ESPN's Cricinfo site for the latest cricket scores from around the globe. View live scorecards, latest matches, and stats.

Web: www.cricinfo.com
Facebook: ESPN Cricinfo Indian Premier League (Page)
Twitter: (None)
LinkedIn: (None)

International Cricket Council

Visit this site for news, tournament events, rankings, and upcoming broadcasts of cricket around the world. You'll find links to league divisions, photo galleries, and video and audio clips.

Web: http://icc-cricket.yahoo.com
Facebook: International Cricket Council (ICC) (Page)
Twitter: (None)
LinkedIn: International Cricket Council (Company)

West Indies Cricket Blog

A nicely done blog site about cricket, including quotes from players and news sources.

Web: www.caribbeancricket.com/weblog
Facebook: (None)
Twitter: westindies
LinkedIn: (None)

CURLING

The Curling News

A great blog about curling, this site is totally dedicated to covering curling competitions from its base in Canada.

Web: www.thecurlingnews.com/blog/
Facebook: The Curling News (Group)
Twitter: (None)
LinkedIn: (None)

14

The Curling Show

If you're looking for a podcast about curling, you'll find it on this site. Podcasts here cover curling championships, interviews with players and teams, and much more.

Web: www.thecurlingshow.com
Facebook: The Curling Show (Group)
Twitter: (None)
LinkedIn: (None)

CurlTV.com

Curling fans can find all the curling info they could possibly want at this site. View game reviews, team competitions and standings, RSS feeds, and bios on curlers and teams.

Web: www.curltv.com
Facebook: CurlTV.com (Group)
Twitter: (None)
LinkedIn: (None)

CYCLING

Le Tour de France

Learn all about the Tour de France, the world's largest cycling race, on this site featuring news about this year's event, the itinerary, video clips, and editorials.

Web: www.letour.fr/indexus.html
Facebook: Le Tour de France (Page, Group)
Twitter: (None)
LinkedIn: (None)

Union Cycliste Internationale

The Swiss-based UCI, or International Cycling Union, is the governing body of competitive cycling sports. The website features news and information about all kinds of cycling competitions, including road cycling, mountain bike, BMX, and indoor cycling.

Web: www.uci.ch
Facebook: Union Cycliste Internationale (Page)
Twitter: (None)
LinkedIn: (None)

VeloNews

At the online journal of competitive cycling, you'll find all the latest news on races, mountain cycling, cyclo-cross, and track cycling. View videos and photos, find out who's leading the pack, and on the forums discuss all things related to cycling.

Web: www.velonews.com
Facebook: VeloNews (Page)
Twitter: velonews
LinkedIn: (None)

DANCE

Movmnt Magazine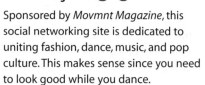

Sponsored by *Movmnt Magazine*, this social networking site is dedicated to uniting fashion, dance, music, and pop culture. This makes sense since you need to look good while you dance.

Web: www.movmnt.net
Facebook: movmnt magazine (Page), Movmnt Magazine - Together as a Facebook Group (Group)
Twitter: movmnt
LinkedIn: Movmnt (Company)

USA Dance

This site, home of DanceSport, the competitive version of ballroom dancing, is dedicated to promoting the love of ballroom dance. Here you'll find news about upcoming events, links to various chapters, competition results, and much more.

Web: http://usadance.org
Facebook: USA Dance Competitions (Group)
Twitter: usadanceinc
LinkedIn: USA Dance

14

DIVING

FINA

Home of the International Swimming Federation, this governing body also heads up diving. Tracking all worldwide diving events, you can find out results, bios, and stats on all the top divers, and a calendar of events.

Web: www.fina.org
Facebook: FINA (Group)
Twitter: (None)
LinkedIn: (None)

Flip N Rip.com

Find diving news about high school, college, and international diving teams here. View meet results, videos, diving info, and forums.

Web: www.flipnrip.com
Facebook: FlipNrip (Page)
Twitter: (None)
LinkedIn: (None)

USA Diving

Surf over to this site for all the latest news about U.S. diving, including clubs, coaches, meet results, upcoming programs, and the diving rulebook.

Web: www.usadiving.org
Facebook: USA Diving (Page)
Twitter: USADiving
LinkedIn: (None)

EQUESTRIAN SPORTS

Stadium Jumping, Inc.

Visit this site for the latest results on the show-jumping circuit. Find entry forms for upcoming events, ticket information, and news stories.

Web: www.stadiumjumping.com
Facebook: Stadium Jumping Inc (Group)
Twitter: (None)
LinkedIn: (None)

FENCING

United States Fencing Association

If swordplay is more to your liking, visit the United States Fencing Association's website. View domestic and international news about the sport of fencing, from youth programs to veteran fencing. Find out national point standings, fencing facts, and how to find a local club.

Web: www.usfencing.org
Facebook: US Olympic Team (Page)
Twitter: USFencing
LinkedIn: (None)

FISHING

Angling Masters

On this social networking site for fishermen, you can join and create your own personal page, called a "cabin," share photos, swap stories with others, and participate in online fishing tournaments.

Web: www.anglingmasters.com
Facebook: Angling Masters International (Group)
Twitter: (None)
LinkedIn: (None)

Bounty Fishing.com

This site features a fast-growing community of competitive fishermen. You'll find plenty of info and forums, tips on competition rules and processes, tournament schedules, leader boards, and records.

Web: www.bountyfishing.com
Facebook: BountyFishing.com (Page)
Twitter: BountyFishing
LinkedIn: (None)

FOOTBALL

Arena Fan

Arena football fans will enjoy this site filled with fan-based message boards, chat rooms, fantasy leagues, clubs, podcasts, history, stats, and much more.

Web: www.arenafan.com
Facebook: ArenaFan (Page)
Twitter: arenafan
LinkedIn: (None)

College Football Podcast.net

When college football season is at its peak, you can catch up on past, present, and future podcasts on this site.

Web: www.collegefootballpodcast.net
Facebook: College Football Podcast (Group)
Twitter: CFBPodcast
LinkedIn: (None)

Fanblogs.com

Stop by this site for some very interesting blogs discussing teams, games, and botched plays.

Web: www.fanblogs.com
Facebook: Fanblogs (Page)
Twitter: (None)
LinkedIn: (None)

NFL

Official home of the National Football League, this site is a good starting point for following your favorite professional teams as they play across the nation. View draft picks, team rosters, player bios, scores, stats, and standings. You can also find video clips of exciting game plays and shop for merchandise.

Web: www.nfl.com
Facebook: NFL (Page, Group)
Twitter: (None)
LinkedIn: (None)

GOLF

The Golf Blog

Visit this site for a fun blog covering all things related to the sport of golf. You'll find video clips, news, and links.

Web: www.thegolfblog.com
Facebook: (None)
Twitter: thegolfblog
LinkedIn: (None)

PGA

Official home of the PGA, Professional Golfers Association, this website is chock-full of news and information on the sport of golf. View video clips, find tournament schedules, and purchase tickets. You can also find an instructor, look for job opportunities, and shop for equipment.

Web: www.pga.com
Facebook: PGA (Page)
Twitter: (None)
LinkedIn: (None)

GYMNASTICS

Inside Gymnastics Magazine

Serving up online content from their magazine, *Inside Gymnastics* brings you the top stories, news about events and standings, blogs, and links to apparel and equipment makers around the world.

Web: www.insidegymnastics.com
Facebook: Inside Gymnastics (www.insidegymnastics.com) (Page)
Twitter: InsideGym
LinkedIn: (None)

14

USA Gymnastics

Serious fans of gymnastics will find plenty to like about the sport on this site, including events, results, and bios on top athletes. The site covers women's, men's, rhythmic, group, trampoline and tumbling, and acrobatic gymnastics.

Web: www.usa-gymnastics.org
Facebook: USA Gymnastics (Page)
Twitter: USA_Gymnastics
LinkedIn: USA Gymnastics (Company)

HANDBALL

US Handball Association

Handball players can find all kinds of stuff on this site, including tournament news, the handball hall of fame, message boards, rules and information about the game, and podcasts.

Web: www.ushandball.org
Facebook: U.S. Handball Association (Page)
Twitter: (None)
LinkedIn: (None)

HANG GLIDING AND PARAGLIDING

Air Sports Net

A great resource into the world of hang gliding, paragliding, ultralights, and parachuting, this site offers lots of links to products and services, including weather forecasting products.

Web: www.usairnet.com
Facebook: Air Sports Net (Page)
Twitter: airsportsnet
LinkedIn: (None)

The Oz Report

Dedicated to hang gliding and the likes, the forum page at this site offers several good message boards discussing hang gliding, sites to pursue hang gliding, and various competitions.

Web: http://ozreport.com/forum
Facebook: The Oz Report (Group)
Twitter: (None)
LinkedIn: (None)

United States Hang Gliding and Paragliding Association

The name says it all—this site offers news about hang gliding and paragliding, including news, chapters and clubs, a calendar of events across the nation, pilot info, articles, and even a link to online shopping for hang gliding equipment.

Web: www.ushpa.aero
Facebook: United States Hang Gliding and Paragliding Association, Inc. (Group)
Twitter: (None)
LinkedIn: (None)

HOCKEY

NHL

At the home of the National Hockey League, you'll find tons of information about the sport on this site. View schedules, scores, stats, player bios, and all the top stories. The Fan Zone area features blogs, newsletters, and online games. You'll also find photo galleries, video highlights, and podcasts to download.

Web: www.nhl.com
Facebook: NHL (Page)
Twitter: (None)
LinkedIn: National Hockey League (Company)

KAYAKING

Kayaking.com

If paddling is your thing, this site is full of news, photos, articles, events, guide-books, gear review, and even contests and giveaways all associated with the sport of kayaking.

Web: www.kayaking.com
Facebook: (None)
Twitter: (None)
LinkedIn: Kayaking.com (Company)

KayakMind

If you're looking for a social network of fellow whitewater kayakers, then look no further than this site. You'll find plenty of other passionate souls who share a love of tiny floating devices and raging river currents with whom to exchange stories, tips, and the like.

Web: http://kayakmind.ning.com
Facebook: KayakMind (Group)
Twitter: (None)
LinkedIn: (None)

LACROSSE

Lacrosse Forums.com

Discuss everything from general men's field lacrosse, recruiting news, game-day coverage, and anything else related to lacrosse on this forum board.

Web: www.lacrosseforums.com
Facebook: Inside Lacrosse (Page)
Twitter: Inside_Lacrosse
LinkedIn: (None)

LaxPower

Tailored to the lacrosse fan, this site lists computer ratings for men's and women's college, boy's and girl's high school, MLL, and NLL. Keep up with scoreboards, tour-nament schedules, awards, video clips, and forums.

Web: www.laxpower.com
Facebook: LaxPower Lacrosse (Page)
Twitter: (None)
LinkedIn: (None)

LaxSpot.com

This social networking spot is dedicated to lacrosse fans and players. Share blogs, photos, and videos; connect with team-mates and friends; buy and sell equip-ment; and find lacrosse events.

Web: www.laxspot.com
Facebook: LaxSpot.com (Page)
Twitter: (None)
LinkedIn: (None)

U.S. Lacrosse

This site is the national governing body of men's, women's, and youth lacrosse. Stop by to view news, events, shop for clothing and equipment, find local chapters, or just learn more about the sport in general.

Web: www.lacrosse.org
Facebook: US Lacrosse (Page)
Twitter: US_Lacrosse
LinkedIn: US Lacrosse (Company)

MARTIAL ARTS

MMA Fighting.com

Fans of mixed martial arts fighting will enjoy this blog. It contains reviews of recent matches as well as links to news items about MMA.

Web: www.mmafightingblog.com
Facebook: MMA Fighting.com - The Mixed Martial Arts News Website (Page)
Twitter: MMAFighting
LinkedIn: (None)

MMA Weekly

Looking for info about mixed martial arts fights? Visit this site. It features daily news, a live radio show, a photo gallery, forums, and live chats with fighters.

14

Web: www.mmaweekly.com
Facebook: MMAWeekly.com (Page)
Twitter: mmaweeklycom
LinkedIn: (None)

The Ultimate Fighting Championship

Here's a knockout site dedicated to the UFC. View video clips, interviews with the fighters, and event schedules. You can also learn more about this exciting mixed martial arts sport and the rules that govern the matches.

Web: www.ufc.com
Facebook: UFC: Ultimate Fighting Championship (Page)
Twitter: ufc
LinkedIn: (None)

United States Judo Association

Supporting both players and clubs, this site features news, forums, club info, hall of fames, and even a list of expelled members.

Web: www.usja-judo.org
Facebook: USJA - United States Judo Association (Group)
Twitter: (None)
LinkedIn: (None)

World Karate Federation

At the home of the World Karate Federation, you'll find a complete history of the organization and its competitions, rules and regulations, videos, news, and links to related sites.

Web: www.karateworld.org
Facebook: World Karate Federation (Page)
Twitter: (None)
LinkedIn: (None)

World Tae Kwon Do Association

Tae Kwon Do students and masters will find plenty of info on this site, including a history of the art, a calendar of events and tournaments, and a photo gallery.

Facebook: World Tae Kwon Do Association (Page)
Twitter: (None)
LinkedIn: (None)

MOTORCYCLE SPORTS

American Motorcyclist Association

You'll find news about motorcycle racing here, including links to all the associated websites, such as superbike, supermoto, motocross, flat track, and hill climb.

Web: www.amadirectlink.com/
Facebook: American Motorcyclist Association (Page)
Twitter: (None)
LinkedIn: (None)

Dirt Rider

You'll find plenty of blogs about the down-and-dirty racers and their flying motocross machines on this site. Riders share their stories and adventures, and talk about their bikes in great detail.

Web: http://blogs.dirtrider.com
Facebook: Dirt Rider Magazine (Page)
Twitter: (None)
LinkedIn: (None)

Moto-Racing on SpeedTV

Find all the details you need about motocross racing here, including standings, results, and upcoming events.

Web: http://moto-racing.speedtv.com
Facebook: SPEEDtv.com (Page, Group)
Twitter: SPEED
LinkedIn: (None)

OLYMPICS

International Olympic Committee

Looking for more information about the upcoming Olympics, or about games from the past? This site gives you the latest news and countdowns to both summer and winter Olympics, as well as history about the games and a virtual tour of the Olympic Museum.

Web: www.olympic.org
Facebook: The Olympic Games (Page)
Twitter: Olympics
LinkedIn: International Olympic Committee (Company)

ORIENTEERING SPORTS

Geocaching.com

Join the millions of geocaching fans around the world at this site, the official global GPS hunt site. If you're new to geocaching, you'll find out how to get started. Locate geocaches near your area, or check out the forums to discuss all things related to geocaching.

Web: www.geocaching.com
Facebook: Geocaching.com (Page)
Twitter: GoGeocaching
LinkedIn: (None)

Podcacher

Here's a great little show about the world of geocaching. You can view this week's episode or catch up with previous podcasts in the archive.

Web: www.podcacher.com
Facebook: Podcacher Listeners Group (Group), The Podcacher Podcast (Page)
Twitter: podcacher
LinkedIn: (None)

PARASAILING

Parasailing Videos at Metacafe.com

Take a gander at this collection of para-sailing video clips from people visiting places around the world.

Web: www.metacafe.com/tags/parasailing
Facebook: Parasailing (Page)
Twitter: (None)
LinkedIn: (None)

RACQUET (EXCLUD

USA Racquetball

At the official site of the U.S. Racquetball Association, you'll find information about upcoming tournaments, a player hall of fame, and links to racquetball equipment.

Web: www.usra.org
Facebook: USA Racquetball (Page)
Twitter: usaracquetball
LinkedIn: (None)

World Squash

Site of the World Squash Federation, here you can learn more about this sport, including rules and regulations, upcoming tournaments, and top players.

Web: www.squash.org
Facebook: World Squash Federation (Page)
Twitter: (None)
LinkedIn: (None)

RAFTING

American Whitewater

Find out all the specifics about the rivers you will be rafting on before planning your experience. The mission of AW is to conserve and restore America's whitewater resources and to enhance opportunities to enjoy them safely. You'll find all kinds of help and information here, especially on safety and what is being done to save the whitewater ways.

Web: www.americanwhitewater.org
Facebook: American Whitewater (Page)
Twitter: AmerWhitewater
LinkedIn: (None)

RODEO

Professional Bull Riders

If riding bulls is your thing, this site is the place to go. You'll find clips of the latest bull-riding competitions, news about upcoming events, ratings and rankings of the circuit's best riders, blogs, web chats, and merchandise.

Web: www.pbrnow.com
Facebook: Team PBR (Page)
Twitter: teampbr
LinkedIn: Professional Bull Riders, Inc. (Company)

Professional Rodeo Cowboys Association

Saddle up and ride over to this website for all the latest information about the professional rodeo circuit. Follow the rodeo careers of your favorite cowboys, covering everything from steer wrestling to roping and riding. Keep track of upcoming events and current standings.

Web: www.prorodeo.com
Facebook: Pro Rodeo.com (Page)
Twitter: (None)
LinkedIn: Professional Rodeo Cowboys Association (Company)

ROWING

Rowing News

Maintained by *Rowing News Magazine*, this site covers everything from NCAA rowing to world rowing championships.

Web: www.rowingnews.com
Facebook: Rowing News Magazine (Page)
Twitter: (None)
LinkedIn: (None)

World Rowing.com

This site lists rowing events and news, tracks the top rowers and results, and details the kinds of rowing found in this worldwide sport.

Web: www.worldrowing.com
Facebook: www.WorldRowing.com (Page)
Twitter: WorldRowing
LinkedIn: (None)

RUGBY

Planet Rugby

Join in on the world's biggest online rugby club and check out news, fixtures and results, tournaments, and forums, and even participate in a fantasy league.

Web: www.planet-rugby.com
Facebook: Planet Rugby (Page)
Twitter: Planet_Rugby
LinkedIn: (None)

The Rugby Blog

This blog site covers all the major rugby players, teams, and tournaments, plus provides links to other rugby blogs.

Web: www.therugbyblog.co.uk
Facebook: The Rugby Blog (Page, Group)
Twitter: TheRugbyBlog
LinkedIn: (None)

Rugbydump.com

This site combines rugby blogging and some excellent video clips of game play. What could be better for rugby fans?

Web: www.rugbydump.blogspot.com
Facebook: Rugbydump.com (Page, Group)
Twitter: (None)
LinkedIn: (None)

RugbyRugby.com

This site is chock-full of rugby news and headlines. Find all the latest results from around the world, read editorials, and shop for your favorite team uniforms.

Web: www.rugbyrugby.com
Facebook: Rugby Rugby (Page)
Twitter: rugbyrugbynews
LinkedIn: (None)

Rugby World Magazine

Dubbed the world's best-selling rugby magazine, this site has an excellent selection of rugby video clips from matches around the globe.

Web: www.rugbyworld.com/clips
Facebook: Rugby World Magazine (Page)
Twitter: Rugbyworldmag
LinkedIn: (None)

scrum.com

Billing itself as the perfect pitch for rugby, this site features news, tournament info, stats, forums, editorial columns, podcasts, video clips, a newsletter, photo galleries, a scrum fantasy league, classifieds, and links to other rugby stuff.

Web: www.scrum.com
Facebook: Scrum.com (Page)
Twitter: Graham_Jenkins
LinkedIn: (None)

USA Rugby

At the official site of U.S. rugby, you'll find plenty of info about the sport in general and about clubs and tournaments, rules and regulations, and scoreboards for men's, women's, and high-school tournaments.

Web: www.usarugby.org
Facebook: The Official USA Rugby Fan Page (Page)
Twitter: (None)
LinkedIn: USA Rugby (Company)

SAILING

Sailing Networks 📖

Dedicated to connecting sailors worldwide, this site helps boats find crew members, and crew members find boats. Plus, you'll find info on upcoming sailing events, classified ads, and forums.

Web: www.sailingnetworks.com
Facebook: Sailing Networks (Page)
Twitter: (None)
LinkedIn: (None)

US Sailing

On this site learn the ins and outs of sailing, including where to find upcoming races and regattas. View sailing news, find links for training, and learn how to get started yourself.

Web: www.ussailing.org
Facebook: US SAILING (Page)
Twitter: ussailing
LinkedIn: US SAILING (Company)

Yachting and Boating World

Visit this site to view sailing news, blogs, boats for sale, forums, weather, and tide reports.

Web: www.ybw.com
Facebook: Yachting and Boating World (Page)
Twitter: (None)
LinkedIn: (None)

SCUBA DIVING

PADI: Professional Association of Diving Instructors

A fantastic site with current information. Updated daily, this site offers dive-center listings, product catalogs, news, and course listings. Also provides plenty of information about PADI diving certification. Site content is divided into three areas: Start Diving, Keep Diving, and Teach Diving. Great site for both novice and expert scuba divers and their instructors.

Web: www.padi.com
Facebook: PADI: Professional Association of Diving Instructors (Page, Group)
Twitter: (None)
LinkedIn: (None)

14

SKATEBOARDING

Thrasher Magazine

Thrasher Magazine's online site offers everything for the skateboarding fanatic, from products to skateboard park locations. Find skateboarding events, message boards, and news.

Web: www.thrashermagazine.com
Facebook: Thrasher Magazine (Page)
Twitter: (None)
LinkedIn: (None)

Transworld Skateboarding

Skateboarders can find plenty of info on this site, from videos and photos to trick tips to message boards.

Web: www.skateboarding.com
Facebook: TransWorld SKATEboarding (Page)
Twitter: (None)
LinkedIn: (None)

SKATING

Golden Skate

An excellent online resource for everything related to figure skating. You'll find news headlines, articles, forums, and a listing of upcoming events.

Web: www.goldenskate.com
Facebook: Golden Skate (Page)
Twitter: goldenskate
LinkedIn: (None)

Roller Skating Association International

If roller skating is more your sport, visit the Roller Skating Association International site. You'll find information about skating competitions and industry news, and you can locate a skating center near you.

Web: www.rollerskating.org
Facebook: Roller Skating Association Int'l (Group)
Twitter: RSAIntl
LinkedIn: Roller Skating Association International (Group)

US Figure Skating

If you're a fan of figure skating, visit this site for news and headlines about the sport. Find athlete bios, events, results, clubs, videos, and discussion boards.

Web: www.usfigureskating.org
Facebook: U.S. Figure Skating (Page)
Twitter: USFigureSkating
LinkedIn: U.S. Figure Skating (Company)

SKIING

Ski Racing

Find the latest news and info about snowsport competition. You can participate in forums, view video and short films and a photo gallery, and read through classified ads.

Web: www.skiracing.com
Facebook: Ski Racing Magazine (Page)
Twitter: SkiRacingMag
LinkedIn: (None)

USA Waterski

This site has it all when it comes to watersports—everything from water-skiing, show skiing, waterboarding, waterski racing, and kneeboarding. View rankings, tournament scores, and photo galleries.

Web: www.usawaterski.org
Facebook: USA Waterski (Page)
Twitter: USAWaterSki
LinkedIn: (None)

Wakeboarding Magazine

Wakeboarding Magazine presents news; feature articles; gear and boat reviews; instructions on wakeboarding, wakeskating, and boating; classifieds; announcements of upcoming events and competitions; photos and videos; discussion forums; and sample articles from its printed publication.

Web: www.wakeboardingmag.com
Facebook: Wakeboarding Magazine (Page)
Twitter: (None)
LinkedIn: (None)

SNORKELING

BSAC Snorkeling

British Sub Aqua Club (BSAC) presents this site to introduce water lovers to the underwater world of snorkeling. Site covers First Steps, Training, Advice, and Activities. Features an excellent collection of snorkeling games that can help you hone your skills while having fun.

Web: www.bsacsnorkelling.co.uk
Facebook: British Sub-Aqua Club (BSAC) (Page)
Twitter: (None)
LinkedIn: (None)

Tropical Snorkeling Blog

This blog reviews various tropical snorkeling locations, providing insider tips for finding the best beaches and reefs wherever your travels take you.

Web: www.tropicalsnorkeling.com/snorkeling-blog.html
Facebook: Tropical Snorkeling (Page)
Twitter: TropicalSnorkel
LinkedIn: (None)

SOCCER

ESPN Soccer Net

ESPN's soccer site has all the latest international soccer news, plus fantasy leagues, stats on players and teams, video clips, and fan forums.

Web: http://soccernet.espn.go.com
Facebook: (None)
Twitter: Soccernet
LinkedIn: (None)

Sams-Army.com

Billing itself as the unofficial website for supporters of the U.S. National Soccer Team, this site includes team news, videos, photos, schedules, polls, and trivia.

Web: www.sams-army.com
Facebook: (None)
Twitter: SamsArmy94
LinkedIn: (None)

Soccer 24-7 🖻

If you want to discuss soccer, visit this site for some lively online conversations about soccer around the globe.

Web: www.soccer24-7.com/forum/index.php
Facebook: Soccer 24-7 (Page)
Twitter: (None)
LinkedIn: (None)

SOFTBALL

Amateur Softball Association

Home of the Amateur Softball Association, this site features news and info about softball tournaments, ranging from youth leagues to adult leagues. Find help with equipment, umpires, and more. This is also the home of USA Softball.

Web: www.asasoftball.com
Facebook: ASA Softball (Page)
Twitter: ASAUSASoftball
LinkedIn: (None)

14

USA Softball

Looking for game results from softball teams across the nation? This site keeps track of news headlines, softball events, and results. The site also features an online store for all your softball equipment needs. This is also the home of the Amateur Softball Association.

Web: www.usasoftball.com
Facebook: ASA Softball (Page)
Twitter: ASAUSASoftball
LinkedIn: (None)

SURFING

International Surfing Museum

At this site, you can view a collection of surf films, surf music, surfboards, and memorabilia. Visit the current exhibit too. If you like this site, consider becoming a member.

Web: www.surfingmuseum.org
Facebook: The Huntington Beach International Surfing Museum (Page)
Twitter: (None)
LinkedIn: (None)

Surfline

Billing itself as "The Best Place on the Net to Get Wet," this site provides up-to-date reports and live webcams of the best places to surf worldwide. The site also features product reviews and plenty of articles about surfing and the world's top surfers. The Surfology area contains an excellent collection of surfing tips and techniques along with a Surfology glossary.

Web: www.surfline.com
Facebook: Surfline.com (Page)
Twitter: (None)
LinkedIn: Surfline (Company)

SWIMMING

CollegeSwimming.com

Keep abreast, no pun intended, of collegiate swimming competitions around the nation on this site. View top times, qualifying standards, team info, and meet results.

Web: www.collegeswimming.com
Facebook: CollegeSwimming.com (Page)
Twitter: (None)
LinkedIn: (None)

USA Water Polo

Gulp down the hottest news on the sport of water polo on this site. Learn about clubs, camps, and clinics; upcoming events; and how team USA is doing so far this year.

Web: www.usawaterpolo.com
Facebook: USA Water Polo (Page)
Twitter: USAWP
LinkedIn: USA Water Polo (Company)

TENNIS

Tennisopolis

Here's a lovely social networking site helping tennis players connect and communicate. Search for fellow players in your area, find a local group, or chat live with other tennis fans.

Web: www.tennisopolis.com
Facebook: Tennisopolis : Tennis Social Network (Page)
Twitter: tennisopolis
LinkedIn: (None)

USTA

At the site of the United States Tennis Association, you'll find tennis info about professionals and amateurs alike. The site even has info for parents and coaches.

Web: www.usta.com
Facebook: (None)
Twitter: (None)
LinkedIn: USTA (Company)

Wimbledon

A must stop on any tennis player's surfing list, the official home of the famous Wimbledon tennis championships offers news, video clips, merchandise, and links.

Web: www.wimbledon.org
Facebook: Wimbledon (Page)
Twitter: Wimbledon
LinkedIn: (None)

TRACK AND FIELD

Track & Field News

If running, jumping, and throwing is your thing, visit the Track & Field News site. You'll find plenty of headlines, results, records, and rankings on everything from indoor and outdoor track-and-field events.

Web: www.trackandfieldnews.com
Facebook: Track & Field News (Page)
Twitter: (None)
LinkedIn: (None)

USA Track & Field

The national governing body for U.S. Track and Field sports, this site keeps track of national championships, Olympic trials, stats, events, and athlete bios.

Web: www.usatf.org
Facebook: USA Track & Field (Page)
Twitter: USATrack_Field
LinkedIn: USA Track & Field (Company)

VOLLEYBALL

USA Volleyball

Encompassing all levels of players, this site brings you the news about national teams, junior teams, and adult teams. You'll also find event schedules, rules and scorekeeping info, and the latest rankings.

Web: www.usavolleyball.org
Facebook: USA Volleyball (Page)
Twitter: USOlympic
LinkedIn: USA Volleyball (Company)

Volleyball.com

View news, polls, and video clips of volleyball games indoors and out. The site includes forums, blogs, products, and tips.

Web: www.volleyball.com
Facebook: Volleyball.com (Page)
Twitter: Volleyball
LinkedIn: Volleyball.com (Company)

WINDSURFING

iWindsurf.com

Avid windsurfers will really find this site useful. It has links to current wind conditions and forecasts, forums, videos, classified ads, and more.

Web: www.iwindsurf.com
Facebook: iWindsurf.com (Page)
Twitter: (None)
LinkedIn: (None)

14

Professional Windsurfers Association

Representing the best in windsurfing around the world, this site offers the latest in news and events, rankings and profiles of the best windsurfers on the circuit, and tips and links.

Web: www.pwaworldtour.com
Facebook: PWA World Tour Windsurfing (Page)
Twitter: (None)
LinkedIn: (None)

Windsurfing Magazine

Windsurfing Magazine hosts this well-rounded site where you'll find news, videos, events, forums, and shopping links for all the equipment and apparel you might need.

Web: www.windsurfingmag.com
Facebook: Windsurfing Magazine (Page)
Twitter: (None)
LinkedIn: (None)

WRESTLING

CBS College Sports

This site features various sports podcasts from colleges around the nation, including college wrestling.

Web: http://cstv.collegesports.com/podcasts/
Facebook: CBS College Sports Network (Page)
Twitter: (None)
LinkedIn: (None)

The Mat

This site is dedicated to wrestling fans. No, not TV wrestling, but real competitive wrestling, from high school to college, men's and women's divisions. View rankings, competition schedules, and match results. View RSS feeds and message boards, or sign up for a wrestling camp near you.

Web: www.themat.com
Facebook: USA Wrestling (Page)
Twitter: USAWrestling
LinkedIn: USA Wrestling Fans & Supporters (Group)

14

TRAVEL

The Internet has made the world a smaller place—and made travel a whole lot easier. The social media outlets listed in this chapter help you stay connected to the best fares and fees and get recommendations from in-the-know travelers. The chapter also includes links to sites where you can make reservations, and buy tickets online. Whether you're looking for a cruise, an eco-vacation, a theme park, or a luxury hotel, you'll find it here. Or if you're in the mood to take a trip without leaving home, check out some of the videos, social networks, and virtual travel sites, perfect for armchair travelers.

AIRLINES

Aer Lingus $

Web: www.aerlingus.com/cgi-bin/obel01im1/bookonline/index.jsp
Facebook: Aer Lingus (Page)
Twitter: (None)
LinkedIn: (None)

Aeromexico $

Web: www.aeromexico.com/en_us/
Facebook: El Nuevo aeromexico.com (Group)
Twitter: AeroMexico_com
LinkedIn: Aeromexico (Company)

Air Canada $

Web: www.aircanada.com
Facebook: Air Canada (Group)
Twitter: (None)
LinkedIn: Air Canada (Company, Group)

Air France-KLM $

Web: www.airfrance.us
Facebook: Air France (Page, Group)
Twitter: AirFrance_ES
LinkedIn: Air France KLM (Company), Air France-KLM (Group)

AirTran Airways $

Web: www.airtran.com/Home.aspx
Facebook: Airtran Airways (Page)
Twitter: AirTranFares
LinkedIn: AirTran Airways (Company), AirTran airways (Group)

Alaska Airlines $

Web: www.alaskaair.com
Facebook: Alaska Airlines (Page)
Twitter: AlaskaAir
LinkedIn: Alaska Airlines (Company)

Alitalia $

Web: www.alitalia.com
Facebook: Alitalia (Page, Group)
Twitter: Alitalia
LinkedIn: Alitalia Compagnia Aerea Italiana SpA (Company)

American Airlines $

Web: www.aa.com/homePage.do
Facebook: (None)
Twitter: AAirwaves
LinkedIn: American Airlines (Company), AAdvantage Road Warriors (Group)

Austrian Airlines $

Web: www.aua.com/us/eng
Facebook: Austrian Airlines Srbija (Page)
Twitter: Austrian_NL
LinkedIn: Austrian Airlines (Company)

British Airways $

Web: www.britishairways.com/travel/globalgateway.jsp/global/public/en_
Facebook: British Airways (Page, Group)
Twitter: BritishAirways
LinkedIn: British Airways (Company, Group)

Cathay Pacific Airways ⑤
Web: www.cathaypacific.com/cpa/en_INTL/homepage
Facebook: Cathay Pacific Airways (Group)
Twitter: cathaypacific
LinkedIn: Cathay Pacific Airways (Company), Cathay Pacific (Group)

China Airlines ⑤
Web: www.china-airlines.com/en/index.htm
Facebook: China Airlines (Page)
Twitter: airchinaasp
LinkedIn: (None)

Continental Airlines ⑤
Web: www.continental.com/web/en-US/default.aspx
Facebook: I Love Continental Airlines (Group)
Twitter: continental
LinkedIn: Continental Airlines (Company)

Delta ⑤
Web: www.delta.com/index.jsp?noFlash=true
Facebook: Delta Airlines (Group)
Twitter: DeltaAirLines
LinkedIn: Delta Air Lines (Company)

EgyptAir ⑤
Web: www.egyptair.com
Facebook: Egypt Air (Group)
Twitter: EgyptAir_Online, EGYPTAIR_
LinkedIn: (None)

EL AL ⑤
Web: www.elal.com/ELAL/English/States/USA/
Facebook: (None)
Twitter: elal_airlines
LinkedIn: EL AL Israel Airlines (Company)

Frontier Airlines ⑤
Web: www.frontierairlines.com/frontier/home.do
Facebook: Frontier Airlines (Page, Group)
Twitter: flyfrontier, Frontier_Air
LinkedIn: Frontier Airlines (Company, Group)

Hawaiian Airlines ⑤
Web: www.hawaiianair.com
Facebook: (None)
Twitter: FlyHawaiian, HawaiianFares
LinkedIn: Hawaiian Airlines (Company, Group)

Icelandair ⑤
Web: www.icelandair.com
Facebook: Icelandair (Page)
Twitter: Icelandair
LinkedIn: Icelandair (Company)

Japan Airlines (JAL) ⑤
Web: www.jal.com/en/
Facebook: (None)
Twitter: japan_airlines, JAPAN_AIRLINES_
LinkedIn: Japan Airlines (Company, Group)

JetBlue ⑤
Web: www.jetblue.com
Facebook: The JetBlue Experience (Group)
Twitter: JetBlue
LinkedIn: JetBlue Airways (Company)

Korean Air ⑤
Web: www.koreanair.com
Facebook: korean air (Group)
Twitter: KoreanAir_KE
LinkedIn: Korean Air (Company)

Lufthansa ⑤
Web: www.lufthansa.com
Facebook: Lufthansa BUE Oldies (Group)
Twitter: Lufthansa_DE, Lufthansa_USA
LinkedIn: Lufthansa (Company, Group)

Malaysia Airlines ⑤
Web: www.malaysiaairlines.com
Facebook: (None)
Twitter: MAS
LinkedIn: Malaysia Airlines (Company)

Mexicana Airlines ⑤
Web: www.mexicana.com
Facebook: (None)
Twitter: MexicanaAir
LinkedIn: Mexicana Airlines (Company)

Midwest Airlines ⑤
Web: www.midwestairlines.com
Facebook: (None)
Twitter: MidwestAirlines
LinkedIn: Midwest Airlines (Company, Group)

Qantas ⑤
Web: www.qantas.com.au
Facebook: Qantas Airlines (Group)
Twitter: QantasUSA
LinkedIn: Qantas (Company), Qantas Airways (Group)

Ryan Air ⑤
Web: www.ryanair.com/en
Facebook: Ryanair (Group)
Twitter: ryanairmobile
LinkedIn: Ryanair (Company)

Scandinavian Airlines (SAS) $

Web: www.flysas.com/en
Facebook: Scandinavian Airlines System (Group)
Twitter: SASGroup
LinkedIn: Scandinavian Airlines (Company), SAS Scandinavian Airlines (Company)

Singapore Airlines $

Web: www.singaporeair.com
Facebook: Singapore Airlines (Group)
Twitter: SQairlines
LinkedIn: (None)

Southwest Airlines $

Web: www.southwest.com
Facebook: Southwest Airlines (Page)
Twitter: SouthwestAir
LinkedIn: Southwest Airlines (Company, Group)

Spirit Airlines $

Web: www.spiritair.com
Facebook: (None)
Twitter: SpiritAirlines
LinkedIn: Spirit Airlines (Company)

Turkish Airlines $

Web: www.turkishairlines.com
Facebook: Turkish Airlines (Page, Group)
Twitter: TurkishAirlines
LinkedIn: Turkish Airlines (Company, Group)

United Airlines $

Web: www.united.com
Facebook: united airlines fan club (Group)
Twitter: UnitedAirlines
LinkedIn: United Airlines (Company, Group)

US Airways $

Web: www.usairways.com
Facebook: (None)
Twitter: usairways
LinkedIn: US Airways (Company), USAirways Frequent Flyers (Group)

Virgin America $

Web: www.virginamerica.com
Facebook: Let Virgin America Fly!! (Group)
Twitter: VirginAmerica
LinkedIn: Virgin America (Company)

Virgin Atlantic $

Web: www.virgin-atlantic.com/en/us/index.jsp
Facebook: Virgin Atlantic (Page, Group)
Twitter: VirginAtlantic
LinkedIn: Virgin Atlantic Airways (Company), Virgin Atlantic (Group)

Nuts About Southwest

A variety of Southwest Airlines employees, from customer service agents and flight attendants to executives, have their say about working for Southwest, current policies, and other travel-related topics.

Web: www.blogsouthwest.com
Facebook: Southwest Airlines (Page)
Twitter: SouthwestAir
LinkedIn: Southwest Airlines (Company, Group)

Under the Wing (Delta)

A behind-the-scenes blog from Delta covering destinations, planning and booking tips, history, operations, and so on.

Web: http://blog.delta.com/
Facebook: Delta Airlines (Group)
Twitter: DeltaAirLines
LinkedIn: Delta Air Lines (Company)

AIR TRAVEL

The Airline Blog

An anonymous blog that offers insightful analysis of airline-industry news.

Web: http://theairlineblog.blogspot.com/
Facebook: The Airline Blog (Page)
Twitter: airlineblog
LinkedIn: (None)

Boarding Area

Focusing on business travelers, Boarding Area hosts several travel blogs of interest to frequent flyers, including The Cranky Flyer, Points Wizard, and View from the Wing.

Web: www.boardingarea.com
Facebook: (None)
Twitter: BoardingArea
LinkedIn: (None)

15

Federal Aviation Administration

It's the job of the Federal Aviation Administration to ensure safe air travel in the United States. Learn about what the FAA does; get news and updates; find out about flight delays and airport closings, research aviation data, and statistics; get tips for travelers; and so on.

Web: www.faa.gov
Facebook: Federal Aviation Administration (FAA) (Page, Group)
Twitter: FAAAviationNews
LinkedIn: FAA (Company)

FlightAware

FlightAware is a free, real-time flight tracker that lets you follow the progress of planes in the air. Here you'll also find airport information—arrivals, departures, and activity.

Web: http://flightaware.com/
Facebook: FlightAware (Page)
Twitter: flightaware
LinkedIn: FlightAware (Company, Group)

FlightStats

Frequent flyers (or even occasional ones) will find this site helpful, whether planning a trip or en route. Before you go, check flight availability, published fares, and promotions. When you're on your way, learn about airport information and delays, parking, and security wait times. Get flight reports and even check ratings of particular flights based on their history. Track flights in progress, get alerts on your cellphone, and download widgets to put FlightStats info on your desktop.

Web: www.flightstats.com
Facebook: FlightStats (Page)
Twitter: flightstats
LinkedIn: (None)

FlyerTalk

Billing itself as "the world's most popular frequent flyer community," FlyerTalk offers discussion forums on travel-related topics, including frequent-flyer programs, reviews, budget travel, and more. Create a profile, chat in real time, and upload photos from your travels.

Web: www.flyertalk.com
Facebook: FlyerTalk (Group)
Twitter: FlyerTalk
LinkedIn: Flyertalk (Group)

AMUSEMENT PARKS AND THEME PARKS

Busch Entertainment Corp. Worlds of Discovery

This site brings together the theme parks operated nationwide by Busch Entertainment Corp.: Discovery Cove, Aquatica, SeaWorld, Busch Gardens, Adventure Island, Water Country USA, Sesame Place. Links take you to individual parks' sites, where you can get more information and buy tickets.

Web: www.seaworldparksblog.com
Facebook: SeaWorld (Group), Seaworld Groupies (Group)
Twitter: seaworldonline, SeaWorld_Parks
LinkedIn: SeaWorld (Company)

California's Great America

In Santa Clara, California, this park offers thrill rides, rides for kids, and live shows. Nickelodeon Central features characters from the popular kids' channel, such as Dora the Explorer, SpongeBob SquarePants, and the Wild Thornberrys. Boomerang Bay is an Australia-themed water park.

Web: www.cagreatamerica.com
Facebook: Great America (Page), great america!! (Group)
Twitter: CAGreatAmerica
LinkedIn: (None)

Canada's Wonderland

Canada's Wonderland has more than 65 rides, including a dozen roller coasters; concerts, shows, and other attractions; and a 20-acre water park. It's located north of Toronto.

Web: www.canadaswonderland.com
Facebook: Canada's Wonderland (Group)
Twitter: WonderlandNews
LinkedIn: Paramount Canada's Wonderland (Company)

Canobie Lake Park

Located 30 miles north of Boston in Salem, New Hampshire, Canobie Lake Park has more than 85 rides, games, and other attractions. Rides range from an antique carousel and other kiddie rides to four roller coasters. Rides' thrill levels are graded Green Circle (mild), Blue Square (moderate), or Black Diamond (high). Preview Black Diamond rides by taking a video "virtual ride."

Web: www.canobie.com
Facebook: Canobie Lake Park (Page)
Twitter: CanobieLakePark
LinkedIn: (None)

Cedar Point

Like roller coasters? Cedar Point has 17 of them—the most, it claims, of any amusement park on Earth. The 364-acre park in Sandusky, Ohio, boasts a total of 75 rides, ranging from mild to wild. The park includes a water park, four resort hotels, a campground, two marinas, and an entertainment complex.

Web: www.cedarpoint.com
Facebook: Cedar Point (Page), cedar point (Group)
Twitter: cedarpoint
LinkedIn: (None)

Disney.com: The Official Home Page for All Things Disney 🏅

This site offers information about Disney parks around the world and, as it promises, all things Disney, including movies, videos, games, and music. You can also read about Disney vacation packages and its cruise line. Disney-themed items are available for purchase in the gift shop.

Web: http://disney.go.com/index
Facebook: Walt Disney (Group)
Twitter: DisneyParks
LinkedIn: The Walt Disney Company (Company), Walt Disney World (Company), Disney Appreciation - Fans of Walt Disney World and other Disney Parks (Group)

Dollywood

Dollywood, named for country singer and co-owner Dolly Parton, is located in the Great Smoky Mountains near Gatlinburg, Tennessee. In addition to rides, Dollywood has stage shows (featuring music from bluegrass and country to rock 'n' roll from the 1950s and 1960s) and demonstrations of traditional crafts such as candle and soap making, woodworking, and glass blowing. The park features five festivals each year: Festival of Nations, KidsFest, Barbeque & Bluegrass, Harvest Celebration, and Smoky Mountain Christmas.

Web: www.dollywood.com
Facebook: Dollywood (Page)
Twitter: Dollywood
LinkedIn: (None)

Hard Rock Park

This rock-themed park opened in spring 2008 in Myrtle Beach, South Carolina. Its different areas celebrate different aspects of popular music, such as the British Invasion (English-style rock), Lost in the '70s (folk, punk, disco, and glam rock), Born in the USA (American rock), and Cool Country. Hard Rock Park has a variety of rides, including five roller coasters, and music venues, including a 10,000-seat amphitheater for daily shows and special events.

Web: www.hardrockpark.com
Facebook: (None)
Twitter: HardRockPark
LinkedIn: Hard Rock Park (Company, Group)

15

Hersheypark

Hersheypark, in Hershey, Pennsylvania, has more than 60 rides, including 11 roller coasters, 13 water rides, and 26 rides just for kids. Use the Ride Search to find the rides you'll like best: You can search rides by height requirements, type of ride, and thrill level. Its Fahrenheit roller coaster has a 97-degree drop—the steepest, the park claims, in the United States. Hersheypark also stages shows, concerts, talent shows, and other entertainment.

Web: www.hersheypark.com
Facebook: Hershey Park (Page)
Twitter: (None)
LinkedIn: Hershey Entertainment & Resorts (Company)

Kings Island

With a variety of thrill rides and family rides, this Mason, Ohio, park boasts the most kid-friendly roller coasters any-where. Its Nickelodeon Universe area has been named Best Kids Area by trade paper *Amusement Today* for seven years in a row. Get acquainted with the park's rides and shows, and then buy your tick-ets online.

Web: www.visitkingsisland.com
Facebook: Kings Island (Page, Group)
Twitter: KingsIslandPR
LinkedIn: Paramount's Kings Island (Company)

Knott's Berry Farm

Once upon a time, this really was a berry farm. Now this Buena Park, California, park has six themed areas: Ghost Town, Fiesta Village, the Boardwalk, Camp Snoopy, Wild Water Wilderness, and Indian Trails. Each area has rides, shows, and places to eat. Use the Fun Finder to plan your day according to your interests and how much time you can spend.

Web: www.knotts.com
Facebook: Knott's Berry Farm (Page)
Twitter: knottsbrryfarm
LinkedIn: Knott's Berry Farm (Company)

LEGOLAND California

As its name suggests, LEGOLAND is a LEGO-themed park, featuring 50 rides and attractions in nine themed areas: The Beginning, Land of Adventure, Dino Island, Explore Village, Fun Town, Pirate Shores, Castle Hill, Miniland USA, and Imagination Zone. Watch videos taken in the park, explore shopping and dining options, and buy tickets online.

Web: www.legoland.com/california.htm
Facebook: Legoland California (Group)
Twitter: LEGOLAND_CA
LinkedIn: LEGOLAND California Resort (Company)

The Season Pass

This weekly podcast features interviews and information relating to amusement parks, rides, and theme park attractions.

Web: www.seasonpasspodcast.com
Facebook: (None)
Twitter: theseasonpass
LinkedIn: (None)

SeaWorld

One site covers three SeaWorld parks: Orlando, San Diego, and San Antonio. View a gallery of visitor-contributed SeaWorld photos, and upload your own. Learn more about shows and programs, and buy tickets online.

Web: www.seaworld.com
Facebook: SeaWorld (Group), Seaworld Groupies (Group)
Twitter: seaworldonline, SeaWorld_Parks
LinkedIn: SeaWorld (Company)

Six Flags Theme Parks

Six Flags Inc. operates more theme parks than any other company in the world, with 20 parks in the United States and others in Canada, Mexico, and the United Arab Emirates. In 2007, Six Flag parks worldwide had nearly 25 million visitors. This site is the hub for any Six Flags park you want to investigate; pick a park to learn about its rides, shows, and special events.

Web: www.sixflags.com/national/index.aspx
Facebook: Six Flags Great Adventure (Page), Six Flags (Group)
Twitter: SixFlags
LinkedIn: Six Flags (Company), Six Flags Theme Parks (Company)

Theme Park Insider

A guide to the world's most popular theme parks, praised by *Forbes* and *Travel + Leisure* magazines, Theme Park Insider includes reviews of rides, shows, and hotels. The site also lists safety data by park and by recent incidents. There's a searchable discussion forum where you can ask questions of experienced park goers.

Web: www.themeparkinsider.com
Facebook: (None)
Twitter: ThemePark
LinkedIn: (None)

Theme Park Review

Packed with information, Theme Park Review serves up photos, videos, reviews, and other information for theme parks all over the world. Read reviews, look at photos and videos, and discuss your favorite parks and rides in the forum. The site also organizes theme park tours and events.

Web: www.themeparkreview.com
Facebook: Theme Park Insider (Page)
Twitter: ThemeParkReview
LinkedIn: (None)

Universal Orlando

If you're visiting Orlando, don't forget to check out the *other* theme park there. Universal Orlando is a world-class complex of parks (Islands of Adventure, Universal Studios Orlando, and Wet 'n' Wild), hotels, and entertainment venues. Explore the parks, buy tickets or vacation packages, and compare Universal and Disney.

Web: www.universalorlando.com
Facebook: (None)
Twitter: universalresort
LinkedIn: Universal Orlando (Company)

Universal Studios Hollywood

Located just north of downtown Los Angeles, Universal Studios Hollywood offers a plethora of entertainment opportunities: a theme park, studio tours, Citywalk (a shopping/dining/entertainment complex), movie theaters, and concerts. This site tells you what's new and gives an overview of all the attractions. You can buy tickets online.

Web: www.universalstudioshollywood.com
Facebook: Universal Studios Hollywood - Official Page (Page)
Twitter: UniversalParks
LinkedIn: Universal Studios (Company)

AQUARIUMS

Aquarium of the Pacific

Located in Long Beach, the Aquarium of the Pacific is southern California's largest aquarium, with a mission to educate people about the Pacific Ocean. Here you'll find information about the museum and its exhibits, news and events, and conversation and education programs. Watch videos (the site has both video and audio podcasts) and read the aquarium blog.

Web: www.aquariumofpacific.org
Facebook: Aquarium of the Pacific (Page, Group)
Twitter: AquariumPacific
LinkedIn: Aquarium of the Pacific (Company)

Florida Aquarium

This colorful, kid-friendly site gives you a virtual tour of the Florida Aquarium, located in Tampa. Preview the aquarium's galleries (Wetlands, Bays and Beaches, Coral Reef, and Sea Hunt) as you plan your visit. Find out about its educational and conservation programs and learn how to become a member.

Web: www.flaquarium.org
Facebook: The Florida Aquarium (Page)
Twitter: floridaaquarium
LinkedIn: The Florida Aquarium (Company)

15

Georgia Aquarium

The world's largest aquarium, which opened in Atlanta in 2005, features all kinds of aquatic life swimming in eight million gallons of water. Explore the aquarium and its many programs, watch beluga whales via webcam, get visitor information, and buy tickets.

Web: www.georgiaaquarium.org
Facebook: Georgia Aquarium (Page, Group)
Twitter: GeorgiaAquarium
LinkedIn: Georgia Aquarium (Company, Group)

Monterey Bay Aquarium Video Library

California's Monterey Bay Aquarium has an extensive collection of videos showing the aquarium's animals, exhibits, and projects. Take a virtual visit to a great aquarium.

Web: www.montereybayaquarium.org/efc/video_library/video_library.aspx
Facebook: Monterey Bay Aquarium (Page), Monterey Bay Aquarium Enthusiasts (Group)
Twitter: MB_Aquarium
LinkedIn: Monterey Bay Aquarium (Company), Monterey Bay Aquarium Members (Group)

National Aquarium in Baltimore

With more than 10,500 animals from 560 species, the National Aquarium provides a fascinating glimpse into the world under the water. This educational site has sections titled Animals, Exhibits, and Conservation, and each contains pages of interesting content. Buy tickets and get directions, learn about volunteering or making a donation, and check out the aquarium's special programs.

Web: www.aqua.org
Facebook: National Aquarium in Baltimore (Page)
Twitter: NatlAquarium
LinkedIn: National Aquarium in Baltimore (Company)

New England Aquarium

The New England Aquarium is one of Boston's most popular attractions. Founded in 1969, the New England Aquarium combines education and entertainment to inform about conservation. Learn about the thousands of animals that live at the aquarium, from penguins and seals to whales and giant octopuses. There are also sections about conservation and research, education, planning your visit, and getting involved.

Web: www.neaq.org
Facebook: New England Aquarium (Page, Group)
Twitter: NEAQ
LinkedIn: New England Aquarium (Company)

BED-AND-BREAKFASTS

BedandBreakfast.com

Whether you're looking for a B&B, an inn, a lodge or cabin, or a farm or ranch vacation, this directory has it. Search by inn name or location, read travelers' reviews (or write your own), check out specials and favorite recipes, or buy a gift card accepted at nearly 4,000 inns. The BedandBreakfast.com Report is a newsletter you can subscribe to or read online.

Web: www.bedandbreakfast.com
Facebook: BedandBreakfast.com (Page)
Twitter: bandb_com
LinkedIn: BedandBreakfast.com (Company)

BnBFinder.com [BEST]

A well-organized and comprehensive directory of B&Bs, packed with information. Find a B&B anywhere in the world and see the 25 most popular location searches. Read B&B-related articles, from traveling with pets to planning a B&B wedding. Besides gift certificates, recipes, and reviews, the site also has an excellent blog.

Web: www.bnbfinder.com
Facebook: BnBFinder.com (Page)
Twitter: (None)
LinkedIn: (None)

BUDGET TRAVEL

Amateur Traveler

More than a thousand people regularly listen to this podcast by Chris Christensen, whose shows are all about "travel for the love of it."

Web: http://amateurtraveler.com/
Facebook: Travel Destinations (Page, Group)
Twitter: tdestinations
LinkedIn: (None)

Backpack Europe on a Budget

To see Europe cheaply, try backpacking. This site prepares you for your trip, with advice about packing, clothes, lodging, transportation, and taking care of tired feet.

Web: www.backpackeurope.com
Facebook: Backpack Europe (Group)
Twitter: backpackeuro
LinkedIn: (None)

BestFares.com

This discount travel site monitors airfares and reports on travel news, cruises, tour packages, hotel rates, car rentals, destinations, and last-minute vacations. To be first to hear about the best deals, subscribe to Hot Deals by email.

Web: www.bestfares.com/index.php
Facebook: Bestfares.com (Page)
Twitter: BestFares
LinkedIn: Bestfares.com (Company)

Budget Travel 🏅

The online home of *Arthur Frommer's Budget Travel* magazine, this excellent site is indispensable to the budget-minded traveler, with articles on destinations, shopping, travel news and advice, and more—all geared to saving you money. Sections include This Just In, Real Deals, Destinations, How-to Handbook, Trip Ideas, Tips & Experts, My Budget Travel, and Magazine (where you can subscribe).

Web: www.budgettravel.com
Facebook: Budget Travel (Page, Group)
Twitter: budget_travel
LinkedIn: Budget Travel (Company)

Cheapest Destinations

Travel writer Tim Leffel reports on affordable destinations, bargain vacations, and international travel deals.

Web: http://travel.booklocker.com/
Facebook: (None)
Twitter: timleffel
LinkedIn: (None)

Hostels.com

Hostels offer basic accommodations at bargain prices, and this site lists more than 23,000 hostels and other budget lodgings around the world. Read travel guides and hostel reviews and join in the forum discussions.

Web: www.hostels.com
Facebook: www.hostels.com (Page)
Twitter: hostels_com
LinkedIn: (None)

Hotwire.com

If you've got some flexibility in your travel plans, Hotwire offers an easy way to get better deals on airline tickets, hotel reservations, and car rentals. Working with leading travel companies, Hotwire resells unsold airfare, hotel rooms, rental cars, and vacation packages. Some bookings are "opaque," meaning that you don't know the name of the hotel or car-rental company until after you've paid, but you do get limited information, such as a hotel's location and number of stars, before you buy.

Web: www.hotwire.com
Facebook: Hotwire (Page)
Twitter: hotwire_deals, hotwire
LinkedIn: Hotwire (Company)

The Indie Travel Podcast

If you'd rather travel on your own terms than join a group or tour, you'll enjoy this weekly podcast about traveling independently.

Web: www.indietravelpodcast.com
Facebook: Indie Travel Podcast (Page)
Twitter: indietravel
LinkedIn: (None)

Last Minute Travel

If you can pack up and go on a moment's notice, visit this site to find the best last-minute deals: flights, hotels, cruises, cars, and packages. There's a discount travel club, newsletter, and blog as well.

Web: www.lastminutetravel.com
Facebook: Last Minute Travel (Page)
Twitter: LMTTweets
LinkedIn: (None)

Priceline.com

This discount travel service lets you search for a flight, hotel, car, cruise, or vacation package, and then compare prices to find the deal you want. If you're flexible, you can try naming your own price. Tell Priceline.com what you want (flight info, hotel or car-rental location, dates, and so on) and the maximum you want to pay. Within hours, you'll find out whether any company has accepted your bid.

Web: www.priceline.com
Facebook: Priceline Negotiator (Page)
Twitter: TheNegotiator
LinkedIn: Priceline.com (Company)

SkyAuction.com

Bid on travel products—plane tickets, hotel rooms, vacation packages, travel gear, and more—in auctions that begin at just $1.

Web: www.skyauction.com
Facebook: SkyAuction.com (Page)
Twitter: SkyAuction
LinkedIn: SkyAuction.com (Company)

STA Travel

Students can find great deals on this site by taking advantage of special student rates that other travel companies don't know about. Here you'll find bookings (flights, lodging, vacations), rail passes, and discount cards—everything young people need to start exploring the world.

Web: www.statravel.com
Facebook: STA Travel (Page, Group)
Twitter: statravelers
LinkedIn: STA Travel (Company)

Travelzoo

Twelve million people subscribe to Travelzoo's free Top 25 newsletter, a weekly compendium of the best deals in travel. The website offers travel information and deals.

Web: www.travelzoo.com
Facebook: Travelzoo (Page)
Twitter: Travelzoo
LinkedIn: Travelzoo (Company)

CAR RENTALS

Advantage Rent A Car Ⓢ
Web: www.advantage.com
Facebook: Advantage (Page)
Twitter: AdvantageRAC
LinkedIn: Advantage Rent A Car (Company)

Alamo Ⓢ
Web: www.alamo.com
Facebook: Alamo Rent A Car Miami (Group)
Twitter: AlamoRentaCar
LinkedIn: ALAMO Rent A Car Middle East (Company)

Avis Ⓢ
Web: www.avis.com
Facebook: AVIS RENT A CAR (Page), Avis Rent A Car (Group)
Twitter: AvisWeTryHarder
LinkedIn: Avis (Company), AVIS WE TRY HARDER GROUP (Group)

Budget Ⓢ
Web: www.budget.com
Facebook: Budget (Page, Group)

Twitter: budgetcar
LinkedIn: Budget Rent a Car (Company)

Dollar ⑤
Web: www.dollar.com
Facebook: Dollar Rent a Car (Page, Group)
Twitter: DollarCar
LinkedIn: (None)

Enterprise ⑤
Web: www.enterprise.com
Facebook: Enterprise car rental (Group)
Twitter: (None)
LinkedIn: Enterprise Rent-A-Car (Company)

Europcar ⑤
Web: www.europcar.com
Facebook: Europcar (Group)
Twitter: EC_Intl
LinkedIn: Europcar (Company)

Fox Rent A Car ⑤
Web: https://foxrentacar.com
Facebook: Fox Rent A Car (Page)
Twitter: foxrentcar
LinkedIn: Fox Rent-A-Car (Company)

Hertz ⑤
Web: www.hertz.com
Facebook: Hertz (Page)
Twitter: ConnectByHertz
LinkedIn: Hertz Rent a Car (Company)

National ⑤
Web: www.nationalcar.com
Facebook: national car rental (Group)
Twitter: nationalcares
LinkedIn: National Car Rental (Company)

Payless Car Rental ⑤
Web: www.paylesscarrental.com
Facebook: Payless Car Rental (Page)
Twitter: PaylessCar
LinkedIn: Payless Car Rental System, Inc. (Group)

Rent-A-Wreck

Rent-A-Wreck is a nationwide franchise car-rental company. The main Rent-A-Wreck lets you search for local franchises based on city and state or ZIP code.

Web: www.rentawreck.com
Facebook: Rent-A-Wreck. (Group)
Twitter: rentawreck
LinkedIn: (None)

Thrifty ⑤
Web: www.thrifty.com
Facebook: Thrifty Car Rental (Page, Group)
Twitter: ThriftyCar
LinkedIn: (None)

CRUISE LINES

American Cruise Lines ⑤
Web: www.americancruiselines.com
Facebook: American Cruise Lines (Page, Group)
Twitter: (None)
LinkedIn: (None)

Carnival Cruise Lines ⑤
Web: www.carnival.com
Facebook: Carnival Cruise Lines (Page, Group)
Twitter: CarnivalCruise
LinkedIn: Carnival Cruise Lines (Company, Group)

Celebrity Cruises ⑤
Web: www.celebritycruises.com
Facebook: Celebrity Cruise Line (Page)
Twitter: (None)
LinkedIn: Celebrity Cruises (Company)

Crystal Cruises ⑤
Web: www.crystalcruises.com
Facebook: Crystal Cruises (Page, Group)
Twitter: crystalcruises
LinkedIn: Crystal Cruises (Company)

Cunard Cruise Lines ⑤
Web: www.cunard.com
Facebook: CUNARD (Page, Group)
Twitter: cunardexpert
LinkedIn: Cunard Line (Company)

Disney Cruise Line ⑤
Web: http://disneycruise.disney.go.com/
Facebook: Disney Cruise Line (Page, Group)
Twitter: DCLNews
LinkedIn: Disney Cruise Line (Company), Disney Cruisers (Group)

Holland America Line ⑤
Web: www.hollandamerica.com
Facebook: Holland America Line (Page, Group)
Twitter: HALcruises
LinkedIn: Holland America Line (Company)

Norwegian Cruise Line ⑤
Web: www.ncl.com
Facebook: Norwegian Cruise Line (Page, Group)
Twitter: NCLCruiseLine
LinkedIn: Norwegian Cruise Line (Company)

Oceania Cruises ⑤
Web: www.oceaniacruises.com
Facebook: Oceania (Page, Group)
Twitter: OceaniaCruises
LinkedIn: Oceania Cruises (Company)

Princess Cruises ⑤
Web: www.princess.com
Facebook: Princess Cruises (Page, Group)
Twitter: PrincessCruises
LinkedIn: Princess Cruises (Company, Group)

Regent Seven Seas Cruises ⑤
Web: www.rssc.com
Facebook: Regent Seven Seas Cruises (Page)
Twitter: regentcruises
LinkedIn: Regent (Company)

Royal Caribbean Cruise Lines ⑤
Web: www.royalcaribbean.com
Facebook: Royal Caribbean International (Page)
Twitter: RoyalHotDeals
LinkedIn: Royal Caribbean International (Company)

CRUISES

About.com: Cruises

Whether you're planning your first cruise or your fiftieth, you'll find helpful information here: news, cruise-line profiles and reviews, destinations and activities, helpful lists (from what to pack to the best cruise lines for families or for romance), a glossary, and recommended reading.

Web: http://cruises.about.com/
Facebook: About Cruises - Cruise Travel Information from About.com (Page)
Twitter: AboutCruises
LinkedIn: (None)

Cruise.com ⑤

Cruise.com's low-price guarantee makes this a must-visit when you're shopping for a cruise. Its gigantic database holds information about thousands of cruises, and you can also learn about cruise lines, ports and shore excursions, special cruises, and more.

Web: www.cruise.com
Facebook: Cruise.com (Page)
Twitter: cruisecom
LinkedIn: Cruise.com (Company)

Cruise Critic

Visit this site before you book a cruise to get the scoop on cruising, with cruise-line profiles, ship reviews, a guide for first-time cruisers, the latest news, and the best deals. You can find a cruise by "cruise style" (family, expedition, romance, senior, and so on) or current specials, or by searching (by destination, cruise line, lifestyle, or price). There are sections on luxury cruises, planning, ports, and other special features.

Web: www.cruisecritic.com
Facebook: Cruise Critic (Page, Group)
Twitter: CruiseCritic
LinkedIn: Cruise Critic (Group)

Cruise Value Center ⑤

News, special offers, and last-minute bargains—check out this site for cruise information and deals.

Web: www.crowncruisevacations.com
Facebook: Crown Cruise Vacations (Page)
Twitter: ccvadvantage
LinkedIn: (None)

Fox World Travel Cruise Videos

This travel agency features promotional videos you can watch online from six major cruise lines.

Web: www.gofox.com/cruises/videos.php
Facebook: Fox World Travel (Page)
Twitter: foxworldtravel
LinkedIn: Fox World Travel (Company)

Freighter World Cruises $

If you're looking for a different kind of cruise, consider a freighter. Informal and uncrowded, freighter travel can also save you money. To learn more, visit this site, which specializes in booking passengers on freighters.

Web: www.freighterworld.com
Facebook: Freighter Cruises (Group)
Twitter: (None)
LinkedIn: (None)

icruise.com $

This site offers hand-picked specials, last-minute deals, and five ways to search for a cruise: by destination, departure port, sail date, cruise line, or cruise ship.

Web: www.icruise.com
Facebook: iCruise.com (Page)
Twitter: (None)
LinkedIn: (None)

ECOTOURISM

Planeta.com

Planeta.com describes itself as "a global journal of practical ecotourism," so if you're interested in traveling in an earth-friendly way, visit this site. Sections include Places, Events, Guides, Travelers, Ecotourism, and Headlines. Includes a wiki you can help build and maintain.

Web: www.planeta.com
Facebook: Planeta.com: Global Journal of Practical Ecotourism (Group)
Twitter: (None)
LinkedIn: (None)

ResponsibleTravel.com

Promoting "holidays that give the world a break," this site offers hand-picked eco-friendly vacations from 270 travel companies. The site is British but also works with American travelers. Whatever your travel interests—beaches, culture, honeymoon, luxury, cycling, walking, and more—you'll find a environmentally responsible version here.

Web: www.responsibletravel.com
Facebook: Responsibletravel.com (Page)
Twitter: r_travel
LinkedIn: (None)

TIES: The International Ecotourism Society

Founded in 1990, TIES promotes travel that "conserves the environment and supports the livelihoods of the local populations." Learn about what TIES does, apply for membership, get facts and statistics about ecotourism, and find an ecotour for your next trip.

Web: www.ecotourism.org
Facebook: The International Ecotourism Society (TIES) (Page)
Twitter: ecotravel
LinkedIn: (None)

FAMILY TRAVEL

FamilyFun: Travel

Let the fun begin! The Travel area of the FamilyFun website has lots of tips and suggestions for creating a fun and memorable trip. Sections include Destinations, Activities & Attractions, Disney Vacations, Camping Trips, and Your Great Vacations (travel stories and ratings from readers).

Web: http://familyfun.go.com/family-travel/
Facebook: "Family Fun Travels" Disney Group
Twitter: FamilyFun
LinkedIn: (None)

Family Travel

Freelance writer Sheila Scarborough and guests blog about seeing the world with kids in tow, with informative posts about specific countries, cities, and destinations.

Web: www.familytravellogue.com
Facebook: Family Travel Logue (Page)
Twitter: SheilaS
LinkedIn: (None)

15

Family Travel Forum $

This site's motto is "Have Kids, Still Travel!" There's lots of free content, from advice for making car trips easier to ideas for different age groups to recommendations for family-friendly hotels, cruises, and activities. When you join the site (it's free), you get access to discounts and last-minute travel deals, as well as twice-a-month email travel alerts. For a small fee ($5.95), you can get custom help with planning your trip from the site's experts.

Web: www.familytravelforum.com
Facebook: Family Travel Forum (Page)
Twitter: familytravel4um
LinkedIn: (None)

Pamela Lanier's Family Travel

This attractive site has lots of info for families who travel. Highlights include Road Food (recipes for on-the-go food that kids will eat), Great Outdoors (ideas for active families), Travel Destinations, and Travel Tips. You can also search for accommodations and sign up for the site's newsletter.

Web: www.familytravelguides.com
Facebook: Pamela Lanier (People)
Twitter: PamelaLanier09
LinkedIn: Marie Lanier (People)

FOREIGN LANGUAGES

Fodor's Travel Guides: Living Language

Learn the basics of the local lingo before you travel. This site covers common expressions useful to travelers—from sightseeing and finding your way to healthcare and personal services—in French, German, Italian, and Spanish.

Web: www.fodors.com/language/
Facebook: Fodor's (Page), Fodor's Friends (Group)
Twitter: fodorstravel
LinkedIn: (None)

Tours.com: Language Tours and Vacation Packages

Use the directory here to find a vacation that focuses on learning the local language while you see the sights.

Web: www.tours.com/tours_vacations/language.htm
Facebook: Tours.com (Group)
Twitter: tours_com
LinkedIn: (None)

Travlang

Choose a language (the site lists dozens, from Afrikaans to Zulu) and learn useful words and phrases for traveling where it's spoken: basic words, numbers, shopping/dining, travel, directions, places, and times and dates. Also has a currency converter, translation tools, information about visa requirements, and user forums.

Web: www.travlang.com
Facebook: (None)
Twitter: travlang
LinkedIn: (None)

GENERAL

Driftr

Driftr is a community where travelers get together to share experiences, advice, photos, reviews, and tips. Research your destination before you go—where to stay, where to eat, what to see, and how to get around—and share your trip after you're back home.

Web: www.driftr.com
Facebook: Driftr (Page)
Twitter: (None)
LinkedIn: Driftr Travel Community (Group)

Expedia $

This online travel agency helps you find the best deals, fares, and vacation packages. Browse today's top travel deals or build your trip by searching for fares and value packages. Has a rewards program for repeat customers.

Web: www.expedia.com
Facebook: Expedia (Page)
Twitter: Expedia
LinkedIn: Expedia (Company)

Extravigator

Extravigator is an open forum for those who enjoy the good life to discuss luxury travel. Membership is free.

Web: http://extravigator.com
Facebook: Extravigator (Page)
Twitter: (None)
LinkedIn: (None)

Fodor's Travel Guides

Here you'll find a world of travel information from the publisher of these popular travel guides: destinations, hotels, restaurants, cruises, travel news, forums, and a link to book your trip on Expedia. Sign up for Fodor's weekly newsletter or browse previous issues. Buy Fodor's books in the online store.

Web: www.fodors.com
Facebook: Fodor's (Page), Fodor's Friends (Group)
Twitter: fodorstravel
LinkedIn: (None)

Frommer's

More than 50 years ago, Arthur Frommer published *Europe on $5 a Day*, and since then the series has grown to more than 300 popular travel guides. The official Frommer's website is packed with travel tips, advice, ideas, and destinations. Besides articles, forums, a store, a database of hotels, and a link to book your trip, you'll find podcasts and a blog.

Web: www.frommers.com
Facebook: Frommer's (Page)
Twitter: Frommers
LinkedIn: Arthur Frommer's Budget Travel (Company)

Hotels.com ⑤

As its name implies, Hotels.com helps you find a place to stay when you travel. When you search, you can narrow results by setting a price rating, star rating, and/or guest rating, and then locate hotels on a map. You can shop for flights and vacation packages here.

Web: www.hotels.com
Facebook: Hotels.com (Group)
Twitter: hotels_com
LinkedIn: Hotels.com (Company)

IgoUgo 🏅

When you join this travel community, 350,000 strong, you can connect with others who share your travel interests. Create a travel journal and submit reviews and photos; this earns points toward frequent-flyer miles, so you can travel some more. If you want to research a destination, IgoUgo has more than 5,500 of them covered. A bonus: The site's editors check reviews and other content submitted by members, so you can trust the info you find here.

Web: www.igougo.com
Facebook: IgoUgo (Page)
Twitter: igougo_com
LinkedIn: IgoUgo (Company)

JourneyPod Luxury Travel

For those who like to live the good life as they travel, this podcast focuses on luxury hotels, gourmet restaurants, and see-and-be-seen hot spots.

Web: http://journeypod.libsyn.com/
Facebook: I Love journeyPod (Group), journeyPod Luxury Travel Guide (Page)
Twitter: journeyPod
LinkedIn: journeyPod (Company)

Kayak ⑤

Kayak is a super search engine that searches more than 140 travel sites, so you can compare results and find the best deal. Even better, you can filter and sort the results in various ways—for example, narrow your price range or the time window for a flight. Also offers last-minute deals, comparisons and statistics, and a free account so you can keep track of your searches. Kayak is not a travel agency; when you choose to make a reservation, you go directly to the site of the company making the booking.

Web: www.kayak.com
Facebook: KAYAK (Page)
Twitter: KAYAK
LinkedIn: (None)

Mobissimo

When you search for something here, Mobissimo scours scores of travel sites to find you the best deals. Search for flights, hotels, cars, deals, or activities (like golf or wine tasting). Has a blog that's updated each weekday.

Web: www.mobissimo.com
Facebook: Mobissimo (Group)
Twitter: (None)
LinkedIn: Mobissimo (Company)

Orbitz ⑤

This online travel agency lets you research, plan, and book a trip, whether for business or pleasure. Find up-to-the minute rates, fares, packages, and deals.

Web: www.orbitz.com
Facebook: Orbitz - Official Page (Page), Orbitz (Application)
Twitter: Orbitz
LinkedIn: Orbitz Worldwide (Company)

TravelBlog

TravelBlog hosts hundreds of blogs journaling travelers' voyages, photos, adventures, and musings. You can read the blogs on the site or create your own. You can search for blogs by region, which is helpful when you're planning a trip and want to read others' experiences with that destination.

Web: www.travelblog.org
Facebook: TravelBlog (Page, Group)
Twitter: (None)
LinkedIn: (None)

Travellerspoint Travel Community

With more than 150,000 members, this large community of travel enthusiasts is a great place to swap travel stories, make like-minded friends, remember past trips, and plan future ones. Create a blog, upload photos, map your trips, ask questions, share advice, and help build the sites' Wiki Travel Guide.

Web: www.travellerspoint.com
Facebook: Travellerspoint (Page)
Twitter: Travellerspoint
LinkedIn: (None)

Travelocity ⑤

A full-service online travel site where you can book vacation packages, flights, hotels, cars, rail travel, cruises, last-minute deals, and activities. Sign up for the Fare Alert service for notification when fares drop between your home airport and your favorite destinations.

Web: www.travelocity.com
Facebook: Travelocity Roaming Gnome (Page)
Twitter: RoamingGnome
LinkedIn: Travelocity (Company)

Travelography

Get commentary on travel-related news from Alan A. Lew's podcasts.

Web: http://podcasternews.com/travelography/
Facebook: (None)
Twitter: Travelography
LinkedIn: (None)

Wikitravel

This wiki offers free travel guides to destinations around the world, written and edited by travelers. Do some research, or jump in and contribute.

Web: http://wikitravel.org
Facebook: Wikitravel (Page, Group)
Twitter: wikitravel
LinkedIn: (None)

HOTELS

Best Western International Hotels ⑤
Web: www.bestwestern.com
Facebook: Best Western (Page, Group)
Twitter: TheBestWestern
LinkedIn: Best Western International (Company)

Clarion Hotels ⑤
Web: www.clarionhotel.com
Facebook: Clarion Hotels (Group)
Twitter: ChoiceHotels
LinkedIn: Choice Hotels International (Company)

Club Med ⑤
Web: www.clubmed.com
Facebook: Club Med (Group)
Twitter: clubmedinsider
LinkedIn: Club Med (Company), Club Med - Official (Group)

Comfort Inn ⑤
Web: www.comfortinn.com
Facebook: Comfort Inn (Page, Group)
Twitter: ChoiceHotels
LinkedIn: Choice Hotels International (Company)

Days Inn ⑤
Web: www.daysinn.com
Facebook: Days Inn (Page)
Twitter: (None)
LinkedIn: (None)

Doubletree ⑤
Web: http://doubletree1.hilton.com
Facebook: Doubletree Hotels (Page, Group)
Twitter: HWhotels
LinkedIn: Hilton Worldwide (Company)

Econo Lodge ⑤
Web: www.econolodge.com
Facebook: Econo Lodge (Page)
Twitter: EconoLodge
LinkedIn: Choice Hotels International (Company)

Embassy Suites ⑤
Web: http://embassysuites1.hilton.com
Facebook: Embassy Suites Hotels (Page)
Twitter: Embassy_Suites
LinkedIn: Embassy Suites (Company)

Extended Stay America Hotels ⑤
Web: www.extendedstayhotels.com
Facebook: (None)
Twitter: (None)
LinkedIn: Extended Stay Hotels (Company)

Four Seasons Hotels and Resorts ⑤
Web: www.fourseasons.com
Facebook: Four Seasons Hotels and Resorts (Page), Four Seasons Hotels & Resorts (Group)
Twitter: FourSeasons
LinkedIn: Four Seasons Hotels and Resorts (Company)

Hampton Inn ⑤
Web: http://hamptoninn1.hilton.com
Facebook: Hampton Inn (Page, Group)
Twitter: HWhotels
LinkedIn: Hilton Worldwide (Company)

Hilton Hotels ⑤
Web: www1.hilton.com
Facebook: Hilton Hotels (Page, Group)
Twitter: HWhotels
LinkedIn: Hilton Worldwide (Company)

Howard Johnson ⑤
Web: www.hojo.com
Facebook: hojo (Page)
Twitter: happyhojoworld
LinkedIn: Howard Johnson (Company)

Hyatt Hotels and Resorts ⑤
Web: www.hyatt.com
Facebook: Hyatt (Group)
Twitter: HyattConcierge
LinkedIn: Hyatt Hotels Corporation (Company)

InterContinental Hotels and Resorts ⑤
Web: www.ichotelsgroup.com/intercontinental/en/gb/home
Facebook: InterContinental Hotels Group (Page, Group)
Twitter: IHGPLC, IHG_Deals
LinkedIn: InterContinental Hotels Group (Company)

Knights Inn ⑤
Web: www.knightsinn.com
Facebook: Knights Inn (Group)
Twitter: WyndhamRewards
LinkedIn: Wyndham Hotel Group (Company)

La Quinta Inns and Suites ⑤
Web: www.lq.com
Facebook: La Quinta Inns & Suites (Page)
Twitter: LQ
LinkedIn: La Quinta (Company)

Marriott Hotels and Resorts ⑤
Web: www.marriott.com
Facebook: Marriott! (Group), Marriott (Page)
Twitter: MarriottIntl
LinkedIn: Marriott International (Company), Marriott Hotels (Company), marriott vacation club (Company)

Motel 6 ⑤
Web: www.motel6.com
Facebook: Motel 6 (Page)
Twitter: Accorhotels
LinkedIn: Accor Hotels (Company), Accor Hotels and Resorts (Group)

Novotel ⑤
Web: www.novotel.com
Facebook: NOVOTEL (Page)
Twitter: (None)
LinkedIn: (None)

Outrigger Hotels and Resorts ⑤
Web: www.outrigger.com
Facebook: (None)
Twitter: (None)
LinkedIn: Outrigger Hotels & Resorts

Peninsula Hotels ⑤
Web: www.peninsula.com
Facebook: Peninsula Hotels (Group), The Peninsula Hotels (Group)
Twitter: (None)
LinkedIn: (None)

Radisson Hotels and Resorts ⑤
Web: www.radisson.com
Facebook: Radisson Blu Hotels & Resorts (Group)
Twitter: (None)
LinkedIn: Radisson SAS (Company), Carlson Companies, Inc. (Company), Radisson Blu (Group)

Ramada Worldwide ⑤
Web: www.ramada.com
Facebook: Ramada Worldwide (Page)
Twitter: WyndhamRewards
LinkedIn: Wyndham Hotel Group (Company)

Red Roof Inn ⑤
Web: www.redroof.com
Facebook: Red Roof Inn (Page)
Twitter: (None)
LinkedIn: Red Roof Inns (Company)

Relais & Châteaux ⑤
Web: www.relaischateaux.com
Facebook: Relais & Châteaux (Page, Group)
Twitter: (None)
LinkedIn: Relais & Châteaux (Company)

Ritz-Carlton Hotels and Resorts ⑤
Web: www.ritzcarlton.com
Facebook: Ritz Carlton (Group), RITZ CARLTON (Page)
Twitter: Ritz_Carlton
LinkedIn: The Ritz-Carlton Hotel Company LLC (Company)

Rodeway Inn ⑤
Web: www.rodewayinn.com
Facebook: RODEWAY INN (Page)
Twitter: ChoiceHotels
LinkedIn: Choice Hotels International (Company)

Sheraton Hotels and Resorts ⑤
Web: www.starwoodhotels.com/sheraton/index.html
Facebook: Sheraton (Page, Group)
Twitter: StarwoodBuzz
LinkedIn: Sheraton (Company)

Super 8 Motel ⑤
Web: www.super8.com
Facebook: Super 8 Motel (Page, Group)
Twitter: Super8hotels
LinkedIn: Wyndham Hotel Group (Company)

Travelodge ⑤
Web: www.travelodge.com
Facebook: Travelodge !!! (Group), Travelodge (Page)
Twitter: WyndhamRewards
LinkedIn: Wyndham Hotel Group (Company)

Westin Hotels and Resorts ⑤
Web: www.starwoodhotels.com/westin/index.html
Facebook: Westin Hotels & Resorts (Page), Westin Hotels (Group)
Twitter: StarwoodBuzz
LinkedIn: Westin Hotels & Resorts (Company)

Wyndham Hotels and Resorts Ⓢ
Web: www.wyndham.com
Facebook: Wyndham Hotels (Page)
Twitter: WyndhamRewards
LinkedIn: Wyndham Hotel Group (Company)

INTERNATIONAL TRAVEL

About.com: Africa Travel

Lots of information here about traveling to Africa, including maps, when and where to go on safari, the top-10 destinations, and much more. There are separate sections for different African countries.

Web: http://goafrica.about.com/
Facebook: About.com (Page)
Twitter: AboutTravel
LinkedIn: About.com (Company)

About.com: South America Travel

Essential information for anyone planning a trip to South America: planning, most popular destinations, festivals and holidays, history, cuisine, wildlife—and that's just scratching the surface of this informative site.

Web: http://gosouthamerica.about.com/
Facebook: About.com (Page)
Twitter: AboutTravel
LinkedIn: About.com (Company)

Australian Travel and Tourism

This well-designed, highly interactive site introduces travelers to all that Australia has to offer. Explore different areas of the country; learn about events attractions, climate, and wildlife; find out about visas and other entry requirements; and locate a travel agent.

Web: www.australia.com
Facebook: Tourism Research Australia (Page)
Twitter: TourismAU
LinkedIn: Tourism Australia (Company)

Canada.travel

The website of the Canada Tourism Commission helps you plan a trip to Canada. Its Explore section has these categories: Natural Wonders, Seasonal Sensations, Luxury Escapes, Refresh & Rejuvenate, Cultural Discoveries, Urban Retreats, and Mountain Tops. There are separate sections for travelers, meeting planners, media, and those in the travel trade.

Web: www.canada.travel/selectCountry.html
Facebook: Team Canada Tourism (Group)
Twitter: canadacomTravel
LinkedIn: Canadian Tourism Commission (Company)

China Travel

A place to learn about traveling to China and meet others who've been there or want to go, China Travel serves up news and facts about China, its cities, and its culture. View photos, read travelers' stories, and find hot travel deals.

Web: www.chinatravel.com
Facebook: China Travel (Page, Group)
Twitter: (None)
LinkedIn: ChinaTravel (Group)

Cool Antarctica

All about Antarctica: facts, news, and amazing photos. The site's Antarctica Cruise and Travel Guide is a great source of information for those planning a trip, covering everything from the basics of Antarctica travel (when to go, what to pack, how much it's likely to cost) to information about specific tours.

Web: www.coolantarctica.com
Facebook: Antarctica (Page, Group)
Twitter: (None)
LinkedIn: (None)

Egyptian Tourism Office

The Egyptian Tourist Authority has put together an in-depth site about the country to help you plan your trip. With videos, news, an events calendar and travel planner, an Arabic phrase book, the LovEgypt Club newsletter, and more, this site will fascinate Egyptophiles.

Web: www.egypt.travel
Facebook: Egypt Travel (Page, Group)
Twitter: (None)
LinkedIn: (None)

France.com

One of the world's most popular tourist destinations, France has something to please nearly everyone. France.com highlights the best the country has to offer, with news, forums, and information about regions, getting there, lodging, and tours.

Web: www.france.com
Facebook: France.com (Page)
Twitter: francecom
LinkedIn: (None)

Germany Travel Guide

If you're planning a trip to Germany, be sure to stop here first. Here you'll find general information about the country, as well as information about culture, destinations, business, and activities.

Web: www.justgermany.org
Facebook: Germany Travel Guide (Page)
Twitter: enjoyGermany
LinkedIn: Germany Travel (Group)

Italy Travel Guide

Here's everything you need in order to plan a trip to Italy: a general travel guide, as well as info on destinations, activities, culture, and doing business.

Web: www.justitaly.org
Facebook: Italy Travel (Page, Group)
Twitter: ItalyTravel
LinkedIn: Friends of Italy (Group)

Japan National Tourist Organization

The Japan National Tourist Organization has put together this attractive and informative site to promote travel to Japan. Learn about destinations, make travel arrangements, prepare for your trip, and get in-depth information about Japanese history, culture, attractions, and events.

Web: www.jnto.go.jp
Facebook: (None)
Twitter: JNTO_London
LinkedIn: (None)

Lonely Planet 🏅

The World Guide of this popular series of travel books is your gateway to international travel. Choose a region and country to go to a page loaded with information about that destination: photos, videos, maps, itineraries, fun facts, travel articles and podcasts, and information about getting there, what to do, and where to stay.

Web: www.lonelyplanet.com/destinations
Facebook: Lonely Planet (Page)
Twitter: lonelyplanet
LinkedIn: Lonely Planet (Company)

Rick Steves' Europe Through the Back Door

Bestselling travel writer and television/radio host Rick Steves guides you through Europe. Plan an independent trip or sign up for a tour, read travel news and events, buy Rick Steves guidebooks, or get info about his shows. Has podcasts and a blog.

Web: www.ricksteves.com
Facebook: Rick Steves (Page)
Twitter: ricksteves
LinkedIn: Rick Steves' Europe (Company)

Travelers' Health

International travelers need to be aware of health risks in various parts of the world. This site, maintained by the Centers for Disease Control and

Prevention, explains about diseases, vaccinations, safe food and water, and so on. Has sections on traveling with children and pets, studying abroad, and concerns related to travel by air and cruise ship.

Web: wwwn.cdc.gov/travel/
Facebook: Centers for Disease Control and Prevention (CDC) (Group)
Twitter: CDCemergency
LinkedIn: Centers for Disease Control and Prevention (Company)

Travel Turkey

Advice, tips, and practical info about visiting this popular tourist destination. Whether you're traveling independently or looking for a tour, this site tells you what you need to know—before you go and during your trip. Use the site's free Concierge feature to email questions and get expert answers.

Web: www.travelturkey.com
Facebook: Travel Turkey (Group)
Twitter: (None)
LinkedIn: (None)

U.S. State Department: Travel

The U.S. State Department's Travel site has information for international travelers: passports, travel tips, health information, and alerts and warnings about world trouble spots.

Web: http://travel.state.gov/
Facebook: (None)
Twitter: good_travel
LinkedIn: (None)

VisitBritain.com

This is a wonderful site to discover all that Britain has to offer. Explore London or other cities and regions of the country, find things to see and do and places to stay, learn how to get around, check out vacation deals, and use the Trip Planner to get the most out of your trip.

The site's unique Friends section presents bloggers from all over the country, writing about their region. Read a local's impressions and favorite places, and respond with questions and your own thoughts.

Web: www.visitbritain.com
Facebook: VISIT BRITAIN!!!!!! (Page)
Twitter: VisitBritain
LinkedIn: (None)

MUSEUMS

American Museum of Natural History

This museum, located in New York City, has more than 40 exhibition halls, a library, and research labs. Its website lists highlights of the museum (including past, current, upcoming, and permanent exhibitions), visitor information, children's programs, and much, much more. You can buy tickets, become a member, and shop the museum store online.

Web: www.amnh.org
Facebook: American Museum of Natural History (Page)
Twitter: atAMNH
LinkedIn: American Museum of Natural History (Company)

British Museum

No trip to London is complete without a visit to the British Museum, and this site is an excellent introduction to the museum and its collections. Explore through online tours and featured galleries and objects, find out about current and future exhibitions, and get directions and opening hours. You can also join the museum and shop in the online store.

Web: www.britishmuseum.org
Facebook: I love the British Museum! (Group)
Twitter: britishmuseum
LinkedIn: The British Museum (Company)

Louvre

Possibly the world's most famous museum, the Louvre has a website that lives up to its reputation. Take a virtual tour, view some of the world's greatest works of art, find out about exhibitions, plan your visit, and purchase tickets online. When you sign up for a free account, you can create personalized albums of your favorite items and articles.

Web: www.louvre.fr
Facebook: Louvre (Group), Musée du Louvre (Page)
Twitter: louvrepourtous
LinkedIn: Musée du Louvre (Company)

Metropolitan Museum of Art

On this site, New York's Metropolitan Museum of Art features a work from its permanent collection each day, or you can search its database of more than 50,000 items. Browse the museum by its departments, special exhibitions, virtual tours, articles, and more. Creating a free My Met Museum account gives you special features, such as a virtual gallery to store your favorite artworks and a customizable calendar of Met events.

Web: www.metmuseum.org
Facebook: The Metropolitan Museum of Art, New York (Page)
Twitter: metmuseum
LinkedIn: The Metropolitan Museum of Art (Company)

Museums USA

This directory lists more than 15,000 museums and 3,000 museum-sponsored events. Includes some smaller museums that you may not find in other directories.

Web: www.museumsusa.org/museums
Facebook: Museums USA (Page)
Twitter: (None)
LinkedIn: (None)

National Civil Rights Museum

In 1991, this Memphis museum opened its doors at the site of the Lorraine Motel, site of the assassination of Dr. Martin Luther King, Jr. Here, you can trace the history of the civil rights movement in the United States and watch video interviews with those who lived the struggle.

Web: www.civilrightsmuseum.org
Facebook: National Civil Rights Museum (Page, Group)
Twitter: ncrm
LinkedIn: (None)

National Gallery of Art

The nation's art museum, located in Washington, D.C., shares information about its collection, exhibitions, and events. Its video and audio podcasts give behind-the-scenes information and in-depth looks at items in the collection. Plan your visit, or simply take an online tour.

Web: www.nga.gov
Facebook: National Gallery of Art (Page)
Twitter: (None)
LinkedIn: National Gallery of Art (Company)

Smithsonian Institution

The Smithsonian, in Washington, D.C., is the world's largest museum, made up of 19 individual museums, nine research centers, and the National Zoo. Its website reflects its size and diversity: The Encyclopedia Smithsonian section provides hundreds of articles related to Art & Design, History & Culture, and Science & Technology—and that's just for starters. Find out about exhibitions, events, research, individual museums, and visiting the Smithsonian and becoming a member.

Web: www.si.edu
Facebook: Smithsonian Institution (Page, Group)
Twitter: smithsonian
LinkedIn: Smithsonian Institution (Company)

United States Holocaust Memorial Museum

This Washington, D.C., museum strives to inspire people to "confront hatred, prevent genocide, promote human dignity, and strengthen democracy" through remembrance of the Holocaust. This site explains about the museum and its programs, acquaints visitors with the history of the Holocaust, and offers resources for educators, students, and activists.

Web: www.ushmm.org
Facebook: United States Holocaust Memorial Museum (Page, Application)
Twitter: HolocaustMuseum
LinkedIn: United States Holocaust Memorial Museum (Company)

PARKS

National Parks Conservation Association

The stated mission of the NPCA is "to protect and enhance America's National Parks for present and future generations." You can learn about the work of this organization, receive Action Alerts about important issues, find out how to support the NPCA, explore national parks, and subscribe to *National Parks* magazine.

Web: www.npca.org
Facebook: National Parks Conservation Association (Page, Group)
Twitter: NPCA
LinkedIn: National Parks Conservation Association (Company)

National Park Service BEST

The U.S. National Park Service (NPS) has done an outstanding job putting together this guide, which covers the NPS, its parks, and educational resources.

Follow links to pages for individual parks, including the most popular, such as Yellowstone, the Grand Canyon, Denali, Acadia, the Everglades, Bryce Canyon, Big Bend, Yosemite, and hundreds more. Find a park by name, location, activity (camping, boating, hunting, and so on), or topic (Civil War, fossils/dinosaurs, or caves, for example).

Web: www.nps.gov
Facebook: National Park Service (Page, Group)
Twitter: NPSVIPNetwork
LinkedIn: National Park Service (Company), US National Park Service fans (Group)

U.S. Forest Service

Learn about National Forests and Grasslands (including where to find them and get maps/brochures), get information about passes and fees, read about the history of the Forest Service and its current work. Has a Just for Kids section featuring Smokey Bear and Woodsy Owl.

Web: www.fs.fed.us
Facebook: forest service (Page)
Twitter: forestservice
LinkedIn: USDA Forest Service (Company)

RESTAURANTS

Fodor's World Restaurant Reviews

Fodor's Travel Guides dish up restaurant reviews for destinations all over the world. Reviews are by Fodor's staff and, when available, by diners like you.

Web: www.fodors.com/world/restaurant-reviews.html
Facebook: Fodor's (Page), Fodor's Friends (Group)
Twitter: fodorstravel
LinkedIn: (None)

Happy Cow's Vegetarian Guide

If you're a vegetarian, use this directory to find restaurants serving up cruelty-free food, whether in your hometown or during your travels. With more than 8,000 listings covering more than 100 countries, Happy Cow is an indispensable guide for vegetarians who want to eat out.

Web: www.happycow.net
Facebook: (None)
Twitter: HappyCowGuide
LinkedIn: (None)

Menuism

A social network for foodies, Menuism lets members share restaurant reviews and photos, make friends with other food lovers, and create a list of your favorite restaurants. You don't have to be a member, though, to search for and read reviews.

Web: www.menuism.com
Facebook: Menuism (Page, Group)
Twitter: menuism
LinkedIn: (None)

The Restaurant Guys

Restaurateurs Francis Schott and Mark Pascal bring you this hour-long show each weekday, featuring conversations and interviews with famous chefs, restaurant operators, and wine and food critics.

Web: www.restaurantguysradio.com
Facebook: The Restaurant Guys (Page)
Twitter: RestaurantGuys
LinkedIn: (None)

Restaurants.com

This site offers restaurant reviews from all over the world. Search by location, then browse restaurant listings and user reviews.

Web: www.restaurants.com
Facebook: Restaurant.com (Page)
Twitter: Restaurant_com
LinkedIn: (None)

ZAGAT ⑤

Zagat Guides are famous for directing readers to the world's best restaurants, and ZAGAT Online continues that tradition. When you open a free one-week trial, you can read user reviews and post your own, make reservations online, look at photos or take a virtual tour of restaurants, and get weekly emails. For about five bucks a month, premium members get access to Zagat's own reviews and ratings and a discount in the online store. The Zagat Buzz is the site's blog.

Web: www.zagat.com
Facebook: Zagat Survey (Page, Application)
Twitter: ZagatBuzz
LinkedIn: Zagat Survey (Company)

U.S. TRAVEL DESTINATIONS

California

California is one of those places that seems to have something for everyone, and you can plan your own California vacation here. Explore the state and the California lifestyle, find things to do, and use travel tools to plan and book your trip.

Web: www.visitcalifornia.com
Facebook: Visit California (Page)
Twitter: (None)
LinkedIn: (None)

Hawaii: The Islands of Aloha

Whether you're looking for the bustle and energy of Oahu's Waikiki, the serene beauty of Kauai, or the mind-blowing volcanoes of the Big Island, Hawaii's official tourism site lets you explore the many facets of the Aloha State. Learn about the different islands, find vacation ideas, and plan your trip.

Web: www.gohawaii.com
Facebook: Hawaii (Page)
Twitter: Hawaii_vacation
LinkedIn: Friends of Hawaii (Group)

Hawaii Vacation Connection

Whether you're planning a trip to Hawaii or just dreaming about one, you'll enjoy this blog and podcast of Hawaii vacation tips and news.

Web: www.hawaii-aloha.com/podcast/index.php
Facebook: Hawaii Aloha Travel (Page)
Twitter: hawaii_vacation
LinkedIn: (None)

I Love New York

From the bright lights of Broadway to the roar of Niagara Falls, this site covers everything you need to plan a trip to New York. Main areas of the site include Things to See & Do, Getaways, Where to Stay, Cities & Towns, Outdoors, and About New York State; each area has helpful articles, information, and tools for travelers. Download maps, make reservations online, or order a customized brochure that addresses your specific interests.

Web: www.iloveny.com
Facebook: I LOVE NEW YORK (Page)
Twitter: I_LOVE_NY
LinkedIn: I Love New York (Group)

Myrtle Beach

Calling itself "America's Beach Playground," Myrtle Beach, South Carolina, offers 60 miles of sandy beaches and more than 89,000 accommodations, as well as golf courses, shopping, amusement and water parks, and more. Take a video tour or peruse the photo gallery, learn about lodging and events, and request a free vacation guide.

Web: www.mbchamber.com
Facebook: Myrtle Beach Area Convention and Visitors Bureau (Page)
Twitter: MyMyrtleBeach
LinkedIn: Myrtle Beach Area Hospitality Association (Group)

Only Vegas

The official tourism site for Las Vegas helps you find all the exciting things to see and do in this city that is visited by nearly 40 million people each year. Whether you're interested in casinos, shows, golf, dining, shopping, nightlife, or a wedding, this site has everything you need to plan your trip. Watch Vegas videos, find a hotel, check upcoming attractions, browse special deals, and make reservations online.

Web: www.visitlasvegas.com
Facebook: Visit Las Vegas (Page)
Twitter: Vegas
LinkedIn: (None)

Orlando Travel & Visitors Bureau

This site is a must-visit for anyone planning a trip to Orlando. You'll find places to stay, things to do, other visitor info, discounts and promotions, an event calendar, and the like.

Web: www.orlandoinfo.com
Facebook: Visit Orlando (Page)
Twitter: VisitOrlando
LinkedIn: (None)

Travel Alaska

The Alaska Travel Industry Association has put together an excellent website to help you plan your trip to America's last frontier. Sections include Discover Alaska, Destinations, Things to Do, Getting Around, and Places to Stay. Sample itineraries, such as Destination Anchorage, Inside the Inside Passage, and The Great Alaska Road Trip, show possibilities for your trip.

Web: www.travelalaska.com
Facebook: Alaska Travel Industry Association (Page)
Twitter: VisitOurRainbow
LinkedIn: (None)

TravelTex

If you're planning a trip to the Lone Star State, this site will get you started with information about cities and regions, activities and events, and places to stay. Check out the interactive map of Texas, watch videos, and read articles on everything from shopping to ranches and rodeos to birding to Texas music. You can sign up for free newsletters and a travel guide.

Web: www.traveltex.com
Facebook: Travel Texas... (Group)
Twitter: texastourism
LinkedIn: Friends of Texas (Group)

VisitFlorida

Whatever you want to see, do, or experience in Florida, this site can help you plan your trip. It's packed with articles and features about the Sunshine State, including events and attractions, regions, beaches, sports, weather information, romantic getaways, tours, and deals. A nice feature is a series of blogs from 10 local experts in these areas: Arts & Culture, Boating & Fishing, Shopping &

Nightlife, Beach & Surf, Family, Authentic Florida, Smart Travel, Golf, Outdoors, and Adventure—so you've got an insider's guide to the activities that interest you.

Web: www.visitflorida.com
Facebook: VISIT FLORIDA (Page)
Twitter: VISITFLORIDA
LinkedIn: Florida's Governor's Conference on Tourism (Group)

VACATIONS

Abercrombie & Kent ⑤

Specializing in luxury vacations, Abercrombie & Kent offers small-group and independent vacation packages to more than 100 countries on all seven continents.

Web: www.abercrombiekent.com
Facebook: Abercrombie & Kent (Page)
Twitter: AKTravel_USA
LinkedIn: Abercrombie & Kent (Company)

Adventure Center ⑤

Those who like active vacations should take a look at this online travel agency, which specializes in adventure vacations: safaris, hiking or cycling tours, overland expeditions, tall ship sailing, and more. Also offers family adventures designed with kids in mind.

Web: www.adventurecenter.com
Facebook: Adventure Center (Group)
Twitter: AdventureCenbbb
LinkedIn: (None)

Away.com

If you're looking for vacation ideas, check out this site. It's packed with insider information and tips on destinations, interest guides, and travel photos and articles. Offers blogs and newsletters.

Web: http://away.com/
Facebook: Away.com (Page)
Twitter: awayblog
LinkedIn: (None)

Golf Vacation Insider

When you register with your email address, this site sends you free reports on any of dozens of different golf courses. The site provides daily tips for those considering a golf vacation, and there's a free newsletter.

Web: www.golfvacationinsider.com
Facebook: (None)
Twitter: GVI_Tips
LinkedIn: (None)

Golf Vacations $

Avid golfers eager to spend their vacation on the links should take a look at this site, which can help you put together a golf vacation package.

Web: www.golfvacations.com
Facebook: Golf Vacations (Group)
Twitter: (None)
LinkedIn: (None)

Gordons Guide: Adventure & Active Travel

Want to spend your next vacation chasing tornadoes or diving with sharks? How about a dog sledding, archeological, or wagon train vacation? Gordons Guide finds dozens of exciting, offbeat, educational vacations and compiles them for you here. Also lists resorts, spas, and retreats.

Web: www.gordonsguide.com
Facebook: Gordon's Guide Adventure Travel - Plan your next vacation!! (Group)
Twitter: GordonsGuide
LinkedIn: Gordon's Guide (Company), Gordon's Travel Guide (Group)

The International Kitchen $

Have you ever returned home wishing you could re-create the wonderful food you enjoyed on vacation? If so, you might be interested in a trip that combines fun, travel, and cooking lessons.

Travel to Italy, France, Spain/Portugal, Morocco, Mexico/the Caribbean and learn to cook the local specialties.

Web: www.theinternationalkitchen.com
Facebook: The International Kitchen (Page)
Twitter: theintlkitchen
LinkedIn: (None)

Ski Vacations $

If your idea of fun is schussing down powdery-white slopes, this travel agency can help you plan your vacation. Get information about resorts (including some videos), talk with other skiers in the forums, play with the cool interactive 3D maps of top ski spots, and book online.

Web: www.ski.com
Facebook: ski.com (Page)
Twitter: Skicom
LinkedIn: Ski.com (Company)

SpaFinder

Consult this directory's "Getaway Spas" to find a relaxing or energizing spa vacation in hundreds of locations around the world.

Web: www.spafinder.com
Facebook: SpaFinder (Page)
Twitter: SpaFinderInc
LinkedIn: Spa Finder (Company)

Volunteer Vacations

This site lists vacations that make a difference, ranging from one to four weeks. Causes for which you can volunteer are sorted into these categories: Animal Welfare, Children's Issues, Community Development, Health & Safety, and Poverty. Choose a cause, and the site offers links so you can find out more.

Web: www.charityguide.org/volunteer/vacations.htm
Facebook: (None)
Twitter: CharityGuide
LinkedIn: (None)

15

ZOOS

Association of Zoos and Aquariums (AZA)

The AZA accredits zoos and aquariums to make sure they meet high standards of animal care, wildlife conservation, science, and education. Visit this site to learn more about the AZA or find an accredited zoo.

Web: www.aza.org
Facebook: Association of Zoos & Aquariums (Page, Group)
Twitter: zoos_aquariums
LinkedIn: (None)

Bronx Zoo

This zoo has more than 4,000 animals and emphasizes conservation. Here you can explore such exhibits as the Congo Gorilla Forest and the Himalayan Highlands Habitat (plus a lot more). Get information to plan your visit, including hours, rates, events, and directions, and listen to behind-the-scenes podcasts.

Web: www.bronxzoo.com
Facebook: Bronx Zoo (Page)
Twitter: TheBronxZoo
LinkedIn: (None)

Denver Zoo

With more than 4,000 animals from 700 different species, this popular zoo receives about 1.6 million visitors each year. Learn about animals and plants, as well as the zoo's education and conservation programs, activities for kids, and planning a visit.

Web: www.denverzoo.org
Facebook: Denver Zoo (Page)
Twitter: DenverZoo
LinkedIn: (None)

San Diego Zoo

The coolest thing about this informative site is its live webcams, which let you observe animals in real time: pandas, polar bears, apes, and elephants. But there's a lot more to explore, too, in these sections: Visit, Calendar, Animals & Plants, Kids, Education, Get Involved, and Donate. The site offers videos, free postcards, online ticket sales, and a store.

Web: www.sandiegozoo.com
Facebook: San Diego Zoo (Page)
Twitter: sdzootrumpet
LinkedIn: (None)

Smithsonian National Zoological Park ⬟

The National Zoo's site offers a world of information about animals and conservation. Twenty webcams let you watch what animals are doing right now, and the Photo Gallery offers tours of the zoo's different areas and exhibits. From backyard biology to rare and endangered species, you can learn about your favorite animals (and some you've never heard of). Find out about zoo events and activities, support the zoo with a donation, or shop in its online store. You can even buy animal-sound ringtones!

Web: http://nationalzoo.si.edu/
Facebook: Pandas at the Smithsonian National Zoological Park (Group)
Twitter: smithsonian
LinkedIn: Smithsonian Institution (Company)

Toronto Zoo

An information-filled site from one of the world's largest zoos, with more than 5,000 animals living on a 710-acre site. The Animals section offers videos and fact sheets on dozens of animals from all over the world. There's also information about events and programs, adopting an animal, zoo camp, conservation, and education, as well as an online store.

Web: www.torontozoo.com
Facebook: the toronto zoo (Page)
Twitter: (None)
LinkedIn: Toronto Zoo (Company)

Index

G

Y

Z